# *Contested Conversions to Islam*

# Contested Conversions to Islam

## *Narratives of Religious Change in the Early Modern Ottoman Empire*

Tijana Krstić

STANFORD UNIVERSITY PRESS
STANFORD, CALIFORNIA

Stanford University Press
Stanford, California



Printed in the United States of America on acid-free, archival-quality paper

Library of Congress Cataloging-in-Publication Data

Krstic, Tijana, author.
Contested conversions to Islam : narratives of religious change in the early modern Ottoman Empire / Tijana Krstic.
pages cm
Includes bibliographical references and index.
ISBN 978-0-8047-7317-1 (cloth : alk. paper)
ISBN 978-0-8047-9332-2 (pbk. : alk. paper)
1. Muslim converts from Christianity—Turkey—History. 2. Conversion—Islam. 3. Islam—Relations—Christianity. 4. Christianity and other religions—Islam. 5. Islam and state—Turkey—History. 6. Turkey—History—Ottoman Empire, 1288–1918. I. Title.
BP170.5.K77 2011
297.5'740956—dc22
2010048409

Typeset by Bruce Lundquist in 10/12 Sabon LT Pro

*Mirjani i Bošku, sa ljubavlju i zahvalnošću*

# Contents

*Acknowledgments*
*ix*

*Note on Transliteration and Pronunciation*
*xiii*

INTRODUCTION
Turning "Rumi":
Conversion to Islam, Fashioning of the Ottoman Imperial Ideology, and Interconfessional Relations in the Early Modern Mediterranean Context
*1*

CHAPTER ONE
Muslims through Narratives:
Textual Repertoires of Fifteenth-Century Ottoman Islam and Formation of the Ottoman Interpretative Communities
*26*

CHAPTER TWO
Toward an Ottoman Rumi Identity:
The Polemical Arena of Syncretism and the Debate on the Place of Converts in Fifteenth-Century Ottoman Polity
*51*

CHAPTER THREE
In Expectation of the Messiah:
Interimperial Rivalry, Apocalypse, and Conversion in Sixteenth-Century Muslim Polemical Narratives
*75*

CHAPTER FOUR
Illuminated by the Light of Islam and the Glory of the Ottoman Sultanate: Self-Narratives of Conversion to Islam in the Age of Confessionalization
*98*

CHAPTER FIVE
Between the Turban and the Papal Tiara: Orthodox Christian Neomartyrs and Their Impresarios in the Age of Confessionalization
*121*

CHAPTER SIX
Everyday Communal Politics of Coexistence and Orthodox Christian Martyrdom: A Dialogue of Sources and Gender Regimes in the Age of Confessionalization
*143*

CONCLUSION
Conversion and Confessionalization in the Ottoman Empire: Considerations for Future Research
*165*

*Notes*
*175*

*Bibliography*
*217*

*Index*
*253*

# Acknowledgments

Since this is a book about conversion narratives, let me begin with my own. Like many converts whose stories will be discussed in the following chapters, I would describe my conversion to Ottoman history not as a moment but as a long and convoluted process. The idea of studying the Ottoman Empire crept up on me gradually, almost in spite of me, since like generations of Balkan school kids I was taught that Ottoman history was an endless string of calamitous events about which we knew everything we needed to know—those were the bad times. The war that ravaged Yugoslavia in the early 1990s while I was in high school made my aversion toward Ottoman history even deeper, as it was the subject of ongoing contestation, malicious misuse, and falsification by nationalists of all stripes. I had no intention to enter the brawl. However, the process of "turning" began in my junior year at the American University of Bulgaria where I attended classes in Ottoman and Middle Eastern history by Professor Fredrick F. Anscombe. He was the first in a series of agents of conversion who made me realize that there was more to Ottoman history than the proverbial yoke and that it was important to deal with one's own perceptions of the Ottoman past.

Still unsure whether I would like to study the Crusades, which were my first academic interest, or go in the direction of Ottoman history, I arrived at the University of Michigan where I became a student of Rudi Paul Lindner—in the context of this story, the great *şeyh* who brought about my conversion. He proselytized Ottoman history to this unwitting novice ignorant of the Turkish and Ottoman languages by introducing me to the great "saints" in the *silsile* of Ottoman historiography (Wittek, Giese, Taeschner, Babinger, and others) and by initiating me into the field through translations of Ottoman sources into German. I am forever grateful to Professor Lindner for taking a chance on me and being the kind of adviser that I could have only wished for—there when you most need him, able to provide expert and coherent guidance and allow for great freedom of exploration and expression.

The process of my becoming an Ottomanist probably would have never gotten off to a good start had it not been for the wonderful people who taught me Turkish and Ottoman Turkish during my years at the University of Michigan. I am particularly grateful to Aslı Iğsız, who not only made the Turkish grammar intelligible and fun but whose friendship sustained me throughout graduate school and continues to do so. Hatice Aynur first taught me how to decipher texts in Ottoman Turkish, which was a turning point in my life. I continued to work on Ottoman narratives and documents with Gottfried Hagen, whose expertise in early modern Ottoman historiography and hagiography has been a great source of inspiration and motivation. I am also grateful to the late Şinasi Tekin, under whose guidance I, along with many of my colleagues, first struggled with Ottoman paleography at the Harvard-Koç summer school in Cunda.

Other professors and students made my time at the University of Michigan an unforgettable and overwhelmingly positive experience. I was fortunate to work with Professor John V. A. Fine Jr., from whose vast knowledge of Byzantine and Balkan history I greatly benefited and whose contagious enthusiasm and optimism lifted my spirits on many occasions. Similarly, I am immensely grateful to Kathryn Babayan, who has been both a great friend and a wonderful adviser. Monica Burguera, Emil Kerenji, Ana Mirkova, Edin Hajdarpašić, the late Mary O'Reilly, Mia C. Lee, D. Grace Davie, and Bhavani Raman made Ann Arbor a dynamic and fun place to live and study.

From Michigan, my search for knowledge on the path of becoming an Ottomanist led me to the University of Chicago, where I arrived as a visiting student but found a second academic home. I am indebted to Professor Cornell H. Fleischer not only for treating me as one of his own students but for generously sharing his vast expertise and unique insights into Ottoman history both in the classroom and in many informal *sohbet*s over the years. It was in his class, trying to divine the meaning of the lofty Ottoman passages by Mustafa Ali, that I met my husband, Tolga U. Esmer, with whom I have been sharing this adventure of exploring Ottoman history ever since. In Chicago, I also met Ebru Turan, a fellow Ottomanist and a fiercely devoted friend without whom I would have never become the same historian. It was also in Chicago that my friend and colleague Natalie Rothman and I began our ongoing conversation about cultural, linguistic, and religious encounters between the Venetian and Ottoman empires, which profoundly influenced my understanding of the early modern Mediterranean world. I thank Natalie and Ebru for challenging me, encouraging me, and teaching me how rewarding it is to work together.

The core research for this book was done in Turkey and Bulgaria between 2002 and 2004, where I met numerous people who solidified my attachment to the professional path and the topic I had chosen. Particular thanks go to Anthony Greenwood, Gülden Güneri, and Semrin Korkmaz of the American Research Institute in Turkey, who made my lengthy stay at this important establishment a wonderful experience. Through their friendship and expertise Günhan Börekci, Sara Nur Yıldız, Holly Shissler, Nina Ergin, Haşim Şahin, and Erik Ohlander made the ups and downs of research seem less steep. I would like to thank the staff of the Süleymaniye Library, Atatürk Library, Başbakanlık (Prime Ministerial) Archive, Topkapı Sarayı Museum Library, and the Islamic Research Center (İSAM) in Istanbul for their help and excellent research conditions. In Bulgaria, I was greatly aided by Stoyanka Kenderova, director of the Oriental Collection at the "SS Cyril and Methodius" National Library in Sofia; the former head librarian, Zorka Ivanova; and Professor Rossitsa Gradeva. My research and its subsequent transformation into this book were made possible by grants from the University of Michigan, the Social Science Research Council, the American Research Institute in Turkey, the Andrew W. Mellon Foundation, and Pennsylvania State University.

This study has evolved through conversation and exchanges with friends and colleagues from various fields. At Pennsylvania State University, where I taught between 2006 and 2009, colleagues David Atwill, Nina Safran, Kumkum Chatterjee, Ronnie Hsia, Gregg Roeber, Matthew Restall, and Jonathan Brockopp provided indispensable feedback on different aspects of my research. Thanks to Skype, Natalie Rothman and Ebru Turan were always there for brainstorming and trying out ideas. In the final stages of preparing the manuscript, I greatly benefited from Ussama Makdisi's challenging and constructive reading of my work. Derin Terzioğlu offered insightful feedback on early modern Ottoman religious trends, while Grigor Boykov and Mariya Kiprovska generously contributed their expertise in Ottoman historical geography and mapmaking. Emine Fetvacı, Sara Nur Yıldız, and, most crucially, Günhan Börekci helped me with finding and obtaining the cover image for the book, while Noel Putnik produced the index.

Friends scattered around the world and too numerous to list made life on the tenure track seem less grim. Special thanks go to David, Yurong, Kate, and Peter Atwill, as well as to Samar Farage and Sajay Samuel for making State College a warm and happening place even during the long, uneventful winter months, and for sharing food and drinks with Tolga and me on so many occasions that we have practically become family. At our new academic home at Central European University in Budapest, Elissa Helms, Niels Gaul, Nadia al-Bagdadi, Aziz al-Azmeh, Volker

Menze, Constantin Iordachi, and Katalin Szende have facilitated the transition and provided a warm and friendly welcome. Nevena Ivanović and Aleksandra Erdeg deserve my particular gratitude for reminding me all these years that there is life outside academia. I would also like to thank my editor, Norris Pope, and assistant editor, Sarah Crane Newman, at Stanford University Press for their support, understanding, and cooperation during the long process of book production, and the copyeditor, Cynthia Lindlof, for her careful reading of the manuscript.

I would have never become an academic had it not been for my parents, Mirjana and Boško Krstić, a literature teacher and a journalist/novelist, who taught me the value and power of the written word. Their love, support, understanding, and genuine interest in what I do helped me endure long periods of separation from them. The same is true of my sister Jana, my grandmother Jelena Milanković, and the Milanković family. In the United States, the distance from my family was lessened by Suna and Erkan Esmer, my parents-in-law, who have embraced me as their own daughter. Our dog, Gretl, who has "supervised" the writing of two Ottomanist books and yet miraculously shows no signs of psychiatric problems, has provided indispensable companionship and diversion. Without Tolga, who has been expertly juggling the roles of partner, best friend, and colleague for the last ten years, getting to this point in my life would not have been nearly as meaningful, fun, and exciting. I can never thank him enough for everything he has shared with me, for the love and support he has given me, and for always making me see the brighter side of life.

# Note on Transliteration and Pronunciation

In order to make this work reader-friendly and accessible to the audience beyond the fields of Ottoman and Middle Eastern studies, Ottoman Turkish, Arabic, and Persian personal names are rendered in their Modern Turkish and Anglicized forms. Thus, I use "Ibn Arabi," not Ibn al-'Arabī; "Ebussuud" rather than Ebū's-su'ūd; and "Birgivi," not Birgivī. Ottoman place-names are generally rendered in Modern Turkish, except for those frequently used in English, such as Istanbul, Sofia, and Gallipoli, which appear in their Anglicized form. For the terms frequently used by scholars working on Islamic history, such as *dhimma*, *hadith*, *shahada*, *sharia*, and *mahdi*, I use the Anglicized version of Arabic rather than Ottoman Turkish forms. However, terms that refer to specifically Ottoman manifestations of Islamic concepts and institutions relevant for the discussion are rendered in Modern Turkish; thus, *vakıf* (not *wakf*), *fetva* (not *fatwa*), and *kadı* (not *qadi*). Titles of works, officials' titles, specific terms that are relevant to the discussion, and quotations from texts in Ottoman Turkish are transliterated following the rules of modified Modern Turkish, which means that only long vowels are marked, along with letters *'ayn* (') and *hamza* (') (e.g., *Mecmū'atü'l-letā'if*). The rules of pronouncing Modern Turkish are as follows:

| | |
|---|---|
| C, c | like *j* in English |
| Ç, ç | like *ch* in English |
| ğ | "soft *g*"; hardly pronounced, but it lengthens the preceding vowel |
| I, ı | "undotted *i*"; pronounced like the vowel sound in *earn* |
| İ, i | like *i* in English *bit* |
| Ö, ö | like *ö* in German or *eu* in French *peur* |
| Ş, ş | like *sh* in English |
| Ü, ü | like *ü* in German or *u* in French |

*Contested Conversions to Islam*

# Turning "Rumi"

## *Conversion to Islam, Fashioning of the Ottoman Imperial Ideology, and Interconfessional Relations in the Early Modern Mediterranean Context*

In a letter sent to the Ottoman grand vezir Rüstem Paşa around 1555, a group of elite Ottoman imperial infantrymen (janissaries) complained that their recently appointed head officer (*ağa*) was an unjust, ignorant "Hungarian infidel who converted to Islam only yesterday and whose breath still reeks of pork."[1] Although the authors of this letter were themselves converts to Islam, recruited through child levy (*devşirme*) among Ottoman Christian subjects in the Balkans and Anatolia, they apparently did not find it problematic to bring up the charge of their *ağa*'s recent embrace of Islam and his supposed ignorance of Muslim faith as a disqualifier for his successful service. Echoes of a similar sensibility toward conversion are also found in a polemical treatise on Islam and first-person account penned in 1556–57 by a Hungarian convert to Islam named Murad b. Abdullah.[2] Perhaps in order to preempt a similar charge as the one leveled at this janissary *ağa*, in his treatise Murad recounts how he was inspired to embrace Islam through learning and reading about Muslim faith. This, he implies, endowed him with great moral capital to criticize what he perceived as lack of piety in Ottoman society.[3]

It is by now commonplace to assert that the early modern Ottoman Empire was remarkably integrationist toward converts in comparison to its Christian contemporaries—there were no "purity of blood" (Sp. *limpieza de sangre*) laws or Inquisition in the Ottoman domains. Converts were integrated into Ottoman society through a variety of patronage mechanisms, given opportunities for upward social mobility, and in the period between the fifteenth and seventeenth centuries were preferred to born Muslims for positions in the Ottoman government. However, that does not mean that conversion to Islam did not pose a challenge to Ottoman Muslim society's constantly evolving sense of community and orthopraxy. The examples given are just two among many Ottoman sources authored by born Muslims and converts to Islam in the sixteenth and seventeenth centuries that use the notion of conversion to advance particular visions of what it meant to be a good Muslim in the age of growing polarization between Sunnis and Shi'ites and increasing complexity of social relations in a bureaucratizing and expanding Ottoman Empire.

Nor were Muslim authors the only ones within the Ottoman domains producing narratives about conversion that sought to define the boundaries of their confessional and political community at this time. In the 1560s, an Orthodox Christian monk from Sofia (today in Bulgaria) recorded a story about a certain local Orthodox Christian named Nikola who converted to Islam while drinking with his recently converted friends but later apostatized and was executed according to Ottoman Islamic law.[4] Nikola's story is one of many neomartyrologies—accounts of the suffering and death of Orthodox Christians who converted to Islam and later reneged, only to be executed by Ottoman authorities for apostasy or blasphemy—produced in the period between the fifteenth and seventeenth centuries. These narratives warned the Orthodox Christian flock against interaction with Muslims (even former friends) lest such relationships result in conversion. Neomartyrologies also instructed those who lapsed and converted in how to atone for their sin by volunteering for martyrdom, thus defying the long-standing Orthodox Christian tradition that frowned upon those who deliberately sought to "witness" for Christ. Besides encouraging resistance to conversion and thus setting firm boundaries between Christianity and Islam, the neomartyrs and narratives about them provided the Orthodox Christian Church with a powerful polemical argument against their Catholic and Protestant contemporaries who claimed that a good Christian could not live under Ottoman rule.

Between the fifteenth and seventeenth centuries Ottoman Muslim and Christian authors and institutions produced a rich corpus of narrative sources like these contesting the meaning and implications of conversion to Islam. These polemical narratives articulated different visions of imperial and communal religious politics, challenging and redefining in the process the boundaries of the authors' confessional entities. The present study explores these competing and constantly evolving concepts of conversion in the early modern Ottoman Empire by drawing on heretofore unknown Ottoman self-narratives of conversion to Islam, little-studied personal miscellanies of Ottoman literati (*mecmū'a*), "catechisms" of Muslim faith (*'ilm-i ḥāl*), hagiographies of Muslim holy men (*menākıbnāme, vilāyetnāme*), Ottoman chronicles and histories, Christian captivity narratives, Orthodox Christian neomartyrologies, Western travelogues and ambassadorial accounts, and Jesuit missionary reports. These attempts to delineate what it meant to be a Muslim or a Christian in the Ottoman Empire transpired in the context of a broader, Mediterranean-wide age of empire building, confessional polarization, and interimperial rivalry between the 1450s and 1690s.

The debates on conversion and religious boundaries did not have the same intensity or overtones throughout the Ottoman domains, and they draw attention to the need for a more nuanced understanding of the empire's cultural geography in the period between the fifteenth and seventeenth centuries. The narratives to be discussed come for the most part from the Ottoman "Lands of Rum" and were produced by "Rumis." Although in early Islamic Arabic and Persian literature the term *Rūm* referred to the "Romans" (*Rūm* = Rome), especially Eastern Romans or Byzantines, and their lands, following the Turkish settlement in Asia Minor in the eleventh century the same term also began to be used for Muslims inhabiting the former Byzantine territories.[5] In the Ottoman context the term continued to evolve, and by the fifteenth century the Ottomans used the expression "Lands of Rum" (*diyār-ı Rūm*) to designate their domains in Anatolia and the province of Rumeli (*Rūm ili*; literally, the "Land of Rum") that was made up of the growing conquests in what is today the Balkans.

The term "Rumi" (*Rūmī*), however, did not refer only to the inhabitants of Rum but had already attained further cultural implications in pre-Ottoman times. More specifically, it came to denote a particular segment of society—"those who spoke Turkish (preferably a refined kind of Turkish, but not necessarily as their mother tongue) and acquired their social identity within or in proximity to urban settings, professions, institutions, education and cultural preferences." As a sociocultural category, "Rumis" differentiated themselves from the "Turks," a term that primarily had associations of "ethnicity-not-transcended and attachment to tribal ways and cultural codes."[6] Mustafa Ali (1541–1600)—one of the most prominent sixteenth-century Ottoman literati—eloquently sums up the development of "Rumi" as a cultural category different from but related to "Turk" in the Ottoman context. In his *Essence of History* (*Künhü'l-Ahbār*), Mustafa Ali writes:

> Those varied peoples and different types of Rumis living in the glorious days of the Ottoman dynasty, who are not [generically] separate from those tribes of Turks and Tatars . . . are a select community and pure, pleasing people, who, just as they are distinguished in the origins of their state, are singled out for their

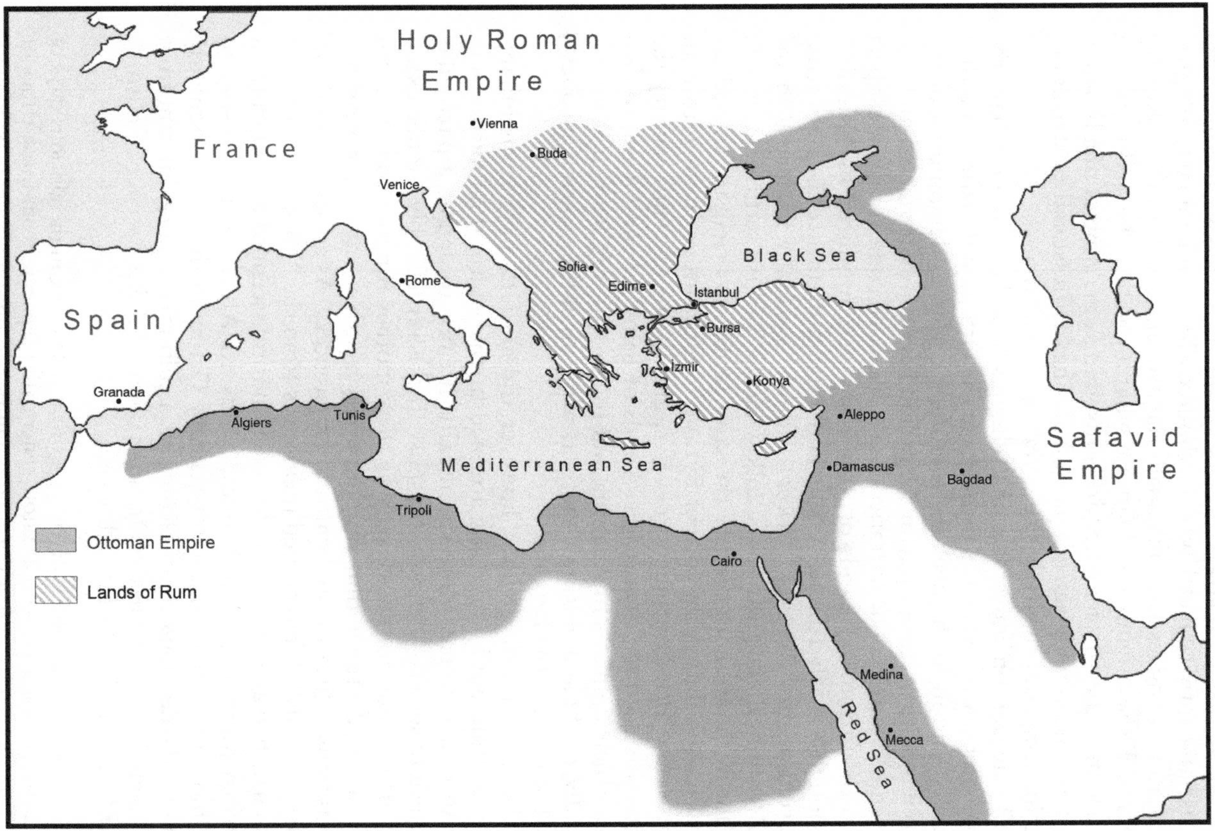

*The Ottoman Empire, ca. 1600*

piety, cleanliness, and faith. Apart from this, most of the inhabitants of Rum are of confused ethnic origins. Among its notables there are few whose lineage does not go back to a convert to Islam . . . either on their father's or their mother's side, the genealogy is traced to a filthy infidel. It is as if two different species of fruit-bearing tree mingled and mated, with the leaves and fruits; and the fruit of this union was large and filled with liquid, like a princely pear. The best qualities of the progenitors were then manifested and gave distinction, either in physical beauty, or spiritual wisdom.[7]

According to Mustafa Ali, Rumis embodied the history of the Ottoman territorial expansion, cultural diversity, and integration under the umbrella of Islam, with conversion playing a central role. Although official Ottoman documents did not use the term "Rumi" to refer to Ottoman Muslim subjects from the Lands of Rum, the latter (both converts and others) often identified themselves as "Rumi" (besides the more generic "Muslim") to people from other regions, and were in turn known as Rumis by other Muslims.[8] As Cemal Kafadar suggests, "Rumi" was a relational category shaped by society and evolved with the changing social and political conditions in the Ottoman Empire and around it.[9] As such, its meaning was wider than that of the more official term "Osmanlı" (Ottoman), which continues to confound historians of the Ottoman Empire because it is unclear to whom it can justifiably be applied beyond the members of the ruling dynasty and the military-administrative elite. However, both "Osmanlı" and "Rumi" had social and cultural implications surpassing "Türk" (Turk)—the term consistently used by Westerners to describe any Muslim from the Ottoman Empire. Although the meaning of "Türk" was not entirely negative—after all, even the language of the elite of the empire was called Turkish—or static, to an urban Muslim living in the sixteenth-century Ottoman Empire the term tended to call to mind the nomadic tribes of Anatolia and invoke notions of boorishness.

Nevertheless, in the cultural usage the primary opposite of "Rumi" was above all "Acem" (*'Acem*), which most frequently referred to Iranians or Safavids but could also designate a foreigner (as in *'acemioğlan*, the official term for *devşirme* recruits who were "sons of foreigners" or non-Muslims), and at times "Arab" (*'Arab*), a term that could denote anybody from nomadic Bedouin to speakers of Arabic regardless of their ethnicity to other broad social categories.[10] Although in the fifteenth and sixteenth centuries the categories of "Rumi," "Acem," and "Arab" served mostly to mark cultural competition and affinity, by the late sixteenth and especially in the seventeenth century the sources began to register increasing tensions among them, particularly along the Rumi/Acem but also Rumi/Arab lines. These tensions stemmed from a variety of sources, including the increasing religio-political polarization between Sunni Ottomans and Shi'a Safavids and changing methods of recruitment for the Ottoman military and administrative ranks.[11] It is therefore important to reflect on the observations of the Venetian ambassador (*bailo*) Lorenzo Bernardo in his report (*relazione*) from 1592 (despite factual mistakes he makes about beliefs of the "Persians"). Bernardo writes:

> In former times, Serene Prince, all Turks held to a single religion. . . . But now the Turks have not a single religion, but three of them. The Persians are among the Turks like the heretics among us [Christians], because some of them hold the beliefs of Ali, and others those of Omar, both of whom were followers of Muhammad, but held different doctrines. Then there are the Arabs and Moors, who claim they alone preserve the true, uncorrupted religion and that the Turks from *Grecia* [Rumeli], as they call these in Constantinople, are bastard Turks with a corrupted religion, which they blame on their mostly being descended from Christian renegades who did not understand Muslim religion.[12]

This book explores how the process of conversion to Islam related to these and other aspects of gradual confessional and political polarization in Ottoman domains through texts from the Lands of Rum produced in the period between the fifteenth and seventeenth centuries. In this sense, I do not claim to provide an empirewide perspective but to reflect on the debates stemming from the areas of the empire most densely inhabited by both non-Muslims and new Muslims and most acutely affected by the ongoing process of conversion. For this reason, although it takes into consideration Anatolia, where the process of conversion to Islam reached back to the eleventh and began to ebb by the sixteenth century (most significantly shaped by factors predating the Ottomans), the book privileges Rumeli, where conversion became a new and important phenomenon in the fourteenth century with the appearance of the Ottomans.[13] That is not to say that throughout the period in question conversion to Islam did not occur in other parts of the Ottoman Empire, especially in the significant Christian population centers in the Levant. However, it was a phenomenon of limited proportions (compared to Rumeli); and in this context, conversion to various denominations of Christianity and encounters with the Catholic and Protestant missionaries become interesting topics of research, especially beginning in the seventeenth century.[14] Importantly, Rumeli was also the location of the seat of the Ottoman government where imperial policies were crafted in dialogue with information from other regions of the empire. The book will explore how the heavy presence of converts from Rumeli and the wider Mediterranean region in the Ottoman capital and among the ranks of the Ottoman government influenced the articulation of imperial policies, in relation to both the empire's western and eastern neighbors in the period under discussion.

Although not all parts of the Lands of Rum were located along the shores of the Mediterranean, I treat them as part of the larger Mediterranean zone—what Braudel called the "Mediterranean of the historian," which stretches far beyond the shores of the sea.[15] In a recent study, Adnan Husain reflects on Braudel's monumental work and suggests that "what renders the Mediterranean zone unique might be [the] *longue durée* of inter-religious contact, interchange, and even competition among the universal claims about history and confessional identity experienced consequentially by Muslims, Christians, and Jews during formative periods of their—far from static—late antique to early modern traditions."[16] It is my contention, drawing both on primary sources and recent research, that the nature of early modern Ottoman history or of the phenomenon of conversion cannot be understood without paying attention to the ongoing dialogue of Ottoman cultural discourse with the Mediterranean heritage of the Lands of Rum, in all its religious, linguistic, political, and cultural complexity.[17] As Ottoman geographic literature suggests, by the sixteenth century the Ottomans came to consider the Mediterranean—the geographic center of the ancient Roman Empire—as central to their imperial authority and legitimacy, particularly as the sultans' aspirations to join the two Romes (Rome and Constantinople) and establish a Universal Monarchy reached its zenith in the era of Sultan Süleyman (1520–66).[18] Although the dreams of an Ottoman-controlled Mediterranean recede after the late sixteenth century, as Evliya Çelebi's writings show, the sea continues to play an important role in Ottoman imperial ideology and cultural imagination throughout the seventeenth century. This ongoing fascination with the Mediterranean culminated in the Ottoman conquest of Crete from Venice in 1669, which gave a new boost to the Ottoman elites' aspirations to the glory of the empire of old, if only for a few years.[19]

## *Contact among the Religious Cultures of the Medieval and Early Modern Mediterranean: A Framework for Inquiry*

Recent post-Orientalist scholarship acknowledges that the sustained contact among religions in the Mediterranean zone has resulted in numerous mutual influences that shaped and continue to shape each of the confessional communities involved. However, contact among religions continues to be examined mostly within a framework that tends to dehistoricize the debate over dogma, or through the anthropological categories of religious practice such as holy places or sacred journeys that localize and schematize the issue of interconfessional contact.[20] In this way, the larger shared conceptual frameworks that resulted from the long history of interaction and "mutually informing dialectics of Mediterranean religious cultures" are easily overlooked.[21] The reconstruction of these conceptual frameworks is a task that new scholarship aspiring to integrate the study of religion into historical inquiry will have to undertake. In the following chapters I initiate this inquiry by focusing on the period between the fifteenth and seventeenth centuries when shared conceptual frameworks were woven at least partly out of expectations of the Last Days, concerns with the spiritual renewal and purification of religion, the language of Neoplatonism and human experience of the divine, and aspirations to a Universal Monarchy. Depending on the historical context and actors involved, these shared frameworks were at times deliberately constructed and maintained, but at times they also existed without the knowledge of those who operated within them.

For instance, the first interconfessional polemical encounter in the Ottoman context on record is the debate between Gregory Palamas (d. 1359), the bishop of Thessaloniki and a great Byzantine mystic who spent close to a year in Ottoman captivity in 1354–55, and the so-called *Chiones*, most probably Jewish converts to Islam who were members of the entourage of the second Ottoman ruler (*emīr*) Orhan (r. 1326–59).[22] The *Chiones* informed Palamas that they had "made themselves Turks" after learning that Turks also adhered to the Ten Commandments given to Moses.[23] They discussed with Palamas Christian concepts of divinity and the nature of Christ. The *Chiones* found the ideas that Christ was God although he was born a man and that God could be contained in the womb of a woman particularly contentious. Attending the discussion himself, *emīr* Orhan inquired why Christians do not accept and love Muhammad, despite the fact that Muslims love and honor Jesus (Tr. İsa) and his mother, to which Palamas responded that Jesus was the last prophet and that Christians cannot accept anyone who came after.[24] The same question was posed to Palamas by a Muslim learned man whom he encountered while roaming freely around Ottoman İznik (formerly Nicaea) and who asserted that Christians intentionally removed the evidence of Muhammad's coming from the Gospels. Palamas diplomatically concluded that it was important to reflect on what had been said, while another Muslim observed that the time would come when they would all be in accord.[25] Both parties understood what was implied—according to the eschatological tradition shared by Christians and Muslims, the crowning event of Jesus' Second Coming and of the Day of Judgment will be the conversion of infidels to one true faith that will unite the world. The question was, of course, which faith was the true faith that would guarantee salvation and entrance into paradise.

Palamas's letter to his congregation in Thessaloniki describing these encounters illustrates how easily he and his interlocutors found common points to discuss and contest. It also previews some of the key topics of religious polemics that will resurface in the Ottoman period: the validity and authenticity of the scriptures, the nature of Jesus, the relationship between Jesus and Muhammad, and the consequences of the Day of Judgment. Of course, many of these topics were tropes from Muslim and Christian polemical literature, already long established by the fourteenth century.[26] However, what makes Palamas's polemical letter to his congregation special is that it was based on a face-to-face encounter—a rare experience for a Byzantine polemicist based in or around Constantinople—that transpired in a remarkably respectful atmosphere in the Ottoman domains during the early stages of Ottoman expansion. In the fourteenth century, Byzantine anti-Muslim polemics, which had thrived since the seventh century, underwent a change as a result of particularly intense relations with the Ottomans, as both foes and allies.[27] Palamas's letter to his congregation in Thessaloniki and the record of his debate with the *Chiones* changed the tenor of the Byzantine anti-Muslim treatises into a more informed, if not more conciliatory, one.[28]

However, even more interesting than the common topics Palamas and his interlocutors did discuss are the topics that they did not touch upon but could have. Gregory Palamas was not just one of the most famous Byzantine theologians but also the foremost proponent of hesychasm—a time-honored eremitic style of Christianity based on the pursuit of inner quietude (*hesychia*) in which victory over passions allows the monk to contemplate and experience the divine.[29] Palamas followed in the tradition of Christian Neoplatonists, most important, Pseudo-Dionysius, but he shunned the latter's belief that God is unknowable and beyond sensory experience. Palamas's hesychast theology explored the limits of biblical anthropology by emphasizing the potential of man, who was created in the image of God, to physically experience divine "energies," which Palamas distinguished from divine "essence."[30] The experience of divine grace came to a hesychast through regulating breathing, fixing the eyes on one point, and repeating the uninterrupted monologic prayer in which one invokes Jesus and remembers God until spirit descends into the heart.[31] Those hesychasts who managed to see God within themselves reportedly saw him in the form of light, such as the light that appeared to the apostles on Mount Tabor, which denoted a prelude to the glory of Jesus in his Second Coming.[32] Hesychasm became popular in Byzantium in the late thirteenth century but attained the status of mainstream Orthodoxy through theological debates in the mid-fourteenth century.

Palamas's hesychast mystical theology and "the prayer of the heart" had an interesting corollary in contemporary Anatolian Sufism strongly influenced by the thought of the famous Andalusian mystic Muhyiddin Ibn Arabi (1165–1240). In the early thirteenth century Ibn Arabi brought the mystical tradition of al-Andalus, infused with Neoplatonic sensibilities, to Seljuk domains in Anatolia.[33] In 1331, more than twenty years before Palamas found himself in İznik, the Ottoman *emīr* Orhan established a religious seminary (Ott. Tr. *medrese*) in this city and appointed Davud-i Kayseri, a renowned connoisseur and interpreter of Ibn Arabi's work, as its first professor (*müderris*). Ibn Arabi's mysticism drew significantly on the Islamic Neoplatonic tradition and the emanationist imagery of God as Light.[34] At the same time, it was emphatically anthropocentric inasmuch as it envisioned human potential to reach perfection in God and thus achieve unity with the divine. A perfect human being (*insān kāmil*) is a "perfected locus of Divine self-disclosure,"[35] the person who actualizes God's goal in creating the universe by recognizing God in his fullness. And the path toward knowing God is remembering him (*dhikr Allāh*) through repeating his names. According to Ibn Arabi, to remember God fully is to find him sitting within the heart, which is God's throne in the microcosm of man.[36] Ibn Arabi's teachings, disseminated by his disciples, had already become extremely influential throughout the Islamic world by the beginning of the fourteenth century.

To what extent were the Byzantine hesychasts and the Anatolian Sufis aware of the parallels in their teachings and practices, and did these similarities advance the interfaith dialogue or even elicit conversions? Although research on the history of hesychasm suggests that it may have been affected by Sufi practices and thus informed by Muslim mysticism along the path of its development,[37] there is no evidence that in the fourteenth century either the Sufis or the hesychasts were aware of or referred to each other's practices. Some scholars who wrote on this subject (which is admittedly insufficiently explored) tried to make a case that the conceptual and structural parallels between Sufism and hesychasm must have resulted in a better interconfessional understanding in the Byzantine-Seljuk and later Byzantine-Ottoman contact zones.[38] However, there is scant evidence that the shared Neoplatonic repertoire, the celebration of human potential to participate in the divine, or even mutually recognizable styles of piety and sanctity centering on venerable holy men, *directly and by themselves* led to conversions or any sort of religious ecumenism, especially on the Christian side. In order for such a synthesis to happen, certain groups or individuals had to actively promote it, and as we will see, that depended on the historical context and configurations of power. Recent studies exploring the parallels between Sufism and Eastern Christianity in general and between Palamas's and Ibn Arabi's mysticism in particular are also careful not to postulate any sort of borrowing or transcendental unity of religions. Rather, they stress the unity with distinctions while pointing to the remarkable convergences.[39]

Nor were the convergences confined only to Sufism and hesychasm. Neoplatonic themes of heavenly hierarchy as well as the concepts of emanation and renewal of religion set in a stark eschatological framework informed works not only of Palamas and Ibn Arabi but also of some Latin mystics such as the Spiritual Franciscans (Fraticelli), who found refuge from inquisitorial persecution in the territories of the Byzantines and various Turkish commanders (*beğ*) in the fourteenth century. The Fraticelli, who settled in Chios and other areas of Asia Minor, were particularly influenced by the thought of the Calabrian monk and mystic Joachim of Fiore (d. 1202).[40] He postulated that history consisted of three ages: the age of the Father (or of the Old Testament), the age of the Son (or of the New Testament up to 1260), and the age of the Spirit, which would be the age of spiritual liberty, renewal, and humanity's complete unification with the divine preceding the Day of Judgment.[41] Although there is no evidence of direct influence, Gregory Palamas shared the Joachimite tripartite vision of history. Also, just as Joachim of Fiore envisioned the virtuous monks presiding over the age of the Spirit, so did Palamas believe that in the era "of manifestations of the Spirit" only the hesychasts would fully comprehend the divine mysteries through their ability to experience divine energy.[42] Ibn Arabi also endorsed the idea of a "quintessence of the spiritual elite," or those whose pursuit of self-perfection in the quest for the divine enables them to understand the inner meaning of the scriptures and attain the Truth.[43] Unlike the Joachimites and hesychasts, Ibn Arabi did not partition history into three ages but asserted that each age has its own "perfect man" in whom unity with God was realized. Nevertheless, he envisioned the arrival of the Imam of the Last Age, *mahdi* (literally, "the rightly guided one"), who will appear when the earth becomes filled with injustice and oppression to breathe the spirit back into the religion of Islam. This imam will be guided in his actions by the spiritual elite, and his arrival will precede the Day of Judgment.[44]

As this short discussion suggests, millenarian tendencies and expectations of spiritual renewal were part of the religious repertoire shared by Muslims, Jews, and Christians in the later Middle Ages. According to Cornell Fleischer, the millenarian expectations shared by religious communities around the Mediterranean began to intensify in the aftermath of the Ottoman conquest of Constantinople in 1453, peaking in the early sixteenth century. These expectations induced political actors from the Ottomans and Safavids, to the Habsburgs, Venetians, the French Valois, and even various popes to aspire to establish a Universal Monarchy and articulate their competing imperial claims in messianic terms.[45] The scenarios of the end, which will be discussed in more detail in Chapter 3, were based on early medieval Byzantine texts, such as the *Apocalypse of Pseudo-Methodius* and the *Visions of Daniel*, that were widely disseminated in both Latin Christendom and Islamdom.[46] Muslim and Christian authors selectively appropriated elements of the apocalyptic texts they shared, just as they did with different philosophical aspects of Neoplatonic texts. Ottoman converts played a particularly important role in producing and mediating interimperial propaganda infused with apocalyptic imagery.

## *"Confessionalization" and "Social Disciplining": Useful Terms for Early Modern Ottoman History?*

In the second half of the sixteenth century the continued expectations of spiritual renewal as well as continued interimperial competition gave rise to the phenomena of confessional polarization and Sunnitization in the Ottoman Empire. While the Habsburgs challenged the Ottoman sultan's ambition to create a world empire under the banner of Islam, the most direct blow to the Ottomans' dynastic legitimacy and claim to leadership in religion came from their neighbor to the east, Safavid shah Ismail and his Turkmen followers in Anatolia known as the "redheads" (*kızılbaş*) because of their red headgear.[47] In 1501, Shah Ismail proclaimed his identity as *mahdi*, the prophesied redeemer of Islam and the awaited hidden imam of the Twelver Shi'a branch of Islam, uniting the spiritual and political prerogatives in his ruling personality. Simultaneously, he initiated the process of conversion of Iran to Shi'a Islam that constituted the first phase in the evolution of Safavid Shi'ism from mystic nonscriptural piety of the *kızılbaş* to the *sharia*-based Imami Shi'ism later in the sixteenth century.[48]

But Shah Ismail was not the only Muslim claiming to be the messianic ruler with the right to worldly dominion. A series of millenarian revolts in Anatolia in the period between 1511 and 1538 exposed the explosive power of politically charged mystic piety, typically focused around a messianic figure claiming the right to the sultanate.[49] These and other challenges to the Ottoman sultan's authority and legitimacy gave rise to the first consistent attempts to articulate and enforce a Sunni orthodoxy in the Ottoman domains and persecute dissenters.[50] The *kızılbaş* and other religious transgressors who were not immediately executed were often deported from Anatolia to various parts of Rumeli (Dobruca, Buda) or the Mediterranean (Cyprus) throughout the sixteenth century, making this a problem that spanned the Ottoman Lands of Rum.[51] The process of confessional polarization and Sunnitization started in the sixteenth century and continued, with varying degrees of intensity and success, throughout the seventeenth century, spearheaded by the so-called Kadızadelis—a group of "puritan" preachers whose agitation and calls to religious and moral reform of the empire shook the Ottoman capital and the Lands of Rum.

If we keep these developments in mind, it appears possible to speak of an "age of confessionalization" in which Ottomans and Safavids faced challenges similar to those of their European counterparts. The term "confessionalization" was coined in the 1970s by two historians of early modern Germany, Wolfgang Reinhard and Heinz Schilling, who sought to capture by it the interconnectedness of religious and political change in the sixteenth century.[52] They argued that in the period between the Peace of Augsburg in 1555 and the beginning of the Thirty Years War (1618–48), church (both Protestant and Catholic) and state cooperated for the twin purposes of social disciplining and state building, thus delineating the boundaries of various confessional entities in the Habsburg Empire.[53] According to Reinhard and Schilling, political elites in various early modern German states, building on the precept of "whose realm, his religion" (*cuius regio, eius religio*) that allowed them to formulate their own religious policy, sought to achieve a tighter politico-religious integration as a basis for community and state building. Since its formulation, the confessionalization thesis, with the accompanying concept of "social disciplining," has been tested and challenged by historians working on other parts of western, central, and eastern Europe, who by and large acknowledge its usefulness as a heuristic device while pointing to numerous regional differences and specificities, especially in terms of the ability of "elites" to impose official religious reforms on the "people" and the notion that the initiative in confessionalization necessarily came from "above" (i.e., from the state).[54] However, there have been no attempts to examine whether and to what extent the concept of confessionalization is relevant to the developments in early modern Islamdom.

I initiate this debate by arguing that the Ottomans experienced analogous developments and even implemented policies leading to integration of politico-religious spheres similar to those taking place throughout the Habsburg and other contemporary European domains. Historiographies of both the Ottoman Empire and early modern Europe typically ignore or treat as a mere coincidence the fact that the Sunni-Shiʿa polarization began to intensify around the same time that Western Christendom experienced the Catholic-Protestant split. In contrast, I argue that this was not a coincidence and that the process of formation of distinct confessional territorial blocks and forging of religious "orthodoxies" unfolded simultaneously in both Muslim and Christian empires in the sixteenth century as a consequence of imperial competition between the Ottomans and Habsburgs on the one hand and the Ottomans and Safavids on the other.

Although the fashioning of Habsburg, Ottoman, and Safavid imperial identities and religious orthodoxies ran parallel, through dialogue with each other, and at a similar pace from the early 1500s on, their more mature articulation can be traced to the second half of the sixteenth century when it became clear that neither side could decisively defeat the other or its respective internal "others." In the sixteenth century, confession building in the Ottoman Empire was a predominantly top-down process orchestrated by the sultan and his advisers, especially in the era of Sultan Süleyman. Similar to the dynamics in contemporary Catholic and Protestant polities, in the Ottoman (and Safavid) Empire religious rhetoric was infused into the processes of state and social formation, resulting in a tendency to sacralize authority exercised by the ruler. The project of Sunnitization and social disciplining initiated by the highest political and scholarly circles of the Ottoman Empire in the mid-sixteenth century was at least partially successful since it dotted the empire with numerous new mosques and *medreses* from which new generations of reform-minded preachers began to emerge. Consequently, in the seventeenth century new initiatives for religious reform and definition of "orthodoxy" began to be articulated "from below."[55] The palace- and Istanbul-bound sultans now came to negotiate leadership in religious reform with other social groups, most notably the mosque preachers who spearheaded the Kadızadeli movement. This new generation of reformers took issue with various practices they perceived as "innovation," particularly in the Sufi rituals and beliefs, but also increasingly targeted non-Muslims. Although the processes of confessionalization and Sunnitization affected most forcefully the Lands of Rum (Rumeli, Istanbul, and Anatolia), their repercussions were felt in other parts of the Ottoman Empire as well, especially Syria and Egypt.[56] As Chapters 5 and 6 will demonstrate, confessionalization in the Ottoman Muslim community was in a close dialogue with the parallel developments in the Ottoman Orthodox Christian community.

The adoption of the terms "early modern" and "confessionalization" from European historiography for the study of Ottoman history carries risks that have to be addressed. The term "early modern" has been criticized by many scholars for its Eurocentric connotations, ties to the problematic notion of "modernity," and general lack of definition.[57] Yet historians of Europe as well as of other parts of the world continue to use it to label the period between (roughly) 1500 and 1800, in the absence of a coherent alternative term that would articulate the evidence of common economic, political, and cultural trends that tied the continents together in ways unseen before the end of the fifteenth century.[58] One of the most controversial aspects of applying the notion of "early modern" beyond Europe in a comparative perspective has been the implied Eurocentrism of most such comparative efforts, since other cultures are typically assessed in terms of whether they lacked or possessed traits of the "West." In order to avoid the pitfalls of uncritical comparative history, Sanjay Subrahmanyam suggested the "connected histories" approach, which proposes to explore the interface between local and regional developments on the one hand and the supraregional or global on the other, aiming to discern how regional histories were connected. He argues that polities across early modern Eurasia could be examined within a common framework, but by keeping in mind social, religious, cultural, and political specificities of each polity and delineating local manifestations of global trends.[59] Trying to tackle the same issue of the dangers of comparative history, Peter Burke, one of the most important historians of the early modern era, suggested that taking other regions of the world rather than Europe as the departure point (or the norm) of the study could also help remedy the problem.[60] Both Subrahmanyam and Burke suggested focusing on noneconomic "linchpins" of the early modern world, such as "millenarianism" or a broadly conceived "humanism."

Heeding these constructive ideas, as well as the call by other critics of "early modernity" to reject the blanket 1500–1800 periodization in favor of a more study-specific time definition, this book suggests the "age of confessionalization and empire building" in a broadly defined Mediterranean region as a framework for study of the connected histories of the Ottoman Empire and its European and Safavid neighbors and rivals. By putting the Ottoman Empire at the center of the investigation, the book proposes to define this "age of confessionalization" based on the Ottoman experience of state and confession building, as well as the key moments in the Ottomans' interaction with their rivals, as an era that lasted from the 1450s, when Ottomans attained their capital with its imperial legacy, to the 1690s, when the Kadızadeli movement collapsed in the aftermath of the failure of the Second Siege of Vienna. The reason for embracing the concepts of "confessionalization" and "social disciplining," which also emanate from European historiography, is not to prove that Ottomans "had it too." Rather, the ensuing discussion draws on the growing literature showing that different parts of western and eastern

Europe had vastly different experiences of the projects of confessionalization and social disciplining. As a further contribution to the debate on the utility of these concepts as heuristic devices, this book will argue that they were not exclusively European phenomena but represented one of those linchpin trends (with specific local manifestations) shared among inextricably connected polities on different continents. In this way, the book challenges the notion that Islamic polities shared only in early modern economic, diplomatic, and military trends, while religion and religious politics set them apart from their Christian contemporaries.

## *"Syncretism," "Toleration," and Conversion in the Historiography on the Ottoman Empire*

In discussing the convergences among Christianity, Judaism, and Islam in different contact zones, and especially in the early Ottoman context, historians have tended to resort to the language of "syncretism," which in its most basic definition refers to blending of elements from different religious traditions.[61] The tendency to focus on "syncretic" phenomena and "toleration" (conceptualized as peaceful coexistence of different religious communities) has been particularly pervasive in recent post-Orientalist literature that seeks to move away from the notion of the "clash of civilizations," which continues to inform much popular and academic literature about the Ottoman Empire and the Middle East. This attachment to the concept of syncretism seems to persist among Ottomanists even though the term has come under heavy criticism in recent years from different quarters of academia because it presupposes purity of religious traditions and ignores precisely the kind of *longue durée* interaction and elaboration of common cultural material just discussed.[62]

In Ottoman studies the concept of syncretism has been associated with the theory about the proselytizing "heterodox" Sufi mystics (dervishes) since the 1930s.[63] According to this theory, antinomian dervishes unconcerned with Islamic orthodoxy incited numerous conversions among Christian peasantry in Anatolia and Rumeli by preaching a heavily "Christianized" Islam.[64] Particularly important sites of the proselytizing activity, according to scholars working in this vein, were the so-called ambiguous sanctuaries scattered around Ottoman Rumeli and Anatolia where Muslims began to worship their own saints at traditionally Christian places of saint worship. Ignoring the possibility of fierce competition and silent resistance on the part of those whose sanctuaries were usurped in this way, historians have postulated that ambiguous sanctuaries were the loci of religious blending and coexistence that frequently resulted in conversion to Islam, largely without any evidence based on nonhagiographic material.[65] In this view, syncretism constitutes a prelude to conversion to Islam.

During the 1990s, the concept of syncretism began to gain new ground among students of early Ottoman history, but this time with respect to the Ottoman state. Many of these studies reacted against Balkan nationalist and Orientalist historiography that portrayed the Ottoman rule exclusively in terms of religious fanaticism and oppression.[66] Others had a specific goal to reconsider the so-called *gazā* thesis based on the studies of the Austrian Ottomanist Paul Wittek from the 1930s and 1940s, which postulated that the principal reason for the emergence of the Ottoman polity was the Ottomans' pursuit of holy war (*gazā*).[67] These studies examined the process of early Ottoman state building and asserted that the Ottomans' political acumen, particularly in the fifteenth century, was decisively "syncretic" and manifested itself both as a lack of concern for religious boundaries and as a smooth incorporation of various non-Muslim military and administrative elements.[68] The concept of syncretism was here used to downplay the Ottomans' fervor for religion, in contrast to the previous generation of scholars who tended to overemphasize it, and to establish the image of the Ottoman state as tolerant and inclusive, unlike its modern successor states in the Balkans and elsewhere.

However, this renewed enthusiasm for syncretism, laudable as its motives may have been, opened a path to new questionable interpretations. In recent studies syncretism is almost by rule coupled with the epithets "heterodox," "unorthodox," or even "non-doxy-minded," implying that only those not "fully" Muslim or Christian had the capacity to be tolerant or reach out to the religious "other." In order for a modicum of coexistence to be achieved, it is implied, the integrity and correctness of the participants' faith must have been compromised. In some cases, discussion of syncretism is joined by the theory about "incomplete" or "superficial" conversions, suggesting that those who converted to a syncretic Islam are not "real, authentic" Muslims.[69] This kind of rhetoric stems from the Christian conceptualization of orthodoxy and overlooks Islam's unique flexibility to absorb Christian elements and make them part of its own tradition to the point that it is meaningless to insist on their Christian origins.[70] It also reveals an unwillingness to deal with the historical reality of religious difference and complexities of religious coexistence. The emphasis on the language of sharing and religious blending as well as on the "inclusive," "tolerant," and "pragmatic" Ottoman state obscures the ways in which competing groups in Ottoman society negotiated their differences and erases the complicated matrix of power relations attendant upon the process of early Ottoman state building.

Despite these criticisms, this book will not entirely reject the concept of syncretism but acknowledge that it remains productively problematic and seek to rethink it along the lines suggested by recent anthropological and historical scholarship. A recent study, for instance, argues that the arena of syncretism is as much the site of fierce competition and politicized difference as of contact and reconciliation.[71] As we have seen, similarities and convergences between different religious groups do not necessarily give rise to conciliation or unification. Depending on the historical context, they can in fact give rise to exaggerated and bitter contestation, precisely because of the need to obliterate the similarities and produce difference where it is scarce.[72] Thus, some scholars have suggested that syncretism be approached as conscious religious politics promoted by specific social groups that cannot be considered in isolation from the discourses of anti-syncretism that arise in reaction to it.[73] In relation to this dynamic and constantly changing dialogue between the politics of syncretism and anti-syncretism, we can also take the discussion on the issue of toleration in the early modern Ottoman Empire beyond the notion of *dhimma* (the pact of protection and freedom of worship extended according to Islamic law to the tax-paying Jewish and Christian subjects of a Muslim state), which has a limited explanatory value. As Karen Barkey points out, toleration in the Ottoman Empire was not something fixed or given by law but "the negotiated outcome of intergroup relations" that emerged and was maintained "both from the top down by the state and from the bottom up by communities where each shared an interest in the maintenance of intercommunal peace and order."[74]

Building on these new theoretical takes on syncretism and toleration, the ensuing discussion will explore how and by whom the shared religious content was appropriated to articulate (anti-)syncretic strategies in the early modern Ottoman polity. On the highest level, the politics of religious synthesis and toleration (as well as the politics of religious tension and withdrawal of toleration) was closely related to the development of the Ottoman imperial ideology, which underwent significant changes from the fifteenth into the seventeenth century, as well as to the constant reconfiguration of the elites and their relationship to the center of imperial power. However, the politics of religious synthesis in the Ottoman Empire was not an exclusive prerogative of the state, Sufis, or any other particular social group or institution. Rather, it was a set of social strategies articulated and rearticulated throughout Ottoman history by a variety of actors in different positions of power, ranging from converts themselves to their family members, friends, fellow-workers or soldiers, and Muslim and Christian communal leaders.

## *"Islam" and "Conversion" in the Historiography on the Ottoman Empire*

Although scholarship routinely refers to the Ottoman Empire as an Islamic state, studies of Islam in the Ottoman context are surprisingly few and largely interested in how the state enforced Islamic traditions of rule, which are imagined as timeless.[75] Although anthropologists have long questioned the notion of Islam as a homogenous religious tradition and explored the characteristics of regional "Islams,"[76] a study of whether or not there was an Ottoman Islam (or Islams), and what characterized it, remains to be written. Historians of the Ottoman Empire have by and large ceded the issue of religion in the Ottoman context to scholars working on Sufism, Islamic law, and Islamic institutions of higher learning. As a result, the interplay between religion and society in the Ottoman Empire is still rather poorly understood, and Islam, for the most part, continues to be studied outside a historical framework. A recent study that proposes to remedy this problem argues that there were four basic sectors producing interpretations of Islam in the Ottoman Empire: the central government (or the state), religious colleges (*medreses*) with their religious scholars (*'ulemā*), Sufi orders (*tarīkas*), and the folk (heir to a traditional culture informed by mythological elements).[77] Even though this fourfold division represents a significant step beyond reductionist portrayals of the relationship between (an essentialized) Islam and (an essentialized) state, it still proposes a static model that identifies what Talal Asad calls the "typical actors."[78] This model schematizes and dehistoricizes the actions of "typical actors," thereby masking apparent contradictions and changing patterns of institutional relations and conditions.

In order to obviate the pitfalls of overschematization, this study will approach Islam (as well as Christianity) in the Ottoman Empire as a historically emergent field of practice and debate.[79] This approach proposes to preserve rather than efface the essential feature of Islamic tradition—constant argument and conflict over the form and significance of practices.[80] Instead of assuming that the typical actors always acted in predictable ways, the ensuing discussion will explore over a period of time the competing Islamic initiatives as well as individual and institutional attitudes toward particular issues, such as conversion. By acknowledging that the Islamic tradition in the Ottoman Empire developed parallel with conquest, in a dialectical as well as dialogic relationship with the local traditions in the territories conquered, we can dispel the notion of a monolithic Islamic tradition ushered in by the conquering

Ottomans. In this way, we also avoid the pitfalls of questioning the level of the Ottomans' commitment to Islam and resorting to the concept of syncretism in the sense of religious blending or even worse, "dilution" of an (imagined) Islamic orthodoxy. The Ottomans began to articulate what constituted orthodoxy and heresy only in the early sixteenth century, and this process has to be historicized within the wider framework of confessional developments in early modern Islamdom and Christendom. In this way, this study proposes to move away from both Islamic exceptionalism (which seeks to understand confessional developments in Islamic societies solely within the framework of Islamic history) and Orientalist theories about an unchanging, monolithic Islam incompatible with other monotheistic religions.

Unlike the issue of Ottoman Islam, conversion to Islam in the Ottoman Empire has been the subject of numerous articles, dissertations, and monographs that have for the most part investigated the social and political dimensions of the conversion process, more often than not with a specific ideological agenda. Since the early modern period, observers and students of the Ottoman Empire have poured much ink on the question of what role the converts and conversion played in the foundation and successes of this polity. The early modern European *Turcica* literature displayed a marked resentment of the "renegades"—especially those European Christians who traveled to the Ottoman Empire to "turn Turk"—who were described as worse than the "Turks" themselves. Nevertheless, at the turn of the twentieth century, European historians began to postulate that renegades were in fact the secret of the Ottoman success, since Turks did not have the "civilizational requirements" to establish an empire.[81] The response of the Turkish historians that ensued sought to minimize any impact converts may have had on the development of the Ottoman enterprise, which was presented as exclusively "Turkish."[82] In many respects, this remains the historiographical orthodoxy in Turkey to this day.

Traditionally, conversion to Islam during the Ottoman centuries has been the favorite topic of the Balkan historians. They have produced numerous important studies based on Ottoman census records (*tahrīr defterleri*) that suggested significant regional differences in the dynamic of the process of conversion, demographic profile of the converts, and their reasons for becoming Muslim.[83] According to information from the Ottoman census records subjected to quantitative analysis, conversion to Islam in Rumeli was minimal in the fourteenth and early fifteenth centuries, increased slightly in the late 1400s, and rose steadily throughout the sixteenth century. It appears that the process peaked in the mid-1600s only to slow down and come to an almost complete stop by the end of the

1700s. However, not all parts of Rumeli witnessed the same dynamic. For example, the region of Thrace (conquered by the Ottomans in the mid-fourteenth century) saw extensive colonization by Muslims from Anatolia but also a steady rise in local conversions over the centuries. Conversely, Bosnia, conquered in the mid-fifteenth century, witnessed only a limited Muslim colonization but experienced a rapid and extensive process of conversion of the local population to Islam that was already complete by the end of the sixteenth century. By contrast, another majority Muslim area, Albania, which was conquered gradually over the course of the fifteenth century, saw a significant onset of conversion to Islam only in the second half of the seventeenth century.[84] In addition to regional variations and differences in the dynamic of conversion between the cities and the countryside, studies based on the census records also suggested that the first wave of converts to Islam were typically former members of the Balkan and Byzantine nobility seeking to become part of the highest echelons of the Ottoman establishment, whereas common people began to embrace Islam only later.[85]

Despite these important studies, it is nationalist historiography that left an indelible imprint on popular notions about the Ottoman period and the phenomenon of conversion in the Balkans. In some cases, nationalist historians "creatively" interpreted the data based on Ottoman census records to argue that the Ottoman conquest was followed by an unprecedented destruction and forced conversion.[86] These and other studies based on various fabricated "historical" narratives alleging the forced nature of conversion in the Ottoman Empire have resulted in a considerable corpus of Balkan nationalist historiography representing converts as either victims of Ottoman oppression or "traitors" to their "nation" and religion—sometimes both at the same time.[87] The child levy plays a particularly important role in nationalist historiography, where it is styled as the principal Ottoman method of conversion designed to rob the subject nations of their best and brightest, even though it was discontinued by the mid-seventeenth century and accounts for only a small number of converts to Islam during the five centuries of Ottoman rule in Rumeli.

In recent decades more balanced accounts that explicitly seek to move away from various biases in Orientalist and nationalist literature and explore new sources have emerged. Drawing on records from the Ottoman courts (*kadı sicilleri*), legal opinions of the Ottoman jurisprudents (*fetva* collections), and converts' petitions to the Ottoman Imperial Council (*kisve bahası* petitions), they make a significant contribution, for example, to our understanding of the institutional, legal, and procedural aspects of conversion in the Ottoman Empire, changes in the way the Ottoman state understood and sought to publicly present conversion, the agency of the converts, the importance of patronage, and the role of gender and slavery in the process of conversion.[88] We now know that it was fairly easy to convert to Islam in the Ottoman Empire and that people of all ages and from all walks of life exercised this possibility throughout the centuries of Ottoman rule, although the profile of the converts varied depending on the period. The technical requirements for conversion were the same, regardless of gender, social status, or age: one just had to lift one's right index finger and pronounce the *shahada*, stating that God is one and that Muhammad is his prophet, in front of two adult Muslim witnesses. Ottoman official documents as well as narrative sources described the act as "to become a Muslim" (*müslümān olmak*) or "to be honored by the glory of Islam" (*şeref-i islām ile müşerref olmak*); in the later sixteenth and seventeenth centuries the phrase "to embark on the right path" (*ihtidā etmek*) appears, perhaps reflecting a new sensibility toward the phenomenon. The act itself triggered a series of changes in one's legal status, and recent studies suggest that in many cases both male and female converts used conversion strategically to achieve desired social goals, especially in the later stages of the conversion process, in the seventeenth century.

Although invaluable in advancing the conversation on conversion to Islam in the Ottoman context, recent studies have privileged the state's perspective on the issue by drawing mostly on the archives of the Ottoman central government and Ottoman courts, which present conversion in highly formulaic administrative language that often completely effaces the converts' own words. In this way, they have perpetuated the notion that "the state" was the key agent of conversion rather than just one of many participants in the process, which involved a variety of social actors and initiatives. Sources of other provenance have either been ignored or used to illustrate the state's role in the process, while the attempts to gain a more "immediate" access to the converts' perspective have been declared futile because of supposed lack of self-narratives of conversion to Islam. For the same reason recent research on conversion to Islam remains largely Ottoman-centric, without references to the wider early modern context. If comparisons are made, they invoke almost exclusively earlier Muslim polities and practices of conversion, thus enhancing (if inadvertently) the notion that conversion to Islam was a sui generis phenomenon.

However, this contention has become untenable in the light of the growing literature on converts, captives, and other cultural intermediaries that has deeply eroded the Orientalist notion of clear-cut religious and cultural boundaries in the early modern Mediterranean.[89] Scholars from other fields, especially Venetianists, have recently highlighted the complementary value of documents from different Mediterranean archives for understanding how contemporary rivals viewed Ottoman conversion practices and their wider impact in the Mediterranean. Several recent studies suggest that the upward social mobility of converts to Islam, and the Ottomans' flexibility in accommodating various non-Muslim groups through granting them autonomy in return for performing valuable services, forced the Venetians and Habsburgs to adjust their own policies toward noncitizens and religious nonconformists in order to compete for the services of the population with a particular technological or political know-how, especially in the contact zones between empires.[90] Converts were particularly valued as recruits into the diplomatic, military, and commercial corps that sought to advance the competing religious, political, and economic agendas in the age of increasing confessional and imperial polarization in the sixteenth and seventeenth centuries. The phenomenon of conversion to Islam thus had a significant impact outside the Ottoman Empire that is crucial for understanding wider early modern political and religious dynamics. Nevertheless, in order to begin to study that dimension of conversion to Islam, it is necessary to significantly expand the analytical framework and delve into a variety of primary sources of different genres, as well as of diverse communal and geographic provenance.

## *Conversion to Islam in the Age of Empire Building and Confessionalization, 1450s–1690s*

Drawing on a variety of previously unknown or unexplored narrative primary sources in Ottoman Turkish, Latin, Italian, German, Serbian, Bulgarian, and French, the present study seeks to expand the conversation on conversion to Islam by raising new questions and introducing new sources to the discussion. By considering narratives produced by different individuals, communities, and institutions of Muslim, Orthodox Christian, Protestant, and Catholic backgrounds, it examines the debate about conversion to Islam and religious difference on a transcommunal and transimperial level within a Mediterranean-wide age of confessionalization rather than privileging the perspective of the Ottoman state. Although the ensuing discussion will be mindful of the dynamics within the Jewish community and among the Jewish and other Ottoman religious groups, the book focuses on Muslim-Christian relations, since Jewish primary sources were unfortunately inaccessible to this author.[91]

Chapters 1 and 2 explore how people learned what it meant to be a Muslim in the early Ottoman polity and how the place of converts in the evolving Ottoman society was negotiated. By focusing on Ottoman catechisms of faith (*'ilm-i ḥāl*), hagiographies of Muslim holy men, and other Ottoman Turkish didactic texts from the fourteenth and early fifteenth centuries, Chapter 1 examines the textual repertoire of early Ottoman Islam, the circumstances of its production and circulation, as well as different modes of interpretation to which it gave rise, leading to the religio-political differentiation within the early Ottoman polity. This chapter traces the development of Ottoman Islam to fourteenth-century Anatolia, with a special interest in the challenge posed to the Ottoman polity in its formative stages by the conquest of its first foothold in Rumeli in 1354. Chapter 2 then examines the narratives produced by Muslims and Christians in response to the absorption of Christian converts of Byzantine and Balkan origins into Ottoman ranks, particularly in the context of the emerging Ottoman imperial project in the era of Sultan Mehmed II, before and after the conquest of Constantinople in 1453. This chapter highlights the variety of syncretic and anti-syncretic strategies articulated by opponents and proponents of the converts' increasingly central role in the Ottoman army and government. These chapters complete the discussion devoted to the Ottoman polity in the fifteenth century.

Chapters 3 and 4 examine the converts' participation in the fashioning of an Ottoman imperial consciousness in the age of intense rivalries with the Habsburgs and Safavids, beginning in the early sixteenth century. Literate Ottoman converts to Islam engaged these issues through a variety of polemical narratives, often anonymous personal miscellanies, in which they creatively interpreted the history of religions to argue that Islam is a perfected version of Christianity and that "true" Christians were actually Muslims. They represented the Ottoman sultan as the prophesied messianic ruler and predicted his victory over his rivals. Chapter 4 introduces five previously unknown or unstudied Ottoman self-narratives of conversion from the late sixteenth and seventeenth centuries that are unique sources for understanding the nature of the converts' participation in the articulation of Ottoman imperial ideology in the age of confessionalization.

The last two chapters focus on the Ottoman Orthodox Christian community, starting in the late sixteenth century. Chapter 5 reconstructs competing Catholic, Orthodox, and Ottoman Muslim discourses on conversion and martyrdom and provides a historical context for the production of neomartyrologies. It examines the attempts of various Orthodox Christian groups to define a good Christian living under the Ottoman rule. Unlike Chapter 5, which focuses more on the Mediterranean-wide age of confessionalization, Chapter 6 explores neomartyrologies from the perspective of the Ottoman religious politics and Muslim-Christian (gender) relations. These chapters argue that neomartyrologies, which have heretofore been largely shunned as "politically incorrect" texts depicting Ottoman excesses against Christians, in fact represent a unique corpus of sources that raise interesting questions about how ordinary Christians and Muslims (and in some cases Jews) mobilized religion and law on an everyday basis in order to manage their daily lives. Neomartyrologies also allow a historian to sidestep the methodological trap of addressing interfaith relations in the Ottoman Empire, and particularly the issue of conversion, exclusively through Ottoman administrative sources and solely in terms of the relationship between the state and its non-Muslim subjects.

CHAPTER ONE

# Muslims through Narratives

## *Textual Repertoires of Fifteenth-Century Ottoman Islam and Formation of the Ottoman Interpretative Communities*

Sometime around 1403 Kutbeddin Mehmed İzniki (d. 1418), an Ottoman scholar from İznik, wrote the work *Mukaddime* (The Introduction)—one of the earliest, if not the first, manuals of faith (*'ilm-i hāl*) in Ottoman Turkish.[1] As its title suggests, *Mukaddime* aspired to be a comprehensive introduction to Islam and gained considerable popularity in the ensuing decades, so much so that in 1458 a copy was prepared for the imperial library at the express wish of Sultan Mehmed II (r. 1451–83), and some early sixteenth-century converts singled it out as the key text that guided them in acquiring their knowledge of Islam.[2] In the customary introduction where the author states the reasons for composing the work (*sebeb-i te'līf*), İzniki relates:

> This poor one saw that there are fine and beautiful books on compulsory religious duties [*farz-ı 'ayn*] but only in Arabic and Persian, and that many people cannot understand their meaning or if they can, they soon forget and cannot relate what they learned. For that reason this poor one wished to compose an introduction to the knowledge of obligatory duties in Turkish, so that it is read to the novices [*mübtedī*] and to the boys and girls who are about to reach maturity until they retain the commands of the law in their hearts and beliefs . . . and after they come of age they act accordingly.[3]

İzniki's *sebeb-i te'līf* presents an interesting snapshot of the Ottoman Muslim community in the early 1400s. It conjures up a developing community striving to meet the needs of the new believers, both novices in faith and the young, but lacking religious literature in the language of its congregants. İzniki's remarks remind the student of Ottoman history of a simple fact that is often forgotten: the development of Ottoman Islam has a history of its own, and this history unfolded parallel to the foundation of the Ottoman polity and Islamization of the domains that came under its rule.

This chapter explores the phenomenon of Islamization or the process by which the religious tradition of Islam became a major factor within the early Ottoman polity by focusing on the production and dissemination of early Ottoman texts seeking to instruct its readers and listeners how to become pious Muslims. These texts ranged from more formal catechetical works such as *'ilm-i ḥāl*s to hagiographies of holy men to various other genres of dogmatic (*'akāid*) literature. Islamization in the early Ottoman Empire was informed by unique political and spiritual currents emanating from thirteenth-century Anatolia—the search for alternative political and religious means of legitimization in the wake of the Mongol destruction of the Abbasid caliphate (1258) and the intellectual and spiritual legacy of the great Sufi master and systematizer of Sufi thought, Ibn Arabi. Furthermore, the processes of Islamization and foundation of Ottoman Muslim communities cannot be fully understood without taking into consideration the competing political and religious agendas that marked the formation of the Ottoman polity in the fourteenth and fifteenth centuries.

The concept of interpretative communities is central to the ensuing discussion. The spread of Islam in the Ottoman domains entailed the formation of multiple "textual" or interpretative communities—micro-societies organized around common understanding of a "text."[4] However, this text did not necessarily have to be a literary artifact—it could also be a group experience (such as participation in the conquest of Rumeli), an individual life story (such as the lives of warriors and saints), or simply a term.[5] The participants in a community shared views and experiences, which allowed them to coalesce around particular texts and determine their meaning and practical implications. The process of the formation of these communities, which constantly evolved and changed form over time around particular texts, accounted for diversity within Ottoman Islam.[6]

By focusing on the concept of a textual or interpretative community, it is possible to break down the distinction between oral and written modes of communication and bring listeners into the realm of written texts. The relationship between the written and spoken registers in Ottoman society was complex and dialectic because the two registers existed side by side rather than developed one after the other in an evolutionary manner. As a cultural milieu with restricted literacy and where the printing press (for texts in Arabic script) started being used only in the eighteenth century,

Ottoman society placed a special importance on the public performance of written texts as a means of disseminating information to those who could not read.[7] Preaching ranged from highly formal exhortatory religious sermons in the mosques to didactic storytelling in a variety of informal venues.[8] Its practitioners and audience also spanned a wide social spectrum and transcended gender boundaries. It is therefore my contention that in order to obviate the cultural models postulating the independence and occasional mixing of the "high" and "popular" cultures, it is necessary to focus on the cultural artifacts shared within a society and their multiple social appropriations.[9]

Several questions are particularly central to this investigation into the formation of the Ottoman Muslim interpretative communities and the repertoire of early Ottoman Islam. Which texts and what kinds of cultural brokers were pivotal in the formation of these communities? What kinds of religious sensibilities did they articulate? Was there anything distinctly Ottoman about them? How did religious interpretation and the understanding of history interact in the formation of interpretative communities in the early Ottoman polity? How distinct were these communities from each other?

Finally, we address two distinct aspects of Islamization, which nevertheless cannot be separated from each other and which operated simultaneously. On the one hand, the process entailed a "universalizing" impulse that sought to regulate belief, maintain Muslim identity through the production of prescriptive texts, and bring the people, both Muslims and those newly entering the community, under the umbrella of Islam. On the other hand, Islamization also entailed an "indigenizing" impulse or adjustment to the local conditions and challenges they posed to Islamic identity as it strove to take hold throughout the Ottoman domains, especially in Rumeli.[10] Although these challenges are often addressed in terms of syncretism or Islam's absorption of elements from local belief systems, we focus here on the impact indigenization had on relations within the Muslim community and the texts that were produced as a result.

## *In Pursuit of a Universal Community of Believers*

Teaching Islam to both "new" and "old" Muslims was central to the universalizing aspect of Islamization. However, as İzniki points out in his introduction to the *Mukaddime*, early Ottoman educators faced the crucial gap between Arabic (and to a lesser extent Persian) as the language of the authoritative Islamic texts and Turkish as the medium for religious instruction of converts and Muslim congregations in the Ottoman context.[11] The Qur'an, rather than the primary instrument of Islamization, was a venerated but ever-remote authority for most new Muslims, both in Anatolia and in Rumeli. This aura of incomprehensibility gave rise to all sorts of magical beliefs surrounding the Qur'an, a phenomenon that also occurred in other non-Arabic-speaking cultures on the path of Islam's expansion.[12] At the same time, the Qur'an could prove frustrating as a precise guide on how to improve one's conduct or lead a pious life. Thus arose the need for texts and individuals who would produce authoritative interpretation of the Islamic precepts embodied in the Qur'an and *hadith* (reports on sayings and deeds of the Prophet Muhammad), which explains how *'ilm-i hāl* literature came into existence.

A survey of library catalogues of Ottoman manuscript collections reveals that *'ilm-i hāl* and *'akāid* literature constitutes a significant portion of all collections and that certain works enjoyed particular popularity. For instance, in the most prominent Rumeli collections, in Sarajevo and Sofia, the list of the most copied works (after the Qur'an) is led by Birgivi Mehmed Efendi's (d. 1573) *Vasiyetnāme* (*Risāle-yi Birgivī*) (The Testament or Birgivi's Treatise) and *Tarīkat-ı Muhammediye* (Ar. *al-Tarīqa al-Muhammadiya*) (The Muhammadan Path); followed by Yazıcızade Mehmed's (d. 1451) *Muhammediye* (The Story of Muhammad); *Kitāb-ı Üstüvānī* (Üstüvani's Book), composed by a student of the Kadızadeli preacher Üstüvani Mehmed Efendi (d. 1661); and Hibetullah b. İbrahim's (fourteenth-century?) *Sa'ātnāme* (The Book of the Hour).[13] Contrary to the widespread belief that every *'ilm-i hāl* is essentially identical to other examples of the genre, these sources from the early Ottoman period suggest that researchers must subject themselves to the constant process of conscious defamiliarization. A brief investigation into the contents of these popular Ottoman manuals of faith will demonstrate several instances of progressive change in religious sensibility from early to late *'ilm-i hāl* literature and flesh out some of the main themes and frameworks that the texts aspired to impart to their audience.

İzniki's *Mukaddime*, written about 1403, was probably the first Ottoman *'ilm-i hāl*. The author himself was one of the first generation of Ottoman scholars educated in the theological seminary in İznik, established after the Ottoman conquest of the city in 1336 and initially led by Davud-i Kayseri (d. 1350).[14] In his introduction to this work İzniki argues for an accessible didactic text in simple Turkish language that would allow the young and the novices to easily comprehend the truths of Islam. In order to stay true to the ideal of simplicity, İzniki begins with the so-called Gabriel *hadith* in which the archangel Gabriel is directed by God to assume the appearance of a man and go to the Prophet Muhammad to ask him what faith is. Gabriel appears to Muhammad and requires of him an exposition of faith. In response, Muhammad declares that faith is belief in one God, in God's angels, in books that descended from heaven, in prophets, in the Day of Resurrection, and that all things good and lawful are because of God.[15] These six articles are then repeated again and again throughout the text as the preconditions for a complete faith. An important aspect of İzniki's work is the eschatological framework within which the question of knowing or not knowing the articles of faith is set. He relates the story of Münker and Nekir, the two angels who will question each person after death regarding the individual's belief in God, the prophet, and the contents of his or her faith. Depending on the answers, the person will be sent either to heaven or to hell. Both the beauties of heaven and horrors of hell are then elaborated to the minutest detail, drawing on the extensive tradition of the "torments of the grave" (Ar. *'azāb al-qabr*).[16]

What is interesting about this emphasis on the Gabriel *hadith* and the "torments of the grave" is the oral aspect of both traditions—one has to not only know the right answers but also be able to enunciate them. This suggests that Islam was most likely taught in a question-and-answer format. Indeed, evidence from Ottoman personal miscellanies confirms that converts memorized their Islam as a set of answers to specific questions on topics such as the contents of faith, obligatory duties, and schools of law. For instance, a personal miscellany of a Hungarian convert to Islam from the sixteenth century contains a catechism in which each entry begins with "If they ask you . . ." and continues with "you should answer them . . ."[17] Drawing from all the legal traditions rather than only Hanefi, İzniki relates the ambiguity regarding the need to profess orally the six articles of faith. He says that according to certain experts on law it is not necessary to say them out loud and it is possible to enter paradise by only believing in them; however, according to other interpretations, which he himself endorses as well, since the worldly government is external (*zāhir*), it is also necessary to outwardly express one's belief if one is to be considered a Muslim rather than an infidel.[18]

Regarding the issue of conversion, İzniki states that an infidel who becomes a Muslim is entirely cleansed of sins.[19] It is interesting that this issue does not normally appear in later catechisms, such as Birgivi's *Vasiyetnāme*, an *'ilm-i hāl* that achieved unprecedented popularity and is still used as a catechism among Muslims in Turkey and the Balkans.[20] At the same time, one can trace a development in interpretation of this particular issue in relation to the earlier *'ilm-i hāl*s as well. For example, a manual of faith dated tentatively to the mid-fourteenth-century Karasi province has a section in which converts, new Muslims, are said to be going directly to paradise without having to answer any questions after death or at the Day of Resurrection (*hesābsuz uçmağa varurlar*). The rules that are supposed to be applicable to all Muslims are therefore bent in the case of new Muslims, which testifies to a great concern and need to boost the spread of Islam. Şinasi Tekin has argued that this tenor of interpretation suggests that the manual was written by earlier converts to attract new ones.[21]

İzniki's comments relating to novices in Islam are completed by a discussion on whether it is essential to understand what is implied when one pronounces *shahada* in the act of conversion. He summarizes the views of Imam Abu Hanifa, who maintains that only the rebellious and obstinate cannot understand or refuse to understand that God is one. Whoever does not learn it or refuses to learn it is an infidel. İzniki also cites al-Ghazali, who asserts that only the faith of those who internalize *shahada* in their hearts leads to salvation. As for those who profess it only outwardly, it is sufficient to make them Muslims in this world, but they would be judged in the hereafter.[22] In conclusion, İzniki says that a believer is considered to be the person who enunciates the six articles of faith, who believes from the heart, and who performs the obligatory duties.[23] This indicates that he attributed particular importance to the condition of being a novice in Islam as well as to the challenges that numerous new Muslims posed to the Muslim community, such as how to know whether someone is a sincere believer or not. The rest of İzniki's work addresses numerous other questions on personal and communal worship, introducing Sufi values and views, and striving to provide the guidelines for a society that appears quite latitudinarian in its implementation of Islamic precepts.[24]

İzniki's attention to new Muslims stands in contrast to later *'ilm-i hāl*s. For example, unlike *Mukaddime*, which conveys the notion of a new and expanding Islamic polity looking outward, Birgivi's *Tarīkat-ı Muhammediye* and the *Kitāb-ı Üstüvānī*, written in the sixteenth and the seventeenth century, respectively, look inward, focusing on the problems of an established Islamic society with many rivaling registers of piety, struggling to impose order on diversity of practice.[25] For instance, Birgivi's *Tarīkat-ı Muhammediye* was written in Arabic and typically used as a manual by imams and judges (*kadı*). It covered the topics of piety and morality as well as the Sufi path to the divine.[26] Once a member of the Bayrami Sufi order himself, Birgivi sharply criticized the innovation (*bid'at*) and superstitions (*hurūfe*) introduced to Sufism by some *derviş* orders of his time and adhered firmly to the Sunni Sufi path as articulated by al-Ghazali, although with some important differences.[27] Birgivi insisted on the Qur'an and *sunna* (the deeds and sayings of the Prophet Muhammad) being the only sources of Muslim faith, dismissing pernicious innovations such as visitation of saint's shrines and accompanying rituals.[28] Moreover, in his *Vasiyetnāme*, he provides explicit rules not only of worship and belief but also of proper conduct, including the rules on what is improper to say, look at, or do.[29] This explicit effort toward social disciplining caused Birgivi's work to become an inspiration for the seventeenth-century Islamic reform movement of the Kadızadelis, who argued for a return to a pristine Islam from the time of the Prophet, devoid of accrued traditions and innovations. *Kitāb-ı Üstüvānī* reflects these Kadızadeli values, sharply criticizes perceived innovations introduced by the Sufis, and cites *Tarīkat-ı Muhammediye* in many places.[30] These texts thus reflect different moments in the history of the Ottoman Muslim community and attendant religious needs.

The works of the brothers Yazıcızade Mehmed (d. 1451) and Ahmed (d. ca. 1465), which broadly fit the genre of the *'ilm-i hāl*, further illustrate the conditions facing the early Ottoman Muslim community and underscore the interplay between the universalizing and indigenizing impulses inherent in the process of Islamization. The brothers hailed from Gallipoli (Tr. Gelibolu, Gr. Kalipolis), the site of the celebrated first Ottoman conquest in Rumeli in 1354, and they were quite the local patriots. Although they are particularly important for understanding the process of Islam's expansion into Ottoman Rumeli because they were the self-appointed "apostles" to the Muslims in Rumeli, the impact of their works was felt throughout the Ottoman Lands of Rum. Produced in the mid-fifteenth century, their literary works and efforts in *'ilm-i hāl* literature closely followed İzniki's. More important, their works are among the earliest examples of Ottoman literature written in Turkish.

In the conclusion to his book *Envārü'l-Āşikīn* (The Illuminations of the Enraptured) (c. 1449) Yazıcızade Ahmed writes that he completed this work in Gallipoli, "the excellent domain of Muhammad Mustafa."[31] He explains how the book came into existence. He had been pleading with his brother Mehmed, who was a "scholar and adept in spiritual mysteries" and privy to the mystical secret of the famous Sufi master Hacı Bayram, to compose a book that people could read. At his brother's insistence, Mehmed then wrote a work in Arabic entitled *Megāribü'z-zamān*. When he completed the book that brought together all the twelve sciences, he encouraged his brother Ahmed to translate it into Turkish so that the folk of "their province" (*bizüm ilün kavmi*) could profit from this diverse knowledge.[32] At this point, using the *Megāribü'z-zamān* as a source, "as if an ocean poured out into two entities," Ahmed put together the *Envārü'l-Āşikīn*, a work in prose, while his brother wrote *Muhammediye*, a work with almost identical content but in verse.

Ahmed also mentions another reason why he and his brother embarked on this enterprise. He says that a group of pious Muslims came to him one day and complained that ignorance and blind imitation in matters of faith and ritual were rife among the folk of their province. Those knowledgeable in religious interpretation were few, while others made the people go astray from God's path. A book was necessary that would explain the stories of the prophets and the laws and make the religious truths explicit. Ahmed says that he knew that many adequate books existed in Arabic and Persian but not everybody could discern their meaning, and that preachers often imparted their misinterpretations to the people. Like İzniki, Ahmed decided that a book in Turkish was necessary to remedy the situation. To this purpose he and his brother collected the wisdom from the Qur'an, *hadith*, *tafsir* (Qur'anic exegesis), and the holy books of *Tevrāt* (the Pentateuch) and *İncīl* (the New Testament).

In conclusion, Ahmed entreats God to be merciful to the people of Gallipoli because they are all either fighters on God's path (*gāzī*s) or martyrs (*şehīd*s). According to the Yazıcızade brothers, there are two kinds of *gāzī*s: some fight the infidels (*kāfirler*) while others battle their own sinful selves (*nefs*). The former then become martyrs in the hands of infidels, while the latter are "martyred" in the hands of God the Pardoner (*gaffār*). By destroying their sinful selves, the latter are annihilated in a spiritual, mystical sense while at the same time achieving the goal of every Sufi mystic, unity with the divine. As another Sufi thinker explains, "When the carnal soul is destroyed, [the seeker] becomes both a martyr and a *gāzī*."[33] Ahmed thereby pleads for a special status for Gallipoli as a land of *gāzī*s and mystics, both struggling on their path to God.[34]

The sense of mission that the two brothers shared comes across clearly and strongly both in the *Envārü'l-Āşikīn* and the *Muhammediye*. It is therefore all the more fascinating that they achieved the planned objective, and much more, of giving the common folk a text they could draw upon in learning and teaching the basics of Islam. Both works had an almost instant success across the developing Ottoman Empire, figuring as the most important sources on Islam next to the Qur'an.[35] It appears likely that in many cases the *Envārü'l-Āşikīn* and the *Muhammediye* actually represented the totality of what a person knew about Islam, with the Qur'an being inaccessible because of the ostensible language barrier.[36] The famous seventeenth-century Ottoman traveler Evliya Çelebi reports that throughout Anatolia people had committed to memory the Qur'an and the *Muhammediye*, drawing attention to the phenomenon of the *Muhammediye* reciter (*Muhammediye-han*). Interestingly, in his description of Gallipoli he emphasizes that in this area the poor and the rich, especially women, learned by heart the *Muhammediye* rather than the Qur'an.[37] A recent study suggests that over time the *Muhammediye* became the favorite religious literature of women and that even today

Muslim women gather in households for reading of this timeless *'ilm-i hāl*.[38] Apparently, the attraction for women was there from the very beginning, as suggested by the fact that some of the early sixteenth-century copies of the text were executed by women, which is a rare phenomenon.[39]

What kind of Islam was introduced in the *Muhammediye* and the *Envārü'l-āşikīn*, and what was the method of presentation? The two works have a slightly different focus but contain much of the same material. Roughly half of the *Muhammediye* is devoted to the Prophet Muhammad, his mission, his family, and his companions. The rest of the account mostly elaborates the events leading to and attendant upon the Last Judgment, developing an intense eschatological framework already introduced in the part concerning the Prophet. A short section at the end of the account is devoted to Sufi teachings and advice on how an individual believer should relate to Divine Truth and tame the sinful self. In contrast to the *Muhammediye*, the *Envārü'l-āşikīn* has more of an *'ilm-i hāl* layout and aspires to be a comprehensive compendium of necessary knowledge about Muslim faith. It is divided into five parts, each explaining, respectively, the Creation, God's commands to all the prophets leading to Muhammad, angels, the Day of Judgment and Resurrection, and the words of God (so-called *Hadīth Qudsī*) on different topics, mostly on who will enter paradise and who will not. Both brothers cite the authorities they are using in compiling the works; the authors who figure most are al-Ghazali and his *Ihyā' 'ulūm al-dīn* (The Revival of Religious Sciences) and Ibn Arabi and his *Futūhāt al-Makkiya* (The Meccan Openings). On matters of law the most often quoted is Abu'l-Layth al-Samarqandi.

The values promoted in the works of the Yazıcızade brothers are characteristic of Sufi sensibility. The ideals of poverty and rejection of the material world pervade both accounts and are given considerable space in the section on who will enter paradise without having to answer the questions at the Day of Resurrection. The respect for the learned ones is also emphasized, but the concepts of learnedness and pious asceticism (*zühd*) associated with Sufis are introduced hand in hand, suggesting that Yazıcızade Mehmed had people like himself and his brother in mind.[40] The correct and informed observation of one's religious duties, patience, and humility also command a lot of attention in the *Muhammediye* and *Envārü'l-āşikīn*. Radical Sufi practices like *melāmet*—avoiding the good opinion of the public by hiding one's good deeds and displaying one's faults in order to attain perfect sincerity in devotion to God—and belief in reincarnation (*hulūl* and *tenāsüh*) are explicitly condemned in the *Muhammediye*.[41] Both works are adamant about respecting Islamic law (*sharia*) and rooting one's piety in it.

Nevertheless, it is the drama of the Last Hour that underlies the works of the two brothers most decisively, just as it does in the Qur'an. In this context, the focus on Gallipoli as a place of special importance in the grand scheme of things is an intriguing feature of the Yazıcızade brothers' texts.[42] In the *Muhammediye*, Yazıcızade Mehmed states that he was among those who fought *gazā* against the "Franks" (Western crusaders) in Gallipoli and pleads with God to allow all the Gallipoli *gāzī*s to enter paradise without having to answer for their deeds.[43] Yazıcızade Ahmed cites the *hadith* that the most important *gazā* campaigns are those fought at sea, that those fallen in such campaigns are the most exalted of all martyrs, and that they go directly to paradise.[44] Both the *Envārü'l-āşikīn* and *Muhammediye* evince the idea that they are written, if we adopt the Yazıcızade brothers' division, by the *gāzī*s struggling on the path to God against their own selves, for the *gāzī*s fighting the infidels. Therefore, "a Sufi parallels, on a higher plane, the virtues of a Muslim warrior,"[45] which accounts for the pronounced rhetoric of *gazā* aiming to encourage the fighters in their endeavor.

The Day of Judgment and related issues of accounting for one's deeds and torments beyond the grave are central to another popular work of the *'ilm-i hāl* genre that has left an indelible mark on popular piety in the Ottoman Lands of Rum yet for some reason has so far escaped the researchers' radar. The text, *Sa'ātnāme*, was written by a certain Hibetullah b. İbrahim, probably in fourteenth-century Anatolia.[46] Although nothing is known about Hibetullah b. İbrahim, it is clear from the *Sa'ātnāme* that he was a Sufi *şeyh* (literally "elder," but it is also the title used for experienced spiritual leaders in Sufi tradition).[47] Another product of the Sufi milieu, this fascinating text written in simple Turkish develops the drama of the Last Hour and outlines what a believer has to do and what prayers he or she has to say every hour of the day to ensure a place in paradise before "The Hour" (*sa'āt*) comes. The central image of the text is the moment when the angels Münker and Nekir question the deceased to determine whether he or she should go to paradise (*Cennet*) or hell (*Cehennem*). The text promises to give guidance on how to do well on this crucial examination and/or how to enter paradise directly without having to account for past deeds (*hesāb*). The importance of this moment of questioning beyond the grave in the Muslim popular imagination should not be underestimated: recent anthropological research among Muslims in Bulgaria suggests that there was a genuine concern among Muslims in Rumeli about the ability to understand the questions Münker and Nekir will ask, since according to the tradition the angels will speak in Arabic. In order to remedy this troubling condition, some Muslim communities in Rumeli apparently developed a tradition about a benevolent intermediary, a translator of sorts, who will instead of the deceased respond to the angels.[48]

Despite its flamboyant fictive sections the *Sa'ātnāme* essentially adheres to the Islamic eschatological tradition as defined in the Qur'an and more so in *hadith*. In fact, the author keeps referring to the Qur'an and the collections of the "sound *hadith*" (*sahīheyn*) of Muslim (AH 202–261 / 817–875) and Buhari (AH 194–265 / 810–870), as well as to numerous unidentified commentaries on opinions of Islamic jurisprudents (*tefsīr-i fetāva*). According to Jonathan Berkey, the inclusion of *hadith*, often fabricated or unsound, was a salient feature of popular preaching.[49] In fact, one of the most contentious aspects of popular preaching in the eyes of the religious scholars was its noncompliance with the standards of transmission of religious knowledge. Even when the transmitted *hadith* was sound, in theory the preacher violated the "golden rule" by not personally hearing it being transmitted but reproducing it from books.[50] This alerts the student of Islam in the Ottoman Empire to the fact that popular preaching covered a lot of "gray areas" that were ignored by the imams preaching in the mosques, especially the so-called *İsrāilīyāt*, the traditions that entered Islam from Judaism and Christianity and became an inseparable part of Muslim piety. However, most frequently, at least in the earliest Ottoman period, the tensions between popular and authorized preaching concerned the authority to transmit religious knowledge rather than its content.

The key of the *Sa'ātnāme*'s appeal and unprecedented success is in an in-built formula that caused the text's multiplication in a manner comparable to that of modern "chain letters" that are supposed to bring you luck if you forward them to your friends. In the introduction, Hibetullah b. İbrahim promises to be the vehicle of the readers' salvation if they oblige to help him save his soul. He says, "I request of every person in whatever place this book is read to pray in the beginning and in the end and to donate the *sevāb* [God's reward for a pious act on earth] to this poor one [i.e., Hibetullah], so that with the benefit of your prayers I may save myself from the torments of the grave and find peace."[51] In return, all those who copy this book in beautiful writing, read it expressively, and listen to it attentively; all those who act according to its stipulations and pray at certain hours; all those who commission its copying and donate it will get their place in paradise in the vicinity of the Prophet. Hibetullah then cites his alleged communication with the Prophet, who promised to put all those who revere this book directly into paradise without accounting for their deeds.[52]

The message was not lost on the people—a survey of the many extant copies of the text reveals the magical aura that the *Sa'ātnāme* attained over time. Preceding or following the text one finds numerous talismans and prayers, calculations, and divination instructions.[53] The most fascinating aspect of the text's history, however, is its potential to communicate and "save" people with vastly different levels of literacy and access to the written word. By offering a chance to everyone from the copyist and listener to the person who commissions and donates a manuscript to find a place in paradise, the *Sa'ātnāme* not only breaks the traditional concept of the book but becomes almost a "multimedia" artifact that cuts across social boundaries. The manuscripts that remain testify to this, as they range from copies on lavish paper in a calligraphic manner in the theological seminary (*medrese*) of Şehzade Mehmed in Istanbul to copies executed in shaky, barely literate handwriting in books that suffered much damage from constant use. Particularly intriguing is the gender aspect—women owned, commissioned, and endowed many copies to local mosques, Sufi hospices (*tekke*s), and *medrese*s. These women's social status is sometimes explicit—for example, one of the copies is said to be endowed by a slave woman (Fatma *cāriye*);[54] in other cases women would be referred to as Emine *kadın*, which may denote a manumitted slave since the usual formula would include the name of the father.[55] Often the text would be commissioned by women from Muslim families, some even related to the local imam.[56]

Another category of literature essential in teaching Islam to novices in the early Ottoman polity was hagiography. Hagiography represented the strongest link between Sufism, society, and the teaching of Islam. Sufism supplied the main impetus for the production of hagiography in the Ottoman Empire because it was interested in the teachings of the past as embodied in the everyday practice of piety. Part of this quest was the emulation of the exemplary Muslims who managed to live in the presence of the divine in the course of their lives. For this reason, the compilation of hagiography had a special instructive and didactic character. In the introduction to one of the most famous compilations of holy men and women's lives, the so-called *Tezkiretü'l-evliyā* composed in the twelfth century,[57] the author, Feridüddin Attar, lays out a number of reasons why he produced this work. He states that in order to understand the Qur'an and *hadith*, one needs special linguistic abilities. However, the words of the *şeyh*s and holy men are the explanation of the Qur'an and *hadith* in the everyday language of the people and are thus particularly beneficial to the general public. He cites people who appealed to him to compile the work because they cannot read and write yet want to hear of the words and deeds of the famous *şeyh*s whose lives provide examples of how to follow God's precepts.[58] The stories of holy men and women, mostly Sufi masters and outstanding mystics, were therefore at the same time the most efficient teaching tool and the most popular reading matter at public gatherings.

In a society with limited literacy, reading aloud or reciting was an important aspect of the communication and articulation of social identity. It is not surprising that this social need gave rise to individuals of different profiles who specialized in oral performance and transmission of texts. The *Muhammediye* was recited in public places and at home gatherings, but its versified character probably made free additions to the core text difficult. Hagiographic and other didactic material was much more elastic and conducive to reshaping at each new performance. In that respect, it was closer to the historico-epic material that was commonly a part of the storyteller's (*meddah*) repertoire, such as the *Battalnāme* (the story of legendary Muslim fighter Battal *Gāzī*) or *Hamzanāme* (the story of Amir Hamza, the Prophet's uncle).[59] The tastes of the reading/listening public, as well as the list of most popular texts up to the end of the sixteenth century, can be gauged from the list of books endowed to the first "public" library, located in Cihangir mosque in Istanbul. The library was endowed in 1593 by Mahmud Bey b. Abdullah, the chief of boatsmen transporting animals and people across Istanbul (*peremeciler kethüdāsı*) and likely a convert, as his name would suggest,[60] and housed about forty books. Among these were *Muhammediye*; *Envārü'l-Aşikīn*; *Mevlid-i Nebī* (epic dedicated to Muhammad's birth); *Destān-ı Kurubaş* (an eschatological versified story with Jesus/İsa as the protagonist, also known as *Hikāyet-ı Cimcime Sultān*); *Destān-ı Ahvāl-ı Kıyāmet* (a poem recounting the events preceding the Day of Judgment); *Kıssa-yı Temmim-i Dāri* (an eschatological poem); *Battalnāme, Ta'bīr-i Rüyā* (a dream-interpretation manual); *İskendernāme* (an epic about Alexander the Great, containing a chapter on the Ottomans); *Tevārīh-i Āl-i Osmān* (the chronicle of the House of Osman); and *Yūsuf ve Züleyha* (a romantic poem).[61] Storytellers who performed these narratives in public often used the text only as a prop rather than actually reading from it.

In Ottoman society an oral performer could be at the same time an entertainer, a religious instructor, and a "historian" inasmuch as he recounted the events of the past and reinterpreted them in accordance with a particular audience's relationship to the past and present, as well as with a view to their specific perceptions of the divine.[62] The story of the past was therefore re-created and negotiated in the dialogue between the storyteller and the audience, making the narrative ever relevant to the conditions in the community that was created around the text. For instance, the chronicle of the Ottoman dynasty (*Tevārīh-i Āl-i Osmān*) authored by Aşıkpaşazade (d. ca. 1484) illustrates this process of negotiation very well because it records the (presumed) questions from the audience:

> Question: Hey dervish, you spoke about the dervishes and religious scholars of the Lands of Rum. Why didn't you mention Hacı Bektaş Sultan?

Answer: The holy men of Ottoman domains were those I mentioned. This Hacı Bektaş did not form a friendship with any of the members of the Ottoman dynasty. That is why I did not mention him.[63]

Here Aşıkpaşazade sets out to discredit the popular belief that the famous Anatolian mystic and holy man Hacı Bektaş (d. ca. 1271) was close to the first two generations of Ottoman rulers. By the end of the fifteenth century, when Aşıkpaşazade was writing, Hacı Bektaş was considered patron saint of the janissaries, but his cult also became the rallying point for a wide range of people discontented with Ottoman rule.[64] In his chronicle Aşıkpaşazade tries not only to undermine the charisma and importance of Hacı Bektaş and his followers but to establish his own Vefai Sufi order as intimately related to the Ottoman dynasty from the earliest period.[65] As this example suggests, the notions of history, present concerns, and religious identity came together particularly in the stories about the lives of holy men, with the distinction between religious and secular heroic figures often very blurred.[66] Thus, popular preaching and storytelling had a distinct political dimension that appealed equally to those who ruled and those who resisted rule.

## *What Was "Ottoman Islam" in the Early Fifteenth Century?*

To what extent were the conditions informing the spread of Islam in the Ottoman polity different from anything previously seen in Islamic history? In recent years scholars have increasingly argued for the necessity of a new analytical language to discuss the early Ottomans' religious environment—a language that acknowledges the historical reality of Ottoman Islam rather than describing it as a syncretic, shamanism-infused aberration from a supposed "normative" Islam, which in the context of the fourteenth and fifteenth centuries is a figment of scholarly imagination.[67] The necessity for this new language stems in part from the profoundly different political makeup of the Islamic world starting in the second half of the thirteenth century, but also from the fact that thirteenth-century Anatolia, the arena in which the Ottoman polity emerged, experienced in this period simultaneous processes of Islamization, Turkification, and an institutionalization of Sufi (or dervish) orders (*tarīqa*). The panorama of Sufism in Anatolia featured a mixture of mystic movements of different origins, from Iran and Central Asia to Andalusia, and was continually redrawn.[68] All of these influences were important for the development of Ottoman Islam.

However, it is of particular significance for the ensuing discussion to elucidate the impact of the intellectual and spiritual legacy of Ibn

Arabi, a Sufi mystic from al-Andalus also known as the Greatest Master (Ar. *al-shaykh al-akbar*), who sojourned in the Seljuk capital of Konya in the first half of the thirteenth century. He was without doubt the single most important influence on the development of Sufi thought from the mid-thirteenth century onward, and consequently on the development of Sufism in the Ottoman Empire.[69] By destroying the caliphate in 1258 as the pivotal Muslim political institution, the Mongols gave rise to a hurried search for alternative political and religious means of legitimization throughout the Muslim community. This need for creative new solutions to political legitimacy problems coincided with the rapid dissemination and unprecedented popularity of Ibn Arabi's thought, which would directly inform religio-political discourse in the Ottoman polity and become the basis for some proposed solutions to the vacuum in power in the post-Mongol Muslim world.

Ibn Arabi produced the most comprehensive exposition of Sufi metaphysics, which was later termed in Arabic *wahdat al-wujūd* or "unicity of being." According to this concept, divine attributes are manifest in all of creation, including humans, and the goal of each seeker of divine truth should be to explore every known path to knowledge in order to experience the infinity of the divine in one's self. Those who excel in the quest for knowledge of the divine are saints (Ar. *wāli*; pl. *awliyā*), to whom Ibn Arabi refers as "the heirs of the prophets" and "friends of God," and they are ordered in a hierarchy based on the degree of their proximity to the divine.[70] The individual able to achieve perfect oneness with God is a "perfect human being."[71] This perfect human being is a mystical axis or pole (*qutb*) who represents God's real deputy (*halīfa*) and heads the hierarchy of saints. Various hierarchies of saints each have their own *qutb*, who is in turn subjected to the "pole of the poles" (*qutb al-aqtāb*). Each age is supposed to have its own *qutb al-aqtāb*, also known as "pole of the age" (*qutb az-zamān*), who is sometimes identified with a messianic world-restorer, *mahdi*. According to Muslim tradition, the *mahdi* will come to revitalize the religion of Islam and prepare the ground for the final hour. Ibn Arabi saw the *qutb* as the fullest manifestation of the universal rational principle (*al-haqiqāt al-muhammediya*).[72]

Although Ibn Arabi's esoteric writings did not explicitly deal with "the practical interrelations between the spiritual realization and the historical forms of Islamic tradition,"[73] nor provide detailed guidance for an application of his ideas to the political community, by attributing to the individual a potential to attain the divine, his teachings furnished the basis for a new political imagination. This new imagination increasingly focused on the search for individuals whose charisma made them likely candidates for the rank of the *qutb*, who would mediate between the seen and unseen worlds. In the absence of a defined political structure in Anatolia, and given the political vacuum that with some interruptions lasted until the end of the fifteenth century, the social expectations of the Turkmen population in the region became increasingly centered on the continuing source of charisma epitomized by the local mystics and Sufi elders who styled themselves as the *qutb*. In the late fifteenth century this eventually led to the rise of Shah Ismail, head of the Safavid religious order and founder of the Safavid Empire (1501–1722), who best articulated the *qutb*-centered religious and political tendencies of the age by uniting the spiritual and political prerogatives in his ruling personality.[74]

How were metaphysical Sufism and Ibn Arabi's teachings disseminated in the Ottoman lands, particularly in the newly conquered Rumeli? As William Chittick points out, "Ibn Arabi's popularity among the Sufis should not be understood to mean that he was widely read by them. In fact, the vast majority were not scholars and did not have the requisite training to study his writings. Generally, however, those with an intellectual calling, who often ended up as guides and teachers, spoke a language that was largely fashioned by him and his immediate followers."[75] Indeed, as Ottoman institutions of higher learning were only in the process of being established in the fourteenth and early fifteenth centuries in cities like Bursa, İznik, and Edirne, many of the early Ottoman literati and legal scholars pursued studies in the colleges and Sufi hospices of Konya, Damascus, and Cairo, where Ibn Arabi left a lasting legacy.[76] Having participated in the international community of itinerant Muslim scholars who gathered in these scholarly centers, these literati would return to the Ottoman lands and often take up prominent positions.[77] The list of the earliest Ottoman commentators on the seminal works of Ibn Arabi includes many of the personalities that profoundly influenced the religious atmosphere in the nascent Ottoman polity: for instance, Davud-i Kayseri, head of the first Ottoman theological seminary; Şeyh Bedreddin (d. 1416), famous Ottoman jurisprudent and rebel; Molla Fenari (d. 1431), who came to be considered the first chief jurisprudent (*şeyhü'l-islām*) of the Ottoman Empire; Kutbeddin İzniki, author of the first catechism in Ottoman Turkish; and Yazıcızade Mehmed, author of the *Muhammediye*.[78]

It is significant that the authors of the first Ottoman catechisms were all devotees of Islamic mysticism in the Akbarian (from Ibn Arabi's title, *al-shaykh al-akbar*) tradition and experts in Islamic law.[79] In this way Sufi sensibility and Ibn Arabi's ideas were successfully imparted to the general public not only through Sufi hagiographies but also through Ottoman catechisms that made the language of Islamic mysticism a socially available discourse rather than an exclusive prerogative of the institutionalized forms of Sufism. As a consequence, early Ottoman society abounded in interpretative communities formed around Ibn Arabi's teachings, whose appropriations and applications to various religio-political agendas varied greatly, from more moderate, as in the case of the Yazıcızade brothers, to revolutionary, as in the case of Şeyh Bedreddin and other mystics with nonconformist millenarian programs. Yazıcızade Mehmed and Şeyh Bedreddin also provide us with good examples of how Ibn Arabi's legacy and Sufism in general facilitated "indigenization" of Islam in Rumeli and perpetuated the debates within the Ottoman Islamic community.

## *Challenges of Indigenization*

Clifford Geertz argued that an essential aspect of Islamization is the "effort to adapt a universal, in theory standardized and essentially unchangeable, and a well-integrated system of ritual and belief to the realities of local, even individual, moral and metaphysical perception."[80] John Renard qualified this phenomenon as an "indigenization" or a "process by which a culture, ethnic group, or region puts its own stamp on Islam, and it accounts at least in part for the diversity within Islamdom."[81] Although this aspect of the Islamization of the Ottoman domains is usually discussed in terms of Muslim-Christian relations and the blending of elements from the two religions that supposedly gave rise to a "syncretic," "Christianized" Islam,[82] it is worth considering to what extent this process affected relationships within the Muslim community itself. A pivotal event in the formation of the early Ottoman polity was certainly the Muslim troops' crossing the Dardanelles into Gallipoli in 1354 and the subsequent expansion into Rumeli—the European domains of the former Byzantine Empire that, unlike Anatolia, had witnessed virtually no exposure to Islam prior to this date. The process of Islam's establishment in Rumeli posed significant challenges to the developing Ottoman Muslim community. By the mid-fifteenth century the conquest of Rumeli became the central experience, a shared "text" around which interpretative communities of different social, religious, and political outlook evolved. Various narratives dating around and after 1450 articulated visions of Rumeli history from the perspective of the frontier lords (*uc beğleri*) and other *gāzīs* who attained glory through the conquest of the province, almost certainly better reflecting fifteenth- than fourteenth-century realities.[83] These texts often differed considerably from the narratives simultaneously or subsequently produced to tell the Ottoman version of the Rumeli conquest. Moreover, the Ottoman version, as enshrined in various chronicles of the Ottoman dynasty (*Tevārīh-i Āl-i Osmān*) from the late fifteenth century, displays choice elements from these dissenting narratives, essentially appropriating and neutralizing them.

The singular importance of Gallipoli for the Rumeli *gāzīs*, as well as the Yazıcızade brothers' Sufi affiliation and *gāzī* sensibilities, has already been mentioned. Several pieces of information in the *Muhammediye* help to further contextualize the two brothers in the politico-social network of mid-fifteenth-century Rumeli. Yazıcızade Mehmed reports that his friends encouraged him to present his work to one of the great sultans of the age—the Persian sultan, the Egyptian sultan, or the "Sultan of Rum, Murad b. Muhammad Han [Ottoman Sultan Murad II (r. 1421–51)]."[84] Mehmed declines, saying that the only door at which he will adore and revere is that of Muhammad, thus refusing to put his intellectual and spiritual charisma in the hands of any secular ruler.[85] In a later work, *Dürr-i Meknūn*, which was composed after the fall of Constantinople, Yazıcızade Ahmed implicitly criticized Sultan Mehmed II's self-image as an emperor in a Christian, Byzantine sense—a model that was contrary to the Muslim ideals of a ruler.[86]

The Yazıcızade brothers' work does not feature any radical Sufi ideology. In fact, it explicitly condemns practices such as *melāmet*, to which Ibn Arabi devoted considerable attention in his opus and which was embraced by another Ottoman interpretative community that formed around Ibn Arabi's ideas—the Melami order of dervishes, which branched off in the fifteenth century from the Bayrami Sufi order to which the Yazıcızade brothers belonged.[87] Nevertheless, the tension between political and spiritual powers, informed by Ibn Arabi's ideas of the holy men's greater proximity to God, is implicit in their work. This is further underscored by the story about the Yazıcızade brothers' Sufi master Hacı Bayram Veli and his visit to Gallipoli. According to *Tārih-i Edirne* and *Hikāyet-i Beşir Çelebi*, Hacı Bayram met with the Yazıcızade brothers on his way to Edirne from Ankara.[88] According to the legend, the reason for his voyage was that someone had slandered him to Sultan Murad II, saying that Hacı Bayram's disciples were multiplying from day to day and that he was likely to fix his gaze on the sultanate itself any day. Hacı Bayram thus went to Edirne to prove his obedience to Sultan Murad. The precedent for a holy man's claim to the sultanate would have been the revolt that had taken place just a few years before, in 1416, during which another famous Sufi mystic, Şeyh Bedreddin, supposedly aspired to conjoin the religious and political spheres in a bid for the sultanate (*saltanat dāvāsı*).

The modern historians' explanations of why Şeyh Bedreddin, one of the most educated Muslim scholars of his time and son of one of the Rumeli conquerors, rebelled have all been partially convincing.[89] However, it seems sensible to view his motives and the reception of his message in the context of the political mood and holy men–oriented *qutb* piety prevailing in the Lands of Rum at the turn of the fifteenth century. Both Timur's devastating defeat of Sultan Bayezid I at Ankara in 1402 and the ensuing civil war among Bayezid's sons (1402–13) left the Muslim community doubtful that the House of Osman had the spiritual and political right to rule. Bedreddin himself got involved in the civil war by serving as a military judge (*kadı'asker*) for one of Bayezid's sons, Musa, from 1411 to 1413. Upon Musa's defeat by his brother Mehmed, Bedreddin was exiled to İznik, only to promptly leave and become associated with several religio-political revolts in western Anatolia and Rumeli from 1413 to 1416, instigated by individuals described in the sources as his followers.[90]

In Bedreddin's hagiography written by his grandson Hafiz Halil around 1460, the author not only unambiguously suggests that the *şeyh* had a Seljuk lineage, which was politically superior to that of the Ottomans, but also states that Bedreddin's grandfather was the teacher of the last Muslim caliph, thus forging a strong legitimizing link between the *şeyh* and the last legitimate ruler of all Muslims.[91] Unlike the winner of the civil war, Ottoman prince Mehmed I, Şeyh Bedreddin had both political charisma, through his Seljuk lineage, and the spiritual charisma, through immense learning and achievements on the Sufi path. These qualifications must have made him in the eyes of many a superior candidate for the sultanate. The duality of his charisma also explains the varied nature of his followers, who ranged from disenchanted Rumeli raiders, descendants of early colonizers in Rumeli, and major political players of the day, to mystical Sufi circles, nomadic Anatolian Turkmen who allegedly settled in the area of Dobruca in the thirteenth century and subsequently embraced Christianity, and supposedly even Christians.[92] Not surprisingly, Bedreddin himself and his teachings, like those of his spiritual master Ibn Arabi, became the focus for the formation of many different interpretative communities during his life, as well as those proliferating to the present day.[93]

Even though the controversy over Şeyh Bedreddin's true goals and teachings still rages in scholarly literature, it is important to keep in mind that he was not executed for religious but for political transgressions.[94] It was perhaps the first time that the question of the boundaries between revolutionary mysticism and heresy surfaced with great vigor in the early Ottoman context and forced contemporary scholars to decide how far a Sufi could go in his religio-mystical preaching before he was called a heretic and/or a political rebel.[95] Given the appreciation of Ibn Arabi's teachings among the Ottoman learned, it must have been extremely difficult for religious authorities to define the boundaries between religious and political "transgressions" inspired by some of Ibn Arabi's theosophical ideas. His teachings on saints as "friends of God" and natural heirs of the Prophet were particularly conducive to endowing charismatic preachers and men steeped in mystical piety, such as Bedreddin, with the aura of holiness and attributes of power in both the material and spiritual worlds. According to the apologetic account his grandson left, Bedreddin was received as the Second Messiah (*mesīh-i sāni*) among both Muslim and Christian populations to which he preached.[96] There are indications that Bedreddin drew on the confluence of millenarian expectations and anticipations of a religious figure who was to renew religious worship and correct the injustices of political regimes on earth that were shared by Muslims, Jews, and Christians alike around the Mediterranean.[97]

As seen from the examples of the Yazıcızade brothers and Şeyh Bedreddin, the polarity between the Ottoman sultans' and sundry holy men's charisma based on a presumed greater proximity to God was articulated in a variety of ways in Ottoman Rumeli, ranging from less explicit to downright revolutionary. The memory of the earliest conquests in Rumeli became the rallying point for the formation of communities that elaborated narrative, religious, and political choices alternative to those of the emerging Ottoman polity. The great *gāzī* frontier lords (such as Mihaloğulları, Turahanoğulları, Evrenosoğulları, and Malkoçoğulları), heirs of the glorious tradition of Rumeli conquests in charge of expanding the boundaries of the province, in certain areas came to form alliances with the Anatolian Turkmen population (*yürüks*) who had been steadily pouring into the province since the mid-fourteenth century, giving the interpretative communities that were forming in Rumeli *qutb*-centered overtones and a sense of independence from political authority.[98] These alternative views came to be expressed in a series of "Rumeli narratives," intimately related to each other through the events and personalities they mention: the *Saltuknāme*, *vilāyetnāme* of Seyyid Ali Sultan (Kızıl Deli); *menākıbnāme* of Şeyh Bedreddin; *vilāyetnāme* of Otman Baba; and *vilāyetnāme* of Demir Baba.

What all of these texts have in common is a sacralization of the conquest of Rumeli as the pivotal *gāzī* event, and of the conquerors—other than the members of the Ottoman dynasty—as men particularly close to God because of their supreme service to the faith. So, for instance, the *Saltuknāme* elaborates the adventures of Sarı Saltuk, the hero who supposedly led the first wave of Muslim Turkmen immigration to the Byzantine territories along the Danube in the 1260s. This text ends with an episode of the Ottoman leader Orhan's son Süleyman Paşa's crossing to Thrace with forty holy men (*erenler*). They are represented as the heirs to Sarı Saltuk's legacy as the legendary conqueror of Rumeli and agent of Islamization. The same motif of forty holy men (*kırklar*), but this time appointed by the Prophet Muhammad himself and blessed by Hacı Bektaş, who crossed to Rumeli led by Seyyid Ali Sultan, is central to the plot of the *vilāyetnāme* of Seyyid Ali.[99] One should particularly notice the narrative sacralization of the event by means of numbers: according to the doctrine of sainthood developed by Hakim Tirmidhi and later elaborated by Ibn Arabi and adopted by different Sufi orders, forty is the number of saints that are invisible guardians of the world.[100] The crossing to Rumeli and the initial conquests also open the *menākıbnāme* of Şeyh Bedreddin, while the *vilāyetnāme*s of Otman Baba and Demir Baba deal with subsequent generations of Rumeli *gāzī*s and *evlād-i fātihān.*

A characteristic feature of the *vilāyetnāme* genre is the merger of a conquering warrior's and a saint's attributes in one charismatic person. These combined spiritual and material powers are juxtaposed to the purely secular powers of the Ottoman sultans. For instance, Seyyid Ali Sultan and Sarı Saltuk are both descendants of the Prophet (*seyyid*s) and possessors of sanctity (*vilāya*).[101] Following in their path, Şeyh Bedreddin—the son of a *gāzī* who participated in the conquest of Thrace—revolts against the Ottoman authorities, reportedly putting forward the idea that the spiritual and political leadership of the Muslim community should be combined in one person. After him, Otman Baba, who proclaimed himself the reincarnation of Sarı Saltuk, is known to have challenged Mehmed the Conqueror from his spiritual center in Thrace by claiming that he is the "pole of the poles" and therefore the ruler of both worlds.[102] This is also the title given to Demir Baba, whom both folklore and the *vilāyetnāme* characterize as the spiritual heir of Otman Baba and Şeyh Bedreddin, whereas Seyyid Ali Sultan (Kizil Deli) and Sarı Saltuk are mentioned throughout the text.[103]

One notable reason why *qutb*-centered piety may have spread into east-central Rumeli and became a distinguishing mark of the Islam that was established in the area is the particular nature of the Muslim conquest of the region. Unlike the conquests of Bosnia and, for the most part, Albania that were accomplished a century later (in 1463 and throughout the fifteenth century, respectively), the takeover of Thrace was not an imperially coordinated affair. Despite the attempts of the Ottoman chroniclers to smooth over the events following the conquest of Gallipoli by the son of the Ottoman ruler Orhan, Süleyman Paşa, and his premature death in 1357, other contemporary sources reveal numerous rival claims and legacies by those who also participated in the conquest of Rumeli and contested the notion of Ottoman political supremacy. For instance, there is an ongoing debate among scholars on who exactly conquered the city of Edirne, which was to become the Ottoman capital in

Rumeli.[104] The special status of the Rumeli conquerors whose energies the Ottomans eventually managed to mobilize for their own cause, such as descendants of Turahan, Malkoç, Mihal, and Evrenos, was evident in the fact that Ottoman sultans recognized their property rights to portions of conquered land that *gāzī* frontier lords had been allowed to transmit to their children since the time of the conquest.[105] In contrast, other Ottoman military dignitaries received a land grant (*tımār*) from the sultan in return for their military service, but upon their death the land grant reverted to the sultan as the proprietor of all the conquered land. Those Rumeli *gāzīs* who refused to submit to Ottoman authority were not only physically but also textually obliterated by being erased from Ottoman historical narratives.[106]

In the absence of a defined political structure, Rumeli Muslims carving their place in the predominantly Christian region sought assurance that their endeavor was divinely approved. Within this context of competing claims to land and leadership, the blessing of a holy man claiming to represent the link between the seen and unseen worlds was of particular political significance for the conquering lords, especially in their negotiation with the Ottoman sultan, who could not easily curb them. Although the relationship between the local Muslim saints and local Muslim potentates began in the early days of Muslim conquests in Rumeli, it became fully explicit and to some extent romanticized in the era when both frontier lords and dervishes, the two pillars of the early Ottoman polity, found themselves overpowered by Mehmed II's efforts at institutionalization and centralization in the second half of the fifteenth century. This era witnessed a concerted effort on the part of the frontier lords to facilitate the creation of interpretative communities, through textual (production of hagiographies of the *vilāyetnāme* genre) and architectural patronage (construction and reconstruction of shrine complexes). These communities were formed around the cults of the holy men who increasingly mobilized elements across Ottoman society that defined themselves, more or less explicitly, in contrast to the politico-religious agenda of Ottoman authorities. Although they were originally informed by Rumeli realities, by the late fifteenth century these communities began to find followers among discontents throughout the empire (most probably as a consequence of frequent military campaigns in both Rumeli and Anatolia), especially among the nomadic Turkmen in Anatolia who also gravitated toward *qutb*-centered piety and disliked the sultans' efforts to make them settle in one place and tax them.[107]

Interestingly, all of the holy men celebrated in these Rumeli *vilāyetnāmes* were gradually incorporated into the Bektaşi network of saints in the course of the sixteenth century, although originally they had very little or nothing to do with the cult of Hacı Bektaş. This process was related to the efforts of Sultan Bayezid II (1481–1512) to impose control on the vast heterogeneous body of those discontented with Ottoman rule, whose propensity for religious antinomianism with political overtones required an urgent solution in the face of the rising Safavid threat in the first decade of the sixteenth century. By encouraging the formalization and reorganization of the Bektaşi order at the beginning of the sixteenth century, Bayezid II hoped to reform the anti-Ottoman politico-religious energies of the discontents within an institutional setting.[108] As we will see, this initiative also has to be considered within the larger framework of the historical development of the concepts of heresy and heterodoxy in the Ottoman context during the early sixteenth century, much influenced by the Safavid Shi'a challenge. An important development that concerns Rumeli in this context is the process of the immigration and forced transfer (*sürgün*) from Anatolia to Rumeli of the Safavid sympathizers (the "redheads"), beginning in the era of Selim I (1512–20).[109] The synergy between these immigrants and local Rumeli discontents brought further changes and negotiations to the Rumeli texts and interpretative communities, shaping the heretofore loosely defined religio-political dissatisfaction more decisively in the direction of Bektaşi and/or *kızılbaş* and/or Shi'a propaganda in its various manifestations.[110] It is therefore not surprising that on the eve of the Battle at Çaldıran in 1514, as Ottoman forces were preparing to face off with the Safavid army, some Ottoman officials suspected raider commander Mihaloğlu and his troops of being in cahoots with the shah and expected him to fight halfheartedly or even desert.[111]

## *Conclusion*

This chapter has shown that discourses of religious instruction in the early Ottoman polity varied greatly depending on the profile of the preacher, storyteller, and other brokers of didactic texts. It has suggested that early Ottoman religious colleges educated scholars who were deeply steeped in Sufi metaphysics, especially in the teachings of Ibn Arabi, and disseminated the vocabulary and imagery of Sufism through didactic texts aimed at common folk. It is therefore unjustified to insist on a distinction between "Sufis" as those who embraced Islamic mysticism and the "religious scholars" as those who had no affinity for it. Rather, it is necessary to acknowledge that those who appropriated and applied different Sufi doctrines were embedded in different structures of power and exercised different socioreligious functions. Scholars in religious colleges founded by the sultans, individuals with Sufi sensibilities, or organized Sufi dervish orders that sought closer relationship with the political authorities, as well as the mystics and dervish orders who wanted nothing to do with the ruling establishment, all vied for recognition as *the* interpretative authority of Muslim faith and (Ottoman) history. The socioeconomic background of these groups also varied greatly, which means that they occupied different positions in Ottoman society, including those on the very fringes.[112] Although the parameters of the debate were changing with the shifting balance of power within the Ottoman polity throughout the fifteenth century, especially with the strengthening of the sultan's authority, the same issues would continue to be discussed in the early sixteenth century, albeit in a somewhat altered political and cultural context.

This multidirectional competition is nicely illustrated in an episode from the treatise by George of Hungary, a captive in the Ottoman Empire in the mid-fifteenth century, who relates a peculiar Sufi perspective. George recounts that in 1444 Sultan Murad II was approached by religious scholars (he calls them "tanismani," from Persian *dānışmend*, "a learned man") and dervishes (members of organized Sufi orders) to resolve a dispute over who should be receiving the offers, alms, and gifts of the people according to the law. The former asserted that since they were in charge of counseling, judging, governing, instructing, and transmitting the law to the people—without which the Ottoman realm would not function properly—they should receive all the donations. The dervishes insisted that they were the heirs and representatives of those who constituted the very foundation of Islamic law and that they interceded with God on behalf of the people, assisted with prayers in time of crisis, and fought off the calamities that threatened the state when all human efforts were futile. Murad II initially ruled in favor of the religious scholars; however, one night shortly after, he experienced horrible stomach pain and rushed to the latrine, into which he then fell as the seat under him cracked. Rather than fall all the way to the bottom, the sultan managed to hang on to a beam and began to shout for help. When no one came to rescue him for an hour, it occurred to him to invoke a saint, who indeed promptly appeared and pointed out to the astonished sultan that it was the "friends of God" rather than legal scholars who always appear in the hour of need. According to the story, after this event Sultan Murad declared that all of the donations should go to the dervishes and withdrew from public life to live as a mystic, leaving the throne to his son Mehmed II. George asserts that unlike his father, Mehmed strongly disliked the dervishes, among other reasons because a dervish supposedly made an attempt on his life.[113]

These passages from George of Hungary's treatise underscore the ambiguous relationship between various religious interest groups in the early Ottoman Empire and the Ottoman sultans. Although the sultan had the power to arbitrate on technical and administrative issues concerning believers and play different groups off against each other when necessary, he was constantly reminded, especially by the maverick Sufis such as those portrayed in the Rumeli narratives, that there were powers greater than he that he could not control and that could reduce him to a mere supplicant in the blink of an eye. In the age of millenarian expectations and *qutb*s who claimed to control both seen and unseen realms, the sultans, being strictly temporal rulers, were at a distinct disadvantage; however, as we will see, by the sixteenth century Ottoman imperial ideologues began to propose creative solutions for this problem.

CHAPTER TWO

# Toward an Ottoman Rumi Identity

## *The Polemical Arena of Syncretism and the Debate on the Place of Converts in Fifteenth-Century Ottoman Polity*

Sometime in the early 1460s, Konstantin Mihailović, an Orthodox Christian who was captured by the Ottomans during the siege of Novo Brdo (today in Kosovo) in 1455 and enlisted in the janissary corps, managed to regain his freedom, return to the Christian fold, and write a memoir of his experiences while in Ottoman service. Among other intriguing observations Mihailović offers his interpretation of the Ottomans' success:

> Turkish or heathen expansion is like the sea, which never increases or decreases. . . . Sea water is dense and salty, so that in some regions they make salt of it; nevertheless, without adding a portion of fresh water to the salt water, salt cannot be made. . . . The Turks are also of such nature as the sea: they never have peace . . . they round up and bring several thousand good Christians amongst the heathens; having been mixed they [the Christians] are spoiled, like the above mentioned water. Having forgotten their good Christian faith they accept and extol the heathen faith. And such heathenized Christians are much worse than true-born heathens. This then adds to the expansion of the Turks.[1]

According to Mihailović, the Ottomans deliberately incite mixing between Muslims and Christians in order to stimulate the latter's conversion to Islam and the Ottoman political cause. He implies that "mixing" is one of the Ottoman methods of conquest and the key to their success. However, by invoking the images of purity and defilement, Mihailović also informs his readers that, in his eyes, mixing is a negative phenomenon and that its end product, the converts, is inferior to any pure, even purely negative form, that is, the born Muslims.

Mihailović's narrative raises a number of intriguing questions. Who were these "several thousand good Christians" who were supposedly targeted for mixing and conversion in the mid-fifteenth-century Ottoman Empire? Who were the "Turks" that allegedly promoted mixing as a method of Ottoman growth and expansion? Was mixing universally endorsed by the Muslim community and condemned by the Christian one? How were the phenomena of mixing and conversion narrated and explained in the texts authored by different fifteenth-century Ottoman Muslims and Christians?

In modern historiography the mixing that Mihailović describes is often characterized as "syncretism"—the term that has become a code word for the latitudinarian nature of the early Ottoman religious politics and seamless incorporation of non-Muslims into the Ottoman state and society. However, such usage of "syncretism" smoothes over what was a considerably rougher fabric of early Ottoman history and glosses over the power struggle and political initiatives that underscored the encounter between different political and religious communities in the context of the Ottoman expansion in the fifteenth century. Building on recent criticism of the concept of syncretism, I will use this term to denote the conscious politics of religious synthesis promoted by specific social groups that has to be studied in conjunction with the phenomenon of anti-syncretism, or the politics of upholding religious boundaries.[2] The chapter reconstructs the Ottoman arena of syncretism as both the site of "politicized difference" and of "contact and reconciliation."[3]

The issue of syncretism in the Ottoman Empire is inextricably related to the phenomenon of conversion to Islam as the most emblematic act of crossing religious and political boundaries. In trying to reconstruct the process of conversion to Islam and incorporation of Christians and converts into the Ottoman ranks in the fifteenth century, scholars have been relying either on Ottoman administrative materials, such as census records, or on hagiographies and histories—rarely both. The reason for using two different source bases is, besides methodological preferences, that they seem to tell two different stories about who spearheaded the process of conversion. Studies based on Ottoman population censuses (*tahrīr defterleri*), the earliest of which date to Ottoman Rumeli in the 1430s, indicate that the process of conversion in this region varied greatly depending on the strategic importance of the area, was only in its inception at the time, and did not significantly impact Rumeli's overwhelmingly Christian demographic character until the following century.[4] These census records also suggest that many early converts exercised a military function, which led a number of scholars to argue for the pivotal role of the "state" in the conversion process.[5] However, fourteenth- and fifteenth-century Ottoman hagiographies (particularly of the *vilāyetnāme* genre) from both Anatolia and Rumeli imply that it was the Sufi mystics, typically in their dual role as holy men and *gāzī* warriors, who effected numerous conversions of Christians, thus creating the image of the dervishes as the most important agents of conversion.[6] The dervishes' roles in the Islamization of the Anatolian and Rumeli space, for instance, through the building of Sufi hospices, is well documented.[7] Nevertheless, there is no substantial evidence, other than hagiographic material, to suggest that dervishes of any persuasion preached overtly to non-Muslims or actively sought anybody's conversion.[8] In Ottoman historiography, both the "state" and the dervishes have also been portrayed as the key agents of syncretism.

The challenge that presents itself is how to approach the Ottoman administrative sources and Ottoman hagiographies together in order to achieve a more complex understanding of the early process of conversion to Islam in the Ottoman polity and of the politics of religious synthesis. Although some scholars have exposed the potential pitfalls of using Ottoman census records uncritically for the study of conversion,[9] hagiographies continue to confound students of the subject. What are we to do with numerous stories about dervish-warriors and charismatic preaching mystics disseminating Islam in Rumeli? Devin DeWeese suggested that rather than hope to demythologize conversion narratives and distill the kernel of historical truth, we must explore the ways their creators, both oral and literary, used religiously charged language at their disposal to express their visions of human and communal truths.[10]

Minding these methodological caveats, this chapter sets up a dialogue between the information from *tahrīr defterleri* (and other administrative sources) and various Ottoman narratives from the fifteenth century. It takes as its departure point scenes of conversion described in hagiographies, accounts of heroic exploits, and other texts and explores their polemical language and imagery in light of other nonnarrative contemporary sources. There are three types of converts that most frequently appear in fifteenth-century Ottoman narratives: the Christian warrior, the Christian maiden, and the Christian priest. Looking beyond these tropes, the chapter discusses contexts of conversion that emerge from the dialogue of sources and seeks to expose competing strategies for and against religious synthesis. It argues that "syncretism" in the Ottoman Empire was not something that was confined to the state, Sufis, or any other particular social and religious group or institution. Nor was it a spontaneous phenomenon that received little consideration by contemporaries.

A close reading of fifteenth-century Ottoman sources reveals a new polity with a diverse political landscape aware of the dire need to increase its manpower, yet at the same time deeply ambivalent toward incorporating those who until yesterday it had to fight. The issue of what and whom to incorporate into the nascent Ottoman Muslim enterprise stood at the center of the debates about the nature of the leadership and future of the polity. Mehmed II's conquest of Constantinople, the city embodying the Roman imperial idea together with the notion of the Christian *oikumene*, posed a challenge of self-definition not only to the Ottoman ruler but to all Ottoman interpretative communities delineated previously. Which of the Byzantine (and other) traditions and subjects should be admitted into the political community of the new rulers, and under what conditions? How can these traditions and people be simultaneously incorporated and their "infidel" past rendered innocuous? Who gets to define who belongs to the community of *gāzīs* and believers and who does not? As a result of these debates among various Ottoman interpretative communities, the parameters of a Rumi Ottoman identity emerged by the end of the fifteenth century, setting the stage for the articulation of an ecumenical imperial cultural outlook in the early sixteenth century.

## *Beyond the Trope of the Converted Christian Soldier: Contentious Politics of Recruitment and the Debate over the Trajectory of the Early Ottoman Polity*

One of the most fascinating fifteenth-century Ottoman narratives is the *Saltuknāme*, a work of the *vilāyetnāme* genre that recounts the accomplishments of Sarı Saltuk, the archetypal missionary dervish-warrior who is credited with the onset of Islamization in Rumeli. In the 1470s, at the request of the Ottoman prince Cem Sultan, a man named Ebu'l Hayr-i Rumi compiled this work from oral legends circulating for at least two centuries. The narrative of the *Saltuknāme* is particularly rich in scenes of Sarı Saltuk's duels with the flower of Christian knighthood and his overwhelming victories upon which Christian warriors, awed by the saint's extraordinary military prowess, convert to Islam. At the very beginning of Ebu'l Hayr-i Rumi's compilation, Sarı Saltuk fights Alyon-i Rumi, a champion of the pope and the Christian king. Upon defeat, Alyon embraces Islam as a sign of submission to Sarı Saltuk's overwhelming power. He receives a new name, İlyas-i Rumi, and becomes the saint's companion. Moreover, he volunteers immediately to fight the Christians in his stead.[11] Later on in the text, İlyas is courted by Christians to rejoin them. Besides killing the person sent to invite him back, he asserts that while he was an infidel, he did not have enough strength to kill fifty tied-up men, but now that he has become a Muslim, his sword is sharper than that of the Christians.[12]

Numerous other examples of converted warriors demonstrating exceptional zeal for their new faith appear in fifteenth-century Ottoman narratives. The most famous among them is probably Köse Mihal, the Christian lord of Harmankaya (near Bursa) and progenitor of the Mihaloğlu family, who became a follower of Osman and whose conversion is discussed in detail by the fifteenth-century Ottoman chroniclers Oruc and Aşıkpaşazade.[13] What should we make of these stories about zealous converted adherents to the Ottoman religious and/or political cause? Recent historiographical discussions dismiss the possibility of religious zealotry as an aspect of the early Ottomans' behavior, stressing instead the inclusiveness of early Ottoman policies. Furthermore, it is by now well established that from Osman's time and throughout the fifteenth century, Christians participated in Ottoman raids against other Christians, partook in the distribution of booty, and received land grants (*tımār*) in return for their services, all without having to convert.[14] Whose narratives, then, are these, and what is their function?

To begin to answer these questions, one has to look more closely at the question of Ottoman military and administrative ranks to see if the prominent profile of a military convert-recruit emerging from the fifteenth-century narratives is substantiated by other contemporary sources. Who in fact constituted the Ottoman army in 1350, in 1400, or in 1450? After the first establishment of the Ottoman forces in Rumeli in 1354, the region was dominated by various frontier raider commanders and their descendants, such as those from the families of Evrenos and Köse Mihal, the two early Ottoman allies of Christian origin, in addition to warriors from the Karasi province and groups of Anatolian Turkmen who came to settle in the region.[15] However, the Anatolian troops could not satisfy the Ottoman need for manpower in the region, and by the early to mid-1400s the picture significantly changed. According to one study, the percentage of Christian *tımār* holders in Rumeli in the fifteenth century varied from 3.5 percent to 50 percent of the overall number of *tımār* holders, depending on the region.[16] The majority of these Christians became Muslims in the course of one or two generations, even though they were not compelled to convert.[17] In many places, the sole defenders of the fortresses were Christians, often with only one or two Muslim officers. It can thus be surmised that in certain areas Christian soldiers (*vojnuk*s) and members of other different non-Muslim groups exempted from taxes for the services they rendered represented the majority of Ottoman troops.[18] The number of non-Muslims in the ranks of the

Ottoman army, especially among the raider (*akıncı*) troops, whose role was to ravage the territory before the advance of the main army, was also reportedly high. There are indications that non-Muslims were actually given preference over Muslims for this position.[19] In the 1450s, the post of grand vizier, the second most important office in the state, became the prerogative of the child levy recruits as well as the converted sons of Balkan nobility.[20] The janissaries, or the sultan's elite fighting infantry units created through *devşirme* levy sometime in the 1390s, were also of non-Muslim origin. In other words, by the early1400s, a great percentage (if not the majority at certain times and places) of the Ottoman military, as well as high-placed dignitaries in Rumeli, were converts to Islam, offspring of converts, or Christian adherents to the Ottoman cause, working and fighting alongside the Muslims from Anatolia.

When we turn to the narrative sources with this knowledge in mind, some intriguing new vistas open up. If we accept the likely theory that the audience relishing the narratives about warriors of faith (*gāzīs*) and their extravagantly violent treatment of infidels were mainly Ottoman soldiers, and if we keep in mind that many of those warriors were Christians and converts, we arrive at a seeming contradiction that is worth exploring in more detail. One should first imagine an Ottoman military camp on the eve of battle against a Christian enemy, with Anatolian Muslims, nomadic Turkmen resettled in Rumeli, and new Rumeli Muslims, as well as Christian troops, cooped up in close proximity to each other, tensions running high. A fifteenth-century Orthodox Christian source about the martyrdom of a certain soldier named George from Sofia gives us some insight into what the atmosphere in such a mixed camp could have been like. It depicts an incident from 1437 in which an altercation between a group of Muslim and Christian soldiers stationed near Edirne as part of the Ottoman army cost George his head because he was provoked to blaspheme against Muhammad and extol Jesus.[21] An Ottoman *gazavātnāme* from the fifteenth century recounting the events of the Crusade of Varna in 1444, entitled the *Holy Wars of Sultan Murad, Son of Sultan Mehmed Han*, also illustrates the challenge of deploying religiously mixed troops in Rumeli, which was still hotly contested between the Ottomans and Hungarians in the mid-fifteenth century. According to the text, Sultan Murad II gave the orders to his soldiers to kill those *vojnuk*s who provided supplies to the advancing crusader army in the region of Sofia.[22]

In addition to Christian troops were converts, caught in the middle between their new and their old communities, inevitably seeking to prove their loyalty to the new and distance themselves from the old coreligionists, both within their own camp and across enemy lines.[23] Familiarity between Christian Ottoman warriors and their adversaries must have resulted in some moral confusion among Christian supporters of the Ottoman cause. Regardless of what religion meant to the Ottomans and their rivals, it is undeniable that both sides ultimately construed difference along religious lines and that Christians on the Ottoman side knew that they were fighting under a Muslim flag. It seems possible that narratives displaying obsession with converting or killing the religious "other" (or simply that other who is not on our side) manifest in the *Saltuknāme* were partly produced and circulated by new converts to Islam, or even Christian affiliates with the Ottoman cause, to "resolve" the implicit contradictions—at least on a narrative level—and to prove their loyalty to the new membership group.[24]

A later source that testifies to the importance of Christian troops to the Ottoman fighting machinery well into the sixteenth century provides a glimpse of a figure of the Christian Ottoman warrior who would have delighted in the stories of the *gāzī* exploits while preparing to fight his fellow Christians. French traveler and geographer Nicolas de Nicolay reports in 1553 a fascinating encounter in Edirne with a prize-fighter (*deli*) of Slavic background from Grand Vizier Rüstem Paşa's retinue.[25] This fierce warrior, bedecked for battle and in search of his next military adventure, was dressed in wide pants (*şalvari*) made of bearskin and wore a long cap of leopard fur that fell onto his shoulders, with eagle feathers attached at the forehead. De Nicolay relates:

> I was moreouer curious to aske him by a Dragoman [interpreter] of what nation he was, and what religion he kept, wherupon wisely he gaue me to vnderstand that he was of nation a Seruian . . . and that as for his religion notwithstanding that hee dissembled to liue with the Turks according to their law, yet was he from his birth of heart & wil, a christian, & the better to make me beleeue it, he sayde in the vulgare Greeke, and in the Esclauon tongue, the Lordes Prayer, the salutation of the Aungell, and the Symbole of the Apostles. Furthermore I asked him why hee did apparrell himselfe so strangely, and with such great feathers, his aunswere was, that it was to shew and appeare vnto his enemies more furious & fearefull.[26]

And the enemies, for the most part, were other Christians.

A similar tendency to "resolve" the contradictions and prove loyalty is evident in the narratives of Christian captives who managed to regain their freedom from Ottoman bondage and return to Christendom. Konstantin Mihailović's memoir is a good illustration of the ambiguity surrounding the figure of the boundary crosser. It has to be remembered that in this memoir Mihailović had the task not only of serving the curiosity of the Christians in the West who eagerly consumed any stories about the "Turks" but also of exculpating himself from suspicions of converting to Islam during his relatively long service with the Ottomans. In other words, through this narrative Mihailović sought to be reintegrated into the Christian community. His characterization of the converts/participants in the Ottoman cause who forget their faith as a "species" inferior in every way to the adherents of either of the supposedly pure religious traditions is a strong anti-syncretic statement designed to prove his loyalty to the Christian community he rejoined and erase any doubts of his perhaps being "mixed" and therefore "spoiled."

Another narrative by a former Ottoman captive that became a "bestseller" in the West and that showcases to an even greater extent the challenges of accounting for one's behavior while living under Muslim masters and the need to resolve the contradictions is the *Tractatus de moribus, condicionibus et nequicia turcorum* (The Treatise on the Beliefs, Customs and Perfidy of Turks) by George of Hungary (ca. 1422–1502), published for the first time in 1481.[27] George hailed from Transylvania, where he was captured in 1438 during a raid by Murad II and taken as a prisoner to Edirne. He was subsequently sold and resold as a slave numerous times and spent twenty years in captivity only to regain his freedom, manage to escape to Rome, and become a Dominican monk. In the wake of the Ottoman attack on Otranto in Italy in 1480, he authored this narrative by which he hoped to strengthen the faith of his compatriots in the face of a possible Ottoman conquest and the impending conversions to Islam.

Unlike Konstantin Mihailović, who decidedly rejects Islam, George of Hungary fills his account with praise for the simplicity of Muslim rites and humility of its practitioners. So enthralled is George with Islam that the only argument he can marshal against it is that Islam's attraction is the evidence of its truly diabolical nature. Although he never explicitly admits it, it is clear from George's account that he actually became an active member of a Sufi (probably Mevlevi) community, only to abandon it after his escape.[28] Significantly, his account, which is in part a captivity narrative and in part a theological treatise, was profoundly influenced by the teachings of Joachim of Fiore, the Calabrian monk whose millenarian writings formed the basis of the early modern eschatological tradition in the West. The account had an eschatological framework that decisively influenced the Western Christian tradition of conceiving of the "Turk" and the appeal of Islam as a sign of the impending apocalypse.[29] George's admiration for Islam was therefore rendered safe by the language and framework of the monastic circles he joined.

The importance of the "language of transformation" or the necessity of adopting the rhetoric of a specific religious or social group one is joining should not be underestimated in the process of fitting in and distancing oneself from the previous membership group.[30] Among the Muslim texts, it is known that the *Battalnāme*, another compendium of stories that fuses the elements of warrior epic and hagiography (recorded in the Ottoman period but with roots in the oral culture of medieval Anatolia), was part of the janissaries' curriculum and was read and performed in the Topkapı palace school. Moreover, janissaries invoked the name of Battal *Gāzī* before charging into battle.[31] Like the *Saltuknāme*, this narrative was replete with imagery of a struggle against infidels and the conversion of valiant Christian fighters to Islam. The choice of this text illustrates how important specific group terminology and religious rhetoric were in the acculturation of converts.

The polemical language and group terminology a convert was exposed to depended on the nature of the interpretative community he entered. For instance, Konstantin Mihailović's account serves as a fascinating record of the janissary corps as a distinct interpretative community and introduces the reader to one of the many variants of Ottoman Islam in the fifteenth century. Of particular interest in this respect is the episode concerning the widow Karavida/Tchernavida and Osman(cık), which is found in an elaborate form only in Mihailović's memoir. According to the story, widow Karavida snubbed Osman, the founder of the Ottoman state, for his coarse farmer's garments and poured slops on him from the top of her castle. She also called him Osmancık (little Osman) in ridicule. In revenge, Osman had her thrown from the highest tower after taking the castle. Interestingly, the elements of the legend make sense only within Christian tradition—in the Muslim cultural context a widow would not be associated with evil, whereas in Christian tradition the widow in black signifies evil, death, or sickness.[32] It appears likely that this legend had non-Muslim origins and was circulated among the janissaries as an allegory for the Ottoman victory over the Christian world, with the black widow representing evil Christianity.[33]

Mihailović also relates some of the Islamic lore in circulation among the janissaries. What is immediately striking is the "Ali-centric" nature of early Islamic history retold by Mihailović. He states, for example, that "the heathens hold Ali to be a prophet like Muhammad" and that upon his death Muhammad appointed Ali as his successor.[34] The rest of the account is pervaded by the legend of Ali's miracle-working sword *dilfficary* (mispronunciation of Ottoman Turkish *zūlfikār*). These features of early Islamic history are also found in an earlier captivity narrative, that of Johann Schiltberger, who spent more than thirty years as an Ottoman captive (1396–1427). Interestingly, Schiltberger even classifies those who believe in "a giant called Aly, who was a great persecutor of Christians," as a separate religion. He also says that Muhammad made Ali "chief over all his people, and sent him to Arabia that he should convert Christians . . . but if any would not be converted, then he should compel them by the sword."[35] Ali was a hero of numerous popular epics that celebrated his prowess as a warrior; this fascination with him does not necessarily betray any Shi'a political loyalties among the janissaries in the fifteenth century.[36] It does, however, suggest the existence of a specific interpretative community that would be further pushed toward Ali-centrism through the intimate relationship between the janissary corps and the Bektaşi order, whose worship focused on Ali.[37] This order was institutionalized in the early sixteenth century with the purpose of absorbing and rehabilitating various religio-political discontents within the Ottoman realm.

It is important to keep in mind that the *devşirme* recruits who entered the Ottoman sultan's household and service were not the only community of converts. The history of the earliest conversions to Islam in the Ottoman realm and the absorption of non-Muslims into its political structures is also the history of early Ottoman state building and the struggles it involved. During the fifteenth century, the frontier raider commanders, who resisted the sultans' centralizing policies, also recruited converts into their households. Conversion thus played into the processes of ideological and religious differentiation already under way in fifteenth-century Ottoman polity. Narrative sources from the period, such as the treatise by George of Hungary, indicate that the phenomenon of enslavement through warfare was at least as important in this process of recruitment for various interest groups as the voluntary crossovers of the Rumeli Christians. George of Hungary describes throngs of merchants armed with chains marching alongside the Ottoman armies, ready to take the slaves off the soldiers' hands and transport them immediately to the closest slave market.[38] When one keeps in mind the Ottoman policy that those who did not surrender willingly to Muslim armies were subject to enslavement, and that many regions and fortresses around Rumeli refused to surrender without a fight, one begins to fathom the extent of the phenomenon. Frontier lords were in a particularly advantageous position to recruit men for their households and armies among the captured slaves.[39]

For example, according to the translation (dated 1496) of the endowment charter for the mosque complex in Plevne (Pleven in modern Bulgaria) of the famous descendant of Köse Mihal, the raider commander Mihaloğlu Ali Bey, the beneficiaries of his endowment—in the event his two sons should die—were to be his freed slaves (*'utekā*) Hızır b. Abdullah and Yusuf b. Abdullah.[40] Incidentally, the same Hızır b. Abdullah appears as the patron of an inscription at the tomb of Seyyid *Gāzī* near Eskişehir in western Turkey, the shrine complex attracting a wide variety of religious and political nonconformists, also patronized by his master, Mihaloğlu Ali Bey.[41] The second half of the fifteenth century witnessed a concerted effort on the part of the frontier lords to facilitate the creation of "alternative" interpretative communities through the patronage of texts and architectural complexes centered on holy men. These venerated figures increasingly mobilized elements across Ottoman society that disagreed, more or less explicitly, with the politico-religious agenda of the Ottoman authorities.[42] Hızır b. Abdullah's actions suggest that he was socialized into a particular interpretative community that shared the ideals of the raider commanders and their spiritual advisers who perceived themselves as the *true gāzīs*.

Several scholars working on early Ottoman history have already pointed out that as a discourse, *gazā*-centered narratives did not belong to one homogenous group, nor were the terms *gazā* and *gāzī* understood in the same way by all those who appropriated them over time.[43] Although the concept of *gazā* has been analyzed by historians mainly in the context of Muslim-Christian relations as "holy war" ideology, as a discourse that had a highly moral resonance, *gazā* rhetoric was much more important for intra-Islamic polemics as a vehicle for legitimization or delegitimization, for support or critique of certain political agendas. The Rumeli raider commanders' understanding of *gazā* and its objectives ran counter to Mehmed II's and his experimentation with non-Muslim forms of political legitimacy, particularly with the Roman and Byzantine imperial traditions that Mehmed sought to co-opt upon the conquest of Constantinople.[44] The converts socialized through the central governmental structures or in the sultanic household—the *devşirme* recruits, sons of the Balkan nobility, and high-profile voluntary converts, such as former Byzantine and Balkan commanders—could and often did stand for vastly different agendas and interpretations of *gazā* that carried more weight with the sultan and frustrated the goals of the "old *gāzīs*," such as raider commanders and different dervish communities.

The conquest of Constantinople in 1453 was an especially significant catalyst for the competing definitions of *gazā*. Moreover, by the mid-fifteenth century the debates about what direction the Ottoman polity should take began to reflect the importance of one's "tenure" in Islam. Thus, Çandarlı Halil, a member of an old Anatolian Muslim family that supplied viziers to the Ottoman throne, opposed the conquest of Constantinople, whereas Zaganos Paşa, a recent convert, encouraged it.[45] The fifteenth-century *Anonymous Chronicle* (*Tevārīh-i Āl-i 'Osmān*), one of the key sources on political and religious debates during this period, expresses the views of the "old *gāzīs*" who saw Edirne, the Ottoman capital before the conquest of Constantinople, as their moral center.

For the "old *gāzīs*," which included many disaffected Sufi mystics like Yazıcızade Ahmed, Constantinople was a city of polytheist idols that posed a distinct danger to the integrity of a Muslim enterprise and should ideally be destroyed upon conquest—an event widely viewed as prefiguring the end of the world.[46] These ideas were circulated in stories about the foundation of Constantinople and Aya Sofya that criticized Mehmed II's aspiration to appropriate the Byzantine imperial tradition embodied by the city of Constantinople and style himself an emperor in the image of infidel Byzantine rulers.[47]

"New *gāzīs*," on the other hand, were mostly former Christians who converged around Mehmed II and aspired to make Constantinople, the city that used to be the center of their old world, into the capital of the new empire. The new convert elite around Mehmed II, employed by the sultan to undercut the influence of the native Muslim aristocracy, left its decisive imprint on postconquest Constantinople, as the earliest available endowment charters for the city make apparent. These also show a remarkable absence of the religious scholars and dervish patrons of public works well into the time of Bayezid II, who sought to reverse Mehmed II's policies.[48] The chronicler Aşıkpaşazade, himself a dervish and participant in the raids in Rumeli, also expresses resentment for the influence converts and Christian associates exercised on Ottoman policy by criticizing Mehmed II for granting too much power to the convert Rum Mehmed Paşa during the resettlement of Istanbul.[49] The prominent profile of the converts in Mehmed II's administration and the "concessions" made to non-Muslims during his reign continued to play an important role in intra-Muslim politics well after the fifteenth century.[50]

Although both Muslims and Christians considered it a cataclysmic event that would prefigure the end of time, the Ottoman conquest of Constantinople also set off the politics of religious synthesis from different quarters. For instance, in a letter addressed to Mehmed II from Rome in July 1453 the Byzantine scholar and humanist George of Trebizond (Trapezunt) invited the sultan to unite humanity in a single religion and thereby realize the political unity of the world, as Alexander the Great did. This was a unique Byzantine text that considered Christianity and Islam on an equal footing, appearing to "recognize the divine origin of the Qur'an and the authenticity of Muhammad's prophetic mission."[51] Disappointed in developments within the Christian community and the failure of unification between Orthodox and Catholic churches in face of the Ottoman threat, George of Trebizond invited the sultan to embrace Christianity as an act of an enlightened ruler destined to surpass all of his Roman, Byzantine, and Turkish predecessors. According to George of Trebizond, that would not have been treason to the sultan's ancestral tradition since, he asserts, the divergences between Christians and Muslims are based less on the faith itself than on reciprocal ignorance, vanity, and knack for quarrel.[52] Pope Pius II echoed this invitation and encouraged Mehmed II to convert to Christianity as the first step toward his recognition as the world ruler, although unlike George of Trebizond's, his invitation firmly upheld the superiority of Christianity over Islam.[53]

The sultan himself showed a remarkable interest in the traditions of his Byzantine predecessors, and the conquest of Constantinople marked a new phase in his relations with both his Christian and Muslim subjects. According to legend, soon after the conquest he appointed Gennadios Scholarios, the champion of the anti-Latin party within the Byzantine ecclesiastical circles, as the first Orthodox Christian Patriarch of Ottoman Constantinople.[54] As a consequence, the Patriarchate would over time become an extended arm of the Ottoman government, and this would cause the debate within the Orthodox Christian community on the limits of intimacy with the "Turks." The Conqueror asked Gennadios Scholarios to produce an exposition, or rather apology, of Christian faith, which was translated into Ottoman Turkish in 1455–56.[55] Another high-profile Byzantine intellectual, George Amiroutzes, the philosopher and imperial official at the Empire of Trebizond (a Byzantine successor state that was absorbed by the Ottomans in 1461), also testified to Mehmed's interest in the matters of Christian faith and even recorded his supposed discussions with the sultan on this topic in 1463–65. Edited and adjusted though they were, the sultan's questions to Amiroutzes still suggest his real and lively interest in the faith of his Christian subjects, whom he felt obliged to protect and of whose cultural and political traditions he became heir.[56] Mehmed II ordered, in addition to religious polemics, a survey of Byzantine monuments in Constantinople and patronized a variety of translations from Greek.[57]

At the same time, it was precisely this experimentation with "infidel" traditions and practical measures taken to achieve the grandeur of a ruler in the mold of the Roman emperors that distanced the sultan from groups that considered themselves the moral and historical core of the Ottoman Muslim enterprise. One of the greatest grudges these critics (many of whom hailed from Rumeli) held against the sultan was his magnanimous policy toward non-Muslims during the repopulation of the conquered city, the forced resettlement of Muslim merchants and artisans from the provinces to Constantinople, and the subsequent decision to impose rents for houses that were initially granted as freehold to the settlers. Different religious brotherhoods were also alienated because of the sultan's decision to confiscate pious endowment (*vakıf*) lands to finance military campaigns.[58] All of this made it difficult for Mehmed II to embrace Byzantine imperial traditions to the extent that he perhaps hoped. It was only in the early sixteenth century, during the reign of Sultan Süleyman, that the central imperial spaces of Byzantine Constantinople, such as the Hippodrome, were fully incorporated into the Ottoman imperial ritual.[59]

Even though the Ottoman sultans engaged in the politics of socioreligious synthesis in their attempt to centralize and define their authority, it is analytically insufficient to view the Ottoman fifteenth century simply as an era of religio-political blending without investigating the challenges that Ottoman polity faced in the process. The incorporation of non-Muslims and converts into Ottoman ranks created tensions *within* the Muslim community that are rarely explored because historiography assumes that the Muslim community was geared toward conversion and spreading of Islam by default. Muslim narratives from the period, especially from the religiously mixed military ranks, showcase these tensions in the form of anti-syncretic discourse punctuated with violent and at times graphic imagery that is often explained away rather than situated in its sociopolitical context. One should only recall, for example, Sarı Saltuk's spearing of four hundred Christian monks and Seyyid Ali's (Kızıl Deli's) turning an infidel on the spit.[60] Adjectives such as *syncretic*, *heterodox*, or *metadox* obfuscate the fact that in many of these anti-syncretic Ottoman narratives difference was constructed along religious lines and firmly—at times even zealously—upheld. This does not mean that those who circulated such narratives were necessarily against conversion, converts, or even Christians among their ranks. In some cases it was the larger political agenda for which such recruits were mobilized that gave rise to religiously charged critiques. The meaning of an Ottoman Rumi identity was negotiated through these frictions. This process can be understood only by exploring the different registers of religiously charged language in these types of Muslim sources instead of celebrating the Ottomans' sagacious collapsing of religious boundaries or rendering religion as an insignificant aspect of Ottoman politics.

## *Bringing Up a Rumi: The Trope of the Converted Christian Maiden and the Domestic Politics of Religious Synthesis*

In 1545 Hayreddin Barbarossa (1478–1546), the famous Ottoman admiral, dictated his memoirs to Seyyid Muradi, who preserved them in a five-volume work entitled *The Heroic Exploits of Hayreddin Paşa* (*Gazavāt-ı Hayreddin Paşa*). Barbarossa's story begins in the aftermath of the Ottoman conquest of Midili (Mytilene) in 1462, when Mehmed II appointed a garrison to guard the island. The soldiers were supposedly lonely and bored, so they sent the sultan a petition complaining about their situation. The sultan then responded with an imperial order (*fermān*) allowing them to take Christian women they found attractive and marry them. If the women were not given over voluntarily, they were allowed to take them by force but without transgressing the *sharia*. In that way, the sultan asserted, Islam would spread and it would be easier for them to guard the fortress. One of those garrison guards was Barbarossa's father, Yakup Ağa, son of a cavalryman (*sipāhī*) from Vardar Yenicesi (Yannitsa in today's Greece). He took a Christian girl unmatched in beauty and had four sons with her.[61]

Regardless of whether the *fermān* cited in the *Gazavāt-ı Hayreddin Paşa* itself has any historical basis, intermarriage was a crucial aspect of the Muslim-Christian encounter and another important kind of mixing, to return to Mihailović's metaphor, that aided the spread of Ottoman control and Islam. Nevertheless, because of the nature of the Ottoman census and other records, which center on the male heads of household and omit women's names (unless they are widows), this dimension of the interfaith encounter is invisible in the Ottoman administrative sources and has to be discerned from narratives.

Intermarriage and concubinage offered benefits both for the state and for men on the ground like Yakup Ağa. It is hardly surprising that examples of women abducted or stricken by love at the sight of Muslim heroes besieging Christian castles abound in popular Ottoman literature for male audiences. The aspirations and imagination of the soldiers in this respect are perhaps best captured in the story of the conquest of Aydos Castle recounted by the chronicler Aşıkpaşazade. In this story, the daughter of Aydos Castle's lord (*tekfūr*) has a dream of a beautiful-faced man who will come and lift her out of a hole into which she fell, bathe her, and dress her in new clothes. The maiden realizes that her dream, which essentially announced her conversion to Islam, has come true when she beholds *Gāzī* Rahman, one of the leaders of the Ottoman troops besieging her father's castle. She helps *Gāzī* Rahman and his soldiers take the castle by ruse, and the lovers are united.[62] Although this story weaves together the religious and romantic aspects of *gazā* and celebrates the idea of mutual love, other contemporary narratives are concerned with more practical aspects of obtaining women through *gazā*. In the episodes about women, storytellers made sure to hint at the rewards to be attained by a warrior willing to participate in the conquests, but they also used the opportunity to explain the limits of what was permissible and lawful.[63]

Unlike the religious laws of Christianity and Judaism, which did not tolerate interfaith marriages, Muslim law stipulated that it was allowable for Muslim men to marry non-Muslim women, or more precisely, women of the Book (*kitābī*).[64] At the same time, however, Muslim women were not allowed to marry non-Muslim men. Unsurprisingly, the practice of taking Christian women in marriage or as slave girls was hardly looked upon favorably by the Christian population. The discrepancy in power and in sexual economy involved in the Ottoman conquest triggered the anxiety of miscegenation, which left a deep trace on popular Christian epics and narratives from the Ottoman period (on this topic see Chapter 6). It posed a great challenge to the guardians of the Christian moral community's boundaries, and women who crossed the religious divide through permanent or temporary (*kebin*) marriages, even without explicitly converting to Islam, quickly found themselves outside the bounds of "orthodoxy."[65] However, it does not mean that they necessarily stopped considering themselves Christian, and it is important to consider their role in the context of the discussion on syncretism and conversion.

Upon marriage, a non-Muslim wife had the same rights as a Muslim wife, and she was permitted to observe the precepts of her religion. Laws suggest that the husband could order his wife not to drink wine or bring the cross into the house but could not legally prevent her from doing so.[66] She would be able to read the Bible as long as she was doing so in a low voice. Whereas the children of an interfaith couple would be Muslim by law, through their mother they would be able to learn a different language, be exposed to the teachings of the New and Old Testaments, and perhaps even be secretly baptized. Some sources even suggest that in cases where the mother was Christian, female children would be baptized and males circumcised, although this would be an explicit violation of the *sharia*.[67] Similar cultural phenomena are reported even in cases where the wife actually embraced Islam upon marriage.[68] Interfaith marriages were therefore important contexts of religious change in which non-Muslim women operated as significant agents of religious synthesis. In these circumstances (anti-)syncretic strategies could become part of family politics and could be used by wives, husbands, and children.

Even though this aspect of Muslim-Christian interaction, interfaith marriages, certainly aided the expansion of Islam, it also profoundly affected the constantly evolving definition of what it meant to be an Ottoman. Although contemporary Christian observers (as do many Western scholars even today) insisted on referring to the Ottomans as "Turks" throughout the medieval and early modern eras, the category of "Ottoman" was steadily transcending the ethnic, linguistic, cultural, and religious boundaries of "Turk." This crucial transformation happened over the course of the fifteenth century as the offspring of mixed marriages and numerous new converts entered the echelons of the Ottoman elite and transformed the cultural outlook of the polity to give it a Rumi stamp. This new Ottoman Rumi culture was remarkably heterogeneous and polyglot, reflecting the cultural and religious diversity of the Lands of Rum, while at the same time uniting the vast Ottoman domains under the umbrella of Islam and the Turkish language. The biographies of people whose life and career illustrate this abound. For instance, the mother of Şeyh Bedreddin is said to have been a daughter of a Christian notable (*ban*); she gave birth to Mahmud Bedreddin in a church turned into a house at the fortress of Simavna (in Thrace, close to Didymoteicho in modern Greece), in AH 760 (1358/59).[69] Şeyh Bedreddin's grandson and hagiographer emphasizes his knowledge of the Greek language and his conciliatory rapport with Christians. In the *gazavātnāme*, Hayredin Barbarossa, whose parents' story was described earlier, is portrayed as a man who spoke Greek, knew the basics of Christian faith, and on one occasion showed care and respect for a wounded and captured Christian captain.

The intimate knowledge of the Christian tradition and languages did not make these two Ottoman cultural heroes less Muslim—on the contrary. As will be further illustrated, it was that acute awareness of other cultural and religious traditions that made Ottoman Islam thrive and represent itself as a perfected and superior version of religious truths revealed previously to Musa (Moses) and İsa (Jesus). A more analytical approach to the tropes of mixing, through Muslim-Christian marriages or otherwise, in the context of the developing Ottoman polity reveals that the characterization of Ottoman Islam in this period as "watered down," "Christianized," or "crypto-Christian" overlooks the competitive nature of Ottoman syncretism and Islam's unique flexibility to absorb Christian elements and make them part of its own tradition to the point that it is meaningless to insist on their Christian origins.[70] Although confusion in matters of religious dogma certainly may have afflicted some contemporary Muslims and Christians coexisting in the Ottoman domains, to characterize the entire spectrum of contemporary Ottoman Islam in those terms is a gross exaggeration. This type of analysis, often informed by Christian sensibility and definitions of heresy and heterodoxy, generally misses that what at first glance may appear as collapsing of religious boundaries is often a subtle polemical argument, as the next section will demonstrate.

### *Finding One's Own Personal İsa: The Trope of the Converted Priest and the Fifteenth-Century Polemical Encounter between Islam and Christianity*

In addition to prize-fighters and beautiful women, fifteenth-century Ottoman narratives are particularly concerned with the conversion of priests. In fact, the trope of the converted priest is featured in virtually every popular text that relates to conversion. In the *Saltuknāme* the priests and monks are proportionally the most frequent targets of Sarı Saltuk's proselytizing efforts, as well as victims of his rage. Interestingly, every episode of carnage or mass conversion of the priests in the account is preceded by a form of contest or debate that demonstrates Saltuk's superiority over his archfoes. A close reading of the episodes about conversion of priests takes us a step further in understanding the issues underlying the Ottoman politics of religious synthesis in the fifteenth century and the process of fashioning a Rumi identity.

Unsurprisingly, Ottoman narratives treat the figure of the priest as the most emblematic representative of the Christian community, in both a positive and a negative sense. On the one hand, the priests are the most hated members of Christendom since they act as advisers to kings and emperors in their politics of defiance toward Muslims and are generally perceived as the most ardent enemies of the Muslim faith. In the popular fourteenth-century text *The Book of the Hour* (*Sa'ātnāme*), there is an episode in which a nonbeliever (*kāfir*) is presented with an opportunity to die as a believer. On his deathbed he receives two visions: one is an angel exhorting him to embrace Islam as the only way to enter paradise; the other is the devil disguised as a Christian priest who claims that only Christians can attain eternal bliss and salvation. The man believes the priest and as a consequence undergoes horrific torments in hell.[71] On the other hand, it is exactly this status as the crème of the Christian community (together with nobility) that makes a priest the most desirable target of conversion. To convert a priest—the supreme connoisseur of Christian teachings—represents the greatest victory for a proselytizing Muslim because it constitutes a confirmation of Islam's truth by its most emblematic opponent. The conversion of priests thus epitomizes the strongest polemical argument for Islam over Christianity and for that reason appears almost inevitably in the hagiographies of Muslim holy men to illustrate their chosen status as mediums of divine inspiration and their ability to make the truth of faith apparent to even the staunchest non-Muslims.

In this second respect, a priest converted to Islam is the most intriguing figure in Ottoman conversion narratives because it reveals the value

Ottomans attached to expertise in multiple religious traditions. This attitude is best captured in a popular narrative, *Life and Deeds of Mahmud Paşa (Menākıb-ı Mahmūd Paşa)*, dating probably from the late fifteenth century. The narrative begins with a scene in which a sultan's emissary, sent to investigate abuses of officials, accidentally comes upon a congregation of three or four hundred monks gathered outside the city of Manastır (Bitola in today's Republic of Macedonia) for their annual competition in knowledge of Christian scriptures. The winner, as the emissary is told, is to be appointed as a high priest. A young man manages to solve the difficult scriptural problem posed to the gathering and is appointed the head of the priests. The emissary returns to the Porte and reports to Sultan Murad Han (Murad II) on what he saw in Rumeli. The sultan then sends the emissary back to Manastır to bring the young man to the court, where his intelligence could best be employed. In the meantime, the youth has a dream in which he sees his own conversion to Islam and future service with Sultan Murad.[72] The story places special value on the youth's knowledge of Christian scriptures—he is given over to Molla Gürani to be taught Qur'anic sciences to an even higher degree of excellence.[73] He eventually becomes Mehmed the Conqueror's celebrated grand vizier, Mahmud Paşa Angelović (fl. 1453–74).

According to studies on Mahmud Paşa, there is no historical evidence supporting the theory that he had been pursuing a career in the Orthodox Church before becoming an Ottoman vizier.[74] The fact that this plot device was used by the anonymous author(s) of the *menākıb* suggests not only that the Ottomans were aware that priests/monks were the cream of Christian society but also that a true Ottoman worthy of the leadership position should possess knowledge of different religious traditions. That would put him in the unique position to be a cultural and political broker and attract new adherents to Islam.

An episode from the *Saltuknāme* captures well this aspiration to master the symbolic language of rival religions to advance one's own. In this episode Sarı Saltuk preaches from the Gospel (*İncīl*) to Christian crowds in churches around Rumeli, moving his audiences to tears and, occasionally, to actual conversion. By taking this story out of its specific context, modern scholars have often read it as an illustration of Ottoman syncretism and conciliatory attitudes toward Christians.[75] A closer analysis, however, shows that its intended meaning is far more ambiguous, if not the exact opposite. Sarı Saltuk travels around Rumeli dressed as a priest and represents himself as a special emissary of Jesus (*Mesīh* in the text) to Christians who congregate to listen to his sermons.[76] He then preaches to them from the Gospel and makes them cry with emotion. However, this is not the Gospel as Christians know it. From Sarı Saltuk's debate with a priest further in the text, we find out that this is the "original, unaltered" Gospel that contains the announcement of Muhammad's prophethood, which, according to the Muslim anti-Christian polemical tradition, was erased from the Christian Gospels.[77] It is from this Gospel that Sarı Saltuk is preaching to the Christians, which is a powerful polemical argument in and of itself. Besides sermonizing, Saltuk tells congregants that the night before in his dreams he saw the *Mesīh*, who told him to discipline his community with the silver-gilded leg of the *Mesīh*'s donkey, a relic supposedly held in high esteem among Christians. Saltuk also tells them that whoever receives the most beatings will enter paradise first, and that a golden coin will be collected from each of them to be given to the *Mesīh*. Upon hearing this, obedient Christians, moved to tears, line up to get the beating and send a coin to the *Mesīh*, believing that it would lead to their salvation.

Sarı Saltuk appears here not as an emphatic proselytizer but as a trickster who manipulates the symbolic language of the infidel religion to intrude into the space reserved for holy men of the infidel community and displace their power.[78] What at a first glance appears as evidence of Ottoman conciliatory behavior toward Christians and acceptance of their scriptures is in fact an important anti-Christian polemical argument known as *tahrīf*, already outlined in the Qur'an, which maintains that Christians altered and corrupted their scriptures. The most powerful aspect of the story, that Jesus is represented as acting against his own community through a Muslim medium, is also a restatement of the Qur'anic idea that Jesus/İsa would explicitly distance himself from the Christians because they referred to him as the "Son of God" and that he is essentially a true Muslim. The story cleverly exploits the ambiguity of Jesus' religious identity to the Muslims' advantage, thereby turning a potentially syncretic theme into an explicitly anti-syncretic one. By posing as a priest, Sarı Saltuk draws attention to the importance of competence in religious polemics and mastery in rites, scriptures, and symbols of different religions if Islam is to prevail over its enemies. The episode also demonstrates the deeply competitive nature of the arena of syncretism.

Regarding the conversion of priests, the debate about Jesus as the key common denominator between Islam and Christianity was central to the (anti-)syncretic strategies of the involved parties. In the Islamic tradition, Jesus, or rather İsa, was the subject of hundreds of sayings and stories, constituting what one author termed the "Muslim Gospel."[79] To understand İsa's difference from Jesus and to commit to it effectively constituted an act of conversion to Islam. Christological miracles, such as walking on water or the resurrection of the dead (people or animals), which are reported in hagiographies of Muslim holy men as the most effective means of converting Christians to Islam, have to be understood in this polemical framework: a supernatural phenomenon replicating one of the wonders performed by Jesus is an argument against Jesus' uniqueness and the Christians' claim that he is the Son of God and God himself.

For this reason, proving the difference between Jesus and İsa point by point was the main substance of the Christian-Muslim debates, especially when it involved people so intellectually and spiritually committed to Christian doctrines as priests. For example, an undated but probably very early Ottoman source entitled by a later copyist as "A Debate between a Monk and a Muslim Elder regarding İsa" possibly represents a manual of how a debate like this was to be approached.[80] The text covers contentious points between Muslim and Christian teaching on Jesus, from the meaning of the word *faraklıta* (Paraclete), which the Muslims interpret as a code word for Muhammad in Christian scriptures, to the mode of Jesus' death, his elevation to heaven, and incarnation. As a result of the *şeyh*'s arguments, the monk converts, renounces the world, and enters the *şeyh*'s dervish order.[81] The text's language and imagery suggest that it was produced in a Sufi milieu.

What do nonhagiographic sources say about the Ottoman policies toward conversion of priests? George of Hungary writes that Ottomans did not really exert special efforts to convert anybody, but they gave better stipends to the monks and priests who converted because they were supposed to be an example to others. He cites the example of a Franciscan monk who received a more generous stipend than others from the royal chamber because he reneged.[82] Other Ottoman sources confirm this notion that Christian priests, both Orthodox and Catholic, converted to Islam and received generous support. Although it is hard to ascertain just how well priests fared upon conversion in the fifteenth century because of limited sources, in the records of important imperial dispatches (*mühimme defterleri*) and records of fiscal transactions (*ruznāmçe defterleri*) from the sixteenth century a number of converted priests can actually be traced.[83] In AH 989 (1581) a priest came to the Imperial Council to convert, reportedly after having dreamt of it—he took the name Mehmed and was given a small *tımār*.[84] In the same year, another priest who was a cousin of the chief of the messengers (*kapu oğlan kethüdāsı*), embraced Islam in the Imperial Council, requested support, and was given a *tımār*.[85] The following year, a seventy-year-old priest accepted Islam and took the name Mehmed. He requested to be given the accruals of the pious foundation of Aya Sofya, which were left unclaimed after the death of the previous beneficiary.[86] The records for the seventeenth century are even more abundant and unambiguously suggest both that priests were frequent converts and that a great ideological value was attached to their conversion.[87]

However, the most telling illustration of the Ottoman authorities' attitude toward Christian priests is found in a seventeenth-century source dating to the reign of Ahmed I (1603–17), which is actually a codex of the janissary corps detailing the history of this institution and the rules according to which janissaries were recruited.[88] The codex states that "according to the law, when the time comes that it is necessary to collect the children of the infidels, one son is taken from them. They should take a son of priests and of all families with good background among the infidels."[89] According to the sources, for example, Sokollu Mehmed Paşa (1565–79), the celebrated grand vizier who served under three sultans, was a *devşirme* recruit chosen exactly for these reasons. He was between sixteen and eighteen years old when he was taken away to Istanbul. At the time he was studying at the monastery of Mileševa where his uncle was the head priest. Born to a family of minor nobility in the village of Sokol (thus Sokolović or Sokollu), Bayo, as he was christened, satisfied not one but both of the preferences mentioned in the janissary manual. The fact that he was taken at a relatively old age compared to the regular *devşirme* conscripts suggests that the collectors attached special importance to this "find."[90]

## *Conclusion*

As the preceding discussion of Ottoman Muslim and Christian narratives suggests, "syncretism" in the fifteenth-century Ottoman Empire did not amount to a simple collapse of religious boundaries, inclusion without resistance, or lack of interest in the matters of religion. It was a complex arena of conflicting interests and initiatives represented by diverse groups of agents ranging from the Ottoman government, its political rivals, converts themselves, mothers and wives, to the Orthodox Church. Extant Ottoman narratives articulate various experiences of the encounter between different religious and political traditions that posed a serious challenge to everyone's definition of individual and communal identity. Even though the focus here is on the fifteenth century, it is important to emphasize that both syncretism and anti-syncretism were social strategies articulated and rearticulated throughout Ottoman history by a variety of actors and from different positions of power. In other words, the arena of syncretism was constantly constituted and reconstituted depending on the changing power dynamics within and outside the Ottoman state. We will see how the issues and agendas of the various participants in the Ottoman politics of religious synthesis change over time.

Although the agents of syncretism and anti-syncretism were multiple and diverse, they all relied on social networks to incite religious change and create a feeling of an (interpretative) community. The importance of the household—common, noble, sultanic, or otherwise—was paramount in this process. This perspective contradicts historiography on conversion to Islam, which views the key agents of syncretism and conversion (the "state" and the dervishes) as external to the communities to which converts-to-be belonged. As the dialogue of narrative and archival sources presented here shows, the importance of social networks in the study of conversion to Islam cannot be overstated. Even in the case of the janissaries, whose mode of recruitment inspires the view of the Ottoman state as an "external" agent of conversion, one could argue that the real religious change happened only within the sultan's household or in the context of homeschooling young recruits received when they were placed in different Anatolian Muslim families to learn Turkish and hard physical work as a part of their training. Other types of social relations, such as professional networks (on this see especially Chapter 6), also played an important role in the process of conversion to Islam.

Islamic mysticism complemented the process of conversion that was based on social and family networks, but individual Sufis and wandering dervishes had a minimal, mostly indirect impact on the phenomenon. George of Hungary, a captive who admits, albeit tongue in cheek, that he had converted to Islam as a consequence of his fascination with Sufism, explicitly states that his master of fifteen years played a crucial role in facilitating his exposure to Islamic mysticism and near conversion. George describes conversations with his master and mistress (who treated him as their adopted son) in which they encourage him to direct his supplications to different Muslim saints.[91] What George's personal narrative suggests is that it was not so much the dervishes in person but the language and imagery of Islamic mysticism made available to potential converts by their owners (if the convert was a slave), master craftsmen, already-converted family members, or fellow soldiers and curriculum instructors in the imperial palace that were important in the process of acculturation and conversion. The terms, imagery, and personalities associated with Sufism were not the exclusive property of the Sufi orders. They found their way into popular Muslim narratives through different registers of oral discourse, ranging from Friday sermons to popular preaching and storytelling. The stories about the lives of holy men like Sarı Saltuk were an indispensable tool for teaching the tenets of Islam to both new and old Muslims and a means of reinforcing their Muslim identity by providing the polemical language of Islam.

The complex politics of religious synthesis, multifaceted debate on the place of converts in Ottoman society, and the power struggles among different Ottoman interpretative communities throughout the fifteenth century eventually gave rise to a new, broader cultural outlook of the Ottoman polity by the early sixteenth century. Although some of the more controversial policies of Sultan Mehmed II were scaled back or reversed after his death by his son Bayezid II, who sought to restore good relations between the sultanic household and various religious circles, the policy of recruiting converts for the key positions in the state, including for the post of grand vezir, continued unchanged. So did the policy of marginalization of frontier lords and attempts to neutralize their followers with *qutb*-centric, Alid tendencies in both Rumeli and Anatolia through institutionalization of Sufi orders under the watchful eye of the state. At the same time, Constantinople's position as the empire's capital solidified as a local Muslim elite that identified with the city but continued to negotiate its relationship with the Ottoman dynasty gradually developed.[92] This new Ottoman Muslim urban elite built its identity—which came to be known as "Rumi"—in a selective and often competitive manner upon the religious and cultural past of its constituents. Rumis came from throughout the Lands of Rum, often (but not necessarily) were converts or descendants of converts to Islam, and often spoke several languages (Greek, Italian, or various Slavic languages) in addition to Turkish. For really accomplished Rumis, such as those educated in the sultan's palace or in numerous religious colleges set up in the capital and other major provincial towns in the late fifteenth and sixteenth centuries, learning Arabic and Persian as well as the basics of Islamic law was also a must. No matter where he or she came from, for a Rumi living in the first half of the sixteenth century, Istanbul (or as learned Ottomans also called it, *Kostantinīyye*) came to be the center of the world, the rightful seat of the empire, and the city from which the glories of the Roman emperors and Persian shahs of old were going to be surpassed by the achievements of the Ottoman sultan.

CHAPTER THREE

# In Expectation of the Messiah

## *Interimperial Rivalry, Apocalypse, and Conversion in Sixteenth-Century Muslim Polemical Narratives*

> Then the Turks will come into the City of Rome; the Romans will be bled dry by the rude and heavy burden. The writing thus says that the Turk will have his horse eat on top of the altar that is the first shepherd's. Our glorious Lady will show a miracle: the horse, now meek, will immediately kneel. When the Turk sees this miracle sent by God he will immediately be baptized and will repent his error.

In the late fifteenth and early sixteenth centuries prophecies such as this Venetian one began to circulate throughout the Mediterranean world, predicting the eventual Ottoman conquest of Rome and the sultan's conversion to Christianity as a prelude to the establishment of a Universal Monarchy (*monarchia universalis*) under the aegis of a single emperor and single religion.[1] George of Trebizond's invitation to Mehmed II to embrace Christianity as a prerequisite for establishing himself as the world ruler echoed this Renaissance revival of the (post-Constantine) Roman imperial model of "one emperor, one religion." The dreams of universal sovereignty began to loom large on the minds of rulers around the Mediterranean as they entered the sixteenth century.[2] The Ottomans' rapid assertion as the key power in the Mediterranean after the conquest of Constantinople brought them an aura of metahistorical conquerors whose seizure of Rome was feared to be imminent, especially after Mehmed II's attack on Otranto in 1480. By the time of Sultan Süleyman's ascension to the Ottoman throne in 1520, Ottoman territories straddled three continents, with the recent conquest of Syria and Egypt (1516–17) by his father, Selim I (1512–20), taking the pride of place. The Ottomans seemed poised to finally turn to the conquest of Italy and join the two Romes under their rule.

Nevertheless, Süleyman's ambition to feed his horse at the altar of St. Peter's was frustrated by the simultaneous rise of rival aspirants to universal rule—the Holy Roman Emperor Charles V of Habsburg (1519–58), who challenged the Ottomans in the Mediterranean and central Europe; and Shah Ismail (1501–24), founder of the Safavid dynasty of Iran (followed by his son Tahmasp [1524–76]), who challenged the Ottomans in Anatolia. This three-way imperial encounter was further augmented by a "millenarian conjunction" that gripped the early modern world from Latin America to India, as all monotheistic religions expected the arrival of the Messiah who would restore religion to its pristine condition, convert the unbelievers, and usher in the Day of Judgment.[3] This expectation, based in part on astrological prognostications, was enhanced by profound changes in the mental horizons of contemporaries across communal boundaries who witnessed repeated outbreaks of plague, church schisms and multiple popes, the spectacular rise of the Ottomans after the conquest of Constantinople in 1453, the discovery of the New World, changes in technology and increased contact between cultures, the expulsion of Jews from Spain, and the Protestant Reformation. These developments ushered in a universal debate about which religion would guarantee salvation at what seemed to be an impending Day of Judgment. Timely conversion to the religion of the expected Messiah was of central significance to one's salvation; however, the choice was far from obvious.

This chapter will explore the ways in which Muslims around the Mediterranean, especially Ottoman converts to Islam but also the Ottoman sultan and his advisers, various Ottoman learned men and mystics, Shi'a Muslims, and even Spanish Moriscos dealt with the issues of the "true" religion, the identity of the Messiah, conversion, and apocalypse in an age of interimperial competition, particularly in the first half of the sixteenth century. These issues emerged simultaneously in Christendom and Islamdom, just as they both began to experience religio-political fragmentation that led to the process of "confessionalization" in the Habsburg, Ottoman, and Safavid domains in the second half of the century. The discussion focuses on the little-studied diversity of Islamic initiatives around the Mediterranean as Muslims entered the tenth century of the Islamic era (1494–1592). This diversity came to the fore especially in the debates on the identity of the expected Muslim Messiah and his relationship to Jesus, who was central to the drama of the Last Days in both Muslim and Christian traditions and who linked Islam and Christianity in ways that some Muslims found uncomfortably intimate while others embraced it. Sultan Süleyman's experimentation with apocalyptic discourse in imperial propaganda constitutes a distinct phase in the processes of fashioning an Ottoman Rumi identity and of defining an Ottoman Muslim community and its relationships with other Muslims and non-Muslims.

Even though it is well known that Ottomans "aided" the Protestant Reformation by making forays into central Europe and thus distracting Charles V from his struggle at home, the Ottomans' intellectual engagement with the issues underlying the Catholic-Protestant split has never been examined.[4] Interest in the original Christian and Jewish scriptures, as well as the nature of spiritual authority, the possibility of spiritual renewal, and the proper role of the emperor and pope in religious and political life, was not confined to early modern European Christian humanists. On the contrary, the Ottoman and other Muslim polemical narratives testify to a much more significant interest and involvement of Muslim literati and politicians in the religious debates among sixteenth-century Christians as a consequence of the Ottoman emperor's aspirations to unite the world under the banner of Islam and arbitrate on matters of religion in his role as world ruler.

Converts to Islam were particularly important participants in these debates. In their writings many discuss the veracity of religious scriptures, salvation, spiritual renovation, and the Day of Judgment as well as the Ottoman sultan's role in these matters. As Ottomans' political eminence grew in the early sixteenth century, so did their ability to arouse expectations and attract converts both within and outside the empire.[5] Labeled by Christians in the West as "renegades," the term that merged notions of religious and political betrayal, as well as, by extension, unreliable character, Ottoman converts to Islam often felt compelled to produce or disseminate polemical works that validated the choice they had made, distancing them from their old and integrating them into their new community. Whereas some converts produced original works and openly promoted them, others copied existing works and edited them to suit their own particular concerns. Such edited and adapted polemical texts can be found in personal notebooks or miscellanies known as the *mecmūʿa*, which abound in Ottoman manuscript libraries and constitute a treasure trove for the study of the Ottoman literate audiences' tastes and personal universes. Altogether these narratives constitute a polemical corpus developed by converts for other converts and reflect concerns about the identity of the Messiah, apocalypse, and the role of the Ottoman sultan in the events of the Last Days.

## *Imperial Rivalry and the Apocalypse in the Converts' Works*

The text *The Story of Cem Sultan's Exile* (*Gurbet-nāme-i Sultan Cem*) provides an intriguing point of departure for an exploration of converts' polemical repertoire in the sixteenth century. The narrative relates the adventures of the unfortunate prince Cem, who after unsuccessfully challenging his brother Bayezid for the Ottoman throne fled the empire and suffered a life of exile and imprisonment in Rhodes, France, and Italy from 1482 to 1495.[6] During this time, until his eventual death in Naples in 1495, Cem was a pawn in the hands of Pope Innocent VIII and King Charles VIII of France in their diplomatic dealings with Sultan Bayezid II. Although the text provides fascinating detail on Cem's itinerary and reception among the European nobility, the main agenda of the narrative appears to be to show that the Ottoman prince did not convert to Christianity during his captivity.[7] The scene that precedes the polemical passages (to be discussed later) is particularly interesting, as it evokes the Venetian prophecy cited at the beginning of this chapter. It takes place at the papal court in Rome, where Cem Sultan allegedly discussed religion and politics with his captors:

> The late prince was given a book of history by one of the Venetian learned men. In this book it was written that after the year 920 [1514] a sultan named Süleyman from the House of Osman will become the emperor and embark on war for faith [*gazā*]. After conquering Hungary and undertaking many campaigns, several times he will try to launch a maritime campaign without success. Afterward he will create a great fleet that no one could oppose. And in whatever direction he goes he will be victorious. And this sultan of the fighters for faith, Sultan Süleyman, will come in person to Rome and conquer it, killing numerous leaders and learned men and the pope of the time. Having had his riding horse drink from the baptismal fountain in the churches, he will annex Rome to all of his protected domains, and he will settle there for a while implementing justice. This was written in their books eight hundred years before the year 894 [1489].
>
> When the late prince recounted this great thing, they seemed to have the same book as well; they fetched it, and on comparison they found the same account with even more detail.[8]

In continuation of the narrative the author writes that the Venetian dignitaries and the pope's advisers insisted on leading Cem Sultan into St. Peter's on a horse and planned to have his horse drink from the baptismal fountain in order to fulfill the prophecy under controlled conditions. They were exhilarated that a member of the Ottoman house actually reached Rome and that the prophecy about the sultan who would convert to Christianity, which they hoped would happen in Cem Sultan's case, was realized as a prerequisite for Christendom to enjoy undisturbed peace. However, the author concludes, they did not realize that the Ottoman sultan would have to fight his way into the city and that the time had not yet come.

Since Byzantine times, Venice had played an important role in diplomatic mediation between Constantinople and the Western Christian world—a role that it retained in the Ottoman period.[9] At the beginning of the sixteenth century, Venice increasingly came to rely on the Ottomans in resisting the pressures of the Habsburg emperor Charles V, who sought to establish his own supremacy over all of Italy. Although it is not precisely dated, the *Gurbet-nāme* appears to have been written in the early years of Sultan Süleyman's reign, sometime after the conquest of Hungary in 1526—a campaign that may have been undertaken by the Ottomans at the behest of the Venetians in order to distract Charles from Venice.[10] It is likely that the author of the text was an Italian-speaking convert who was well acquainted with the political atmosphere in Rome and Venice, even with local vernacular prophecies, and possibly involved in diplomacy. A sentence in the text suggests that the author was a companion of Cem Sultan during his exile in Italy and that he remained in Rome after the Ottoman prince's departure to Naples, where he died in 1495.[11] In the fifteenth and sixteenth centuries, as the Ottomans' diplomatic contact with Western Europe increased, they came to increasingly rely on converts to Islam who possessed the requisite linguistic backgrounds and skills for translation and diplomatic mediation.[12] It is possible that the author of the *Gurbet-nāme* was one of them.

Another such convert was Murad b. Abdullah, a Hungarian captured by Ottoman forces at the Battle of Mohács in 1526 who later became an official Ottoman imperial interpreter for Hungarian, Latin, and German and authored a polemical treatise arguing for Islam's superiority over Christianity. In this treatise written in 1556 Murad refers to contemporary Christian prophecies about Ottoman doom, which he says will not be realized:

> *Benī Asfer*,[13] of whom the infidels speak, will come out and, managing to get far into the Muslim territory, will subject the Muslims to the sword and conquer them, but the *Benī İshak* will come from Medina, and one group will engage the enemy. Finally breaking the enemy they will be victorious and will conquer Istanbul, shouting "God is Great!" [*tekbīr*]. As they cry out the *tekbīr*, the walls will crumble. Then while everybody is plundering, there will be a cry that the Antichrist [*Deccāl*] is coming, and everybody will leave their booty. Then they will turn toward that region, and in sum six years will pass between the coming of the *Benī Asfer* and *Deccāl*'s appearance. If within those six years their government does not attack, the people of Islam will rule again. Then İsa [Jesus] will descend to the Earth, and his prayer to God that he be made one of Muhammad's

community will be answered. After becoming a Muslim, he will kill the *Deccāl*. And then Gog and Magog [*Ye'cūc ve Me'cūc*] will come forth, and İsa, having said a prayer, will kill them too. After that the twelfth caliph [*halīfe*], who is the Messiah of the Age [*mehdī az-zamān*], will appear, and his reign will be the time of security and piety, abundance and low cost, and the wolf will walk together with the sheep. İsa announced this twelfth *halīfe* in the Gospel [*İncīl*], and this twelfth one is supposed to portend the decline of the community or the end of time.[14] And the Christians have been observing the successors coming from the Ottoman family and our current emperor [*pādişāh*] Sultan Süleyman, may God protect him and make him last until Judgment Day, being the twelfth since Osman, they expect the demise of the Muslim community and believe that this was announced in the *İncīl*. . . . The infidels' hopes that in the end the world will be at their disposal are based on this.[15]

In this passage Murad combines both sixteenth-century Christian and Muslim prophecies about the end of time and the Ottoman sultan's role in it. Numerous scholars have studied various European apocalyptic discourses about the rise of the Ottomans, especially after the conquest of Constantinople in 1453.[16] However, it is less known that the contemporary Muslim leaders, including the Ottomans, also conceived of their own rise in apocalyptic terms and used the apocalyptic idiom to wage propaganda war on their enemies in both Christendom and Islamdom. As Cornell Fleischer and Sanjay Subrahmanyam have shown, the Muslim world entered the tenth century of the Islamic era in anxious anticipation of the Last Days and a renewal (Ar. *tajdīd*; Ott. Tr. *tecdīd*) of the religious and political system that would be brought about by a Muslim messianic ruler whose coming was foretold by the ancient prophecies.[17] This anticipation was translated into political and religious propaganda that the Ottomans aimed at both the Habsburgs and Safavids, in addition to using it to strengthen Ottoman dynastic claims internally among their Muslim, Jewish, and Christian subjects. These multiple audiences account for the complexity of Ottoman apocalyptic discourse, which drew on both Judeo-Christian eschatological traditions and texts, such as the *Pseudo-Methodius* and the *Book of Daniel*, and on the Muslim, often mystically infused traditions, especially the eschatological teachings of Ibn Arabi.[18] Although the key message that the spiritual renewal awaited by all monotheistic religions in the late fifteenth and sixteenth centuries would be universally fulfilled by an Ottoman sultan was central to the political competition with both Christians and other Muslims, specific contexts brought out different features of the Ottoman apocalyptic propaganda.

Millennial expectations began to be associated with Ottoman sultans in the late fifteenth century, but the first to ride the wave of apocalyptic excitement was Sultan Selim I, who after his conquest of Syria and

Egypt in 1516–17 came to be styled in Ottoman documents as a "master of conjunction" or "world conqueror" (*sāhib-kırān*).[19] After Selim's death in 1520, his only son, Süleyman, with the help of his friend and grand vizier İbrahim Paşa, engaged in an image-making project that consciously drew upon the apocalyptic expectations that converged on him and were supposed to culminate in AH 960 (1552/53).[20] Throughout his reign, Süleyman had a court geomancer (*remmāl*), Haydar, who was privy to the most important political decisions and served as the sultan's confidante. His prognostications only enhanced Süleyman's belief that he was destined to unite the political and spiritual prerogatives in his own persona—last held simultaneously by the Prophet Muhammad—as expected of the messianic last ruler.[21] The image of Süleyman as a prophesied world conqueror and messianic renewer of religion (*müceddid*) was also disseminated through the works of numerous other Ottoman state officials, poets, and popular authors.[22] Foreign envoys' reports from Istanbul in the sixteenth century testify to the ubiquity of prophetic lore and gossip centering on the sultan and his chief men on the streets of the Ottoman capital.[23] Ottoman imperial apocalyptic propaganda had success among non-Muslim audiences as well. For instance, some contemporary Jewish authors, such as the Cretan Romaniote Rabbi Eliyahu Capsali, embraced the idea of the Ottoman sultan as the prophesied conqueror who would usher in the messianic era and bring about the salvation of the Jews.[24] Although the Orthodox Christians produced numerous apocalyptic works in the post-Byzantine period foretelling the return of the "Last Emperor" who would overthrow the Ottomans, they nevertheless conceived of and depicted the Ottoman sultans as the heirs of Byzantine emperors within an apocalyptic framework.[25]

However, Selim and Süleyman were not the only individuals within Islamdom aspiring to the title of the Muslim Messiah or *mahdi*. According to Islamic dispensation, the *mahdi* was the "pole of the poles" (*qutb al-aqtāb*) who would combine knowledge of the divine with supreme martial capabilities. At the dawn of the sixteenth century Shah Ismail, founder of the Shi'a Safavid state in Iran, captured the loyalties of the Turkmen population in Anatolia, the so-called *kızılbaş*, by uniting the spiritual and political prerogatives in his ruling personality and proclaiming himself the *mahdi*. It was traditionally the Shi'a community that felt most comfortable with the idea of a messianic ruler who would unite the spiritual and material realms under his dominion.[26] However, the Ottoman sultan's claim to being the messianic ruler was also challenged by Sufis with radical millenarian beliefs, especially various *şeyh*s from the Melami-Bayrami order, whose revolutionary messianic agendas peaked as the millennium according to the Islamic calendar was drawing near.[27] These *şeyh*s claiming to be the *qutb* and asserting their right to the sultanate, together with millenarian revolts among the Turkmen in Anatolia between 1511 and 1537, persuaded Süleyman that harnessing the ambient apocalyptic discourse was a must if the extent of the Ottoman dynasty's conquest was to match their political control and claims to religious legitimacy.[28] To this purpose, the sultan began to engage not only in ideological propaganda but also punitive measures such as heresy trials of rebellious Sufis, executions of Shi'a agents, banishment, resettlement, and other lesser punishments.[29]

While he faced his Muslim competitors as the *mahdi*, Süleyman stood up to Charles V of Habsburg, who became a focus of millennial expectations in his own right, as the prophesied Last Emperor appearing in the foundational Christian apocalyptic text of Pseudo-Methodius.[30] According to this prophecy, the Last Emperor was to be the savior and redeemer of the Roman Empire against the "Ishmaelites." He was also to summon all the non-Christians to baptism and set up the cross on all of their temples; those who refused to convert would be punished. This and a constellation of other prophecies, such as that of the Second Charlemagne and prophecies inspired by the teachings of Joachim of Fiore, came to focus on Charles V because he was elected Holy Roman Emperor in 1519 and united vast territories in Europe and the New World into what promised to be a new universal empire, despite his lack of real control over much of the German lands. Charles's apocalyptic charisma was further enhanced, especially among the reform-minded circles in German lands, after he sacked Rome in 1527, which confirmed his expected image as the renewer of religion and chastiser of the pope.[31]

In both Ottoman and Habsburg imperial propaganda the intensity of apocalyptic expectations peaked in the early 1530s, only to subside after the failed Ottoman siege of Vienna in 1532 when it became clear that neither Süleyman nor Charles had the power to inflict a decisive victory over the other.[32] However, as Murad b. Abdullah's account and other converts' narratives demonstrate, the debate on the messianic role of the Ottoman and Habsburg (and Safavid) rulers did not disappear—depending on political developments it would surge and subside well into the late seventeenth century. Moreover, it was not just the Ottoman authors who wrote about it. The Mediterranean-wide interest in the issues of interimperial rivalry, authenticity of religious traditions that these imperial rivals represented, and the Ottoman sultan's reputation as the savior is also manifest in the literary and prophetic texts issuing from the Muslim communities in Spain and North Africa in the sixteenth and early seventeenth centuries.

In the 1590s a series of twenty-two lead tablets bearing inscriptions in a rare Arabic script (Solomonic) but purporting to be ancient Christian relics were unearthed from a hill in the vicinity of Granada—a place afterward named Sacromonte, or Holy Mountain.[33] The discovery of these *Lead Books* was preceded in 1588 by the discovery of a parchment featuring a large cross at the top and the text in Arabic entitled "Prophecy by John the Apostle."[34] The accompanying commentary in Latin explained that the relics found along with the parchment were given to San Cecilio, the supposed first bishop of Granada, by the Virgin Mary. One of the lead books (as reconstructed in the sources), known in Arabic as *Kitāb haqīqat al-injīl* (Book of the Truth of the Gospel), contained an interesting prophecy recounted in the text by the Virgin Mary:[35]

> The Conqueror is one of the Kings of the Arabs, but he is not an Arab. He dwells in the Eastern lands of the Greeks, and is a great enemy of the Persians (*'ajam*), and their communities and beliefs and differences in matters of religion. He will have the laudable intention of obeying Allah and of securing victory for his righteous religion. Allah has strengthened him with His victory, and given him dominion, among all created things, over all people at that time. . . . Any believer who prays for his victory and who either assists him himself or spends money for that purpose, and who dies in that condition, will have all his sins forgiven by Allah, who will grant him in Heaven the reward of those who have died as martyrs for the faith.[36]

The story about the conqueror of the East is of course a thinly disguised reference to the Ottoman sultan who is expected to play a crucial role in the events preceding the revelation of the Truth of the Gospel. Although he is not identified as the individual who will reveal the hidden meaning of the Gospel, the great conqueror of the East was to provide the conditions for the Truth to be revealed through his unrelenting obeisance to God's commands and implementation of justice throughout his universal dominion. In this way he would allow the original law of the Messiah Jesus to be fulfilled.

Although there is still much unknown about the *Lead Books*, scholars today mostly agree that these artifacts posing as "authentic" indigenous Christian relics were in fact forgeries produced by Moriscos—Spanish Muslims who were forcibly converted to Christianity and in some cases continued to secretly practice Islam.[37] The *Lead Books* were an elaborate syncretic strategy to represent Islam as an original, lost ancient form of Christianity and thus create religious and political space for Muslims in Habsburg Spain. Throughout the sixteenth century, since the fall of Granada in 1492, Iberian Muslims suffered increasing pressure to abandon their religion, ways of life, and even names. The pressure on the Moriscos to assimilate became particularly prominent in the wake of the Rebellion of Alpujarras in 1568. This text highlights the expectations that Iberian Muslims, suffering increasing pressure to conform to the hegemonic policies of the Habsburg monarchs, had of Ottoman rulers who styled themselves as protectors of Muslims worldwide,[38] as well as the extent to which the issues of religious and imperial struggle became connected in the sixteenth century.

The eschatological import of the encounter between the Muslim and Christian contenders for the title of messianic emperor incited some groups and individuals caught in the middle, like Moriscos and Ottoman converts to Islam, to a variety of creative polemical arguments pertaining to issues of authenticity of scriptural traditions. While the *Lead Books* posed as original Christian relics, Murad b. Abdullah thought of a different way to legitimate Islamic and Ottoman rule via ancient Christian traditions. In his account Murad argues that God gave Jesus the keys to heaven and earth, which Jesus then passed on to Simon (Peter), who became the first pope or the *qutb* of the Christian community. However, Murad argues (in a manner reminiscent of the Protestant anti-Catholic polemics), the pope and his cardinals over time became too invested in worldly dominion and corrupted their scriptures and their religion by removing Muhammad's name from the Gospel. They forgot that the key to heaven was not a material key, and they lost the right to it with Muhammad's arrival. As the new holder of the key to heaven, Muhammad passed it on to Abu Bakr and other righteous caliphs. Finally, the key came into the hands of the Ottoman sultans, and only those who obey them can enter heaven.[39]

The emphasis on the Ottoman sultan as the holder of the keys to heaven and the person who would resolve the tensions between Christianity and Islam by revealing the true meaning of the scriptures speaks to the expectation among some Muslims that the sultan would play an active role in the religious debates of the sixteenth century. Although these debates are typically construed as uniquely Christian and European, or along the lines of Islam versus Christianity, Ottoman sources suggest that Sultan Süleyman envisioned a more global role for himself, which some converts readily embraced. The *Gurbet-nāme* allows us to explore this point more closely, together with the repertoire of polemical tropes appearing in the writings of the Ottoman converts.

## *Reconstructing the Polemical Universe of the Sixteenth-Century Ottoman Converts: The Quest for the True Religion of İsa*

The author of the *Gurbet-nāme* was most likely a convert of Italian origin who was close to the Ottoman household. The emphasis on the supremacy of Islam over Christianity suggests that the text was compiled by someone for whom interreligious rivalry was a burning concern and who was anxious to demonstrate that Cem Sultan did not betray his faith despite finding himself in a precarious position and under pressure to convert to Christianity. After citing the prophecy about Süleyman and his conquest of Rome, the author of the *Gurbet-nāme* sets up a fictional dialogue between the pope and the Ottoman prince that gives the latter an opportunity to demonstrate the superiority of Islam through a series of polemical stories engaging the issue of conversion in intriguing ways. This long interpolation immediately follows the prophecy, lending the entire ensuing debate an apocalyptic framework. In the narrative, the pope gives Cem Sultan a cue by asking: "We hear that you [Muslims] recognize our faith. Is that true?" The prince responds: "Yes, we respect the faith of exalted İsa, may peace be upon him. But that is not the faith decided upon by 318 bishops who gathered at Nicaea [in 325]! If you will not take offence at hearing about it, shall I proceed to tell and explain?"[40]

What follows is a chain of interlinked episodes addressing the issues of the original, true scriptures, the nature of Jesus/İsa, and the process by which the true law of Jesus was corrupted, causing Muhammad to appear and restate God's commands through Islam. The first episode introduces the subject of *tahrīf*, a concept found in the Qur'an and in Muslim polemical works, signifying the corruption of Jewish and Christian scriptures. Although it was a time-honored trope of Muslim anti-Christian and anti-Jewish polemics, the notion of *tahrīf* gained particular relevance in the context of the early sixteenth-century debates about the consequences of translating the Bible into different vernaculars and the need to return to the original language of the scriptures. The text argues that the Gospel existed in five versions: the one that came down to İsa that was the only true Gospel, and four written by Mattaa (Matthew), Markos (Mark), Luka (Luke), and Yuhanna (John). These four false Gospels then were translated into different languages in order to proselytize. According to the author, the original Gospel came down in Hebrew, but through numerous translations its truth was lost. In contrast to this, the author argues, the holy book of Islam, the Qur'an, cannot be translated into any other language or read in any other language, which makes its truth incorruptible. This narrative episode ends with an explanation that from the group of believers in the original Gospel only a few men survived, and eventually only one old person continued to believe, living on a mountain as a hermit withdrawn from the entire world.

According to the text, Salman the Persian (*Salman-ı Farsī*) came across this old monk while hunting in the mountains one day.[41] As the old man was reading a book, Salman became curious about its contents. When he learned that it was the Gospel that came down to İsa and that all other

Gospels in circulation were false, Salman repented for worshipping idols and became a Christian on the spot. The old hermit also informed him that the book contained signs of a new prophet's coming and that he should submit himself to Muhammad when he comes because Muhammad would renew the Truth that the Christian community perverted over time. This fascinating story, which probably originates with some of the earliest Christian converts to Islam, serves in the *Gurbet-nāme* not only as a polemical argument against Christians but also as a justification for conversion, presenting Islam as a purified version of Christianity, or rather, a religion that renews the true law of Jesus/İsa. The message is obvious, if implicit: a *true* Christian is a Muslim.

The old monk also volunteers to tell the story of who corrupted Christian scriptures, which is a transition into the next narrative, the one about Accursed Paul (Bolus La'īn), known to Christians as Saint Paul. Not surprisingly, Paul's "changing" the original law of İsa was one of the most popular tropes in Christian converts' accounts. According to the story replicated in various other narratives authored by converts, when a powerful Jewish general (in some stories he is the vizier of a Jewish king) who spent his entire life persecuting Christians reached his old age and was no longer able to fight with weapons, he decided to resort to a trick that would throw the Christian community into confusion. Pretending to have become a penitent convert to Christianity, Bolus infiltrated the Christian community and gained the trust of its members. After a while, he declared that he was receiving visions from İsa every Sunday and that therefore Sunday should be a special day for Christians. In subsequent "revelations" İsa supposedly related to Bolus that the consumption of wine and pork is allowed, that the direction of prayer is the East rather than Jerusalem, and that the sign of the cross should be adored as a reminder of İsa's suffering—all of this constituting a deliberate deviation from the "original" sacred law. In addition, Bolus invited Melka, Nastur, and Mar-Yakub,[42] the three wisest men of the Christian community, to visit him one by one in his hermitage. To each of them he told a different thing about İsa, causing fractures in the Christian community. Having done irretrievable damage, Bolus disappeared, leaving the Christians to wonder whether Jesus was fully divine, fully human, or both fully divine and human. After stating that Jesus was not killed on the cross but ascended to heaven in his body, only to return at the Day of Judgment, the text offers a fairly well-informed ecclesiastical history of the Christian community from Bolus's disappearance until Constantine the Great's time, detailing the religious dispute over Arianism and the issue of the Trinity.

This story is not complete in the existing manuscript, but it appears that the text sides with Arius, who claimed that Jesus was created by

God the Father and not coeval with and of the same substance as God the Father, which coincides with the Qur'anic stance that Jesus was fully human. Far from being a simple reference to the early disputes in the Christian Church, the story about Arius, his anti-trinitarianism, and his denial of Jesus' divinity had far-ranging implications in the context of sixteenth-century Christian confessional politics, especially in Venice, where one of the most widespread manifestations of reformed evangelical zeal was anti-trinitarianism and the denial of Jesus' divinity.[43] Similar beliefs were also popular in different parts of the Habsburg Empire (Heidelberg), Poland, Hungary, and Transylvania.[44] Early on in Süleyman's reign the Ottomans developed a keen interest in religious and political developments in Reformation Europe, and as an Ottoman report from 1530 suggests, they were well aware that a person named Martin Luther had "created a religion of his own."[45] By the second half of the sixteenth century, a substantial group of European anti-trinitarian refugees formed in Istanbul, where they fled to safety and converted to Islam, demonstrating in the process that the theological differences between Islam and Christianity were not insurmountable and that shared understanding of Jesus' nature can lead to religious synthesis.[46] Moreover, Süleyman saw a role for himself in the religious turmoil that ripped Europe: as his grand vizier İbrahim Paşa told the Habsburg envoy to Istanbul in 1534, Süleyman planned on convoking and presiding over an ecumenical council where the pope and Martin Luther would come together to resolve their conflict.[47] Like Constantine, from whose city he aspired to rule the world, Süleyman was going to bring about the unification of religions under imperial and presumably Islamic auspices. Active involvement in religious issues was from Süleyman's perspective central to his role as emperor—a concept that he would insist upon even more rigorously later in his reign.

The representation of Islam in the *Gurbet-nāme* invokes an ecumenical, irenic religion that went hand in hand with the message of imperial universalism that the Ottomans began to espouse in the first half of the sixteenth century. Rather than simply aiming to convert the nonbeliever, the religious polemic featured in this text was also aiming to delineate the space for the "other" within the ecumenical imperial system—Christians are just imperfect Muslims who would eventually see the light. This conceptualization of Islam was, nevertheless, the product of a particular historical and political moment in which Ottoman control of the entirety of Christendom seemed imminent and was in many ways closely tied to Süleyman's larger-than-life image both domestically and internationally. For this reason, it is perhaps surprising to learn that the core of the text in the *Gurbet-nāme* appears to have been taken from another contemporary polemical narrative. The exposition on Islam's superiority attributed in the *Gurbet-nāme* to Cem Sultan exists as an independent text in a compilation authored by a certain Serrac b. Abdullah, probably early in the reign of Sultan Süleyman, and is known as the *Collection of Pleasantries* (*Mecmū'atü'l-letā'if*). When these two texts are juxtaposed, the contours of a corpus of polemical narratives, promoted and circulated by converts, begins to emerge.

Personal narratives of conversion to Islam authored by Ottoman converts were very rare. In fact, Ottoman converts rarely identified themselves as such in their writings, reflecting both their desire to blend into the Muslim community and their general ability to do so—unlike converts to Christianity in contemporary Europe, especially Spain. For this reason, a curious researcher is typically left to follow random clues and forced to piece the puzzle of the authors' religious background from contextual evidence. Perhaps the most intriguing investigation into the personal universe of the often anonymous Ottoman converts leads through the so-called *mecmū'a*, personal miscellanies omnipresent in the Ottoman manuscript collections. Some Ottoman *mecmū'a*s represent handwritten collections of poetry and stories, often saints' lives, that the owner enjoyed reading or wanted someone close to read; some contain information on practical things such as recipes and lucky charms intertwined with religious texts; and some are designed as manuals for professional men, such as scribes or judges, containing copies of important letters and legal opinions by leading Ottoman jurists. Every *mecmū'a* has its own character and introduces the reader to the world of its owner. As *mecmū'a*s are intended for personal use, most of their owners did not care to record their names on the covers of the book, thus preventing anyone from identifying them. It is through this medium that one has access to many of the literate male Ottoman converts and learns of their anxieties about their non-Muslim past, albeit in a mediated way.[48]

The following excerpt is from the contents list of a *mecmū'a* dating to the reign of Murad III (1574–95), found in Vienna:[49]

1. A short Persian-Turkish dictionary
2. A short catechism of Islam in the form of question and answer
3. A section containing Christian liturgical texts, "Our Father," and various other prayers in German, Latin, Hungarian, and Croatian
4. A collection of German, Hungarian, and Croatian religious poems, with several Hungarian-Turkish *gazel*s (short, rhymed, lyric poems in couplets)
5. A weekly prayer cycle in Arabic
6. A section on fortune telling by numbers [*fāl*]

7. A list of the Ottoman sultans in Turkish
8. Dates of the prophets; dates of the conquest of Istanbul, Bursa, Edirne, Selanik, and Gelibolu in Turkish
9. A section on unlucky days of the month in Turkish
10. A section explaining on which days of the month it is good or bad to cut one's nails

The list continues with numerous other entries, such as a prescription against rheumatism, lucky charms, and the positions of the planets. At first glance, nothing might seem unusual about this list—many Ottoman *mecmūʿa*s contain entries like these. However, a closer look reveals that the owner of this compilation had an unusual interest in Christian prayers and also knew Hungarian, German, and Croatian.[50] The entries on Christian theology and poems are juxtaposed with the texts inducting one into Islam and Ottoman culture, such as the catechism, the prayer cycle, and the list of Ottoman sultans. All this suggests that the compiler had a mixed religious and linguistic background that he tried to reconcile by translating Christian prayers into Turkish and framing them with Muslim prayers and basics of the Muslim faith. The fact that the Christian poems, which reflect a marked Protestant spirit, found their place in this compilation testifies to the owner's implicit belief that parts of his Christian past are compatible with his Muslim present and that a total distancing is unnecessary or impossible, at least at the point when this compilation came into existence. If one were to draw a portrait of this *mecmūʿa*'s owner, one could describe him roughly as a Protestant Hungarian, probably from a German- and Croatian-speaking area in western Hungary, who became a Muslim as a consequence of Ottoman military activities in the area in the mid-sixteenth century.

In the case of the *Collection of Pleasantries* several clues suggest that the author, Serrac b. Abdullah, is a convert, even though he himself does not explicitly say so. First, there is his name: although Abdullah did eventually become a common Muslim name, for most of the early Ottoman period the patronymic Abdullah, or "the slave of God," denoted a convert to Islam. Besides the name is the information that he offers in his "reasons for writing" (*sebeb-i teʾlīf*) section. He states that in an hour of leisure it occurred to him to compose a *mecmūʿa* drawing on Jewish, Christian, and Muslim scriptures; lives of the prophets; the *hadith*; the advice to the kings; and merits of *gazā*, primarily in order to polemicize with Christian and Jewish learned men. He then says that he "translated" (*Türkçe tercüme kıldum*) sections from the New Testament, the Psalms of David (*Zebūr*), and the Pentateuch into Turkish. Unless he translated these sections from Arabic translations of the said scriptures, which does not appear likely given the simplicity of his Turkish and lack of Arabic expressions throughout the text, this information places Serrac b. Abdullah in the convert category with greater certainty. As mentioned earlier, most of the translation work involving the Jewish and Christian scriptures or other non-Turkish and non-Arabic sources was done by converts. In fact, it is at the end of the translations of *Zebūr* that in a couple of cases I found the rare Ottoman self-narratives of conversion authored by former Jews.[51]

Although most *mecmū'a*s are unique, the *Collection of Pleasantries* surprisingly survives in a number of copies preserved in different regional libraries within and outside the former Ottoman Empire, from Istanbul and Sofia to Vienna and Paris. The earliest copy I could find dates to AH 950 (1543/44), which means that sometime after its initial compilation early in Sultan Süleyman's reign, this collection became an independent work that was widely copied and disseminated.[52] It was even translated into French by one of the French dragomans (*jeunes de langues*) in Istanbul in 1737.[53] The *Collection of Pleasantries* is divided into five chapters that each develop a set of polemical arguments,[54] but the fourth and fifth chapters were particularly popular and interpolated in other works. The same sections appear in the *Gurbet-nāme* and another *mecmū'a* dating to the mid-seventeenth century that seems to have belonged to a convert.[55] The relationship between this particular series of polemical texts and authors choosing to incorporate them into their own separate works hints at the existence of a narrative corpus written by converts for the benefit and education of other converts.

The popularity among converts of the arguments discussed in the *Collection of Pleasantries*, and incorporated verbatim into the *Gurbet-nāme*, is illustrated in the work of Murad b. Abdullah, the Hungarian convert to Islam who became an Ottoman imperial interpreter. He discusses at length, among other things, the role of Paul/Bolus in corrupting the original Gospel and Jesus' teachings.[56] He also further develops arguments about the pernicious effects of the translation of scriptures. Here he is again in dialogue with the corpus of polemical stories featured in the *Collection of Pleasantries* and the *Gurbet-nāme* as he delivers his arguments through a story about a *şeyh* Vasıl, a Muslim sage captured by the Byzantine emperor, who also appears in these two texts. In the narrative cycle, this *şeyh* was asked to engage in a discussion on Jesus/İsa with the wisest of the emperor's priests. Through a series of questions, *şeyh* Vasıl demonstrates that many other prophets performed the same miracles as İsa and that either they should also be adored as gods or İsa should not be considered more than a prophet.[57] Given that disengaging the Muslim İsa from the Christian Jesus was central to the Christian converts' efforts to make Islam a religion of their own, this emphasis on Jesus is not surprising in the corpus of converts' polemical works. However, this endeavor to circumscribe a Muslim Jesus became increasingly challenging with the advent of the Muslim millennium.

## *The Messiah Contested: Jesus/İsa versus Muhammad as the True Messiah*

The millenarian conjunction that marked the sixteenth-century religio-political ambiance brought an intensified interest in Jesus, as the central character of both Christian and Muslim eschatological traditions, and his relationship to Muhammad. The most intriguing contemporary source in this respect is the so-called *Gospel of Barnabas*. Today widely recognized as one of the world's most elaborate religious forgeries, this text bears the strong influence of Muslim beliefs about the nature of the scriptures and Jesus' mission. It purports to be the True Gospel, the Gospel relating the truth about Jesus and his teachings according to one of his disciples, named Barnabas. Although the authorship and principal provenance of the original text are still unknown, its Mediterranean coordinates are evident: the oldest surviving manuscript, dating approximately to the last decade of the sixteenth century, is written in the Tuscan dialect of Italian bearing Venetian influences, but it conforms to Muslim scribal tradition, with marginal notes in Arabic and an Ottoman Turkish binding.[58] The second surviving manuscript is an eighteenth-century copy in Spanish, but through the writings of a Morisco intellectual from North Africa we know Moriscos in this region were aware of a text in Spanish by 1634.[59] Additionally, the surviving Spanish copy indicates in the introduction that the text was translated from Italian in Ottoman Istanbul by a certain Mustafa da Aranda.[60] Many theories exist about the origins of the *Gospel of Barnabas*; however, it appears to be incontrovertible that the text is a work of an individual (or individuals) who adhered to Islam but whose religious education encompassed both Muslim and Christian scriptural traditions, most likely due to conversion. Although speculations about the identity of the author continue among scholars, several features of the text suggest a Morisco provenance for the narrative.[61]

The key to the argument for the Morisco influence on the text is the doctrine it espouses that Muhammad is the Messiah—a doctrine that does not conform to the Sunni Muslim tradition and can be traced only to the circle of postexpulsion Morisco intellectuals in North Africa.[62] In the *Gospel of Barnabas* Jesus explicitly tells his disciples that he is not the Messiah and that the true Messiah is the messenger of God whose arrival Jesus is supposed to announce. He then identifies the Messiah as Muhammad.[63] This claim departs from the Sunni tradition, which maintains that the messianic figure expected to usher in the Day of Judgment is either Jesus, who is referred to as *al-masīh* (messiah) throughout the Qur'an, or someone from the lineage of Muhammad—never Muhammad himself. Moreover, according to eschatological traditions expressed in both the Qur'an and the *hadith*, it is Jesus/İsa who will return at the Day of Judgment in body and spirit, whereas Muhammad, who was buried in Medina, is never expected to return as a prelude to the Last Days. According to the early Islamic traditions, İsa, who only apparently died (a Jew was crucified instead of him), was elevated to heaven and will descend again prior to the Day of Judgment to kill the Antichrist (Ar. *al-Dajjāl*) and invite Christians and Jews to embrace Islam, İsa's true religion. He will make justice reign for forty years. According to some *hadith*s, he will marry, have children, and then die a natural death. The Muslims will bury him in Medina, next to Muhammad.[64] This basic story line proved to be quite elastic during the Islamic centuries leading to the Ottoman era. In the meantime, the disputes in the Islamic community gave rise to the Muslim version of the Messiah—*mahdi*—whose relationship to İsa and the events leading up to Judgment Day was never entirely clear. Was İsa the *mahdi*, or was the *mahdi* a separate person?—this is the question that Muslim authors handled differently depending on the period and their religio-political affiliation.[65]

The issue of the Messiah's identity became acutely important as the Islamic millennium was approaching in 1591, further enhanced by the political situation that pitted Muslims against the Habsburgs in the Mediterranean and against each other in Anatolia and Iran. Interestingly, Muslims in Spain and North Africa and Muslims in the Ottoman Empire reacted to the problem in very different ways. Faced with the superiority of the Spanish Habsburg monarchy and its religious policies of forced conversion and expulsion undertaken in the name of Jesus, Moriscos formulated a new doctrine of salvation that sought to undermine the pivotal importance of Jesus in the drama of the Last Days and enhance the role of Muhammad—their vilified prophet who was seemingly unjustly deprived of the soteriological status he deserved. The trauma of forced conversion and suffering for following Muhammad instead of Jesus found in this way a religious expression in the Morisco circles of Venice, North Africa, and Istanbul.

At the same time, among the Muslims in the Ottoman Empire the situation was quite the reverse—a series of Muslim mystics and even scholars proclaimed that Jesus was a prophet superior to Muhammad and argued for the sanctity of the Christian Gospel. Although Western sources report a number of cases, only a few incidents involving this form of religious nonconformity can be traced in Ottoman sources, the most famous of which is the trial and execution of Molla Kabız in 1527. According to the testimonies of Ottoman chroniclers and polemical treatises of Kemalpaşazade, the chief jurisprudent (*şeyhü'l-islām*) of the time, this religious teacher (*molla*) argued for İsa's superiority over Muhammad on the basis of both the Qur'an and the Bible. Ottoman sources testify to the fact that those Ottoman administrators learned in Islamic law had such a difficult time in argumentatively refuting Molla Kabız's assertions that the supreme religious authority, *şeyhü'l-islām* Kemalpaşazade, had to be brought to the Imperial Council to prove him wrong.[66]

The details of Molla Kabız's teachings are unfortunately not available. A surviving *fetva* by Ebussuud Efendi (chief jurisprudent from 1545 to 1574) condemning the teachings of a certain Hakim İshak for believing that the Jewish and Christian scriptures had not been altered, contrary to what the Qur'an asserts, testifies that Molla Kabız was not alone among Ottoman learned men in believing that the Bible could serve as the basis of religious truth.[67] Testimonies of Western commentators pointing to other similar cases may be helpful for reconstructing some of the ideas constituting this "heresy."[68] A Franciscan chronicle reports on the proceedings against another Muslim preacher tried in Constantinople in 1537 on charges reminiscent of those against Molla Kabız:

> It happened in this same year, 1537, in Constantinople that a Turkish cleric [*religioso turco*] preached freely that our Lord Christ was worthy of greater veneration than Muhammad, because Christ was born of a Virgin and he was alive in heaven with God, and that it was not Christ who was crucified, as Christians believe, but a Jew, as Turks also maintain, and that Christ would never find himself in sinful human flesh. In turn, he said that Muhammad was born in sin, out of a carnal relationship, and that he was not alive in heaven, like Christ, but was dead and his body was in Mecca [*sic*], while it was not certain where his soul was.[69]

Similar cases apparently occurred throughout the sixteenth century. Stefan Gerlach reports that in late May of 1573 Ottoman authorities beheaded a Muslim man who was preaching "that Muhammad is not a true prophet . . . and defending Our Lord Jesus' and Holy Ghost's being God. Thousands of Turks, especially in the army and janissary corps believed in this. This man began to spread his beliefs in the Buda [Hungary] region."[70] This particular episode seems to refer to one of the followers of Hamza Bali, a Melami-Bayrami *şeyh* executed as a heretic in 1561, whose impact was nevertheless felt for decades after his death and whose followers may have been responsible for the assassination of Grand Vezir Sokollu Mehmed Paşa in 1579.[71]

Despite their Western provenance, these references to the Muslim clerics' and mystics' teachings sound quite plausible when one calls to mind Ibn Arabi's ideas about Jesus, as well as his theorization and endorsement of the so-called Christic (Ar. *'īsawī*) piety.[72] According to Ibn Arabi, İsa was the only man ever born without sin. He was therefore pure sanctity and spirit, a perfect human being, and the most saintly of all prophets—the one who will come at the end of time from his abode in heaven to seal the line of universal sainthood. In the metaphysical system of Ibn Arabi, which had informed all levels of religious discourse in the Ottoman polity since its very foundation, Jesus attained metahistorical and metareligious proportions. Ibn Arabi himself wrote that he "converted" to the mystical path in the hands of Jesus, who was a model for every Muslim ascetic and wielded powerful moral capital in Sufi sayings, traditions, and the mystical science of letters.[73] Jesus' high status in the teachings of the most revered of Sufi authors and mystics combined with his role in the drama of the Last Days may have induced some Muslims anxiously anticipating the Day of Judgment to believe in Jesus' superiority to Muhammad, who was not to be resurrected and play a central role in the final hours. Rather than illustrative of crypto-Christianity, as some scholars have argued, the outbursts of Christic piety in the sixteenth-century Ottoman Empire emanated from mystical traditions within late medieval Islam, especially Ibn Arabi's systematization of the doctrine on universal sainthood. Thus, it is not surprising that the works of the "Greatest Master," as he was known among the Sufis, found themselves at the center of the debate on Sunni orthodoxy as it was developing in the sixteenth century. Already in the early sixteenth century the *şeyhü'l-islām* Kemalpaşazade was warning that the esoteric writings of Ibn Arabi were not for the ears and eyes of the common folk, who could easily be led to heresy. Several generations later, some piety- and reform-minded Ottoman agents of Sunnitization, like the Kadızadeli preacher Çivizade, went so far as to declare his works heretical.[74]

It seems that because of the apocalyptic expectations, both in Constantinople and in other parts of the Mediterranean world, by the mid-sixteenth century the notion of heresy came to revolve in part around the understanding of Jesus' nature and mission. Just as Italian Anabaptists and anti-trinitarians began to develop a theology that redefined Jesus' role in the salvation of humankind, arguing that Jesus Christ was a perfect human being filled with divine virtue but not God incarnate, and that through the imitation of Christ every man and woman can be saved,[75] Ottoman mystics, scholars, and even some wider segments of the population began to embrace this image of Jesus as the perfect human being and the Messiah, a figure central to salvation in the final hour. Indeed, several sixteenth- and seventeenth-century visitors to the Ottoman Empire report on the existence of the "lovers of the messiah" (*hubmesihleri*) among the population of Istanbul and Slavic-speaking Muslims in Bosnia, as well as along the border with the Habsburg Empire.[76]

## *Conclusion*

As the narratives discussed here demonstrate, imperial competition and the anticipation of an imminent Day of Judgment affected dramatically the ways in which Muslims in different positions of power and of different social backgrounds interpreted such fundamental Muslim traditions as the events of the Last Days and the roles of Jesus and Muhammad in them. Persecuted and converted by force to Christianity, Spanish Moriscos produced and circulated narratives that extolled the roles of both the Ottoman sultan and the Prophet Muhammad in the drama of the final hour, depriving Jesus of his status as the Messiah. At the same time, in the multiconfessional Ottoman capital of Istanbul some Muslim mystics and scholars argued for Jesus' precedence over Muhammad in a series of public professions that outraged the Ottoman authorities and prompted them to begin to define the notion of a Sunni orthodoxy and set up trials against heresy. In addition to these displays of Christic piety, from Rumeli to Anatolia numerous Muslim mystics with more radical leanings portrayed themselves as the *mahdi*, the messianic figure of the Muslim tradition, explicitly rejecting the claims of the Ottoman sultan to the same role. This diversity of Islamic beliefs must have been somewhat confusing for converts to Islam as they strove to carve out their own polemical Jesus and Muhammad and perform their new Muslim identity. For some converts to Islam, Jesus' prominence in the Muslim eschatological tradition and Sufi thought must have been an attractive bonus and facilitated the transition. Nevertheless, for many of the convert authors it was crucial to prove that the Christian Jesus and Muslim Jesus were two very different personalities, which accounts for the prominence of Jesus in the narratives by and for converts. Narratives like those included in the *Gurbet-nāme* and the *Collection of Pleasantries* combined the syncretic strategy of presenting Islam as a perfected version of Christianity and a religion that embraces rather than abrogates the previous revelations with the anti-syncretic strategy of disengaging İsa from his Christian counterpart.

This aspiration to universality at a time when both Islamdom and Christendom were fracturing internally had much to do with Sultan Süleyman's vision of the Ottoman imperial identity, and it did not entirely disappear even when it became clear that the dream of a universal world empire was unrealistic. By the mid-sixteenth century the reality of religious divisions between Sunni Ottomans and Shi'a Safavids, and Muslim Ottomans and Catholic Habsburgs, set in and became more entrenched, as both Charles and Süleyman realized that they would not be able to decisively defeat each other or those who challenged their authority within the Christian and the Muslim communities, respectively. However, it is important to understand the differences in the Ottoman and Habsburg visions of what a Universal Monarchy or Empire was supposed to look like. The Habsburgs were inspired by Justinian's model of *imperium* as a theocratic monarchy based on the principle of "one emperor, one law, and one religion."[77] This model did not tolerate religious diversity and resulted in the forced conversion and expulsion of Jews and Muslims from Habsburg Spain, in addition to persecution of the Protestants. In the Habsburg German territories the principle of "one ruler, one religion" was upheld at the Peace of Augsburg in 1555, which proposed to resolve Charles's conflict with Lutheran princes by not allowing for religiously mixed territories, with the motto of *cuius regio, eius religio*. The Ottomans, on the other hand, were inspired by a pre-Christian ideal of Roman imperial rule, one that embraced diversity and plurality provided that the religion of the ruling establishment was recognized as supreme. This ideal also coincided with the shariatic concept of *dhimma* (pact of protection), whereby Jews and Christians were allowed to worship freely in Muslim-controlled territories in return for the payment of a poll tax. For this reason, religious diversity among Ottoman non-Muslim subjects remained the cornerstone of Ottoman imperial identity and was fully upheld even at the height of the age of confessionalization in the second half of the sixteenth century. In AH 1002 (1593/94) the Ottoman court historian (*şehnāmeci*) Talikizade listed the unparalleled diversity of communities living peacefully under Islamic Ottoman imperial rule as one of his twenty arguments for the Ottoman dynasty's unrivaled greatness and imperial legitimacy among all preceding and contemporary Islamic and non-Islamic dynasties.[78] This diversity was seen as a testimony to Ottoman prestige and ability to bring about the unity of religious groups under the umbrella of Islam, prefiguring the final religious synthesis and victory of Islam at the Day of Judgment, whenever it may transpire. Although the Ottoman elites that made up the state sometimes wavered in this commitment, especially during the more extreme phases of confessionalization in the seventeenth century, they never fully abandoned it.

However, while Ottoman imperial ideology had a place for Jews and Christians, it had no place for rival claimants to the leadership of the Muslim community. As a consequence of the Ottoman rivalry with the

Safavids, Islamdom became increasingly polarized along Sunni-Shi'a lines, as both sides engaged in competing articulations of an Islamic orthodoxy and began to police communal boundaries.[79] By 1555, at the same time that Charles recognized the territorial integrity of the Protestant princes, Süleyman came to recognize the sovereignty of the Safavid shah within the latter's territories by signing the Treaty of Amasya. With this treaty the new religious divisions within Islamdom became increasingly territorialized, while Ottoman and Safavid rulers devoted themselves to the multipronged projects of state and confession building backed up by various measures of social disciplining. Although Süleyman's sixteenth-century successors at times endorsed a more flexible Sunni orthodoxy and the empire continued to tolerate a significant Shi'a population in Mt. Lebanon, the tenor of Ottoman religious politics was profoundly changed.[80] In light of these changes, which resulted in increasing ideological and territorial definition of Sunnism and Ottoman imperial identity, the phenomenon of conversion underwent a transformation as well. Beginning in the second half of the sixteenth century, one was not simply converting to Islam in the Ottoman Empire—he or she was converting to an Ottoman Sunni Islam.

CHAPTER FOUR

# Illuminated by the Light of Islam and the Glory of the Ottoman Sultanate

## *Self-Narratives of Conversion to Islam in the Age of Confessionalization*

In 1556–57, Murad b. Abdullah (1509–ca. 1586), a Hungarian convert to Islam, penned a polemical treatise, *The Guide for One's Turning toward Truth* (*Kitāb tesviyetü't-teveccüh ilā'l hak*), in which he introduced the essentials of the Muslim faith by arguing for Islam's superiority to Christianity and Judaism. In the conclusion to his work Murad states that by writing this treatise he hopes to bring about the conversion of Christians from different parts of Europe (*Firengistān*, "Land of the Franks") and secure the salvation of their souls by bringing them to Islam. With this goal in mind, ten years after completing the text in Ottoman Turkish, Murad translated it into Latin, inscribing the translation onto the margins of the Ottoman text so that Christians in the remotest parts of *Firengistān* could understand it and be drawn to the true faith. To this curious bilingual work he then added an autobiographical section, in both languages, describing the process of his own conversion to Islam and appointment as an imperial interpreter (*tercümān*) for the Ottoman Porte.[1]

To a student of early modern European history the story sounds ordinary enough: polemical autobiographical narratives of conversion from one Christian denomination to another were a staple of the propaganda wars waged among states and religious factions in the era of a confessional polarization that swept across Christendom in the sixteenth century.[2] From the standpoint of Islamic and Ottoman history, however, Murad's account is an unusual find. Although different autobiographical narratives, such as diaries, captivity narratives, travelogues, dream books, and records of mystical visions are well attested to in Ottoman manuscript collections,[3] this is one of only a few autobiographical narratives of conversion to Islam (from Christianity or Judaism) in premodern Islamic history and the earliest source of this kind written in Ottoman Turkish discovered so far.

So what accounts for the appearance of Ottoman self-narratives of conversion—albeit in small numbers—starting in the second half of the sixteenth century? Several Ottomanists have already pointed to a marked surge in autobiographical narratives in Ottoman Turkish beginning in the second half of the sixteenth century and especially in the seventeenth century.[4] Their authors came from a variety of social milieus, ranging from Ottoman Sufi mystics—whose levels of literacy and time-honored tradition of self-reflection in the quest for the divine made them the most likely adherents to this genre—to various Ottoman bureaucrats and literati. Some scholars have therefore suggested that the profound socioeconomic, political, and cultural transformation of Ottoman society during and after the reign of Sultan Süleyman (d. 1566) provided incentives for literate Ottomans to seek new genres to express their views of the world around them.[5] But which developments in particular influenced the emergence of the Ottoman self-narratives of conversion? Is it a coincidence that they appear at the time when Catholics and Protestants, in the aftermath of the Council of Trent (1545–63), resorted to polemical self-narratives by converts as principal tools of proselytization and theological dispute?

Building on the previous discussion of interimperial rivalries and the production of polemical texts by converts, this chapter argues that this concurrent appearance of Ottoman self-narratives of conversion was not accidental. The analysis is based on five heretofore unstudied and/or unknown texts of this genre dating from the late sixteenth through the early eighteenth centuries: in addition to the work of Murad b. Abdullah, self-narratives authored by Mehmed, a former Orthodox Christian student of theology and philosophy from Athens; Yusuf b. Abi Abdüdeyyan, an Ottoman Jewish intellectual turned Sufi mystic; Mehmed, a former priest who traveled to Istanbul to convert, become a mystic, and later receive visions of the Ottoman dynasty's future; and İbrahim Müteferrika, a Unitarian priest who founded the first Ottoman Arabic script printing press. A close reading of these narratives further substantiates the argument that some Ottoman converts readily entered the debate about the correct rituals and the most authentic, scripture-based path toward salvation, which modern scholarship often considers germane only to post-Reformation Christendom. In their conversion narratives they promoted Islam as the religion that promises salvation and the Qur'an as *the* true word of God by bringing together the tradition of medieval Islamic anti-Christian polemics (the so-called *reddiye*) with Christian humanist sensibilities for textual criticism, the study of scriptural languages, and the call for return to the original sources to bear on questions of the authenticity of religious scriptures.

This development was not a result of the simple transference of a post-Tridentine Christian genre to an Ottoman setting but a manifestation of Ottoman participation in the age of confessionalization—the era of simultaneous state and confession building that transpired in both Christendom, where it resulted in the establishment of Lutheran, Calvinist, and reformed Catholic states, and in Islamdom, where it gave rise to the formation of Ottoman Sunni and Safavid Shi'a empires. The fashioning of an Ottoman Sunni state identity started in a more concerted way in the 1540s. However, the process lasted well into the seventeenth century and seemingly reached its conclusion in the 1690s, at the end of the last wave of the Kadızadeli movement. It entailed measures of social disciplining that came both "from above" and "from below," depending on the changing political situation and the structures that made up the Ottoman state. This chapter outlines some aspects of confessionalization in the Ottoman Empire as it situates the self-narratives of conversion to Islam in this historical context.

## *Murad b. Abdullah, a Hungarian–Turned–Ottoman Interpreter*

According to his own story, Murad b. Abdullah was captured by the Ottoman army at the Battle of Mohács in 1526 when he was seventeen years old.[6] A recent study reveals that his Hungarian name was Balázs Somlyai and that he was born in Nagybánya (today in Romania).[7] As he later related to Stefan Gerlach, the Lutheran chaplain to the Habsburg embassy to Constantinople, Murad studied in Vienna before he was captured by the Ottomans.[8] It is unclear what turn his life and career took immediately after the Battle of Mohács—he seems to have received a solid education in Islamic faith and the Ottoman Turkish language, possibly as a recruit in the janissary corps. His appointment as an imperial translator came only later, in the early 1550s, and followed a thirty-month captivity in Transylvania, where he was sent on a diplomatic mission by Rüstem Paşa, the Ottoman grand vizier (1544–53; 1555–61). Rüstem Paşa ransomed Murad and brought his linguistic and diplomatic potentials to the attention of Sultan Süleyman, whose reign witnessed the expansion of Ottoman diplomatic personnel and other branches of bureaucracy.

Murad b. Abdullah describes his acceptance of Islam in the following way:

> When I was offered the Muslim faith, I did not have the courage to accept it because I was familiar with the ways of that [i.e., Christian] side but never had any inkling about this [i.e., Muslim] one. I educated myself through profuse reading. God granted me grace [*'ināyet*], and it is my hope that my last profession of faith [*hātimemüz*] will be sealed with belief [*īmānla hatm ola*]. This is all to say that the reason why many infidels find the idea of becoming a Muslim repulsive is their lack of knowledge about Islam [*Müslümān olmakdan nefret itdükleri bilmedüklerindendür*].[9]

Murad understood his turning toward Islam not as a specific point in time that would resemble Saint Paul's experience of sudden enlightenment but as a process that unfolded parallel with his learning more about Islam and eventually attaining grace, in the manner of Saint Augustine. He admits that at first he did not have the "courage" to accept Islam when it was "offered" to him. Sixteenth-century Western reports from Istanbul mention that captives while still in shackles were routinely invited to embrace Islam. This would not immediately result in their freedom, but in some cases it allowed for more lenient treatment and frequently a contract for eventual manumission.[10] Nevertheless, Murad may also be referring to the period that lapsed between his formal profession of allegiance to Islam and his intellectual acceptance of Islam, since he would not normally be given the chance to receive instruction in the Muslim faith prior to being circumcised. He describes his eventual commitment to Islam as the outcome of intense study and argues that the education he received before falling captive posed the greatest obstacle to his openness to Islam. He relates his journey to Islam as an intensely intellectual, rational experience, although his introduction to it may not have been exactly voluntary.

How unique was Murad's account of his own conversion, and what, if any, precedents does the genre of autobiographical narrative of conversion to Islam have in Islamic tradition? Recent studies exploring how conversion to Islam was narrated in early medieval Muslim sources argue that in contrast to conversion to Christianity, with Paul's and Augustine's accounts serving as models, conversion to Islam was a narrative nonevent and that none of the stories hint at a catechetical preparation or exposure to the message of the Qur'an.[11] These studies raise the question of whether we can assume that all "religions of the Book," despite numerous shared sensibilities, actually share an understanding of religious conversion. They suggest that the verb *aslama* (Ar. "to surrender"), which is used to signal acceptance of Islam in the Arabic sources, can be interpreted as "to enter Islam" and that this "entrance" is only the departure point for becoming a Muslim over a period of time through participation in the rituals and social life of the Muslim community.[12] While effectively denoting conversion to Islam, the Arabic term *aslama* carries none of the meanings traditionally associated with religious conversion defined in a classic study by Arthur Nock as a transformation of the heart and soul—a definition implying that conversion is a dramatic event or process that can be isolated and narrated in the manner of Saint Paul or Saint Augustine.[13]

Other scholars working on different religious and cultural contexts have also questioned the universality of this definition of conversion. They point out that it is a product of a particular historical and cultural milieu and represents the post–Council of Trent formulation of Christian conversion that emphasizes a "sincere" intellectual commitment to one's new religion *before* actual admittance into the community.[14] In contrast, as one prominent scholar suggests, in early Muslim sources conversion was a (narrative) nonevent because "in a sense, a convert first became a member of the Muslim community and later discovered, or tried to discover, what it meant to be a Muslim."[15] Although the expectation of finding autobiographical narratives of conversion to Islam à la Paul or Augustine may be informed by specific (Christian) cultural expectations, it is equally misleading to assume that there was a "timeless" Islamic tradition of conversion narratives and that the relationship between conversion and narration in Islam did not change over time. As a recent study shows, narratives of conversion within Islam, from a less committed to a more pious lifestyle or from a legalist to a mystical understanding of Islam, constituted an important subcategory of premodern autobiographical literature in Arabic.[16] More pertinent to the discussion, there are two widely known full-length self-narratives of conversion to Islam in Arabic from the pre-Ottoman period that directly affected two of the Ottoman narratives to be discussed here.

One of these medieval conversion narratives is *Silencing the Jews* (*Ifhām al-Yahūd*) by Samuel ibn Abbas ha-Ma'aravi (Samaw'al al-Maghribi), a twelfth-century Jewish convert to Islam. The other is *A Unique Find for the Intelligent Mind: A Treatise of Riposte to the People of the Cross* (*Tuhfat al-adīb fī al-radd 'alā ahl al-salīb*), an early fifteenth-century work by Anselm Turmeda, a former Franciscan monk from Majorca who after his conversion in Tunis became known as Abdallah at-Tarjuman.[17] Both Samuel and Anselm Turmeda were learned members of their communities, and their entrance into Islam was intimately related to their pursuit of higher learning. In this respect their narratives are similar to medieval and later early modern narratives of conversion to Christianity by other male intellectuals, suggesting that long-term interconfessional contact in the Mediterranean led to similar polemical and textual sensibilities.[18] These narratives display marked influences of Muslim autobiographical, philosophical, and polemical traditions, which suggests that the Muslim autobiographical narrative of conversion developed as a genre intimately related to Muslim polemical literature.[19]

So how different were the Ottoman narratives from these antecedents? Although Murad does not seem to be aware of these older examples of the genre, some of the later authors were demonstrably inspired by Anselm Turmeda's *Tuhfa*. Like Samuel's and Anselm's accounts, all Ottoman narratives of conversion display familiarity with the Muslim anti-Christian and anti-Jewish polemical tradition, and they almost universally develop the same metaphor of learning as the path that led them to Islam. Nevertheless, in arguing for Islam's superiority and striving to present it as the best possible spiritual option, Ottoman converts espouse and seek to implement the ideals of the reform-minded sixteenth-century Christian humanists who applied their philological expertise and principles of textual and literary criticism to scripture.[20] Similarly, Ottoman converts celebrated a thorough knowledge of scriptural traditions and familiarity with scriptural languages (especially Latin, Greek, and Arabic) and advocated a return to the original sources (*ad fontes*) as well as a systematic comparison of different scriptural traditions in their polemical writings. One of the authors to be discussed also had a thorough familiarity with Greek philosophy. The issue of translation, hotly debated among Catholics and Protestants, also figures prominently in the polemics presented by Ottoman converts. Moreover, unlike the earlier accounts, Ottoman narratives are steeped in the politics of the day, most notably in the interimperial rivalry with the Habsburgs, and they argue for the Ottoman sultans' supremacy over other contemporary rulers through proving Ottoman Islam's superiority over other religions. Each of the narratives therefore inextricably binds the convert with Islam and the Ottoman sultanate—a feature that is entirely new and points to the politicization of religious discourse characteristic of the age of confessionalization.

Murad b. Abdullah's *Guide for One's Turning toward Truth* was the earliest and in many ways the most original Ottoman self-narrative of conversion. Although Murad is mentioned in several studies that touch upon his work as an imperial interpreter and his literary production, his 150-folio polemical treatise-cum-autobiography has never received more than a cursory analysis.[21] Murad writes that the religious disputations he had with Christians as a captive in Transylvania stimulated him to write his treatise.[22] Indeed, underlying Murad's entire work is the belief that conversion is a rational matter that should logically follow upon sufficient "proofs" of Christianity's inferiority and falsehood on the basis of its own scriptures. Referring to his own experience of initial rejection followed by gradual realization of "the truth," Murad states that his work

> will first proclaim the glory of Islam and then prove the falseness of their [infidels'] religion with verses from the Qur'an and *hadith*, with evidence and rationality, and with their own books. There cannot be a better invitation than this book because these are the reasons that obstructed this humble one from embracing Islam in the beginning. Now the issues that the infidels still resist and that were revealed to this poor one will enter their ears. And it is hoped that nobody will be afraid for his soul. Removing prejudice from reality, having understood it impartially, and learning the path of Islam and its stipulations, they will become aware, and only the most ignorant and obstinate infidel would not accept it.[23]

Murad had commenced his studies in an intellectually turbulent era, at the beginning of the Protestant Reformation. Through his education in Vienna and Hungary, Murad became aware of humanist ideas that seem to have shaped his intellectual outlook even as a Muslim. Murad engages in the ongoing humanist debate on how scriptural sources should be treated and upholds the *ad fontes* ideal—albeit with a personal twist. For instance, at the very beginning of the *Guide* Murad introduces the issue of *tahrīf*.[24] He consistently argues that the process of translation of the Old and New Testaments into numerous Christian vernaculars should be blamed for the corruption of Christian scriptures and omissions, such as the removal of Muhammad's name from the Gospels. Although the idea of translation as a source of the scriptures' corruption appears in the older Muslim anti-Christian and anti-Jewish polemical works, Murad recounts how he personally witnessed a mistranslation of the Bible into Hungarian and confronted the Christian interlocutor on that issue.[25] To the rampant process of translation under way in Reformation Europe Murad juxtaposes the untranslatability of the Qur'an and insists that the Muslim scriptures are therefore the true divine message. According to Muslim tradition, the Qur'an is the word of God delivered in the sacred Arabic language and cannot be reproduced or "translated" into various human languages. Any translation of the Qur'an immediately ceases to be the word of God. For this reason the Qur'an must be memorized and recited in its original form even by those who do not understand Arabic.[26]

Murad's exposure to reformed Christian ideas did not necessarily cease with his captivity. Sixteenth-century Ottoman Istanbul teemed with European diplomats, merchants, travelers, and "renegades," all of whom brought news about religious and political developments in Europe, and alternatively, mediated information from the Ottoman Empire to European courts and the general population. From Stefan Gerlach's diary, which spans the years 1573–78, we know that Murad was assigned as an interpreter to the Habsburg embassy in Istanbul, where he had a chance to discuss Christian theology with Lutherans, such as Gerlach, and even anti-trinitarians, such as the infamous Adam Neuser, who fled to the Ottoman Empire, converted to Islam, and became the inspirational leader of a sizable circle of German converts to Islam in the Ottoman capital.[27] A comprehensive study of Murad's opus and information about the later stages of his life suggest, in fact, that he may have harbored Unitarian sympathies. This is particularly evident from the hymns celebrating the unity of God, which he wrote in parallel Ottoman Turkish, Latin, and Hungarian translations.[28] It seems that Murad was aware that Christian unitarianism, which insisted on the single personality of God (and was therefore anti-trinitarian) and the essential humanity of Jesus, was gaining followers in the second half of the sixteenth century throughout Italy, Habsburg lands, Poland, Ottoman Hungary, and Transylvania.[29] The compatibility of various strains of anti-trinitarianism with Muslim beliefs on these issues, especially the doctrine of God's oneness (Ar. *tawḥīd*), escaped neither its adherents nor its critics at the time. The hymns devoted to God's oneness that Murad wrote in the early 1580s and presented in parallel Hungarian, Latin, and Ottoman Turkish versions suggest that he envisioned a non-Muslim audience for his work, most probably among Unitarian Transylvanians.[30]

Murad's account bears testimony to the way general spiritual inclinations are translated from one religion to another in the cases of conversion, for instances of his weaving together Muslim and reformed Christian sensibilities do not stop at his comments on translation. While his *ad fontes* motto serves to enhance his argument for the authenticity of Muslim scriptures, his exposition of Islam is informed by a mystical sensibility drawing upon personal discipline and a regime of self-examination revived by the late medieval Christian mysticism of *devotio moderna* and closely paralleled by Sufism in the Islamic tradition. Sufism represented Islam's spiritual reform inasmuch as it sought to bring to life religious ideals and to embody them through everyday activity.[31] Its stress on the internalization and intensification of Muslim faith and practice made an indelible impression on Murad, who cites numerous Sufi authors who guided him in the process of becoming Muslim.[32] Although it was not the principal impetus for his entrance into Islam, Sufism allowed Murad to reflect upon his own reformed Christian sensibilities and implement them as a Muslim. His numerous references to himself as a sinner conform both to Sufi literary conventions of self-doubt and humility and to the disciplinary regimes of Reformed Christianity with their emphasis on self-control, inward piety, and belief in justification by faith.[33]

In addition to humanist and Reformed spiritual ideals, Murad's account echoes other developments of the era, most notably the intense interimperial competition. Murad refers to the Western prophecies about the demise of the Ottoman dynasty, which was supposedly going to transpire in the reign of Süleyman as the twelfth ruler of the Ottoman line.[34] In response to Christian prophecies, Murad upholds the claim of the Ottoman sultan to be the messianic world conqueror. Moreover, he argues that after Jesus gave the keys of heaven to Peter, the power "to bind and loose in heaven and on earth" was passed on to Muhammad as the last prophet, then to the caliphs, and finally to the Ottoman sultans as the legitimate representatives of the Muslim community.[35] In this way, like many other Ottoman converts to Islam writing nonautobiographical narratives in this period, Murad integrated the post-Reformation debate on legitimate spiritual authority with the imperial competition between the Habsburgs (backed by the pope) and the Ottomans.

By referring to the Ottoman sultan as the legitimate successor of the caliphs, Murad hints at the new development in Ottoman imperial ideology beginning in the 1540s. Until the mid-1530s Süleyman was engaged in an intense struggle with both the Habsburg emperor Charles V and the Safavid shah Ismail for the title of the prophesied messianic Last Emperor who will unite the world under the banner of a single empire and faith. When it became clear that Süleyman could not decisively defeat either of his rivals, he began to replace his messianic charisma with a ruling persona whose majesty was derived from faithful implementation of justice and Islamic law.[36] With the help of the chief jurisprudent Ebussuud Efendi and other members of the bureaucratic elite, Süleyman began to equate the Ottoman sultanate with the institution of the caliphate—the only political formation that implied universal sovereignty over the Muslim community.[37] Although the Ottoman sultans could not trace their descent to the old caliphal dynasties and had never before dared experiment with the concept of being the "successors of the Prophet" and "vicegerents of God," Süleyman and his image makers believed that the regime of justice that his reign introduced bestowed caliphal sovereignty on him. The imperial law (*kānūn*) was now harmonized with holy law through Ebussuud's relentless legislative activity.[38] These attempts at sacralizing the ruler were paralleled in the contemporary Habsburg and Safavid empires. Both Charles V of Habsburg and his son Philip II believed that they ruled by divine right.[39] At the same time, the Safavid shah Tahmasp (1524–76) appointed Ali Karaki (d. 1534) as the "seal of the *mujtahid*s," the Shi'a equivalent to the Ottoman chief jurisprudent, who worked to present the shah as the returned twelfth imam himself—the ultimate form of sacralization in the Shi'a tradition.[40]

Süleyman thus brought his rule as close to being sacralized as possible in the Sunni Islamic context. This process was concomitant to the fashioning of the dynastic image for the Ottomans as protectors of Sunni Islam. Although the Ottomans did not institute an Inquisition as the Habsburgs did, Süleyman dedicated special attention to the transgressions traditionally associated with Safavid Shi'a supporters known as the *kızılbaş* and radical messianism. Previously quite ecumenical when it came to the variety of Muslim beliefs, in Süleyman's reign the Ottoman Empire witnessed a boom in heresy trials and concerted efforts to define the boundaries of belief.[41] This latter goal was achieved through different processes of social disciplining, such as the promulgation of a new criminal law code that policed the boundaries of orthodoxy and public morality, the promotion of mosque worship through the imposition of new fines for irregular attendance, and the construction of an unprecedented number of mosques in order to stabilize mosque congregations and monitor them easily.[42] Provincial Anatolian records testify to the fact that the city neighborhoods (*mahalle*) were renamed (and reorganized) according to their most prominent house of prayer (*mescid*) or mosque.[43] These measures closely corresponded in spirit to those taking place in Carlo Borromeo's Milan and in the Habsburg lands in the aftermath of the Council of Trent, aiming to establish an "orthodox" Catholic community.[44] In addition to the local *kadıs*, certain Sufi orders carried out the policies of Sunnitization and community monitoring.[45]

A similar process also unfolded in the Safavid Empire. Although Shah Ismail officially converted Persia to Shi'a Islam in 1501, this was a process that continued throughout the sixteenth century, and the most notable strides were made in Shah Tahmasp's reign. Ali Karaki, the "seal of the *mujtahid*s," changed the direction of prayer, appointed an imam in every village to teach Shi'a prayer, and set out to constitute a Shi'a confessional and political community through similar disciplining and Islamicizing measures.[46] The principle of *cuius regio, eius religio* was therefore generally upheld in the Ottoman and Safavid empires as well (although exceptions certainly existed), while the debates over spiritual authority in the Muslim community, correct rituals, and even the original text of the Qur'an began to be debated in language reminiscent of Catholic-Protestant and Muslim-Christian polemics. This is how the imperial *tercümān* Ali Bey explained the differences between Sunnism and Shi'ism to Stefan Gerlach:

In their beliefs there is no difference, but Persians do not want to recognize as their caliphs Abu Bakr, Umar, and Uthman, only Ali, who was Muhammad's son-in-law and whom they believe the only rightful heir of political authority. They also say that when angel Gabriel brought a section of the Qur'an down from heaven, he made a mistake and gave Muhammad the section that he was supposed to bring to Ali. Because the Qur'an did not come down all at once, but several verses or several leaves at a time.[47]

At the same time, in the 1570s, one of the most prominent Safavid religious scholars, Mir Husayn, produced a treatise in which Caliph Umar was portrayed as "the forger of the Qur'an who pleased Christians, Jews and Zoroastrians."[48]

During his service under the sultans Süleyman, Selim II (1566–74), and Murad III (1574–95), Murad b. Abdullah witnessed intensifying imperial competition, the reconfiguration of the relationship between the state and religion, and the "theologization" of political discourse. Beginning with Süleyman's reign, these developments profoundly changed the concepts of religious allegiance and religious conversion in the Ottoman Empire. In his advanced age Murad may have been present at the imperial circumcision festival in 1582, the most elaborate Ottoman imperial spectacle ever staged, where Sultan Murad III displayed his piety and largesse by having thousands of poor and orphaned Muslims, including voluntary converts and *devşirme* recruits, circumcised publicly on the same day as his son, the Ottoman prince.[49] Deliberately staged to bolster the image of the dynasty at a time of financial and military crisis, with the war against Safavids going on intermittently since 1578, this festival featured the public conversion of members of the Safavid embassy to Ottoman Sunni Islam. One of the converts even delivered a speech in which he praised the Ottoman sultan and reviled the Safavid shah. According to the sources, this staged conversion scene was a great success and was apparently repeated a week later.[50]

A contemporary source, the *Imperial Festival Book* (*Sūrnāme-yi hümāyūn*) by İntizami of Foça, reports that the ambassador of the "evil-doing king of Vienna" objected to being seated next to the Safavid ambassador on the grounds that the chief Ottoman jurisprudent had issued a legal opinion (*fetva*) proclaiming that the killing of one *kızılbaş* was more meritorious than killing seventy infidels.[51] The Habsburg ambassador therefore recognized the Ottoman vision of a hierarchy of "orthodoxies." The three imperial and confessional projects converged on this occasion in the Ottoman capital to expose the fact that they all drew on the same conceptual language and acknowledged the essential link between imperial sovereignty and religious orthodoxy.

Murad's account not only reflects these new anxieties surrounding religio-political orthodoxy, conversion, and public morality in the Ottoman Empire but also illustrates a convert's ability to tap into these developments to secure much-needed financial support in the age of new patronage opportunities. It should not be forgotten that Murad first wrote his account in Ottoman Turkish and only later translated it into Latin, which suggests that the account had a dual target audience—both the Ottoman establishment and (unspecified) Christians in the West.[52] His description of the moral degeneration that supposedly beset Ottoman society late in Süleyman's reign—he criticizes the venality of Ottoman judges and even rants against sodomy—calls to mind other political commentaries from the late sixteenth century, both the "advice for kings" (*nasīhatnāme*) genre and the less formal politico-religious tracts issuing from the Sufi milieu.[53] But why did an otherwise humble and self-effacing Ottoman servant assume the right to criticize Ottoman society?

As a convert who comprehended the majesty of Islam, now on a mission to present the advantages of embracing Islam to non-Muslims, Murad insists on being a voice of conscience for the Ottoman establishment that witnessed a new commitment to Islamic orthodoxy in this period.[54] Murad must have been aware that in the West it was widely believed that Islamic law did not condemn sodomy and that the Turks were seen as sodomites par excellence.[55] His vociferous critique of sodomy in Ottoman society therefore aims to show that Islam does not tolerate the "sin of Lot's people" and to rally the Ottoman dignitaries in persecution of it. At the same time, through the moral capital he accrued as a convert in an age when religion and politics were intimately intertwined, Murad was also hoping to obtain the patronage of a powerful statesman. In the second half of his reign Sultan Süleyman ushered in a new era of impersonal sultanic rule by establishing a bureaucratic elite that would run the empire.[56] In the subsequent period sultans relinquished their central role in day-to-day politics to the bureaucratic elite, much to the chagrin of contemporary political commentators. This was especially true after the *devşirme* was discontinued in the late sixteenth or early seventeenth century and the new elite, both in Istanbul and in the provinces, began to recruit voluntary converts into their own retinues and train them for various bureaucratic and military positions, thus supplanting the sultan's monopoly on recruitment for state functions.[57] Indeed, after his patron Rüstem Paşa's death, Murad was perpetually in search of a new protector.[58] Although he specifically honors Sultan Murad III in the *Guide*, in trilingual hymns on the unity of God he offers praise to the grand viziers Sokollu Mehmed Paşa and Sinan Paşa for their generous patronage.[59]

Nevertheless, this does not mean that his desire to bring about the salvation of Christians in the West was pure rhetoric. Indeed, Stefan

Gerlach reports that on at least one occasion Murad was instrumental in bringing about the conversion of a Christian from *Firengistān*—in 1575 he took to the Imperial Council a servant of the French king desiring to convert and informed Grand Vizier Sokollu Mehmed Paşa about his intention.[60] As his treatise survives in only one complete and one partial copy, both located in libraries outside Turkey, it is hard to surmise what kind of audience and what impact it had.[61] However, the fact that he produced at least two copies of the account in his own hand suggests that Murad saw himself as a bridge between two religions, implementing the Christian belief that a convert should not be satisfied with his personal salvation but serve as an apostle for his newfound faith.

## *Mehmed b. Abdullah, a Student of Theology–Turned–Muslim Jurist*

Another conversion narrative testifying to the confessional and imperial competition in which converts increasingly began to take part is the polemical treatise by a learned Orthodox Christian convert from Athens named Mehmed. Significantly shorter than Murad's work, Mehmed's treatise is nevertheless a fascinating source because it provides a direct link with the account of Anselm Turmeda and offers a glimpse into the dynamic movement of people, ideas, and texts in the late sixteenth- and early seventeenth-century Mediterranean world. Although the author mysteriously dates the text to the "year 23 of the Gospel," the context suggests that the narrative was written soon after the death of Sultan Ahmed I (1603–17), possibly in 1623, because the author refers to him as "deceased."[62]

In the introduction to this self-narrative of conversion–cum–anti-Christian polemic, the author reveals that he was born in the city of Athens, "the source of philosophical sciences" (*menba'-yi 'ulūm-i hikemīye*). Here he embarked on the study of Christian theology, which he pursued until he was middle aged, only to turn most passionately to ancient Greek sciences (*fünūn-ı Yunānīye*).[63] As an Orthodox Greek from a provincial town under Ottoman rule, the author had limited choices for pursuing advanced education. Since the 1570s, Orthodox Christians desirous of learning could choose between the Patriarchal Academy in Constantinople and the Greek College founded by Pope Gregory XIII in Rome to advance Catholic missionary activity among the Orthodox.[64] The author states that it was impossible for him to go to "the other side," probably referring to Rome, and that he pursued his education in Athens. At the turn of the seventeenth century, Athens established its own academy where the most celebrated professor, Theophilus Corydalleus, was a neo-Aristotelian educated in Padua.[65] The author seems to have belonged to a small group of Orthodox Christian humanist theologians educated in Athens around this time.

Mehmed states that ancient philosophy enhanced his understanding of the scriptures and that with this new critical apparatus he began to discern in the Old Testament, New Testament, and Psalms verses that suggested the authenticity of Muhammad's prophetic status.[66] He then engages in an extended argument about the line of prophecy from the Old Testament prophets onward, which dwarfs Murad's bilingual treatise in detail and linguistic complexity; it interpolates passages in Greek (written in Arabic script), Persian, and Arabic, with some occasional Latin. Among other arguments, he states that the truth about Muhammad's coming is contained in the Gospels but the Christians intentionally misinterpreted it. Continuing with his conversion story, the author tells us that despite this realization he "did not have the courage to become a lamp lit by the light of Islam" (*nūr-i İslām ile efrūhte çerāğ olmağa cesāret olmayup*). Instead, he embarked on a long journey around the Lands of Rum, going from city to city and village to village in search of knowledgeable Orthodox Christian monks and priests who might explain the verses in question differently. However, despite encounters with learned Christian monks, he was not persuaded, while his confusion was growing greater and his desire to pledge himself to Islam more intense. He describes his mental anguish and yearning for divine guidance in great detail suggestive of the post-Tridentine Christian confessional style that emphasized the believer's transparency before God and the sincerity and completeness of penitence.[67]

Finally, he was advised to go to Rome, the seat of the papacy and Christian learning, where his doubts, he was promised, would be resolved. He stayed in Rome for four years, which suggests that he had ample opportunity to be exposed to the spirit and theology of Catholic renewal.[68] Nevertheless, he says that even there everybody misinterpreted the verses of interest to him. Desperate to find someone who would confirm his understanding of the verses, he heard of an old monk who had the reputation of helping those with questions in the matters of religion, and he decided to seek him out. Upon taking a look at the verses, the old monk started lamenting the fact that the Christian community strayed from the path of its ancestors and transgressed the boundaries of truth through a willful misinterpretation of the scriptures. This finally convinced our author to openly embrace Islam, and he sped to Istanbul, "the center of the circle of the axis of Islam and the seat of caliphs."[69] Here the author accepted Islam in the Imperial Council in the presence of Sultan Ahmed, exchanged his

Christian ecclesiastical robes for the robes of honor bestowed upon him by the sultan, and received the name Mehmed. Since he did not know Ottoman Turkish (*zebān-i Turkī*), he was apparently offered the opportunity to study the language and Qur'anic sciences in the imperial palace and was later rewarded with appropriate gifts.

Although the account bears features idiosyncratic to the author's experience as an educated Orthodox Christian from the Ottoman Empire, the narrative in question is closely modeled on the *Tuhfa* of Anselm Turmeda. A comparison of the two narratives reveals that the episode in Turmeda's *Tuhfa*, in which his teacher explains the meaning of the passages from the scriptures as the announcement of Muhammad's prophecy, is featured almost verbatim in Mehmed's story about the old monk.[70] Evidence about the transmission of Turmeda's work suggests that it is entirely possible that Mehmed had access to it—a translation into Ottoman Turkish was commissioned in Tunis by a prominent intellectual, Abu al-Gays Muhammad al-Kaşşaş, who presented it to Sultan Ahmed I on the occasion of his enthronement in 1603, with the hope that the sultan would aid the cause of the Moriscos facing expulsion from Spain for their tenacity in the Muslim faith.[71] Having been introduced to an Ottoman audience, the account of Anselm Turmeda became the single most popular conversion account in Ottoman lands, surpassing other Ottoman narratives in number of copies and renown.[72] Mehmed's account also survives in a number of copies in former Ottoman manuscript collections, making it the second most copied Ottoman conversion narrative.[73]

Whereas these texts reiterate the same model of intellectual male conversion familiar to us since the medieval period and draw on the Muslim anti-Christian polemical tradition, Mehmed's narrative and the commissioning of a translation of Turmeda's account testify to the new historical context in which conversion transpired. Like Murad's account, they speak about a world in which confessional polarization is enhanced by imperial competition and in which conversion is a highly public and political statement rather than an individual or at best local communal affair. Mehmed's account alludes to the spiritual and scriptural inferiority of both Orthodox and Catholic Christianity compared to Islam and refers to Rome as the "Red Apple" (*Kızıl Elma*)—a metaphor from popular Turkish prophecies that signifies the last Ottoman earthly conquest to be followed by the Day of Judgment.[74] At the same time, Ottoman Istanbul is referred to as the center of Islam and the seat of caliphs, the heirs of the last prophet, Muhammad. Mehmed's conversion to Islam in front of Sultan Ahmed, as well as the choice of Turmeda's conversion account as an appropriate gift for the sultan whose help against the Habsburgs was expected, suggests that conversion to Islam in the age of confessional proliferation increasingly meant allegiance to the Ottoman sultan.

By the mid-seventeenth century the ritual of conversion in the Ottoman Imperial Council was fully developed, with a surgeon in attendance to carry out the circumcision on the premises and with officials being ready to distribute new clothes to the converts.[75] It seems that the institutionalization of conversion was already well under way in Sultan Ahmed I's time, as the first detailed records of names and exact amounts donated to the converts date to AH 1018 (1609).[76] This trend continued throughout the seventeenth century as the sultans, gradually marginalized in day-to-day politics by their administrative elites, strove to project the image of pious protectors of the Muslim community in an era of numerous external and internal political challenges that intensified the calls for return to strict observation of the holy law.[77]

Moreover, when compared with other contemporary conversion narratives from around the Mediterranean, Mehmed's account testifies to the homogenization of conversion practices and narratives in an age of confessional and imperial competition. For instance, in 1604, just a few years before Mehmed penned his account, Uruc Bey, a member of the Safavid shah's embassy to the courts of Europe also known as Don Juan of Persia, published in Valladolid his account of conversion from Shi'a Islam to Catholicism in front of the Habsburg king of Spain, Philip III, and his queen. It is important to emphasize, however, that unlike Murad or Mehmed, Don Juan was not the sole author of his account—because he was not entirely fluent in Castilian, he received help from the court chaplain to the king and queen, Don Alvaro de Carvajal. It is entirely possible that the wording in which Don Juan describes "an inordinate longing in [his] heart to seek and find His Divine Grace" came from de Carvajal.[78] Regardless of the issue of authorship, however, the account provides an interesting description of the ceremony that surrounded the occasion of Don Juan's conversion. In addition to the circumstances that led him to embrace Christianity—most notably attending the church services that amazed him—Don Juan and his coauthor describe the new white satin clothes he was given as a convert and sponsorship of the Spanish majesties.[79] At the same time, Venetian authorities were also distributing new clothes upon the conversion of Ottoman subjects to Christianity in Venice and linking converts into patronage networks through the sponsorship of notable Venetian families and institutions.[80] These occasions were symbolic victories in the context of the interimperial struggle for subjects, especially those with particular technical, theological, or political know-how.

## *Yusuf b. Abi Abdüdeyyan, a Learned Jew–Turned–Sufi*

Another Ottoman conversion narrative from the seventeenth century that survives in numerous copies—in one case even bound together with Mehmed's and Turmeda's texts—was authored by an Ottoman Jewish intellectual who upon conversion adopted the Muslim name Yusuf b. Abi Abdüdeyyan.[81] Yusuf writes that since his childhood, whenever he read in the Old Testament the verses about the prophets, something in them seemed illogical, and he disliked reciting these passages. He says that due to his youth he did not dwell on it much, but with every new reading his heart would beat violently. Later, when his reasoning became more mature and he learned the deceitful ways of the world, none of the explanations of these passages seemed satisfying, and he began to rebel against Jewish custom. Seeing the orderliness in Muslim laws and rituals, he began to contemplate embracing Islam. In order to take his mind off this problem, he devoted himself with great persistence to the study of Jewish religious and practical sciences, hoping for divine guidance. However, no matter how much he strove in study of exegetical treatises, he could not make his heart accept the explanations for the verses in question. He states that he realized that those and other places in the Pentateuch had been altered and that he became aware of the truths of Muhammad's prophecy and the Qur'an, as opposed to the misinterpretations of the Jews. This shook the faith that his parents had instilled in him, and he turned away from his ancestral religion. As he says:

> And having made me turn onto the right path, the guidance of God became a friend that saved me who felt aversion to mankind and sociability, loneliness in religion and community, and confusion in open spaces and the valley of wilderness. It showed me the way to the peaceful courtyards of Islam and adorned me with the robes of God's oneness and excellent qualities of the followers of Muhammad's law. It made the eyes of my clear vision shine with a kohl-like luster of the words "there is no God but God" and with the eye balm of the bright words of "Muhammad is the Prophet of God."[82]

Eventually, under the pretense of trade, Yusuf disposed of all his possessions and donated money to the pious endowment (*vakıf*) of a Muslim saint. He withdrew to a Sufi convent (*zāviye*) to spend his old age in prayer and worship. It is here that he authored the polemical work that demonstrates the veracity of Muhammad's prophecy through the verses from the Old Testament and the Psalms, to which his autobiography is appended.

One surviving manuscript of Yusuf's account suggests that the text was originally written in or before AH 1061 (1651).[83] This date coincides with a turbulent era in the religious politics of the Ottoman Empire that affected particularly adversely the Ottoman Jewish community. In 1648 a new wave of the so-called Kadızadeli movement flared up, promoting a return to the ancestral practice of Islam devoid of innovations as an answer to the military, financial, and political crises that the empire faced in the late sixteenth and early seventeenth centuries.[84] Despite its prominence throughout the seventeenth century, the Kadızadeli movement, as well as the sociopolitical profile of those who embraced it, is still very poorly understood. However, it is clear that the Kadızadelis drew their inspiration from and built upon the sixteenth-century reformists working in the Hanefi legal tradition, such as Birgivi, and represent a new chapter in the Ottoman history of confessionalization and social disciplining.[85] Although the movement was ostensibly championed by Istanbul's mosque preachers and graduates of provincial *medreses*, particularly targeting innovations such as saint worship and the use of music in Sufi rituals, it was far from a simple anti-Sufi lobby group.[86] Kadızadelis called for reform of a society that they perceived as steeped in the sins of incorrect practice of Islam and inappropriately intimate relations between Muslims and non-Muslims, especially in the multiconfessional Ottoman capital.[87] They were not alone in this call, and the participants in this ongoing debate over the form and practice of Islam, as well as over who had the right to define Islamic orthodoxy, to enjoin the right and forbid the wrong, included other *sunna*-minded social actors, ranging from members of some Sufi orders to Ottoman officials, Sultan Mehmed IV, and his mother to common folk. Different social groups thus vied for a monopoly over discourse on public piety and morality, articulating the process of confessionalization from both above and below. Although at times the religious politics of the Ottoman sultans and imperial elites coincided with that of the Kadızadelis, and they joined forces in disciplining Ottoman society, at other times the political elites sought to suppress the movement.[88]

A recent study suggests that in addition to certain Sufi orders who were blamed for introducing innovations to the Muslim faith, the Kadızadeli movement especially targeted Jews, who unlike the Orthodox and Catholic Christians in the Ottoman Empire did not have the protection of European ambassadors in Constantinople.[89] It is well known that Sultan Mehmed IV's personal *şeyh*, Kadızadeli preacher Vani Mehmed Efendi, played an instrumental role in the conversion of Sabbatai Zevi, the famous Jewish rabbi and cabalist who proclaimed himself the long-awaited Jewish Messiah in 1648 but converted to Islam under duress in 1666.[90]

Zevi's conversion to Islam led to a wave of disillusionment among Jewish communities around Europe and in the Ottoman Empire, resulting in a noticeable increase in conversions of European Jews to Christianity and of Ottoman Jews to Islam.[91] Although Yusuf does not specifically invoke these events, his audience, especially the Ottoman Jews, must have been aware of them.

Yusuf's account is yet another example of a male intellectual's narrative of conversion to Islam. Although there is no evidence that it is directly modeled on Samuel al-Mahgribi's, Turmeda's, or Mehmed's account, Yusuf's story follows the same pattern of illumination and conversion through his pursuit of a deeper understanding of the scriptures. It also strikingly resembles contemporary Jewish accounts of conversion to Christianity in that it emphasizes the education and learning that Yusuf received as a Jewish youth—detail designed to counter speculation about base motives for conversion and potentially raise the author's stature in his new community.[92] It is likely that with the new emphasis on the issues of religious orthopraxy and conversion, and with the new pressure on the Jewish community, Yusuf's account assumed a theological value in proselytization similar to the one attached to conversion narratives of Jewish converts to Christianity in post-Tridentine Germany.[93] Even though it is not clear how wide a circulation this manuscript had in the seventeenth century and whether it affected the conversion of other Jews, the fact that three early nineteenth-century copies from the region of the Black Sea survive testifies to the possibility that together with Mehmed's and Turmeda's texts, Yusuf's treatise became a popular instrument of proselytization for Islam.[94]

## *Mehmed, a Priest-Turned-Sufi*

As an educated Orthodox priest and a learned Jew, respectively, Mehmed of Athens and Yusuf b. Abi Abdüdeyyan were not ordinary converts. As we have seen, the trope of the converted priest (and less frequently, a rabbi) was prominent in many other Ottoman narratives about conversion from the earlier periods, but it attains particular importance in seventeenth-century texts. For instance, another popular self-narrative of conversion from the mid-seventeenth century, *The Priest's Story* (*Papasnāme*), was authored by a priest–turned–Sufi mystic who experienced premonitions of the Ottoman dynasty's imminent collapse due to widespread bribery and a breakdown in public morality.[95] When he related these anxieties to his spiritual master, the latter shared with him a prophetic vision of the Ottoman dynasty's future in which seventy more sultans were destined to rule before the Day of Judgment.[96] The master then entrusted the former priest with writing down and communicating this vision to the world in order to stem rumors about the Ottoman dynasty's end. He also insisted that the former priest, as a new convert, was the perfect person to do that because he had seen the Prophet Muhammad in a dream and became a Muslim after "forty-seven years of worshipping idols," and because he had left his family, friends, and possessions in order to come to Ottoman lands after a five-month journey.[97]

This narrative, infused with mystical vocabulary and apocalyptic imagery, is a complex text that engages the real political issues plaguing the Ottoman sultanate in the early to mid-seventeenth century, such as the assassination of Sultan Osman II in 1622; the debate over modes of imperial succession; anxieties about the survival of the dynasty due to Sultan İbrahim's (1640–48) initial inability to produce an heir; the ongoing military rivalry with the Habsburgs, Safavids, and Venetians; and the debate regarding what constitutes Muslim orthodoxy.[98] This debate was part of the broader discussion on "what went wrong" in the Ottoman sultanate that arose in the wake of multifaceted military, financial, and political changes in the late sixteenth and seventeenth centuries.[99] Sufis especially came under fire from the Kadızadeli "puritan" movement. The author of the *Papasnāme* therefore seeks to demonstrate that it is in fact a Sufi mystic, rather than those accusing Sufis of impiety, who is blessed with the foreknowledge of the Ottoman dynasty's future and in charge of its well-being.

Judging from the number of surviving copies, it was a very popular text that circulated from Vienna to Tunisia.[100] It is therefore important that a converted priest would be chosen as the special emissary to relate news of an auspicious future to the Ottoman sultans in a time of crisis. Similarly, a historian from the reign of Mustafa II (1695–1703), Silahdar, reports in his *Nusretnāme* that in mid-April 1695 a Christian (Greek Orthodox) priest arrived in Edirne, where the sultan held his court, to announce that he had a message to deliver to the sultan. He related that he, the priest, had covertly converted to Islam because he saw a vision of the Prophet Muhammad and of the late sultan Mehmed IV, the incumbent's father, in his dream. The Prophet invited the priest to Islam, while the deceased sultan told him to go and declare his Islam to Mustafa, who would superbly reward him. Mehmed IV also entrusted the priest to tell Mustafa that his sultanate would endure for a very long period and that during his reign many an enemy domain would be conquered and recovered.[101] Since the Ottoman-Habsburg war had been going on since 1683 (and would end in 1699 with great losses for the Ottomans), this conversion story was supposed to both boost the Sultan's morale and persuade the Ottoman military and bureaucratic elites in control of the government that Mustafa's active military and political leadership was indispensable. In this way, the Ottoman sultan's enterprise received legitimization and endorsement from the greatest of all authorities—its own converted enemy.

## *İbrahim Müteferrika, a Unitarian Priest–Turned–Ottoman Printer*

The legitimizing power of a converted priest and his relationship to the Ottoman political project are also illustrated by the career and self-narrative of conversion to Islam of İbrahim Müteferrika (1674–1724), the famous founder of the first Ottoman Arabic script printing press, who hailed from the city of Kolozsvár in Transylvania and was most likely a Unitarian.[102] Since his *Treatise on Islam* (*Risāle-yi islāmīye*) was written in 1710 before he climbed the Ottoman honorific hierarchy to attain the title of *müteferrika* (member of the learned elite associated with the court), it is possible that Müteferrika saw it as a convenient means to jump-start his career. His abundant praise of Sultan Ahmed III (1703–30) and unequivocal endorsement of the Ottoman enterprise suggest that Müteferrika had a very specific audience in mind. In fact, as this work survives in only one copy despite Müteferrika's subsequent fame, it appears that it never reached a wider audience than originally envisioned.[103] One could almost say that it was written for the sultan's eyes only.

Müteferrika's narrative represents the culmination of the Ottoman polemical self-narrative of conversion genre in that it combines the elements of all the texts discussed so far. There is a great possibility that Müteferrika, who had access to the imperial libraries of the Ottoman capital, was familiar with these earlier Ottoman narratives. Like Anselm Turmeda, Mehmed of Athens, and Yusuf, he elaborates on his education in theology and study of scriptures in Greek and Latin, in which he finds evidence of Muhammad's prophecy.[104] Like the priest-turned-Sufi, nevertheless, he gives his narrative a prophetic tone, foretelling the Ottoman dynasty's destiny to rule the known world and vanquish all enemies.[105] Finally, like Murad, he engages his knowledge of contemporary European power struggles and religious politics and argues that the Ottoman rivals will collapse because of constant religious and political turmoil. He writes that in the end all the infidels will be brought to believe in the unity of God, which was also Jesus' true message before the scriptures were corrupted. For Müteferrika, who was a Unitarian-turned-Muslim and combined these sensibilities in his religio-political tract, the Ottomans were the only guarantors of purity of belief, especially against Rome, the accursed "Red Apple," and its Habsburg agents, who would succumb to the Ottomans before the Day of Judgment.

## *Conclusion*

The authors of these narratives were by no means typical Ottoman converts. They were literate men, mostly former Christians educated in theology and the Christian polemical tradition, which they could later explore and criticize as Muslims arguing for Islam's superiority. Despite their exceptional backgrounds, these authors and their texts suggest that in the later sixteenth century sensibilities toward conversion and converts in the Ottoman Empire began to change. This is also borne out by other contemporary sources, including court records and converts' petitions to the sultan.[106] Ottoman imperial and religious competition with the Habsburgs and Safavids, as well as the domestic challenges that Ottoman sultans faced in the later sixteenth and seventeenth centuries, were the two most crucial developments that contributed to this change. These developments also directly influenced the emergence of Ottoman self-narratives of conversion to Islam, which, unlike the earlier examples of the genre, inextricably bound together the convert, his new religion of Islam, and the Ottoman state/sultan as Islam's symbolic face.

Given that most of the authors specifically seek the sultan's patronage in their narratives, it is not surprising that both the texts and their authors can be traced to the religious and political milieu of Ottoman Istanbul. However, their impact was not as localized as one might expect. A closer look at manuscript distribution reveals that these narratives, although little known and understudied by modern scholars, were in fact noticed, not only by the sultan and the authors' Muslim contemporaries but also by foreign travelers and diplomats who procured copies for developing European royal and imperial libraries. The majority of the texts discussed here can today be found (in some cases even exclusively) in various Oriental manuscript collections in Western Europe rather than in Istanbul. This testifies to the fact that the debate in which the converts to Islam engaged in their narratives was far from irrelevant beyond Constantinople.[107] In fact, recent research shows that the intellectual debates, conversations, and manuscripts exchanged in early modern Ottoman Istanbul (as well as in other Ottoman trade and cultural hubs such as İzmir and Aleppo) among the members of the Ottoman administrative and intellectual elite, converts to Islam, and Ottoman slaves on the one hand, and various European diplomats, travelers, and dragomans on the other, directly and in a decisive manner shaped the production of knowledge about the "Orient" in Europe.[108] This dialogic nature of the proto-Orientalist European literature and the Ottoman elites' role in its production is emerging as a new and productive field of research that challenges the notion of a fundamental separation between the "East" and "West" and forces researchers to think about the nature of cultural, political, and religious contacts in the Mediterranean in a new way.[109]

In producing self-narratives of conversion that wove together Jewish, Christian, and Muslim polemical traditions and religious sensibilities, the Ottoman converts discussed here were not simple cultural brokers between discrete worlds invested in producing difference in order to advance their own agendas. In their narratives they both drew upon and perpetuated shared conceptual frameworks and debates that marked the Mediterranean-wide age of confessional and imperial polarization in the sixteenth and seventeenth centuries. Catholic-Protestant, Muslim-Christian, and Sunni-Shi'a debates in the age of confessionalization all addressed issues related to spiritual and temporal authority, "correct" rituals, and the authenticity of scriptural traditions employing a shared conceptual vocabulary. Within this common conceptual framework, spaces, texts, and political ideas were contested to form communities of difference that nevertheless acknowledged that they were competing for the same moral and religious capital—universal imperial rule and the status of the only true religion that guarantees salvation.

CHAPTER FIVE

# Between the Turban and the Papal Tiara

## *Orthodox Christian Neomartyrs and Their Impresarios in the Age of Confessionalization*

In 1606 a young Orthodox Christian named Christophoros Angelles arrived from one of the Greek islands to Athens, "where gray-eyed Minerva spake & prophesied . . . by the mouth of learned Grecians," to pursue an education in theology. However, he arrived in an inauspicious moment of tension between the Athenians and their Ottoman "captain" and was arrested as a possible spy for the Spanish. According to the narrative he published in 1617 as a refugee in Oxford, England, he was offered Islam under torture. He describes how he was wrongfully accused, apprehended, and tied up, and how he was asked to reconsider his decision to refuse Islam three times, as was customary according to Ottoman law. Furthermore, he relates that his captors tempted him with promises of great honors and wealth should he convert. However, Christophoros decided to remain steadfast and to die in the religion of his parents. Finally, he gives the details of how he was scourged with rods dipped in salt water and how he feared that he would not persist in his love for Christ. Luckily for Christophoros, his Ottoman captors were amenable to bribery, and thanks to the efforts of Athenian Christian merchants, he was able to escape from Athens. He finally decided to seek refuge in England because France, Germany, and Italy "have continually civil warres," but also because he was told that the English sympathized with the Greeks' plight under the Ottomans.[1]

Christophoros's account makes references to several intellectual, political, and religious trends prevalent at the turn of the seventeenth century. Although by this time humanists in Europe spoke and wrote better Greek than Greek-speaking scholars from the Ottoman Empire, Christophoros "reminds" his readers in England that the ancient Athenians are intimately related to the Orthodox Greeks living under Ottoman rule and that the latter are therefore especially worth saving from their plight.[2] Furthermore, Christophoros refers to the religious wars that beset Europe in the age of confessionalization and draws a parallel between the religious oppression that the Ottomans inflicted upon Orthodox Christians and the tyranny of the Catholics over Anglicans. Christophoros invokes the theme of forced conversion to Islam popular with Christian audiences in the West, and increasingly relevant to readers in England. The late sixteenth century witnessed intensified commercial relations between England on the one hand and the Ottoman Empire and the Barbary Coast on the other, followed by the conversion of many Englishmen to Islam.[3] Furthermore, Christophoros resorts to the language and imagery of martyrdom—the religious idiom that gained new importance with audiences from the New World to Safavid Persia in the sixteenth and seventeenth centuries. In writing this self-martyrology, Christophoros drew not only on the stories of the martyrs familiar to his English audience but specifically on the genre of neomartyrology, which began to gain extraordinary popularity in this period among Orthodox Christians in the Ottoman Empire.

This chapter explores how Orthodox Christians, Catholics, and Protestants contested conversion to Islam and martyrdom in the Ottoman Empire by producing and circulating neomartyrologies, narratives about the suffering and death of Orthodox Christian men and women who were imprisoned and executed by Ottoman authorities, mostly for converting to Islam and later apostatizing or for refusing to convert to Islam after being accused of blasphemy. Special emphasis will be placed on how different segments of the Orthodox Christian community in the Ottoman Empire used the genre of neomartyrology to reshape the boundaries of their community and assert their own definition of what it meant to be an Orthodox Christian in an age when conversion to both Islam and Catholicism was on the rise. These efforts were in direct dialogue with the attitudes of Catholic and Protestant missionaries in the Ottoman Empire toward the phenomenon of new martyrdom in general and the production of neomartyrologies in particular. The discussion situates the phenomenon in the wider framework of confessional politics that encompassed both Christendom and Islamdom in the sixteenth and seventeenth centuries and argues that the idiom of conversion and martyrdom was an essential feature of a transregional age of confessionalization.

## *The Phenomenon of New Martyrdom in the Early Modern Ottoman Context*

When in 313 Constantine recognized Christianity as a licit religion in the Roman Empire, he brought an end to the era of early Christian martyrs, or "witnesses for Christ." In the centuries leading up to the Ottoman conquests, Christians experienced and documented few comparable cases of martyrdom.[4] However, Ottoman conquests and the Protestant Reformation ushered in a new chapter in the history of Christian martyrdom and its narrative record. New martyrs were not simply Christian anymore—they were Orthodox, Catholic, or of various Protestant denominations, but they all claimed the ancestry of the early Christian "witnesses for Christ." This noble lineage was a crucial argument in the multidirectional polemics over the "true" religion that encompassed early modern Christendom in the second half of the sixteenth century.[5]

It is important to mention, however, that martyrdom became an important facet of the contemporary Sunni-Shi'a polemic as well. In the Ottoman Empire, jurists began to proclaim those fallen in battle with the Shi'a Safavids as martyrs for faith.[6] At the same time, in the Safavid Empire we see a new emphasis on the martyrdom of Imam Hussein, the son of Ali and grandson of the Prophet Muhammad. His brutal death at Karbala (in 680) was reenacted in the ritual drama or passion play known as *ta'ziyeh*, which became central to the Safavid imperial ritual and the Shi'a religious identity.[7] The Ottomans gave the Shi'a tradition its "Second Martyr" by executing the scholar Zayn al-Din b. Ali al-Amili in 1558 as a heretic, forcing Shi'a scholars traversing the Ottoman territories to conceal their true religious affiliation and practice dissimulation (*taqiyya*). This was not the only Shi'a scholar publicly executed—in 1536 two Shi'a learned men were bound to a post and burned alive in the square below the citadel in Ottoman Damascus, their ashes thrown into the river.[8] Although the Jewish legal tradition did not condone martyrdom in the sense of deliberately seeking death, the sixteenth and seventeenth centuries also witnessed new cases of consciously dying for the Jewish faith, especially among the Marranos of Iberia, who were influenced by the tradition of Christian martyrdom.[9] The "age of martyrs" therefore went hand in hand with the "age of confessionalization."

The phenomenon of neomartyrdom emerged with the onset of conversions to Islam during the first decades of Ottoman expansion in Anatolia and the Balkans in the fourteenth century, although there are also some references to earlier Orthodox neomartyrs from the Seljuk era.[10] During the thirteenth and fourteenth centuries, the Orthodox Christian Church demonstrated a great deal of compassion for those who converted to Islam out of fear or perceived threat. The phenomenon of crypto-Christianity was especially endorsed as a strategy that would help preserve the Christian rite in new Muslim territories. With this in mind Patriarch John XIV Aprenos generously accepted back into the Christian fold Christians from Bursa who had converted after the Ottoman conquest of the city in 1331 and later repented. The patriarchal letter points out that those not brave enough to voluntarily become martyrs for faith should not be condemned.[11] Orthodox patriarchs were therefore initially demonstrating an understanding of the lot of their flock, perhaps hoping that Christianity would eventually triumph and that Muslim conquests would be a temporary setback; however, it soon became obvious that the Ottomans were there to stay and that tolerating crypto-Christianity meant assisting the spread of Islam. For this reason, martyrdom eventually began to receive more enthusiastic support among some segments of the Orthodox Christian ecclesiastical establishment, especially in the sixteenth and seventeenth centuries. By the end of the eighteenth century, in the first comprehensive compilation of neomartyrologies from the Ottoman era, *Neon martyrologion* (The New Compilation of Martyrs' Lives; Venice, 1794), the compiler, Nikodemos Hagiorites of the Holy Mountain (fl. 1784–1809), was able to include more than one hundred stories about neomartyrs.[12]

Nikodemos Hagiorites provides the most comprehensive discussion of the neomartyrs, their relationship to their ancient precursors, and their "message" in his *Neon martyrologion*.[13] As he points out, the appeal of the neomartyrs is that people had often known them intimately, had eaten and drunk with them, and were present at their martyrdoms.[14] The new martyrs were of significantly lower social status than the early witnesses for Christ, who almost invariably came from patrician families. They were common men and women, usually artisans, craftsmen, and traders from the provinces, typically from Rumeli and the coast of Anatolia. The main difference between the martyrs from the Ottoman period and their ancient precursors was that the former typically accepted Islam and then apostatized or were accused of apostasy after they supposedly became Muslims. However, Hagiorites asserts that the suffering of the new martyrs in every way matches the sacrifices of earlier martyrs and in some ways even surpasses them since the struggle "against the single-person monotheism of those of another faith . . . that can easily deceive the mind" is greater than that "against polytheism and idolatry . . . that can deceive a logical mind only with difficulty."[15] The new martyrs facing the temptation of Islam as a monotheistic religion are therefore even superior to those of old who had to argue against the polytheism of the Roman state. Nevertheless, Nikodemos Hagiorites of the Holy Mountain was not the first to recognize and articulate the neomartyrs' message—he was building on generations of other neomartyrs' impresarios from the era of confessionalization whose identities, mission, and target audience are explored here.

## *The Neomartyrs' Impresarios*

One of the earliest surviving texts of this genre, the martyrology of George the Goldsmith from Kratovo (today in the Republic of Macedonia), who died in Sofia (Bulgaria) in 1515 and whose story was recorded in the late sixteenth century, offers a colorful illustration of an impresario at work.[16] George, who lost his father while still young, had to leave his studies and dedicate himself to work as a goldsmith. His mother sent him to Sofia to live with an educated priest, Father Peter. Under Father Peter's auspices George became an exemplary Orthodox Christian. However, his dedication did not go unnoticed, and soon a group of Muslims irritated by his piety plotted to convert him to Islam. Pretending to be friendly, a Muslim initiated conversation with George and invited him to convert to Islam. George, however, far from being impressed, tried to prove to the Muslim that Islam is a path of destruction and that he should not be inviting anybody to join him on that path. Enraged, the Muslim reported George's words to the local judge (*kadı*), who in turn repeated the invitation to Islam and presented George with the consequences should he refuse.

Upon the end of the first interrogation and George's stubborn refusal to become a Muslim, he is taken to prison. Meanwhile, Father Peter asks the *kadı* to be allowed to counsel George, promising to give him advice on what is best for him.[17] After his request is approved, Father Peter visits George in prison and exhorts him to "rejoice" since he will have a chance to glorify Christ. To this enthusiastic monologue George responds that he is afraid of fire and does not believe he will be able to withstand a painful and humiliating execution, but the priest encourages him not to relent but to be patient in order to be able to "dance with Christ eternally."[18] Throughout the rest of the narrative Father Peter plays the main role in orchestrating George's defense. Interestingly, however, these efforts come across as quite ambiguous, and it is unclear whether Father Peter wants to save George or ensure that George stays adamant in his refusal of Islam. This particular neomartyrology offers a valuable insight into the saint-making process, as it records the social transactions taking place behind the scenes of the main drama, in which George refuses to convert even after the second and third interrogation by the *kadı*. Thus, for example, while the Muslim crowd is cheering for George to be instantly executed for his insulting comments on Islam, Father Peter, unable to stay close to George, asks one of the Muslims in the crowd who, according to the text, is a secret Christian and loves Father Peter, to stay close to the prisoner and report to him what the Muslims say to George and what he answers.

As the account nears its end, George the man loses importance in the general anticipation of George the Martyr, whose dead body becomes the point of contestation between the Muslim and Christian actors in the drama. After George dies in a huge pyre, suffering much physical and verbal abuse, Father Peter and a group of Christians plead with the *kadı* to allow them to bury George in the Christian way. However, the Muslims, well aware that Christians want to bury George as a martyr and establish his remains as holy relics, refuse angrily and add the carcasses of dead animals into the fire so that George's remains would become indistinguishable from the animal ones.[19] But this is where George's holiness becomes apparent, as his body remains whole while the animal carcasses turn into ashes. Impressed by this miracle, the *kadı* eventually allows Father Peter to bury George's remains.

Although this narrative recorded in the late sixteenth century raises a variety of questions regarding the problem of neomartyrdom, I focus on the role of the spiritual adviser in the events that led to the final drama. In the vita of George of Kratovo, Father Peter's actions are portrayed as at least as significant as George's: the narrator follows his every step and reports all of his words and actions. From the point of view of the narrative's author, Father Peter is clearly an equal partner in the process of martyr making, as he provides logistics for the whole event: he encourages George to accept the role of a neomartyr, he takes necessary steps to be informed of the dialogues that transpire between George and his torturers (presumably in order to be able to write it down later), and he goes to enormous lengths to recover George's body in the end. The deliberation and almost Machiavellian character of Father Peter invites the question of what motivated this seemingly well-integrated priest (the *kadı* is supposedly his acquaintance!) to encourage and aid in such a socially disruptive event as George's martyrdom. How seriously are we to take this emphasis on the priest's role in the process of martyr making?

Other neomartyrologies from the late sixteenth and seventeenth centuries testify to the role of spiritual advisers and monasteries in the phenomenon of new martyrdom and reconversion of converts.[20] Ottoman sources also confirm that the role of spiritual advisers, which is not at all prominent in fifteenth-century narratives and seems to come to the fore only in later sixteenth-century neomartyrologies, is not to be underestimated.[21] For example, an Ottoman imperial rescript (an entry in the *mühimme defterleri*) from 1565 suggests that the two individuals who helped an escaped janissary cadet (*ʿacemioğlan*) reconvert to Christianity were both linked to clerical circles: one was the son of a priest, Kaya Keşiş oğlu Nikola from the village of Sarımsaklu near Kayseri; the other was actually a priest himself, Sarımsaklı Papazı Papa Pavlos. Both were condemned to the galleys.[22] Another imperial rescript from 1582 confirms the story about the martyred nun Philotei from Athens (d. 1589), who sheltered women who had converted to Islam as slaves or wives of prominent Athenian Muslims. Philotei helped these women to convert back to Christianity and organized their escape to Venice.[23] Contemporary Jesuit sources also offer a compelling perspective on this issue. For instance, in a report to his superiors in France on the activities of the Society of Jesus in the Ottoman Empire, the Jesuit father Thomas-Charles Fleurieu writes in 1695 of a young man from Morea who was induced to apostatize by his "Turkish" friends while drunk. He later repented and confessed to a priest, who obliged him to renounce his Islam in public and embrace martyrdom. Upon doing so, he was immediately apprehended by Ottoman authorities and thrown in prison, where a priest obtained permission to visit him and managed to give him communion in secret.[24]

Neomartyrologies suggest that the role of monks from Mount Athos was particularly decisive. Mount Athos, also known as the Holy Mountain, was the center of Byzantine spirituality, located on the peninsula of the same name, today in northern Greece. The first monastic communities were established there in the ninth century, and their numbers grew under the patronage of Byzantine emperors in ensuing centuries. Over time, the monasteries of Mount Athos acquired significant tax and other privileges as well as independence from the Byzantine emperors, which they managed to partially retain in the Ottoman period by maintaining good relations with early Ottoman sultans.[25] According to the oldest known title of privilege (*berāt)*, dating to Murad II's reign in 1430, the monasteries gained the privileges of not having the *tımār* system established on the peninsula and not having to allow any Ottoman official to enter the peninsula, whereas the properties of the priests and monks were recognized as religious endowments (*vakıf*) and private property (*mülk*), which meant that the monks did not have to pay either the poll tax or taxes for the products they produced locally.[26] In an age when they still sought to legitimate themselves to the local populations in Rumeli, the Ottoman sultans gained much social capital by recognizing the privileged status of the Athonite monasteries. In addition to immaterial benefits, they gained reliable taxpayers who in exchange for extraordinary privileges committed themselves to paying the tax as an annual lump sum (*maktu*ʿ), which was a very important contribution to the imperial treasury.

Owing to its geographic inaccessibility, distance from significant urban centers, and virtual freedom from Ottoman officials, the Holy Mountain soon became an ideal hiding place for all sorts of fugitives from the Ottoman authorities. Imperial rescripts show that from early in the Ottoman rule Mount Athos became an attractive refuge for Christian boys taken to the janissary corps and converted to Islam. They would often flee to the Holy Mountain, where they would return to Orthodox Christianity and spend the rest of their lives as monks.[27] Sources also testify that Ottoman authorities were well aware of this trend and scrutinized closely the activities of the monks, as the accusation of converting Muslims to Christianity demanded the most extreme punishments. A certain monk Isaiah wrote at the turn of the sixteenth century that the Ottoman emperor was preventing Athonite monks from turning the "imperial fugitives" into monks.[28] Implication in helping escaped prisoners and apostates from Islam made the Athonite monks a perpetual target of punitive attacks, although their privileges were never summarily revoked.

However, in the later sixteenth and especially the seventeenth century, Mount Athos came under tighter control of the Ottoman government, which began to contest a great deal of the privileges and independence that the monks had enjoyed previously. The Athonite monasteries began to feel the impact of the centralizing and Sunnitizing reforms initiated in Süleyman's era when in 1568 Sultan Selim II ordered the confiscation of monastic properties based on *şeyhü'l-islām* Ebussuud Efendi's attempts to create a unified system of taxation and redefine its general principles. Ebussuud argued that the monasteries had not been paying taxes obligatory under the Holy Law and thereby damaged the treasury of the Muslims.[29] In the legal negotiations that ensued, Athonite monks managed to get the Ottoman government to concede them some privileges by threatening to "scatter all around the world," abandon their monasteries, and not pay any further lump-sum taxes that the treasury valued so much.[30] Nevertheless, they had to repurchase their properties under the new legal terms, which started a long era of ever-growing extraordinary taxes exacted on the monasteries as the financial troubles of the Ottoman state, and of the monasteries as well, continued to mount throughout the seventeenth century. The tax records that document this process suggest that in the atmosphere of general social turmoil that marked this era, the Ottoman authorities needed a reliable taxpayer such as the Athonite monasteries and, for this reason, were perhaps willing to overlook the monks' various transgressions.[31] As neomartyrologies suggest, during the seventeenth century, Mount Athos became a significant site for the production of witnesses for Christ.

By the end of the eighteenth century the practice of counseling penitent converts seems to have attained a programmatic character, since in his preface to the *Neon martyrologion* Nikodemos Hagiorites, an Athonite monk himself, advises a person who had converted to Islam and repented to go to an "experienced and virtuous confessor" and tell him of intended martyrdom. The five-step program for a repentant convert also included receiving a second anointing with Holy Unction; going into seclusion combined with fasting, vigils, and ardent prayers to God for mercy and encouragement in the face of martyrdom; receiving Holy Communion with contrition and reverence; and finally "rising up" and going to the very same place where the convert originally "denied Christ" and there denying the religion he accepted, thereby confessing the faith of Christ. Hagiorites concludes: "And with this confession spill your blood and die."[32] Apparently, a penitent convert would be escorted to the chosen place of martyrdom by fellow Athonites, where he would ceremonially trample upon his turban, the symbol of his Muslim identity, in front of the Ottoman judge and declare his apostasy. In addition to making sure that the martyr-to-be did not waver at the last moment, these companions' roles were to initiate the process of canonization following the trial and execution—collecting the martyr's remains, writing his vita, and painting his icon. The story of the new martyr, composed in popular language, would then be disseminated among the Christian population by the wandering Athonite monks (*taxidiotes*).[33]

From the writings of nineteenth-century apologists of new martyrdom it is clear that both Muslims and Christians throughout the Ottoman period heavily criticized the phenomenon. The most common criticism, it appears, was that new martyrs died needlessly as sacrificial lambs of the Athonite ideology, the implication being that the Athonite monasteries exerted pressure on these people who were already in a precarious psychological state as apostates and fugitives from the law. Another common complaint was that new martyrs were guilty of hubris, seeking to attain eternal life in heaven through suicide rather than through a lifelong expiation of sins.[34] The debate on the extent to which it was appropriate for a Christian to seek persecution and martyrdom dated to the early days of Christianity. Although early church fathers initially endorsed martyrdom, by the third century the position of Clement of Alexandria, who maintained that salvation knew no shortcuts and that martyrdom was a daily act involving an individual's entire life, prevailed. In the evolving Orthodox Christianity this position inspired asceticism and the attitude that death should not be courted but avoided.[35] Indeed, unlike the Catholic tradition, the Byzantine Orthodox Christian tradition of saint making decisively resisted the idea of a warrior-saint—a person killed while fighting against the infidels was not accepted as either a martyr or a saint.[36] This tendency, backed by abundant patristic literature, significantly reduced the saint-making options in the post-Byzantine Orthodox Christian world conquered by the Ottomans and diverted the theory of martyrdom in the direction of passive rather than active resistance. By promoting martyrdom, the impresarios of neomartyrs sought to redefine orthodoxy and orthopraxy associated with this phenomenon in the Orthodox Christian tradition. They also challenged the notions that resistance can be only passive as well as that harmony between church and state should be preserved at all costs.

In addition to a long tradition against seeking martyrdom, this practice was frowned upon by clerics from the Ottoman era because of the multiple risks it involved: there was a danger that the intended martyr would not withstand the trial that awaited him and that other members of the church would be implicated, which would not bode well for the status of the Orthodox community under the Ottomans.[37] This is precisely the view expressed by the first priest of the Patriarchate in the sixteenth-century neomartyrology of John the Tailor from Ioannina (d. 1526), written by Nikolaos Malaxos, the metropolitan of Nauplion and famous canonist. In response to John's desire to become a martyr, he states that the holy canons did not permit Orthodox Christians to seek martyrdom on their own because it was questionable whether such an endeavor could be completed successfully.[38] Other neomartyrologies also suggest the contentious nature of martyrdom and the controversial position of both those who sought it and those who endorsed it. The author of the vita of Makarios the Tailor, who died in 1590, goes out of his way to suggest that the idea to die as a martyr came from Makarios himself rather than his spiritual adviser from the Holy Mountain. The text maintains that the priest, after initially refusing to bless his endeavor, was won over by Makarios's determination.[39] In order to counter criticism, apologists of neomartyrdom emphasized the primary importance of free will and intent in the process, explaining that simply dying at the hands of an infidel does not make one a martyr.[40] This accounts for the strong emphasis in the neomartyrologies on the martyr's desire to witness for Christ, whereas the role of the spiritual adviser is not always pronounced.

At the same time, however, the rhetoric of the neomartyrs' impresarios left very little to imagine in terms of the spiritual adviser's position. By the end of the eighteenth century Nikodemos Hagiorites felt entitled to address converts in the following words:

> For you who have denied Christ, we would like to add the following; that is, it is not so strange that you have been defeated, brethren, and have fallen into the

state of denial, because in this world there is a continuous war between the devil and man. . . . What is truly strange and a great evil is to remain in that pitiful faith to which you have fallen and not wish to rise up from it.[41]

And to rise up meant to die. In other words, Hagiorites does not admit any remedy short of outright apostasy for those who converted to Islam. No repentance is deemed sufficient to erase the sin of denying Christ.[42] By the end of the eighteenth century, martyrdom thus became a legitimate culture of resistance that was openly promoted.

Not surprisingly, the perspective of the Orthodox patriarchs stationed in Constantinople, at the center of Ottoman power, was necessarily different and more ambiguous than that of Athonite monks. Although Mount Athos managed to retain some independence as it transitioned to Ottoman rule, with the fall of Constantinople the Orthodox Christian Patriarchate was co-opted into the Ottoman administrative and fiscal system, and the patriarchs had to be approved by the Ottoman sultan. After the conquest of Constantinople in 1453, Sultan Mehmed II appointed the first patriarch, Gennadios Scholarios, formerly leader of the anti-Latin party in the late Byzantine period.[43] Initially, the patriarchs in Constantinople were (at least theoretically) given jurisdiction over all Christians in the Ottoman Empire, thus becoming "ecumenical" leaders of the eastern Christians, not including the Armenians.[44] Nevertheless, as the Ottoman domains expanded to include Egypt and Syria and the diverse Christian communities in these areas, the ecumenical control of the Patriarchate of Constantinople was challenged. Over time, most of the Christian communities in the Arab provinces requested and were granted the status of a group or community (*tā'ife*), which entitled each to have its own communal leadership, collect taxes, and arbitrate in the legal cases involving only its own members.[45] In 1557, through the intervention of the Ottoman grand vizier, Sokollu Mehmed Pasha, the ecumenical appeal of the Patriarchate in Constantinople was further undermined by the restoration of the Serbian Patriarchate in Peć. This fragmentation of eastern Christendom was reinforced from the seventeenth century onward by the arrival of Catholic and Protestant missionaries.[46]

The patriarchs themselves came from different walks of life; some came from the long monastic tradition of Mount Athos, and others from nonclerical backgrounds.[47] Most often, they were puppets for other major players, usually powerful descendants of Byzantine families, such as the Kantakouzeni.[48] Only with the backing of these interest groups could a candidate for the Patriarchate succeed in obtaining the position, as installment in the rank involved stupendously high fees paid to various Ottoman officials. A recent comprehensive study on the character of the Orthodox Patriarchate as an institution under Ottoman rule qualifies it as a "tax farm" that was the object of competition rather than the focus of communal leadership, since the patriarchs were responsible for determining and collecting taxes from the Orthodox and were able to pocket the difference after paying the established sum to the Ottoman government.[49] Sources suggest that Orthodox patriarchs journeying around the empire in an attempt to raise taxes from their flock needed janissary escort to both protect them and enforce their mandate.[50] The close relationship with the Ottoman establishment and the perpetual insecurity of the patriarchal position suggest that patriarchs generally stood to lose from incidents that, like martyrdom, disturbed the status quo and could anger Ottoman authorities. Patriarchs could therefore not openly endorse the practice, but they could try to control and manipulate it in their own interests in the context of the stormy politics surrounding their appointments to the patriarchal throne.[51] There is some evidence that new martyrdom could have been used somewhat strategically in fights for this coveted position.[52]

## *Contesting the Neomartyrs' Message (and Body)*

What concrete historical developments incited the provincial priests and Athonite monks to become the neomartyrs' "impresarios," and who was their target audience? Several trends converged in the late sixteenth and seventeenth centuries that can account for the increased attention to the phenomenon of new martyrdom and its literary record. The period ushered in important changes in the Ottoman Empire, some of which were peculiar to the Ottomans, whereas others were of a more global nature, particularly in the spheres of the economy and the military. An economic crisis in 1585–86 and the subsequent social discontent, the war with the Habsburgs from 1593 to 1606, and a series of Celali and other internal revolts began the Ottoman seventeenth century.[53] At the center of Ottoman power, the sultans became increasingly palace bound and forced to contest their political prerogatives with their family members, courtiers, and grandee households. Fears of the dynasty's survival also resurfaced on several occasions throughout the century because some sultans had failed to produce an heir by the time they were enthroned.[54] Politics in the Ottoman Empire began to be conducted through factions and interest groups that sought to exploit the changes in the dynastic succession from fratricide to seniority, and influence the sultan and the Ottoman military establishment, especially the janissaries. These factions were responsible for deposing no less than four sultans and assassinating two during the seventeenth century.[55]

As in other contemporary Mediterranean polities, the changes in economic, political, and social dynamics prompted Ottoman pundits from various segments of society to seek and identify the causes for the seeming "decline."[56] Ottoman intellectuals lamented the demise of the meritocratic system of promotions, nepotism and rampant bribery, blurring of the clear boundaries between the tax-exempt military (*'askerī*) and tax-paying commoner (*re'āyā*) segments of society, the increasingly palace-bound sultan unwilling to lead military campaigns, and changing recruitment patterns in the Ottoman military.[57]

Other critics blamed the "decline" on a supposed lack of piety in Ottoman society. With fragmentation of central power, other *sunna*-minded groups in Ottoman society, such as the Kadızadeli mosque preachers and graduates of provincial religious colleges whose followers ranged from commoners to imperial elites, came to vie for the initiative in religious reforms with the Ottoman sultan. They used the discourse of religious reform to target their principal opponents in religious economy—the Sufis—but also to create a broader political consensus on the definition of Muslim "orthodoxy." Both economic and religious developments in this period increased competition and tensions among the Ottoman religious communities and led to the tightening of policies regarding non-Muslims. The Ottoman government undertook new measures to police public morality by closing coffee houses and taverns and implementing more strictly the existing sumptuary laws and other measures aiming to delineate the boundaries between Muslims and non-Muslims.[58] It is possible that these methods of social disciplining and new pressures on non-Muslims at least in part influenced the notable rise in the number of trials for apostasy and subsequent martyrdoms among former Orthodox Christians.[59] However, ascribing the new prominence of neomartyrs and narratives about them in the late sixteenth and seventeenth centuries solely to the new sensibilities toward heresy and blasphemy in the Muslim community would be an oversimplification.

The latest research with Ottoman and Orthodox Christian sources from the seventeenth century suggests that the fears voiced by certain segments of Ottoman society, claiming that the boundaries among religious communities were being increasingly blurred, were not entirely unfounded. Both Orthodox ecclesiastical sources and Ottoman court records show that during the seventeenth century the acculturation of Christians into Ottoman society peaked, and that Christians, especially women, were frequently using the Muslim court system to manage their legal affairs.[60] Ottoman census records and converts' petitions to the Imperial Council demonstrate that the rate of Rumeli Christians' conversion to Islam peaked at the same time. Anton Minkov recently argued that the reason for this was not forced conversions, as Balkan nationalist historians have often postulated, but significant changes in the distribution of power in the Ottoman imperial center (decentralization of power in the hands of newly emerging grandee households) and the resulting changes in patterns of recruitment for the state. According to Minkov, when the child levy was discontinued as the primary avenue for the rise of new Muslims through Ottoman ranks, it was replaced by multiple new recruitment channels leading into the households of numerous Ottoman grandees who offered opportunities of entering new patronage and military networks to young males willing to convert.[61] Minkov believes that this may account for the rise of conversion rates in the seventeenth century, although it cannot serve as a comprehensive explanation.

Since the mid-sixteenth century the Ottoman Empire had also experienced a surge in the diplomatic and economic activity of different European polities in various parts of the empire, particularly in Istanbul/Constantinople, the Aegean coast, and the Levant. As one of the key Mediterranean ports and trading route nodes, Constantinople was a hub for exchange of both goods and ideas. Although Italian merchants, especially the Venetians, had maintained their presence in the city since Byzantine times, in the second half of the sixteenth and early seventeenth centuries Constantinople (as well as İzmir and Aleppo) became a destination for thousands of French-, English-, Dutch-, and German-speaking merchants and diplomats. They came in the wake of new trade and diplomatic privileges, known as the capitulations, bestowed by the sultan on the representatives of their governments as a sign of goodwill.[62] Capitulations were ostensibly relevant mostly to trade and diplomacy, but they also led to greater concessions for European Christians while residing in the Ottoman Empire, as well as for the local commercial and cultural intermediaries who facilitated their business. Although these treaties from the late sixteenth and early seventeenth centuries cannot be blamed exclusively for the tense dynamics among the Ottoman religious communities, in the long run they did empower large groups of local Christians who became privileged trading partners and intermediaries for the European merchants at the expense of Jewish and Muslim commercial circles.[63] The competition for opportunities to participate in and benefit from the globalizing early modern economy, therefore, also led to confessional tensions in the Ottoman Empire.

With participation in the global early modern economy also came exposure to global religious trends and missionaries. Confessional divisions plaguing western Christendom found their way into the Ottoman Empire after the Council of Trent and the onset of the Catholic

Reformation. Protestant and Catholic missionaries commenced their activities among the Ottoman Orthodox Christians, competing with each other over access to the Orthodox patriarchs in hope of achieving a union of the churches, drawing on the support of various ambassadors to the Ottoman Empire representing embattled Catholic and Protestant European polities. The Society of Jesus, established in 1540, found its first ally in Patriarch Mitrophanes (1565–72), who was willing to take the Orthodox Church in the direction of union with Rome.[64] However, Mitrophanes was deposed by the ecumenical synod, who felt that the talks of union had gone too far. The Catholic cause was strengthened by the foundation of the Greek College in Rome in 1577, offering higher education to Greek boys. As there was no comparative institution able to provide a solid education in Constantinople, many Orthodox parents decided to send their children to Rome. Since the fall of Constantinople, a substantial Greek community had also existed in Venice, an important center for Greek publishing, where a Greek college opened at the end of the sixteenth century that prepared students for studying at the University of Padua.[65] Not all of these college graduates embraced Catholicism, but many did and began to work on bridging the gap between Catholic and Orthodox churches, undermining the anti-Latin cause dear to some segments of the Orthodox ecclesiastical circles and to Athonite monks.[66] Jesuits established their first missionary enclaves in the Levant in the 1590s and spread their influence considerably during the seventeenth century, mainly with the assistance of the traditional Ottoman ally, France.[67]

Protestants did not sit idle, either. Their first significant overtures to the Orthodox transpired during the first tenure of Patriarch Jeremias II (1572–79, 1580–84, 1586–95), who was approached by the Tübingen Lutheran theologians led by Martin Crusius via Stefan Gerlach, chaplain of the Habsburg emissary to the Ottomans. Jeremias II's contacts with Protestants did not remain a secret to the Orthodox clergy, among whom the union with Lutherans had some supporters but many more opponents, or to the Catholic circles.[68] Although Jeremias II was not interested in a union with Lutherans and was in contact with Rome as well, several decades later a Protestant union with Orthodoxy became a reality. In 1621, Cyril Lukaris, who was educated at the University of Padua, came to the patriarchal throne and in 1629 professed his allegiance to the Calvinist doctrine, attempting to bring it into harmony with Orthodox theology. Lukaris was a close friend of the Dutch ambassador, Cornelius Haga, and a particular fan of the Anglican Church. He was executed by the Ottoman authorities in 1638 as a result of the scheming of a pro-Catholic candidate for the Patriarchate.[69]

The events of the late sixteenth and early seventeenth centuries exposed the significant ideological splits within the Orthodox Christian community itself. These splits were not new and only enhanced the extant differences between the higher clergy, reluctant to formulate a coherent policy of resistance against the Ottoman authorities and Catholic missionaries, and the local parish clergy, who kept much closer relations with their congregations. These rivalries could attain serious proportions, especially when clerics vying for more lucrative positions in the church hierarchy showed no inhibitions about slandering each other or involving the Ottoman authorities as arbiters.[70] Differences between the often poorly educated monks at Mount Athos and the Patriarchate became even more apparent as the clergy who studied in Rome and Venice began to assume high ranks in the hierarchy of the Orthodox Church and experiment with dogma in the late sixteenth century.[71]

Patriarchs often came from Mount Athos or sought refuge there after their deposition, and the boundaries between the monks and patriarchal clergy were not always entirely clear-cut. Nevertheless, by the early seventeenth century different strategies of resistance to conversion of the two key leadership circles within the Orthodox community began to crystallize. The patriarchs and their clergy explored the "official" means of fortifying the Orthodox Christian community and defining the boundaries of belief. The patriarchs were repeatedly making pronouncements against Christians' using the Ottoman legal institutions for matters that were traditionally regulated by canon law (marriage, inheritance, divorce, etc.) and resorting to non-Christian traditions such as concubinage (*kebin*) agreements.[72] Alarmed by the rates of conversion, but also by the Orthodox clergy's ignorance of canon law and even tenets of their faith, the Patriarchate stepped up the education program that stressed the penitential, conscientious practice of Christianity both for the clergy and for the common people. In 1593, Patriarch Jeremias II summoned a council at which it was decided that the Orthodox metropolitans should take definitive steps toward founding schools. It was the first time after the Byzantine period that the church assumed an active role in the education of the Orthodox population.[73]

One could argue that in this new initiative the patriarch was also influenced by the post-Tridentine Catholic reforms that emphasized the education of priests as vital for the correct observance of faith. Because the Jesuits began to establish themselves in the Ottoman domains in the late sixteenth century, the patriarch and his clergy had an opportunity to observe their methods firsthand. The first Jesuit mission appeared in Constantinople in 1583, and its members remarked on the insufficient instruction in faith provided by the Orthodox clergy. They observed that religious teaching consisted mainly of stories about saints and that nothing like catechism existed.[74] A report written in Constantinople in 1612 by Father François de Canillac describes the warm welcome that the Jesuits received from Patriarch Neophitos and his clergy, many of whom had been educated in Rome and were sympathetic to the Catholic cause. Later reports relate Jesuit successes and excellent reception in Naxos, Paros, Nauplion, and Athens in the 1640s. In 1664, Father Robert Saulger writes that the success of the Jesuit mission in Constantinople has been greater than he could have ever imagined. He stresses that many "Greeks" have more confidence in the Jesuit priests than in their own and that women are especially likely to come to Jesuits in order to "escape the avarice of their own priests."[75] In general, all the reports lament the ignorance that both the common people and the Orthodox clergy display in matters of doctrine.[76] It is therefore likely that the Orthodox patriarchs' efforts to reeducate the clergy were inspired by the example set by the Jesuits.[77]

As a result of this renewed interest in education, in the early seventeenth century Athens established its own academy, building on the strong local traditions of humanist learning. This is where both Mehmed, whose story was discussed in the previous chapter, and Christophoros studied in the first two decades of the seventeenth century. Most of the teachers in Athens and in the Patriarchal Academy in Constantinople were graduates of the University of Padua, which was under Venetian influence and less aggressive in converting its Orthodox students to Catholicism than the Greek College in Rome.[78]

At the same time, however, the Athonite and provincial monks seized upon the phenomenon of new martyrdom and its narration as the centerpiece of a multifront resistance to the concomitant advancing acculturation of Christians into Ottoman society, often resulting in conversion to Islam, and Jesuit proselytization. The cult of saints was traditionally the privy of monks both in the Byzantine and post-Byzantine periods. From the monks' perspective, more than any learned tract on dogma, stories of saints and especially martyrs expressed the power of faith and taught believers how to live pious lives. This idea is reflected in the *Treasure*, the single most popular dogmatic text from the second half of the sixteenth century, written by Damaskinos Studitis from Selanik (today Thessaloniki in Greece), a monk at the monastery of Studion. Striving to improve knowledge on the fundamentals of faith among priests and common people and to emphasize the conscientious practice of Christianity, Studitis compiled a collection in the vernacular Greek language with thirty-six headings covering the basics of Christian dogma, explanations of religious holidays, and most important, early Christian martyrs' lives. The *Treasure* was first published in Venice in 1568, but regional variants and translations into Slavic languages had already appeared in the late sixteenth century. New versions and translations brought new additions and regionally specific features, especially in terms of inclusion of Turkish words. Stories of old martyrs told by using specifically Ottoman concepts, such as *ferman* instead of *decree*, *kadı* instead of *judge*, or *sipahi* instead of *captain* of the imperial guards, must have sounded very contemporary to the Christian audiences.[79] The monks became particularly active in disseminating these dogmatic texts, which seem to pay particular attention to the moral and chaste behavior of women.[80] Neomartyrologies' production and promotion reflected the same logic.

The value of martyrdom in Orthodox Christian polemics against Roman Catholicism had already become obvious in the late Byzantine period, before the Ottoman conquest of Constantinople in 1453. After the end of Latin rule in Constantinople (1204–61), the Byzantine emperors made several efforts to heal the schism that had existed between the Catholic and Orthodox churches since the eleventh century, first in order to prevent a new Latin attack on their capital but later to ensure papal help against the advancing Ottomans. Each of the attempts at union failed because of the resistance of the people and segments of the clergy, especially the Athonite monks, who, for the most part, continued to oppose union with Rome during the Ottoman period as well.[81] For instance, in a report from Smyrna in 1658 one of the Jesuit fathers states that the monks of Mount Athos are "great enemies of the Roman church" and that there is a great competition for the souls of merchants traveling from Rumeli, where the influence of the Athonite monks was stronger, to Smyrna, where many merchants embraced Catholicism.[82] In 1367, during discussions between the papal legate Paul and the Byzantine emperor John VI Kantakouzenos, the legate scorned the Christians living under Ottoman rule because they daily tolerated blasphemies against Jesus. The emperor replied that Orthodox Christians living under Ottoman rule were more honorable than those living under Christian rule because they persisted in their faith even while subjugated by the infidel.[83] Nothing illustrates this point more eloquently than the stories about neomartyrs. One of the first Athonite monks in the post-Byzantine period to bring together the issue of martyrdom in polemical texts against both Islam and other Christian denominations was Pachomios Russanos (1508–53), who was associated with the Athonite monastery of Iviron. He compiled several works on neomartyrs from the Ottoman period to provide his fellow Orthodox Christians with examples of persistence in faith and to prove that Orthodox Christianity was superior to the Lutheran, Catholic, or any other Christian denomination.[84] By becoming the impresarios of the martyrs in the course of the later sixteenth and seventeenth centuries, the polemicists (many of whom were Athonite monks) armed themselves with an ideology that resonated far and wide in the age of confessionalization.

By the 1550s confessional wars in Europe had reawakened the phenomenon of martyrdom as the ultimate proof of one's commitment to one's faith in the manner of ancient martyrs. Four major Protestant martyrologies appeared from 1552 to 1559, leaving an indelible mark on early Protestant sentiments in France, England, and the Low Countries.[85] A Catholic response ensued in the wake of the Tridentine reforms in the 1560s, with Rome being reinvented as the showcase of the history of martyrdom, and Jesuits and Franciscans diligently collecting reports of heroic deaths of Catholics throughout Europe.[86] However, evidence suggests that the stories of Orthodox Christian neomartyrs and their experiences with Ottoman authorities made a particularly great impression on Western audiences, especially as the phenomenon of "turning Turk" became a reality in the wake of increased commercial activity between European states (such as England, the Netherlands, and France) and the Ottoman Empire, starting in the second half of the sixteenth century.[87]

This trend is illustrated well by Christophoros Angelles's self-neomartyrology. His account of martyrdom is followed by an encomium to England, which he likens to the head of the Christian world, "for a man according to Aristotle, is a little world." He also calls England the "heaven of comfort to poore Grecians oppressed with the tyrannie of the Turkes." Christophoros adds that England excels in wisdom and virtue as "the Grecians of old did" and suggests that "Grecians" and the English share the same blood because Constantine the Great and his mother, Helen, hailed from Britain. Styling himself as a "Grecian," he says that he "was once dead through the cruell scourging of the Turkes for faith of Christ" and yet "never denied Christ, the true God." The English would, he argues, "also die for their religion, but never turn from their true worship of God," just like "Grecians."[88]

In this way Christophoros strikes several important chords that would have resounded well with his patrons in Oxford. He alludes to England's spiritual kinship with and resemblance to the "Grecians" of past and present, thus appealing to his patrons' humanist sensibilities, while at the same time implying that the English are steadfast both in their resistance to Islam (encountered by many an English captive and merchant in North Africa and the Ottoman Empire) and in their adherence to Anglicanism in the continuing clash with remnants of "popery," both at home and abroad. He also unambiguously suggests an affinity between the Orthodox and Anglican churches, an issue of great relevance in this very period as the Archbishop of Canterbury, George Abbot, and the Orthodox Patriarch, Cyril Lukaris, were exploring the possibility of the union of the Orthodox and Anglican churches.[89] In fact, in 1618, even before becoming a patriarch and exactly when Christophoros was writing, Lukaris sent his first student to study theology in England at the expense of King James I.[90] A few years later, in 1620, two English playwrights, Thomas Dekker and Philip Massinger, published *The Virgin Martir*, a play that revived the hagiographical drama (which had heretofore been considered an overly Catholic genre) on a Protestant English stage with the story of an early Christian saint who was martyred for constancy in her faith in Cesarea, Cappadocia (central Turkey). The play saw four reprints during the seventeenth century and definitively brought home the story of Christian martyrs dying in "Turkey" for refusing to convert.[91] Christophoros's narrative therefore engages the humanist fascination with ancient Greeks but also publicizes the hardships of his contemporary fellow Greeks, who are typically ignored in humanist treatises, through a skillful analogy between the "Papists" and the "Turks" widespread in English Protestant polemical literature of the time.[92]

Theatrical performances enacting the lives of early Christian martyrs were central to the Jesuit proselytizing strategy. Both the Jesuit reports from Constantinople and the Aegean islands and the surviving dramas from the late sixteenth and seventeenth centuries testify to the thriving martyrological theater in Greek vernacular. For example, after establishing a base on the island of Naxos in 1628, the Jesuits set up a performance of a tragedy whose central character was a "converted sinner."[93] Some of the plays were about the martyrdom of saints worshipped mostly, if not exclusively, by the Orthodox Christians, like Saint Demetrius.[94] Commenting on the performance of a play about the childhood of Saint John of Chrysostome, another popular Orthodox Christian saint, staged in Constantinople in 1624, François Aurillac states that "to gain more easily the hearts of the Greeks, the whole play was given in their vernacular language and on the same day when they celebrate the feast of St. Chrysostome."[95] The authors of these plays were Greeks who received education at the Greek College in Rome, at the Jesuit college on the island of Chios, or in Catholic schools in Constantinople.

Nevertheless, both Protestant and Jesuit missionaries to the Levant were also aware and covetous of the powerful message articulated by the Orthodox Christian neomartyrs. Stefan Gerlach, the Lutheran chaplain to the Habsburg embassy who stayed in Constantinople from 1573 to 1578, came with the task of investigating the possibility of union between the Lutheran and Orthodox confessions. Soon after his arrival in

1572, before his hopes of union were let down, he sent his mentors in Tübingen an elaborate account about the martyrdom of a Saint Damianos—probably the monk Damianos who was executed in 1568.[96] Nevertheless, as the prospect of union with the Orthodox faded, Gerlach chose to describe the executions of Orthodox Christians in Constantinople during his stay in plain language without invoking any notion of martyrdom, although at least one incident among several that he mentioned in his diary was classified as martyrdom in the Orthodox collections.[97]

Neomartyrs also show up in a Jesuit report from Smyrna in 1658, which first outlines the proof that the Greeks of Smyrna are in union with Rome and are therefore blessed with unique signs of God's mercy. The proof of their superior faith, the report says, is the martyrdom of Nicolas Caseti, a native of Smyrna, which took place the year before, in 1657. What follows is a long account featuring the key genre markers of a neomartyrology.[98] In conclusion, Father Vabois makes a claim for the neomartyr as a hero of the Catholic Church, rather than any other. He writes: "One of his [Caseti's] children is now in the school of the fathers of our Company: that suffices to show that he was in the path of the Roman church."[99] Not surprisingly, the story of Nicolas's martyrdom is also included in Nikodemos Hagiorites' *Neon martyrologion*, where there is no mention of his allegiance to the Catholic Church and where he is named "Nicholas Karamanos."[100]

In 1695, Jesuit father Charles Fleurieu reports on several other cases of martyrdom. One of them is also recorded by Ioannes Karyophilles (ca. 1600–1693), the Great Logothete of the patriarchal church in Constantinople, who was also the author of the first compilation of neomartyrologies in the Ottoman era.[101] According to the story, Nicholas the Grocer of Karpenesi died in Constantinople in 1672 after being tricked into reading the *shahada* from a piece of paper and subsequently killed for refusing to remain a Muslim. Fleurieu concluded that such examples of most heroic Christian virtues suggested that the land of the Orthodox Christians was not nearly as "sterile" as was believed in France.[102] Indeed, judging from the postmortem odyssey of Nicholas of Karpenesi's body described in detail by Karyophilles, this "fertility" was carefully cultivated: after the execution and suitable bribe to the *kadı*, Christians were allowed to dip their handkerchiefs in Nicholas's blood; his body was then taken by a group of Christians, who buried it in the monastery of Theotokos on the island of Chalke. His head, however, was taken by a priest from the patriarchal church who had ties to the Athonite monastery of Xeropotamou. After spending some time in Constantinople, and being contested by various parties, the head was finally given to the monks of Xeropotamou.[103]

## Conclusion

As these examples show, the bodies and stories of the martyrs were sites of a fierce confessional contestation that involved the Muslims, the Orthodox, the Catholics, and the Protestants. Through the combination of an increase in the actual incidence of "martyrdom" during the seventeenth century due to new interfaith tensions and its promotion by monks and provincial clerics, Orthodox neomartyrs became a powerful weapon in the war for Orthodox souls. Although Athonite monks were aware of the Jesuits' prominent usage of martyrologies in their proselytizing outreach, they also knew that nothing substantiated the truth of faith in the eyes of believers so much as an ever new supply of martyrs—an advantage that Jesuits did not have in the Ottoman context. By familiarizing the Orthodox population with stories of the new martyrs, wandering monks also supplied ideas of resistance and patterns of behavior that a person contemplating martyrdom should emulate. The narratives of new martyrs instructed the penitent converts how to "recycle" their sinful lives into glory for Christ, and they pointed to Mount Athos as the place to go if one could not live with the burden of conversion to Islam. The extensive ascetic training that the new martyrs were subjected to underlies the symbolic relationship between the human and social bodies, as well as the impresarios' need to control the latter through the former. By encouraging the annihilation of the martyr's body, the impresarios made it the site of a powerful anti-syncretic public statement. By "incorporating" the practices described in the narratives, the martyr's body became a site of "memory of bodily experiences transmitted through texts as pertaining to religious memory."[104]

CHAPTER SIX

# Everyday Communal Politics of Coexistence and Orthodox Christian Martyrdom

## *A Dialogue of Sources and Gender Regimes in the Age of Confessionalization*

Various compilations of neomartyrologies feature Philothei, a nun from Athens, as the earliest female Orthodox Christian martyr from the Ottoman era.[1] Philothei, whose secular name was Regula (also cited as Revoula), came from a wealthy Athenian family. Even though, according to her vita, Regula was opposed to the idea of marriage and desired to keep her virginity, her parents pressured her into a marriage with a rich man who turned out to be cruel to her. Regula patiently endured the torture for three years, when her husband suddenly died. She remained a widow for ten years, and after her parents' death she decided to build a nunnery, and later a hospital and a hostel for the needy. The vita asserts that at this time (in the 1570s) many Christian women captured in various parts of the Ottoman Empire were being brought to Athens as slaves and concubines. Four such women, who were also under pressure to convert to Islam, heard of Philothei and her charity work, escaped from their masters, and sought refuge in the nunnery. However, they were traced, and Philothei was brutally beaten and thrown into prison. She was going to be executed, but influential Greek community members interceded on her behalf and paid the Ottoman district governor sufficient money to release her. She returned to her charity work and built another nunnery outside Athens. However, her great piety supposedly irritated some Muslims. One day, a crowd entered Philothei's nunnery and beat her nearly to death. Even though she did not die immediately, Philothei remained bedridden for the rest of her life and died in 1589.[2]

Philothei is one of only six women who appear as new martyrs from the Ottoman period in various collections of neomartyrologies. In contrast, the most recent compilation recounts the stories of close to 170 men who are said to have been martyred in the period between 1437 and 1860.[3] What accounts for this stark disparity in numbers between male and female neomartyrs? Even though Philothei herself was not a convert, her story, as well as other female neomartyrs' stories, is inextricably related to the phenomenon of religious change. Did Christian authors imagine and narrate female conversion to Islam and martyrdom differently from that of males? How did other communities and institutions in Ottoman society relate to what Orthodox Christians claimed to be martyrdom? Did Muslim authors differentiate based on gender and age in their accounts of conversion to Islam? Are the details of Philothei's story plausible in light of contemporary Ottoman sources? If yes, how does a source like this challenge the established narratives about coexistence and tolerance in the Ottoman Empire?

Intriguingly, Suraiya Faroqhi recently found a document among the imperial rescripts dated to 1582 that referred to a nun (*rāhibe*) named Rusula who lived in Athens along with her sister nuns. According to the rescript, numerous Muslim dignitaries accused Rusula of "having attracted the recently islamized slaves, slave women and sometimes even wives of local Muslims, and enticed them back to Christianity." She also provided these women with monastic clothes and means to secretly travel to *Firengistān*. The text relates that a secret chamber where one of the fugitive slaves was hiding was revealed. The judge of Athens and the governor were ordered to investigate the facts and punish the responsible individuals. The nunnery was going to be immediately closed down.[4]

Faroqhi identifies the nun Rusula with Philothei, whose secular name was Regula. However, she wonders whether it is possible that the Ottoman document is talking about the sainted Athenian nun, since it would appear from the rescript that one is dealing with the prelude to the nun's arrest and execution. Indeed, the magnitude of Philothei's crime (converting Muslims to Christianity) in the eyes of Islamic law makes it difficult to imagine that she incurred anything short of the death penalty. However, the neomartyrology, first published in 1775, suggests that she was saved by Christian community leaders who paid a bribe for her release. Further contextualization of the story in contemporary sources demonstrates that this course of events was entirely possible since Philothei/Regula belonged to the Benizelos family, which was connected to the Byzantine Paleologian dynasty and some of the more prominent Italian families.[5] Another near-contemporary narrative—the self-neomartyrology of Christophoros Angelles that dates to 1617 but describes the events taking place in Athens in 1606—testifies that the Athenian Orthodox Christian aristocracy and merchants wielded considerable influence with Ottoman authorities, both in Istanbul and locally.[6] This included the ability to procure liberty, mostly through bribery, of accused and even convicted individuals such as Philothei and Christophoros. Sources also demonstrate that in the first half of the seventeenth century Athens had around ten female monasteries, which lends credence to the setting for Philothei's story.[7] Moreover, given the ties of the Athenian merchants and Orthodox Christian ecclesiastical circles to Venice, which became particularly strong in the sixteenth and seventeenth centuries, we can even surmise that this was the destination in *Firengistān* where Philothei sent her wards.[8]

Faroqhi's discovery is one of many interesting and unexpected convergences between the neomartyrologies and Ottoman sources recently brought to light by Ottomanists, suggesting that the stories about the martyrs and the circumstances of their demise in the hands of the Ottoman authorities should not be dismissed out of hand as anti-Ottoman, Orthodox Christian propaganda.[9] As Philothei's story shows, through a dialogue with the Ottoman and other sources neomartyrologies can offer insights into the locally negotiated nature of Ottoman justice and politics of coexistence. Furthermore, Philothei's neomartyrology opens up interesting new vistas when juxtaposed with sources on women's conversion from other early modern Mediterranean contexts, drawing attention to the gender dimensions of conversion narratives and institutional practices.

This chapter sets up a dialogue between Orthodox Christian neomartyrologies and Ottoman Muslim legal sources, especially *fetva*s, or opinions of the empire's leading jurists, and considers relevant sources from the wider Mediterranean region dating from the sixteenth to eighteenth centuries. Building on the previous chapter, which focused on neomartyrologies in the context of intra-Christian rivalries in the age of confessionalization, the discussion here explores neomartyrologies as sources for the study of Muslim-Christian relations and everyday communal politics of coexistence in the early modern Ottoman Empire. In contrast to recent scholarship, which conceptualizes tolerance in the Ottoman Empire primarily as an expression of imperial policy that both articulated and accommodated religious difference through the mechanisms of imperial and Islamic law, the ensuing discussion shifts the focus away from the state to examine what tolerance meant in various local contexts where Ottoman Muslims and Christians struggled to adapt to and negotiate this legal framework.[10]

Particular attention is paid to the gender dimensions of this issue as envisioned by neomartyrologies and other contemporary Ottoman sources, since women's conversion to Islam was a phenomenon that challenged the communal and family sense of honor and cohesion in different ways than men's, and highlighted different aspects of inequalities built into the modes of coexistence and tolerance in the Ottoman Empire. By focusing on narrative strategies of various Muslim and Christian authors (the neomartyrs' impresarios, Ottoman judges, court scribes, and other authors mediating the converts' hopes and desires), this chapter examines the ways Ottoman Muslims and Christians engaged religious discourse and competing legal and gender regimes to delineate the boundaries of their communities in the age of confessionalization.

## *Tolerance and Coexistence in the Ottoman Empire in Light of the Orthodox Christian Neomartyrologies*

Even without being juxtaposed with Ottoman sources, neomartyrologies raise interesting questions about the mechanisms of Muslim-Christian coexistence in the Ottoman context. A closer inspection of various texts from the sixteenth to eighteenth centuries shows that rather than testify to a perpetual persecution of the Christians, neomartyrologies depict a closely intertwined space in which Christians have Muslim friends, customers, and apprentices. The authors of the narratives and impresarios of the new martyr cult do not shy away from suggesting that it is exactly this blurring of boundaries that poses the greatest danger to a Christian soul and that stories about neomartyrs are meant to warn against the dangers of interaction with Muslims.

For instance, in 1555 an Orthodox Christian named Nikola was martyred in Sofia, the seat of the Ottoman government in Rumeli. Nikola journeyed from his home town, Ioannina, in Thessaly (today in Greece) to Sofia, where he settled down, got married, and attained renown as the best shoemaker in the region. Because of his talent he had many apprentices, both Muslim and Christian, whom he generously instructed in the tricks of his trade. The narrative asserts that Nikola had such a close relationship with his Muslim apprentices that he happily visited their houses and joined them in their merrymaking. On one such celebratory occasion in a local tavern, Nikola got drunk and woke up in the morning to realize that his friends had had him circumcised while he was unconscious, effectively making him a Muslim. Mortified by shame and grief, Nikola withdrew into the privacy of his home, scorned and ostracized by fellow Orthodox Christians. Nevertheless, Nikola secretly continued to practice

Orthodox Christianity and encouraged his wife to continue to attend church services. A year later, on a Friday, a zealous local Muslim came to visit him at home because he had noticed that no one from the Muslim community talked to Nikola or saw him much in public, especially in the mosque, since he had become a Muslim. The visitor stated that this neglect was forgivable since Nikola was a novice, and he admitted that the Muslim community shared the blame because no one had ever come to instruct him in the matters of Muslim faith. However, Nikola refused to own up to being Muslim. He was then brought to the *kadı*, and after a protracted legal procedure powered more by an incensed mob than the judge's decisions, he was executed as an apostate.[11]

As Nikola's and numerous other stories demonstrate, according to the authors of neomartyrologies it was the liberty to penetrate Muslim circles and have seemingly equal opportunities, as well as the tendency to forget that there were borders and hierarchies that should be observed, that led to the downfall of many a Christian. The reasons for the sudden resurgence of religiously defined borders after they were perceived as gone or blurred were many, but as the narratives suggest, they most often involved engagement in a discussion on Islam, Muhammad, or Jesus or, more mundanely, professional jealousy. These moments of withdrawal of tolerance and emergence of politics of anti-syncretism show, as Ussama Makdisi points out, that tolerance and coexistence in the Ottoman Empire were in perpetual tension, ebbing and flowing depending on local, communal, or imperial politics.[12] Withdrawal of toleration did not end the coexistence. On the contrary, as some scholars have argued regarding other premodern multiconfessional contexts where religious difference was accommodated but with discriminatory mechanisms designed to confirm the prerogatives of the dominant group, coexistence was predicated on periodic withdrawals of toleration and even open expressions of violence by the group in power.[13] In the Ottoman context, these moments served to restore balance to a system in which each community had its own place, with Muslims at the top and Jews and Christians at the bottom, whenever a Muslim group or individuals perceived that their prerogatives and communal boundaries had been violated. As previous chapters have argued, the threshold for the withdrawal of tolerance accorded to Jews and Christians as the beneficiaries of the "pact of protection" (*dhimma*) within the Ottoman imperial and Islamic legal system constantly changed depending on both domestic and international developments.[14] With the onset of various Muslim initiatives for social disciplining and community building in the second half of the sixteenth and especially in the seventeenth century, this threshold was generally lowered and the redrawing of communal boundaries became more determined. However, on the local level, such withdrawals of toleration did not necessarily have to follow the fluctuations in imperial ideology and had a dynamic of their own. The notion of tolerance in the Ottoman Empire is incomprehensible without taking into account that it was constantly negotiated from above, from below, and laterally.

How did this work in practice? Many martyrs are said to have been the victims of their Muslim colleagues' envy. This motif occurs in numerous narratives, and typically the hero is a Christian craftsman who makes a greater profit and is more skillful than his Muslim colleagues. Both Nikola and his comrade in martyrdom from Sofia, George the Goldsmith, who was executed in 1515, were targeted for this reason, at least according to their hagiographers.[15] Their success was supposedly perceived as an offense to Islam since it implied that being a Christian was a greater blessing. The strategy that neomartyrs' opponents resorted to was to gradually involve the hero in a discussion about Jesus and Muhammad, hoping that they would provoke him to blasphemy or conversion. Based on what neomartyrologies relate, such provocations were often successful. In fact, one finds other Christian sources that assert that Muslims incited non-Muslims' conversion to Islam by false testimonies. For example, in his 1538 work written in Italian, *On the Origin of the Ottoman Emperors*, Theodore Spandounes observes that Muslim "law expressly forbids a Jew or a Christian to talk about anything relating to the Mahometan religion. But they [Muslims] are always keen to bring over a Christian to their faith; and they use various methods, including false testimony to a *Kadi* [judge] which results in the Christian being punished and forcibly converted or martyred."[16]

Even though this might seem like an expression of Christian anti-Muslim sentiment typical for this genre, a closer reading reveals that the social and religious relationships depicted in neomartyrologies are more complex. With surprising candidness narratives relate that many accusations against Christians came from their fellow Christians rather than only from Muslims. So, one sees jealous brothers reporting on each other, or even more interesting, Orthodox Christian clergy denouncing each other to the Ottoman authorities in competition for church offices or for other petty reasons.[17] This particular phenomenon is of special importance since it exposes the differences that existed in the Orthodox Church structure between the high-placed salaried clerics often acting as Ottoman administrators and local priests and monks, and it also gives clues as to whose perspective neomartyrologies tend to represent. As we have already seen, neomartyrologies are far from one-dimensional pro-Christian narratives—they are an expression of struggle against both internal (Christian) and external (Muslim and Jewish) enemies.

This tendency to target all possible enemies is further clarified when one considers how the texts refer to Jews. There are at least two neomartyrologies that display marked anti-Jewish sentiment among Orthodox Christians, and both recount the death of a martyr from the city of Trabzon (Trebizond) on the Black Sea. According to the vita of John the Merchant from Trabzon, who supposedly died in 1492, the martyr was tied behind a horse and dragged through the streets of the city of Akkerman (today in Ukraine, fifteen kilometers from the Black Sea) and through its Jewish quarter. The text asserts that Jews were throwing various objects at him and that one Jew drew a sword and cut off John's head. It can be established that these particular details are pure fiction.[18] Nevertheless, the story of Symeon the Goldsmith from Trabzon, who was executed in 1653, was recorded by a seventeenth-century impresario of neomartyrs, Ioannes Karyophilles, who writes that a Jew was instrumental to the new martyr's indictment and death. Karyophilles writes that Symeon made some passionate anti-Jewish comments and asserted that Jews harbored malice against Christians.[19] This and other similar references give credence to the theory that anti-Jewish sentiment in Ottoman society often came from Christian converts to Islam.[20] Late sixteenth- and seventeenth-century sources from Ottoman Istanbul confirm that there was considerable tension between the Ottoman Christian and Jewish communities in the city as they both vied for the status of being the preferred non-Muslim group.[21] Furthermore, in the seventeenth century, Orthodox Christians managed to take over the economic roles traditionally played by Jewish commercial intermediaries in Ottoman society, thus increasing animosity between the two communities.[22] These aspects of neomartyrologies prompt further reconsideration of the notions of tolerance and coexistence in the Ottoman Empire as phenomena that should not be theorized only in terms of Muslim–non-Muslim relations but in terms of a broader "economy of tolerance" in which the fortunes of the participants tended to fluctuate according to the domestic and international political situations.

According to extant narratives, another segment of the population often involved in denunciations that could lead to conversion and apostasy were new Muslims who kept their relations with their old Christian friends. Thus, for example, Iordanes the Coppersmith from Trabzon (d. 1650) lost his life for invoking Muhammad's help while gambling with some of his friends who had become Muslims. After the game, one of them reported Iordanes's irreverent usage of Muhammad's name to the local *kadı*.[23] Angeles the Goldsmith from Constantinople (d. 1680) unwittingly lost his life after he participated in a Christian festival celebration that was joined by new Muslims who could not abandon old customs. In the heat of the celebration and dancing, Angeles exchanged hats with some of his Muslim friends. According to neomartyrologies, the donning of Muslim headgear effectively implied conversion to Islam. Angeles was therefore expected to start behaving like a Muslim, and when he failed to do so, he was accused of apostasy.[24] Contemporary Ottoman sources from the sixteenth and seventeenth centuries demonstrate that relatives and acquaintances were indeed pivotal to the process of conversion and that the agents of conversion were most often the people with whom a convert-to-be was familiar. For instance, numerous rescripts of important imperial affairs suggest that the sultan ordered a landholding or stipend to be given to new converts who were cousins of officials already working in imperial service.[25]

How realistic are these stories and the circumstances of conversion described in them? The most intriguing interlocutors for neomartyrologies are the Ottoman jurists who made decisions in response to questions posed by people from all segments of Ottoman society, *fetva*s. Both neomartyrologies and *fetva*s are concerned with drawing clear boundaries between different religious communities and could therefore be labeled as anti-syncretic texts. However, it is intriguing to what degree they correspond with each other. For example, referring to the previously mentioned cases, Ottoman chief jurisprudents since Ebussuud (1545–74) had issued *fetva*s against the participation of new Muslims in Christian celebrations such as Easter, suggesting this was a practice that persisted and demonstrating the effort to prevent any blurring of religious differences.[26] *Fetva*s confirm the allegations found in neomartyrologies that donning Muslim headgear was considered conversion. They also substantiate the claim that conversion to Islam while drunk,[27] conversion to Islam by pronouncing the *shahada* without understanding its meaning (being tricked into it),[28] and conversion to Islam under threat[29] were all considered valid in the eyes of the Ottoman jurisprudents, especially from the seventeenth and eighteenth centuries.

However, in some cases earlier and later *fetva*s are not in perfect accord. For instance, Ebussuud's legal response regarding the wearing of Muslim headgear states that if a Jew (*Zeyd-i yahūdī*) rolls the white turban cloth around his head out of fear, he should not be ordered to become a Muslim. But if a nonbeliever (*kāfir*) changes his clothes (into Muslim dress, presumably) and when asked, "Are you a Muslim or a *kāfir*?" he responds out of fear that he is a Muslim, he has to become, or rather remain, a Muslim. From these two cases it would seem that Ebussuud placed importance on the explicit pronunciation of the words "I am a Muslim," even if it were out of fear, whereas he considers the mere donning of headgear and clothes an insufficient statement of conversion.[30] Unlike Ebussuud, later chief jurisprudents of the seventeenth and eighteenth centuries treat dressing as a Muslim as tantamount to conversion, regardless of whether the "convert" expressed the adoption of Islam in words. For later chief jurisprudents, conversion by trickery and force appears perfectly acceptable, although it violates the Qur'anic principle that "there is no compulsion in religion."[31] Interestingly, the chief jurisprudent Ali Efendi (1674–86) responds affirmatively to the question of whether a person who accepts Islam "involuntarily" should be considered a Muslim, but he emphasizes that if such a person later reneges, he should not be killed but "driven into Islam by force."[32]

These differences in legal decisions by Ottoman jurists from different eras and their tendency to grow less concerned over time with the circumstances that led to one's conversion, even when it involved coercion, corroborate some of the allegations stated in neomartyrologies. They also testify to the evolution and progressive radicalization of initiatives toward social disciplining and confessionalization in the Ottoman Empire and their impact on legal practice. However, *fetva*s did not necessarily reflect the reality of legal practice in the Ottoman Empire because they did not have the force of the law. Even though *fetva*s issued by the chief jurisprudent of the empire had a general validity and served as guidance in similar cases, a judge decided whether the *fetva* presented by one of the litigants was relevant to the particular case and whether to apply it or not.[33]

A neomartyrology from the late sixteenth century that details the fate of Makarios the Tailor from Chios mentions that he went to obtain a *fetva* from a jurist in Constantinople about whether a person who was forced to deny his faith was allowed to return to his former faith without any hindrance. The answer he received was supposedly affirmative, but despite it, Makarios lost his life.[34] This sequence of events merits consideration, as it sheds light on the process of dispensation of justice in an Ottoman locale. In Makarios's case, the *fetva* he obtained initially convinced the judge that Makarios should be released because he was forced to become a Muslim, but the Muslims who had brought him to the court did not give up easily. The following day they gathered in the judge's presence and supposedly threatened him with the following words: "You are not a true Muslim. Instead of forcing people to come to Islam, you release unpunished those who once came and then returned to their former faith as you did with the monk the day before yesterday. We will report you to the Sultan to punish you as an enemy of the faith."[35] As in the story of Nikola's martyrdom, this pressure from the crowd supposedly changed the judge's mind, so he invited Makarios back to the court, and after the latter's persistent refusal to return to Islam he was sentenced as an apostate and executed.

The lenient, law-abiding judge and the enraged, conversion-or-death-disposed Muslim crowd are the staple motifs of many neomartyrologies. In general, every narrative of a martyr's death is a drama in which actors have traditionally defined roles.[36] In this sense, neomartyrologies are no different from the old martyrologies; however, whereas the older generation of hagiographers disliked the benevolent-judge type,[37] its incidence in the texts from the Ottoman period is much greater. The polarity between the lenient judge and raging crowd calls to mind the trial of Jesus Christ by Pontius Pilate. However, to what extent could this pattern be reflective of the situation on the ground around the Ottoman Empire, and what would be the implications of the tensions between a *kadı* and the local Muslims?

By emphasizing many a *kadı*'s reluctance to implement the extreme measures prescribed by the *sharia* and sentence the alleged blasphemer to death, the hagiographers demonstrate awareness of the *kadı*'s function—he is the chief negotiator of the imperial and local political exigencies and the main broker of the communal modus vivendi.[38] Even though scenes in which the judge is tempting the martyr-to-be to renounce Christianity with promises of great material rewards and social advancement are common in early Christian texts, some of the *kadı*s in neomartyrologies are ready to put in danger even their own careers in order to prevent an unjust or deliberately provoked execution. Many *kadı*s are portrayed as well-integrated members of the community and personal acquaintances of the accused or of the Christians involved. Viewed from this angle, it is understandable that they would be reluctant to disturb the communal balance and radicalize interfaith relations.[39] The texts often also make it clear that the *kadı* is aware of the trickery involved in the case and is ready to rule according to the precept that "there is no compulsion in religion." This is the case with the judge in Nikola's martyrology. However, the judge is also portrayed as unable to do so because his legal authority is manipulated by the group of Muslims involved and their strategic deployment of testimonies.[40] It was often difficult for a *kadı* to investigate the truthfulness of testimonies presented, and it is likely that his suspicion would have enraged the Muslim community.

As both *fetva*s and neomartyrologies suggest, it was not uncommon for Muslims of a certain place to denounce a *kadı* or an imam if they found his actions unsatisfactory or un-Muslimlike.[41] At the same time, the Muslim crowd in neomartyrologies as a rule seems unaware of the nuances in Islamic law regarding the issue of conversion, and, in accordance, with the psychology of the masses, the crowd becomes more and more radical as the events unfold. Even though the *kadı* had absolute authority in handling the legal procedure and wide interpretative powers in the sphere of law, the presence of the learned men of the community at the court acted as a check on his power. Although this was significant in the case of corrupt *kadıs*, the learned men could also determine the tenor of public reaction to a *kadı*'s ruling in cases of apostasy, as any lenience could be interpreted as lax "Muslimness." Ottoman sources confirm the possibility of large groups of locals being present at the court on any given day.[42] It was in fact in this "space" among the legal tradition embodied by the *sharia*, its interpretation by the *kadı* and his mindfulness of the local conditions, and the involved Muslim party's pressure that the dispensation of justice transpired. For this reason, it would be wrong to talk about the relationship between the state and its non-Muslim subjects when it comes to the issues of conversion and apostasy without taking into consideration this negotiation process. Although the political language and the discursive framework of Islam and of the *dhimma* pact were certainly relevant, they were never static, and their particular expression could vary from situation to situation.[43]

## *Asserting the Communal Boundaries through Narratives about Women's and Children's Conversion to Islam*

The discussion so far has focused on male neomartyrs because the majority of the surviving narratives detail the destinies of men—typically young urban males moving from smaller cities or rural areas to larger cities in search of better fortune. Other contemporary Ottoman sources from the sixteenth to the eighteenth centuries also suggest that this was the segment of the population most susceptible to conversion to Islam.[44] The neomartyrs' stories imply that urban settings introduced young men to opportunities for professional advancement that were closely tied to one's social contacts in a religiously heterogeneous environment (often in contrast to the more religiously homogenous contexts from which these men came). Both neomartyrologies and other sources suggest that most often conversion to Islam was motivated by a desire to be placed in a more advantageous social network, either because one had no connections and was in search of a support group or because one already had friends and relatives within a Muslim social network. In the case of most adult males whose stories are discussed in neomartyrologies, social and family networks play a key role in the process of conversion. Although neomartyrologies invoke the trope of forced conversion and portray some men as victims of circumstances that emanated from their involvement in economic and political life—professional jealousy being the most prominent motive for scapegoating—men are not typically represented in the neomartyrologies as passive either in the process of religious conversion or in undergoing martyrdom. In depicting men's conversion as a result of a conscious pursuit of religious change and martyrdom, neomartyrologies echo the male self-narratives of conversion. However, what about the representations of women's and children's conversion?

Neomartyrologies discussing children's conversion—a phenomenon that is otherwise rarely visible in Ottoman sources—suggest that family and social networks were particularly important in the cases involving minors. Neomartyrologies often emphasized the dangers of sharing space, work, and entertainment with members of a different faith. Narratives about children's conversion take this subject a step further by focusing on the households in which some members accepted Islam and others did not. Several texts relate that the neomartyr-to-be was pressed to convert to Islam as a child by his or her family members who had become Muslim. For example, Kyrillos the Tanner from Selanik (Thessaloniki in modern Greece) is said to have became an orphan at the age of ten and was forced to live with his mother's brothers, who were of different faiths, one Muslim and the other Christian. Young Kyrillos was put to work as a tanner by his Muslim uncle and later worked for another craftsman. Unhappy with this life, Kyrillos escaped to the Holy Mountain where he became a monk. When he later traveled to Selanik with several fellow monks, he was spotted by his uncle, who shouted out to the Muslims around him that Kyrillos once used to be a Muslim. Grabbed and taken to the local *kadı*, Kyrillos refused to "return" to Islam and consequently died as an apostate in 1566.[45]

To what extent do Ottoman sources substantiate this emphasis on family in the cases involving conversion of minors? In the eyes of Islamic law the validity of a child's conversion depended upon the evaluation of his or her mental capacity at the time of conversion. Since the age of reaching the mental ability to discern the implication of conversion and understand the tenets of the Muslim faith was not fixed by Islamic law (unlike that of sexual maturity), cases had to be reviewed on an individual basis.[46] As Eyal Ginio's research on the Ottoman court records (*siciller*) from Selanik shows, the most problematic group included children age seven to ten.[47] The judge would have to present the child with the basic articles of faith (*telkīn-i īmān*) and assess the child's comprehension of them (*ta'akkul-i dīn*). On this basis the judge would decide whether the child should become a Muslim or not. In some cases, such as those of Onofrii, a Bulgarian boy who converted to Islam as an eight-year-old to spite his parents, or a Jewish boy of the same age who converted to Islam in seventeenth-century Jerusalem, the child was returned to his parents despite the great protest of the Muslim community.[48]

Ginio indicates that the practice of poor parents handing over their children to be apprentices in craftsmen's workshops or to work as house servants was widespread in eighteenth-century Selanik. He maintains that when the master was a Muslim and the child was not, it was entirely possible that "such a dependent and hierarchical relationship . . . might compel or encourage the child to convert to Islam."[49] The case of Kyrillos faithfully corresponds with the cases regarding children's conversion in the court records from the same city two centuries later.[50] Even though the court records do not hint at instances of coercion, they reflect the fact that young adolescents were the most numerous group of minor converts to Islam and most prone to change their religion in search of career opportunity and integration. This vulnerability of young non-Muslim men is also underscored in the vitae of Christian neomartyrs, who usually converted at a young age for a variety of reasons. In many cases the texts do not deny that martyrs-to-be initiated conversion themselves, without physical coercion—however, they discuss cases in which those young converts later changed their minds.[51]

The challenges of living as a minor in a religiously mixed household are also illustrated in a narrative about a female neomartyr, Akylina from Zagliveri near Selanik, who died in 1764. While she was still young, Akylina's father killed a Muslim in a brawl and had to convert to save himself from the death penalty. Her mother, however, remained a Christian and encouraged Akylina to persist in being Christian. When Akylina grew up, her father's Muslim friends exerted pressure that she confirm her Islam; despite her father's insistence the young woman refused to accept Islam and was encouraged by her mother in this decision. Soon after, a group of Muslims came for her and took her to the *kadı*, where she refused to convert and underwent a beating from which she eventually died.[52]

Akylina's story refers to a situation that must have been fairly common: a convert's undiscerning minor children (below the age of seven) were considered converts through their affiliation to their father. In addition, their conversion was considered valid on the grounds that it was deemed beneficial to the child.[53] Again, the contemporary *fetva*s suggest that the plot of the neomartyrology was entirely plausible. Abdürrahim Efendi, a *şeyhü'l-islām* from the early eighteenth century, stipulated that after a Christian accepts Islam, his minor children are considered Muslim.[54] Another *fetva* confirms that a minor daughter was expected to confirm her Muslim religion when she came of age. If she refused, she was to be imprisoned and beaten as a female apostate.[55] According to Islamic law, both male and female children who came into Islam as undiscerning minors as a consequence of their parents' conversion were expected to confirm their adherence to Islam when they came of age and were to be imprisoned and beaten but not killed in the case of refusal. This was in contrast to the stipulation for the willful adult apostates, who were to be killed if male and imprisoned and beaten if female.[56] Although these were the juristic views on the issue, their implementation, as we have seen, could vary depending on local circumstances.

Akylina's story brings us to the question of female neomartyrs. Interestingly, only Philothei's story predates the eighteenth century and displays features that are more similar to the earlier Byzantine hagiographies of sainted nuns than to later female neomartyrologies.[57] Another four vitae are introduced for the first time in the late eighteenth-century *Neon martyrologion* of Nikodemos Hagiorites, and one dates to the early nineteenth century.[58] Although the scarcity of female neomartyrologies in general, and for the sixteenth and seventeenth centuries in particular, ostensibly makes them a poor source on the question of women's conversion to Islam in the Ottoman Empire, precisely this lack, when juxtaposed with other contemporary Ottoman Muslim and Christian sources, speaks volumes. There is also other valuable information in these female neomartyrologies that allows one to critically assess the discussions on gender and conversion in the Ottoman Empire that have heretofore been based almost exclusively on Ottoman sources, especially court records and converts' petitions to the Ottoman sultan.[59]

Except for Akylina, all other female neomartyrs supposedly lost their lives as a consequence of uninvited sexual advances by various Muslims, usually of high rank. Argyre of Bursa (d. 1721), for example, was a beautiful, recently married young woman with whom a Muslim neighbor had fallen in love. Having been refused many times, the neighbor finally went to the local judge and testified falsely that Argyre had promised to convert to Islam. Even though she denied the charges, Argyre was imprisoned, while her husband, in hope of securing a fair trial for her, arranged that she be tried in Constantinople. However, the outcome was not positive, and Argyre was questioned and imprisoned because she insisted on remaining a Christian. In the prison in Hasköy she was regularly beaten, but she also excelled in her perseverance and gave comfort to other imprisoned women. After many years of imprisonment she died at the age of thirty-three.[60] A similar faith was shared by Kyranna of Avysokka near Selanik (d. 1751), who supposedly became the object of desire of a janissary, the military commander (*subaşı*) of her village; Chryse from Moglen (today in Bulgaria) (d. 1795), who was abducted by a Muslim while gathering wood; and Maria (d. 1826), who was allegedly a victim of an "Albanian Muslim."[61]

An obvious common characteristic of all these narratives is that they represent the female neomartyrs as sexual objects and passive victims of circumstance. Few as they are, none of the future female witnesses for Christ convert to Islam voluntarily, unlike their male counterparts. They are all virtuous women steadfast in their religion. When considered on their own, Orthodox Christian neomartyrologies about female witnesses for Christ therefore pose a dilemma: were the cases of women's conversion to Islam, whereby women actively pursued a change of religious allegiance, indeed so rare as these sources would have us believe, or is this lack of variety in the narratives of female new martyrs when compared to the stories about their male counterparts an indication of something else? Is women's resistance to conversion, insisted upon in these texts, reflected in other sources? Finally, how realistic is the story line, especially regarding the legal procedure described in the narratives?

Ottoman sources again prove to be fascinating interlocutors for female neomartyrologies. Although details about Argyre's, Kyranna's, and Chryse's imprisonment and torture may have been exaggerated for the purposes of greater emotional impact, the situations in which they found themselves and the punishments they received cannot be entirely dismissed as fictional, as they are in line with the recommendations of Islamic law regarding female apostates. A *fetva* of Abdürrahim Efendi, chief jurisprudent of the Ottoman Empire at the beginning of the eighteenth century, around the time when Argyre and Kyranna supposedly died, specifically says that if a Christian woman accepts Islam and later becomes an apostate, which was the accusation hurled against all of these women, she should be imprisoned and forced into Islam.[62] At the same time, however, Ottoman sources suggest that by emphasizing only women's resistance to conversion and omitting any notion of their initiative in embracing Islam, neomartyrologies grossly overstated their case. Numerous Ottoman court records demonstrate that female converts frequently availed themselves of the services of Ottoman courts and enlisted them as help in resolving the circumstances arising from women's private lives. According to the *sharia*, a female convert to Islam was entitled to a divorce and custody of her children in the event that her husband refused to convert with her. By registering conversion in court, a female slave could change her circumstances by demanding that her owner be a Muslim (rather than a Christian or a Jew).[63] Furthermore, seventeenth- and eighteenth-century converts' petitions to the Imperial Council asking for financial support and money for new clothes traditionally allotted to new converts abound in the cases of female supplicants.[64]

By representing Muslims as sexual predators eager to ravage not only Christian women's bodies but also their souls by forcing them into Islam, neomartyrologies reveal the perennial fear of miscegenation on the part of the Orthodox Christian ecclesiastical establishment and point to women's conversion to Islam as a major point of convergence of community, family, and individual honor. A seventeenth-century English diplomat with long residence in the Ottoman Empire, Sir Paul Rycaut, captures these fears in his writings:

> It hath been usual for the Turks, especially in the parts of Greece called now Romania, and in Turkish Rumeli, to take Greek Women to Wife, marrying them according to the Mahometan Law; which Custome was become so frequent, that the Christian Women, little regarding that Caution given them by the Apostle, of being unequally yoked, freely enter into *Kabin* with the Turks, and without scruple designed the fruit of their Bodies to the service of the Antichrist, and by the infidelity of their Children, seemed half-content to become themselves Apostates. To prevent and remedy which inconvenience, the Patriarchs and Metropolites often consulted together, but contribute little to their redress, whilst the Turks, who were masters both of their lives and fortunes, made the bodies of the men subservient to their Labor, and of the Women to their Lusts.[65]

This narrative underscores the importance of non-Muslim women in the Ottoman political (and sexual) economy.[66] Muslim law stipulates that it is allowable for Muslim men to marry or take as concubines non-Muslim women, or more precisely, women of the Book, but not vice versa.[67] Although women who were married to Muslims did not necessarily have to convert, such an expectation was implicit. It appears that this was particularly true in cases when the husband was actually a new convert, like Nikola of Ioannina.[68] However, during the Ottoman period, the institution of concubinage (known as *kebin*), which was pervasive among Ottoman Muslims, slowly infiltrated Orthodox Christian society. As Vryonis explains, "It was a contractual arrangement for a fixed period and for which the male paid a cash sum to the father of the woman."[69] This and similar arrangements contracted in the Muslim courts terrified the church, which was struggling to remain the main legal authority for its own flock.

Numerous seventeenth-century cases are known of Orthodox Christians registering marriage and divorce with Muslim judges rather than with Orthodox church authorities so that later they could use the benefits of Islamic law regarding divorce and inheritance.[70] Christian women were particularly ready to use the Ottoman legal system to their own advantage because Islamic law provided more favorable stipulations for women on issues ranging from inheritance and marriage to property transactions and divorce.[71] The discrepancy between the laws provided non-Muslim women with opportunities to temporarily overturn the equations of power within their communities and escape the control of domineering fathers and husbands through converting or just opt-ing for cohabitation with a Muslim. This practice apparently gained so much popularity that by the 1670s the Orthodox Christian patriarch had to ask for an imperial order ruling that only the patriarch had judicial power to grant divorce between Christians.[72]

A rather graphic illustration of the church's position regarding female Christians' interaction with Muslims is found in a nineteenth-century manual for icon painters of Dicho Zograph, where among the different sinners who had to be depicted in hell were "many men and women who have adopted Mohammedanism" and who were to be represented as tortured by devils. Special attention was to be devoted to women who suckled Muslim babies, as that was considered a particularly grave transgression. For example, a mural in the sixteenth-century church in the village of Kalotina (Bulgaria) features wet nurses of "Turkish" children in the scenes of hell; on the mural in the village church of Vojnica (Bulgaria) a woman is portrayed standing helpless with her breasts naked and two snakes viciously biting them. The inscription under the scene reads: "Because she suckled Turkish children."[73] These apocalyptic images correspond well with Rycaut's assertion that Christian women put their bodies in service of the Antichrist—apparently the church authorities also maintained that women who have sinned in this way could find their atonement only on the Day of Judgment.

This suggests that neomartyrologies about women have been heavily sifted through the patriarchal "filters," resulting in conservative texts of a prescriptive and anti-syncretic nature. This strictness of form and content was probably meant to scare into submission an Orthodox Christian female audience that by the seventeenth century apparently displayed considerable willingness to avail themselves of various advantageous stipulations of Islamic law. The attempt to educate Orthodox believers in a penitent and conscientious practice of faith had already begun in the late sixteenth century with works such as the *Treasure* by Damaskinos Studitis, which was copied and amended in subsequent centuries and whose stories about saints and martyrs often critiqued women's tendency to gossip, superstition, and other "sinful" behavior.[74] The Orthodox Christian authorities identified miscegenation and interfaith marriage as one of the most menacing problems eroding the cohesion, morale, and dignity of the community. Thus, it is not surprising that "abduction" (real or imagined) of Christian women by Muslim men represents one of the omnipresent tropes in Christian narration of the community's suffering under Ottoman rule.

However, one has to be careful not to summarily dismiss the image of an unwilling female convert depicted in neomartyrologies and embrace the narrative of Ottoman courts, featuring pro-active female converts seeking changes to their legal status, as a reflection of social realities. If the dialogue of sources is expanded to include contemporary portrayals of women's conversion to Islam in other Mediterranean contexts, it becomes apparent that any careful study of this subject must consider how various institutional representatives imagined women's conversion and what "feminine strategies" women may have employed in institutional settings where their conversion was registered and discussed.

As Philothei's and other neomartyrologies show, some male and female apostates from Islam sought refuge in *Firengistān*—most often in Venice. Venetian archives document the experiences of those men and women who arrived at their destination. Many of their stories are found in the inquisitorial records, since they were treated as renegades who had to be brought back to the Christian fold. They had to spend some time in a sort of "halfway house," the *Casa dei Catecumeni*, where they were taught the basics of the Catholic faith. The records of the *Casa dei Catecumeni*, established by Jesuits in 1557, and other Venetian inquisitorial archives reveal that most female converts to Islam from the territories on the fringes of the Venetian Dominion of Levant, more precisely from Dalmatia, Bosnia, and Cyprus, claimed to have converted in the family context.[75] For example, Maddalena, a fifty-year-old from Sebenico (Šibenik) on the Croatian coast, of Christian parents, lived with the Muslim relatives of her father after becoming an orphan at the age of five or ten. She was given a Muslim name and later married a "Turk" and lived according to the "Turkish rite." However, according to her sister's information, she had been baptized as a child and wanted to become a Christian again in Venice in 1647.[76] Another interesting case is of a Cypriote, Fiorenza Podocattaro, who was captured by a "Turkish general" in 1570 and brought to Bulgaria, "where she pretended to be a Muslim in order to avoid the 'martyrdoms to which Christians were exposed, [such as] to spit on the Cross.'" She lived there for twenty-two years and had three children, all of whom were baptized and taught not to cross themselves for fear of being recognized as Christians.[77] Another study points out that most women appearing as renegades in the inquisitorial records from archives around the Mediterranean described their conversions in the context of marriage, especially if they were enslaved. Often, the converted slave would be freed on the day of marriage. In the worst case, she would acquire her freedom if she gave birth to a child as the status of "mother of the child" (*ümm-i veled*) stipulated, and she would be able to claim a share of her master's property after his death.[78] A pattern emerges from the inquisitorial sources suggesting that family and social networks, or lack thereof, were crucial in the process of women's conversion to Islam.

Furthermore, rather than take any kind of initiative, women are represented as passive objects of circumstance.

Natalie Rothman has suggested that the Venetian inquisitorial sources reflect both the ways local inquisitors imagined conversion to Islam and the ways Ottoman converts to Islam who found themselves in Venice understood conversion. The two views were mostly complementary: the inquisitors readily expected conversion to Islam to be effected at sword's point in the case of men or through some form of male coercion in the women's case, whereas the former Ottoman subjects described their conversion to Islam as a result of some contingency, such as change of family or geographical setting. In both cases, conversion—both to Islam and to Catholicism—was narrated by converts coming from the Ottoman Empire and recorded by the inquisitors as arising from unforeseen circumstances rather than premeditation and conscious pursuit of religious change.[79] This lack of interest in the motivation for conversion, so central to the narratives of Protestant and Jewish converts to Catholicism processed by the same inquisitors in Venice, was also in line with the attitude of Islamic law toward conversion, which considered the pronunciation of the *shahada* as the only relevant indicator of one's conversion, without problematizing motivation.[80]

In inquisitorial records one therefore finds a sort of "collusion" between the inquisitors and Ottoman converts, especially women, whose future in Venice depended on the way they told their life stories. One of the exculpating mechanisms, which must often have coincided with reality, was to claim that she converted to Islam as an undiscerning child, or as a wife wanting to please her Muslim husband. Interestingly, at the same time, for a male renegade marriage to a Muslim woman while in captivity or simply during sojourn in Muslim lands was the most incriminating evidence in the eyes of the Inquisition, as it was perceived as the marker of assimilation and intention to remain Muslim, par excellence.[81] In contracting marriage with a Muslim, men were therefore always seen as initiators while women were imagined as lacking the same potential, although Venetian sources of other genres and provenances clearly disprove that contention.[82] Presenting themselves as weak and bound by patriarchal and familial constraints thus strengthened women's argument for exemption from punishment. By accepting this story line and rehabilitating female converts to Islam, Venetian inquisitors acknowledged these women's "helplessness" and sought to protect them by placing them into alternative, Venetian-sponsored kinship contexts, thus restoring the Christian patriarchal order.

The Ottoman sources documenting women's conversion to Islam present a similar case of a patriarchal state seeking to protect women who in turn adapt the gender asymmetry inherent in Islamic law to their own needs. Leslie Peirce has recently suggested that entries on women in the Ottoman court records should not necessarily be considered reflective of actual events in the court but as normative or "morality" tales.[83] Drawing on Peirce's work, Marc Baer has argued that by recording women's conversions and their outcomes, such as divorce or attaining custody of the couple's children, "the shariah court had an opportunity to offer lessons to Muslims and non-Muslims alike about how the different groups that made up society were supposed to interact."[84] The courts were concerned not only with protecting the socially vulnerable (women and children) and promoting themselves as the ultimate authority on social issues but also with preserving community boundaries and upholding the system of religious and gender distinctions. By portraying women as fully cognizant of their legal rights, Ottoman officials did not seek to undermine the patriarchal framework but to point out the desired and expected outcome of a woman's conversion, especially divorce from a non-Muslim husband in order to prevent unlawful sexual economy. At the same time, by asking for the court's intervention, women both satisfied their own legal needs and provided the court with an opportunity to assert itself as an agent of Ottomanization and as a reference point for all categories of Ottoman subjects.

However, the scope of "feminine strategies" in both Venetian and Ottoman sources should not be reduced to women's desire to "trick" the patriarchal system. As Saba Mahmood points out, "The key problem is the assumption implicit in many studies that all women, regardless of which discursive formation they are product of, hold the desire for freedom from relations of domination and male subordination as their coveted goal."[85] By celebrating women's agency and success in overturning the patriarchal tables, regardless of how temporarily, extant studies on women's conversion have failed to appreciate to what extent through conversion to Islam women actually sought protection and/or asked to be bound by the very forces and structures of power that subordinated them.[86] This is particularly obvious in the case of widows, orphans, and divorcées.

According to a recent study based on petitions for the *kisve bahası* (cash equivalent of the price of new clothes) submitted to the Imperial Council during the seventeenth and early eighteenth centuries, widowed women often converted to Islam and petitioned the sultan to provide them with some livelihood.[87] The study suggests that men were at least four times more likely to convert than women, and that 85 percent of all the petitioners were single. Among ninety-four adult female petitioners, seventy-seven were single or single with children, overwhelmingly widows and divorcées.[88] It is interesting to note that these widowed women were asking the sultan for a means of subsistence (*nafaka*), which usually would be provided by their husbands as a part of a marriage agreement. Thus, in a way, by converting to Islam, a widowed woman was "marrying" again, this time to the state, or rather, the sultan. Since most of the female petitioners came to Istanbul to submit their request and expressed the desire to stay in Istanbul, it is clear that they perceived themselves as uprooted, without close family and kin.[89] If they did not receive protection from the authorities or were not given a chance to start a new life in a new environment, these women could face dire situations. A sixteenth-century case recorded in an imperial rescript illustrates the vulnerability of a female convert who was left without protection: the daughter of Mihal, a resident of Çatalca, converted to Islam with her two daughters, but apparently her family and neighbors then either killed or kidnapped her. An investigation was ordered, suggesting that the sultan took this case very seriously.[90]

Together, Orthodox Christian, Ottoman, and Venetian sources point to the phenomenon of women's conversion to Islam as a particularly contentious aspect of coexistence and interfaith contact in the Ottoman Empire, one that demanded the communal patriarchs' undivided attention as they strove to maintain the cohesion, morale, and honor of their communities in an age of fierce battles for the souls and bodies of converts. Although these sources reveal different and at times mutually contradictory perspectives on women's conversion, they also expose important commonalities in early modern gender regimes. Rather than a striking ideological gap in terms of gender discourses, which is typically emphasized in comparisons of Christian and Muslim societies, sources suggest significant convergences and even commensurability in patriarchal and religious sensibilities informing the notion of female conversion around the early modern Mediterranean.[91] Furthermore, the importance of kinship ties and contingency in women's conversion to Islam featured in Venetian as well as Ottoman Christian and Muslim sources suggests significant mutual influences in terms of institutional practices and narratives.[92]

## *Conclusion*

The dialogue of various Muslim and Christian sources has presented further perspectives on the issues of conversion to Islam, syncretism, and toleration in the Ottoman Empire during the age of confessionalization. Both neomartyrologies and other sources reflect the desire of communal patriarchs in the Ottoman domains, as well as in the contact zones between the Ottoman and other polities, to define and police confessional boundaries through production of narratives about conversion with an explicitly gendered vision of interfaith relations. At the same time, when juxtaposed, the same sources reveal different gender-specific strategies of Muslim and Christian men and women interacting with various institutional representatives and each other in incidents of conversion.

By combining perspectives from "above" and "below" emerging from these sources, it has been argued that tolerance and coexistence in the Ottoman Empire were phenomena that attained meaning in local contexts depending on a complex interplay of (inter)communal, imperial, and international conditions informing particular cases of conversion and apostasy, as well as on the age, gender, and religion of those involved. General imperial and shariatic principles, such as that of *dhimma*, were negotiated, accepted, modified, or contradicted in local contexts through interactions among members of various religious communities who had to deal with the reality of religious difference and adapt to it in order to reach a modicum of coexistence.

# Conversion and Confessionalization in the Ottoman Empire

## *Considerations for Future Research*

This book is about conversion to Islam in the Ottoman Empire, but it is also about how "Islam" and the "Ottoman Empire" were defined and redefined in the period between the fourteenth and seventeenth centuries in response to the process of conversion. The analysis of various narratives from the Ottoman Lands of Rum pertaining to the issue of conversion to Islam has addressed the evolution of the debate on who was a Muslim and how the boundaries of the Muslim community were to be defined and enforced in the Ottoman domains. This process paralleled and was in direct dialogue with analogous debates within the Ottoman Orthodox Christian community that sought to articulate its own identity in relation to both Islam and various other Christian denominations. The perceptions of conversion and the ways of narrating the act of entrance into Islam changed over time; there was no single stable Ottoman concept or narrative of conversion throughout the period under consideration. These debates and the ongoing reconceptualization of conversion in the Ottoman context cannot be fully understood or explained without considering the broader religio-political framework in which they transpired, that of the early modern Mediterranean "age of confessionalization."

The dialogue between Ottoman and various Christian concepts of conversion that intensified during the era of interimperial and confessional rivalry in this age of confessionalization continued well after the seventeenth century, albeit under very different circumstances and informed by new configurations of power. Beginning in 1839, the Ottoman Tanzimat reforms ushered in a set of regulations that aimed to ensure that the act of conversion to Islam was "voluntary." According to these regulations, converts were supposed to profess allegiance to Islam in the presence of their next of kin and representatives of the highest authority of their previous confession, who would be given the opportunity to dissuade the convert-to-be.[1] This procedure that emphasized the voluntary, conscious nature of conversion was a far cry from the ad hoc, informal acts of entrance into Islam narrated in fifteenth-century sources or from seventeenth-century *fetva*s, which seemingly sanctioned conversion under duress in special cases. Rather, it echoed the emphasis on conscious acceptance of faith and its interiorization characteristic of post-Tridentine Catholic Christianity. Ottoman self-narratives of conversion from the sixteenth and seventeenth centuries displayed similarities to the contemporary Catholic conversion narratives; however, as suggested, these narratives were of a polemical nature, espoused the superiority of Islam and the Ottoman sultanate, and reflected Ottoman participation in the age of confessionalization that entailed a certain balance of power. By the Tanzimat era such a balance no longer existed, and Ottoman practices and narratives of conversion from this period appear defensive and concerned with fending off any accusations of forced conversion that could be used by foreign Christian diplomats as an excuse for further interference in Ottoman internal affairs. The synchronization of the Ottoman and post-Tridentine (especially Catholic) Christian concepts of conversion in the nineteenth century does not therefore represent a natural evolution of the trends from the age of confessionalization discussed here but rather a serious change in the nature of the relationship and balance of power between the Ottomans and their imperial rivals, at the expense of the former.

Despite the emphasis on the concept of confessionalization, the preceding chapters have only scratched the surface of this issue in the Ottoman context. The nature of confessionalization and multiplicity of religious initiatives both for and against social disciplining in the Ottoman Empire remains to be explored in greater detail. Since Ottoman historians have heretofore largely left the topics dealing with ideologies of Ottoman Sufi orders, varieties of religious experience, and reform discourses to scholars of Islam, there is much work to be done before we can claim a deeper understanding of these issues in a historical perspective.[2] Case studies based on different regions of the vast Ottoman domains will probably reveal interesting regional differences in the manifestation of the phenomena in question. Connected histories of the Ottoman, Safavid, and Mughal empires that would provide insights into varieties of experiences of state and confession building in the three contemporaneous imperial Muslim polities are also sorely lacking. The following recapitulates some of the preliminary conclusions about conversion and confessionalization in the Ottoman Empire and suggests directions for future research.

The steady evolution of the debates on communal identity can be traced through Ottoman Muslim and Christian sources discussed throughout this book. From the earliest days of the Ottoman polity in the fourteenth century onward, didactic narratives about Islam (especially works of the *'ilm-i ḥāl* genre), hagiographies of Muslim holy men (*menākıbnāme*, *vilāyetnāme*), and epics about famous warriors (*gazavātnāme*) were central to the education of converts and formation of different Ottoman Muslim communities. One typically became a Muslim through learning the in-group language, practices, and narratives of the particular interpretative community one joined. At any given time there were many different Muslim communities under the umbrella of "Ottoman Islam," with the distinctions among them being based on the interpretation of certain texts and religious experiences as well as on the position of their members in the Ottoman political spectrum. Mehmed II's centralizing measures particularly polarized religio-political dynamics in the early Ottoman state by politically marginalizing certain groups, like the frontier lords, and in the process radicalizing their and their followers' variety of Islam, which had mystical and millenarian overtones. Converts contributed to the creation of these communities and maintenance of their boundaries by producing didactic narratives, written in the language of their own immediate milieu, that encouraged other potential converts to embrace Islam, taught them the basics of Muslim faith, and equipped them with polemical arguments against their former religion.

In the early sixteenth century, rivalry with the Habsburgs and Safavids pushed the Ottomans to articulate their imperial and religious identity, leading to attempts to reshape, narrow down, and police the varied spectrum of Ottoman Islam, especially its millenarian streak. Some sixteenth- and seventeenth-century learned Ottoman converts, whose first-person narratives and personal miscellanies were introduced and explored for the first time in this study, connected the notions of Ottoman imperial sovereignty and the divine plan for humankind, representing the sultan as the expected Messiah destined to usher in the Day of Judgment and guarantee spiritual salvation for his subjects. In the context of the Mediterranean world, which witnessed heightened expectations of the apocalypse and intense imperial rivalry beginning in the late fifteenth century, narratives like these echoed beyond the frontiers of the Ottoman domains, amplifying the ongoing religio-political debates in the post-Reformation age. These and other sources discussed suggest that contrary to the established narratives of the early modern period, Ottoman elites took a keen interest in both the political and theological aspects of the debates raging in western Christendom. Literate converts to Islam were particularly engaged in attempts to introduce Islam to disillusioned Christians in the post-Reformation age and portray it as the most authentic scriptural religion that guarantees salvation at the end of time. Their presentation of Islam as a universal religion in a polemical language reminiscent of Christian humanists was particularly prominent in the sixteenth century, matching the Ottomans' contemporary claim to Roman imperial legacy and aspiration to achieve a Universal Monarchy premised on full domination of the Mediterranean.

Since by the second half of the sixteenth century the Ottomans, as well as the Habsburgs, had failed to conclusively defeat their imperial rivals and establish a Universal Monarchy that would erase religious differences, the reality of new religious divisions in Christendom and Islamdom set in and was recognized through a series of peace treaties. The Peace of Augsburg in 1555 ended Charles V's struggle with Lutheran princes and recognized the religio-political divisions within the Holy Roman Empire on the principle of *cuius regio, eius religio*. In the same year, Süleyman the Magnificent and Shah Tahmasp signed the Treaty of Amasya—the first signed peace treaty between the Ottomans and Safavids—in which they recognized each other's legitimacy within their respective domains, set the boundary between the two empires, and agreed to peace for a duration of twenty years. This peace did not preclude production of Ottoman anti-Safavid and anti-*kızılbaş* polemical literature or initiation of further wars, but it set a precedent that became more permanent after the last Ottoman-Safavid war ended in 1639. Although the Ottomans and Habsburgs continued to periodically clash in central Europe and the Mediterranean, no Ottoman campaigns to conquer Vienna were undertaken until 1683. For these reasons, in the second half of the sixteenth century, each of the imperial contenders was given a chance to focus on its own domains and engage in simultaneous projects of religious reform, social disciplining, and state building. Ottoman narratives suggest that at this time, conversion to Sunni Islam gradually became central to Ottoman imperial ceremonial and was institutionalized in ways unseen before.

In the 1540s Süleyman launched a series of Sunnitizing and social-disciplining measures through his reform of the empire's legal system and harmonization, thanks to Ebussuud Efendi, of the *kānūn* and *sharia*. However, the sultan and his advisers were not the only ones championing a religious "orthodoxy" in the Ottoman Empire. Others articulated their positions from the standpoint of Hanefi law and used their authority as legal scholars to declare certain actions or concepts irreligious. This is particularly apparent in the high-profile dispute between Ebussuud Efendi and his predecessor in the post of the empire's chief *müfti*, Çivizade Muhyiddin Efendi (d. 1547), over the legality of the cash endowment for pious purposes (*vakıf*)—a practice widespread in the Islamic world. Along with Mehmed Birgivi, whose writings later served as the key inspiration for the Kadızadelis, Çivizade argued that the cash *vakıf* constituted a violation of Islamic law and issued a *fetva* to this effect.[3] Although technically Birgivi and Çivizade were right, their opinion was not accepted, as it was not considered in the interest of the public, the state, or its Sunnitizing measures.[4] In fact, it was precisely this institution of the cash *vakıf* that maintained Muslim piety in poor neighborhoods and supported vast numbers of Friday mosque preachers in Rumeli, where Muslims were less numerous than non-Muslims. Cash *vakıf* was thus key to the process of Sunnitization of this province.[5]

This one-upmanship in religious orthodoxy had wide social consequences visible both in the imperial administrative culture and beyond. The Sunnitizing measures coincided in the second half of the sixteenth century with the changing social and political realities in the Ottoman Empire, especially the processes of bureaucratization, increased competition for administrative positions, and the rise of elite households who developed their own channels of recruitment. The role of converts in the Ottoman government had been contentious since the mid-fifteenth century, when Sultan Mehmed II turned over his government to the newly converted members of the Balkan nobility and *devşirme* recruits, who were the Sultan's "slaves" (*kul*s), in order to create a loyal base without alternative allegiances and undercut the influence of Muslim notables. From that time, favoring of the *kul*s over other accomplished Muslims and descendants of the Muslim dynasties for positions in the Ottoman government became the norm. However, criticisms of this practice do surface in Ottoman political commentaries and other sources well into the second half of the sixteenth century, informed by the new religio-political challenges the empire faced. Some sixteenth-century authors perceived the appointments of recent converts as a violation of a "tradition" of promotion and career advancement, often at the expense of other competent Muslims who also happened to be converts but of longer tenure in Islam and Ottoman service. Using somebody's recent conversion to Islam as an argument to undermine that person's religious and political loyalty became particularly attractive in the second half of the sixteenth century as the competition for offices in government and patronage of the Ottoman grandees increased, coinciding with the ongoing ideological and military clash with the Safavids.

It is therefore not surprising that in a letter submitted to Grand Vezir Rüstem Paşa sometime before the Treaty of Amasya in 1555, a group of janissaries contrasted their newly appointed commanding officer's short tenure in Islam and proclivity to distribute positions to other newcomers with the serious religious challenge the empire was facing from the Safavids and the need for leaders with exceptional religious integrity and a proven record of service.[6] Similar criticisms brought on by the Safavid challenge are also found in a work dedicated to "the glorious deeds" of Sultan Selim I (*Me'āsir-i Selīm Hāni*, or *Selīm-nāme*), written by the epitome of faithful service to the Ottoman imperial bureaucracy and propaganda machine chancellor (*nişāncı*) Celalzade Mustafa, sometime around 1565. In this work, Celalzade blames Sultan Bayezid II (1481–1512) for initiating the practice of indiscriminate appointments of the *kul*s over *merdümzāde*s—accomplished, deserving Muslims of either common or noble descent from the Balkans and Anatolia—even when those *kul*s' religious integrity, as well as intellectual and administrative capacity, was in question.[7] Celalzade implies that the practice of promoting the undeserving *kul*s instead of opening the government to all pious, "genuine Muslims" (*hakīkaten müslümānlar, pāk i'tikādları*)—the qualities he associates with *merdümzāde*s—cost the Ottomans the support of the Anatolian Muslim notables who were thus incited to embrace the Safavid shah.[8] Although converts by no means ceased to fill up the government and military ranks in the sixteenth and seventeenth centuries, the infiltration of Muslims into the ranks of the janissaries and other institutions previously closed to them, as well as the new preference for the recruits from the Caucasus, marked this era and led to the redefinition of the concept of the *kul* and discontinuation of the practice of *devşirme*. The second half of the sixteenth century thus ushered in the struggle for power among various types of *kul*s and ended the privileged status of converts.

This competition for advantageous positions in the political and religious hierarchy of the empire and multiple impulses toward Sunnitization preceded and informed the emergence of the Kadızadeli movement in the seventeenth century. Perhaps most crucial for this phenomenon was the imperial project begun in Sultan Süleyman's time of increasing the number of mosques and mescids throughout the empire and new support for the institution of Friday prayer as the key distinguishing feature between the Ottomans and their Safavid rivals, who had shunned Friday prayer because it was forbidden until the return of the hidden imam. In order to enforce attendance at Friday prayer, Ebussuud issued a number of *fetva*s proclaiming that regular mosque worship was absolutely necessary and that anyone missing Friday prayers or denying their validity was to be persecuted as an apostate.[9] Mosque preachers, strengthened in number and status, emerged thereby as key agents of Sunnitization and Sunni communal identity in the Ottoman Empire. They would become the standard-bearers of the Kadızadeli movement and command a considerable popular following, challenging the role of all other brokers of piety in the Ottoman Empire, including the sultan, the *'ulemā*, and particularly their main competitors in the religious economy of the empire, the Sufis. As Terzioğlu argues, this shows that there was a considerable continuity between the processes of confessionalization and social disciplining in the sixteenth and seventeenth centuries, and that the Kadızadelis were not a seventeenth-century anomaly that appeared out of nowhere, as they are often portrayed in current literature.[10] Although the process of Sunnitization was neither linear nor uniform, since Sultan Süleyman's sixteenth-century successors adopted a more relaxed attitude toward pursuit of "orthodoxy" and regional differences in methods and targets for social disciplining certainly existed, it nevertheless bore tangible results by the early seventeenth century.

Interestingly, the same period was also characterized by a steady rise in the status of high-ranking religious scholars, who often stood on the opposite side of the confessionalization spectrum from the Kadızadelis.[11] Further study of the Ottoman *'ulemā* and polemical literature produced by the Kadızadelis as well as their Sufi and non-Sufi opponents, expanding upon some recent pioneering research on the seventeenth century, promises to significantly enrich our knowledge about the Ottoman religious and legal debates from this era.[12] Additionally, it is important to keep in mind that although the Kadızadeli movement lost the support of the imperial establishment and its followers were banished from the capital after the defeat of the imperial armies at Vienna in 1683—the campaign promoted and encouraged by the Kadızadeli leader Mehmed Vani Efendi—this was not the end of Kadızadeli influence on Ottoman religious life. For instance, well into the second half of the eighteenth century, sources from Ottoman Bosnia testify to clashes between imams with Kadızadeli ideas and Sufis in the mosques of Sarajevo.[13] Gottfried Hagen has suggested that "Kadızadeli Islam became one of the most influential strains of modern Turkish Islam."[14] However, because we still know very little about the processes that led to this development, it is a key topic for future research.

One of the principal questions for further research is also whether and to what extent confessionalization and social disciplining were transpiring in other parts of the Ottoman Empire, beyond the Lands of Rum; how they were implemented; and in what ways they were resisted. Stefan

Winter recently shed light on this issue regarding Syria, where upon conquest, Ottoman administrators faced the specific challenge of incorporating and efficiently taxing a large and heterogeneous Shiʿa population (consisting of Twelver Shiʿites, Nusayris, Ismailis, and the Druze) with their respective tribal leaders, in addition to Christian Maronites. Winter persuasively argues that even though the imperial and legal framework for persecution of the Shiʿites existed, the implementation of such policies in Syria (and possibly elsewhere) was mitigated by the exigencies of efficient rule on the ground. This meant that depending on the local circumstances, persecution through physical or tax measures could take place but was not the rule. Moreover, he suggests that the Ottoman administrators on the ground were not applying blanket charges of heresy to all Shiʿa groups but creatively approached the issue in relation to a particular group's function in the local administration. He connects this approach to the historical ambivalence toward Shiʿism in the Ottoman Empire and argues that the Ottoman policy toward Shiʿism in the sixteenth and seventeenth centuries cannot be understood solely in terms of Ebussuud's *fetva*s but that it "morphed and adapted continuously according to specific, usually local contingencies."[15] Winter suggests that the choice of exercising persecution or tolerance toward Shiʿites was part and parcel of the Ottoman experience of centralization and state building.

As was suggested, various aspects of the Kadızadeli movement are still poorly understood both in its Rum context and elsewhere. However, there is evidence that the clashes between the Kadızadelis, as devoted followers of Birgivi, and various Sufi orders reverberated beyond the boundaries of the Lands of Rum. In Syria and Egypt they not only manifested themselves as a struggle over who had the authority to "enjoin the right and forbid the wrong" and define the limits of orthodoxy but also played into economic and regional differentiation between the local population and Rumi settlers. The great Damascene Sufi *şeyh* and traveler through Ottoman Arab lands Abd al-Ghani al-Nablusi (d. 1731) wrote several polemical works countering the arguments of the Kadızadelis and a long commentary on Birgivi's *Tarīqat al-Muhammadīya*, which he completed in 1683. Al-Nablusi pleaded for peace within the community of believers (*umma*) and warned against charging other Muslims with unbelief, as some Rumi preachers settled in Damascus were apparently doing against various local Sufis. He was a loyal supporter of the Ottoman enterprise, and his letters from Damascus to Grand Vezir Mustafa Köprülü, in which he warns against excessive lenience toward Serbs in Rumeli during the operations against the Habsburgs, are good examples of the transregional political and religious connectivity of the Ottoman Empire. However, at the same time, he seems to have viewed the Kadızadeli movement as a "Turkish" and "Rumi" folly out of place in Damascus and other Arab domains. In his response to an "ignorant Rumi" (*al-Rumī al-jāhil*) who criticized Sufi *dhikr*, al-Nablusi writes that the Rumi should remember that it was the Arabs who brought Islam to Anatolia. He continues by saying that perhaps the Rumi forgot this since he "probably only recently left off eating pig, deifying Jesus and worshipping idols."[16]

Al-Nablusi's letters and polemical works reveal the complicated, layered nature of political loyalty in the Ottoman Empire and rival cultural, institutional, and regional views on the notion of religious orthodoxy. They are also in an interesting dialogue with the remark of the Venetian *bailo* Lorenzo Bernardo from the late sixteenth century that Arabs viewed Rumis as corrupted Muslims because the latter often descended from converts to Islam. In this case, however, the Rumis' fault does not appear to be that they were too "Christianized" but that they were trying to appear to be greater Muslims than the "true Muslims."

In Egypt, where the Cairene Jewish community became an important medium for the dissemination of Sabbatai Zevi's messianic ideas throughout the early modern Mediterranean and beyond, confessionalization and social disciplining had yet a different manifestation. Jane Hathaway has demonstrated that the fiscal reforms in Egypt initiated by Kadızadeli-inspired Ottoman grand vezir Köprülü Fazıl Ahmed Paşa coincided with the suppression of Sabbatai Zevi's messianic career and the increasing pressures on Ottoman Jewish communities. As part of the reform measures, Köprülü eliminated the long-established position of the *çelebi*—the financial officer of the Jewish community who was also often the key financier of the Egyptian governor. By undermining the financial alliance between the local governor and a minority banker, Köprülü achieved the dual goal of curbing the influence of a non-Muslim group, in accordance with the Kadızadeli agenda, and establishing stronger control of the center over the province.[17] This is a good example of how groups and individuals in the government used religion and social discipline to further their political and state-building goals. Furthermore, it appears that in Egypt Kadızadeli ideas appealed most of all to the Ottoman soldiers from Anatolia who were deployed to Egypt as a result of fiscal reforms, after they were demobilized following the campaigns in Europe. In 1711, these soldiers, who were reportedly inspired by Birgivi's writings, caused an incident in Cairo by attacking the local *'ulemā* and Sufi leaders and destroying Sufi tombs.[18]

As these examples from outside the Lands of Rum suggest, the story of confessionalization in the Ottoman Empire cannot be told without keeping in mind the reconfiguration of the central government and the goals of the state-building elites from the fifteenth to the seventeenth centuries, as well as region-specific experiences of the Ottoman administration. A close review of the Köprülüs' use of religion in carrying out fiscal reforms in Egypt and Syria, or in the incorporation of Crete (conquered from the Venetians in 1669), promises to reveal new, interesting insights into aspects of Ottoman confessionalization. In Crete, for instance, they insisted on the implementation of the shariatic laws instead of the *kānūn* stipulations on land ownership because it both endowed them with the aura of religious orthodoxy and allowed them to appropriate more resources for themselves.[19] Just as with the Ottoman state, the process of confessionalization in the seventeenth century seems to have been decentralized, with various social players—such as the Köprülüs, Sultan Mehmed IV, his mother, and the Kadızadelis—dividing the playing field to each further his or her own goals in the struggle for the upper hand in the government and political economy.

Baki Tezcan has recently issued a call to stop treating the period of the second half of the sixteenth and the seventeenth century as an era of "transition" (from what to what? he asks).[20] Studying confessionalization initiatives of various sociopolitical groups jockeying for power in the seventeenth century as well as how and by whom the confessionalist policies were continued in the Lands of Rum after the failure of the Kadızadeli movement following the Siege of Vienna is an important part of the call to acknowledge this period on its own terms instead of treating it as a "transition," "transformation," "aberration," or "decline." Further research on the Ottoman process of confessionalization will have to take into account the peculiarities of the Ottoman experience of state building marked by various forms of negotiation and accommodation (regarding both non-Muslims and non-Sunnis) not seen on an equal scale in other contemporary polities, as well as reflect the complex field of political and religious players that vied for the exclusive prerogative to enjoin the right and forbid the wrong and thus define both the Muslim community and the Ottoman state.

# Notes

## *Introduction*

1. Gökbilgin, "Rüstem Paşa ve Hakkındaki İthamlar," 48.

2. In the fifteenth- and sixteenth-century Ottoman Empire, the patronymic "bin Abdullah," meaning in Arabic and Ottoman Turkish "the son of God's slave," was a common indicator of one's convert background. However, by the seventeenth century "Abdullah" becomes a frequent male name, which makes it difficult to surmise the religious past of a "bin Abdullah" in sources dating after 1600. In writing, "bin" is often abbreviated as "b."

3. Murad b. Abdullah, *Kitāb*. For Murad's conversion experience, see 148a–153b. For his criticism of sodomy (*livata*) and bribery (*rüşvet*) in Ottoman society, see 89a–b.

4. For a detailed discussion of this neomartyrology, see Chapter 6.

5. el-Cheikh and Bosworth, "Rūm." See also İnalcık, "Rūmī."

6. Kafadar, "A Rome of One's Own," 11. For an insightful discussion of the terms "Rūm" and "Rūmī" in Ottoman sources, see also Özbaran, *Bir Osmanlı Kimliği*, especially 99–108.

7. Quoted in Fleischer, *Bureaucrat and Intellectual*, 254. See also Kafadar, "A Rome of One's Own," 14.

8. See Özbaran, "Ottomans as 'Rumes' in Portuguese Sources," 64–74; and Casale, "Ethnic Composition of Ottoman Ship Crews," 122–44.

9. Kafadar, "A Rome of One's Own," 12.

10. On the term "'Acem," see ibid., 15. On the term "'Arab," see Hathaway, "The *Evlād-i 'Arab* ('Sons of the Arabs') in Ottoman Egypt," 203–16.

11. See Hathaway, "The *Evlād-i 'Arab* ('Sons of the Arabs') in Ottoman Egypt," 203–16. For instance, in the seventeenth century the issue of recruitment for the imperial military and administration brought head to head the *Rūm kulları* (slaves, servants from Rum) and the *evlād-ı 'Arab*, as well as the *Rūm kulları* and the recruits from the Caucasus.

12. In Albèri, *Relazioni degli ambasciatori Veneti al senato*, series 3, vol. 2, 367. For an English translation, which I used but modified, see Davis, *Pursuit of Power*, 157.

13. On the process of conversion to Islam in Anatolia, see Vryonis, *Decline of*

*Medieval Hellenism*; Çetin, *Sicillere Göre Bursa'da İhtida Hareketleri ve Sosyal Sonuçları*; and Lowry, *Trabzon Şehrinin İslamlaşması ve Türkleşmesi.*

14. See Masters, *Christians and Jews*, 68–97.

15. Braudel, *The Mediterranean and the Mediterranean World in the Age of Philip II*, 17–18.

16. Husain, "Introduction: Approaching Islam," 6. The debate on whether or not the Mediterranean can and should be conceptualized as a unit of analysis has intensified in recent years. For the reassessment of Braudel's thesis about the unity of the Mediterranean, see Horden and Purcell, *The Corrupting Sea*; Harris, *Rethinking the Mediterranean*; and Husain, "Introduction: Approaching Islam," 1–23.

17. On this topic, see especially Necipoğlu, "Creation of a National Genius," 141–84.

18. See Emiralioğlu, "Cognizance of the Ottoman World," 89–138.

19. On Evliya Çelebi's and other Ottoman and Muslim authors' visions of the Mediterranean, see Brummett, "Visions of the Mediterranean," 9–55. See also Murphey, "Ottoman Resurgence in the Seventeenth-Century Mediterranean," 186–200.

20. For an insightful critique of the methodological disconnect among anthropologists, historians, and scholars of religion in the study of Islam, see Bowen, *Muslims through Discourse*, 4–11.

21. Husain, "Introduction: Approaching Islam," 6.

22. See Philippidis-Braat, "La captivité," 109–218.

23. Ibid., 169. On *Chiones*, see Balivet, "Byzantins judaïsants et juifs islamisés," 151–80.

24. Philippidis-Braat, "La captivité," 182–84.

25. Ibid., 160.

26. See Khoury, *Les théologiens byzantins et l'Islam.*

27. Ibid., 41–43.

28. The theological discussion Palamas had with Muslims was well known to his contemporaries. Subsequently, Byzantine emperors John Kantakouzenos (1347–54) and Manuel II Palaiologos (1391–1425) both authored anti-Muslim polemical texts, the latter's being based on an actual dialogue with a Muslim professor (*müderris*) in 1391. See Zachariadou, "Religious Dialogue between Byzantines and Turks," 289–304; and Argyriou, "La littérature grecque de polémique," 253–77.

29. See Meyendorff, *A Study of Gregory Palamas*, 134.

30. Ibid., 202–27.

31. Ibid., 141.

32. Ibid., 193–94.

33. See Addas, *Quest for the Red Sulphur*, 57–59. On Ibn Arabi's sojourn in Anatolia, see ibid., 226–27.

34. It may be argued that the terms "theophanies" or "manifestations" (*tajalliyat*) of the divinity, rather than "emanations," are a more accurate rendering of his thought.

35. Samsel, "A Unity with Distinctions," 223.

36. See Chittick, "On the Cosmology of *Dhikr*," 62.
37. Meyendorff, *A Study of Gregory Palamas*, 139–40.
38. On supposed religious conciliation between hesychast monks and Sufis in fourteenth-century Anatolia, see Balivet, *Romanie byzantine et pays de Rûm turc*, 144–49.
39. See Nasr, "The Prayer of the Heart in Hesychasm and Sufism," 195–203; and Samsel, "A Unity with Distinctions," 190–91.
40. See Zhukov, "The Cathars, *Fraticelli*, and Turks," 188–95.
41. See Reeves, "The Abbot Joachim's Sense of History," 782–96. See also her *Influence of Prophecy.*
42. See Clucas, "Eschatological Theory in Byzantine Hesychasm," 324–46. Joachim's teachings may have reached Byzantium through monks from Calabria (a former Byzantine territory), who maintained close ties with Byzantium and took part in religious debates over unification of Catholic and Orthodox churches.
43. See Morris, "Ibn 'Arabi's 'Esotericism,'" 41–43.
44. See Ibn al-'Arabi, *The Meccan Revelations*, vol. 1, 69.
45. See Fleischer, "Shadows of Shadows," 51–52. I thank Professor Fleischer for making available to me his unpublished article "Imperialism and the Apocalypse, 1450–1550," which expands upon the theme of apocalypticism that he discusses in other articles. See also Finlay, "Prophecy and Politics in Istanbul," 1–3. For the intersections of apocalypticism and political propaganda in the sixteenth century, see also Yates, *Astraea*; Pagden, *Lords of All the World*, 26; Reeves, *The Influence of Prophecy*, 359–76; Jacobs, "Exposed to All the Currents of the Mediterranean," 33–60; and Fleming, "Two Rabbinic Views of Ottoman Mediterranean Ascendancy," 99–120.
46. See Alexander, *The Byzantine Apocalyptic Tradition.* On dissemination, see Yerasimos, "De l'arbre à la pomme," 153–92.
47. The classical background study is Alouche, *Origins and Development of the Ottoman-Safavid Conflict.* See also Dressler, "Inventing Orthodoxy," 151–76.
48. On this process, which Kathryn Babayan calls the "waning of *kızılbaş*," see her "Sufis, Dervishes and Mullas," 117–38. See also Abisaab, *Converting Persia.*
49. Imber, "A Note on 'Christian' Preachers in the Ottoman Empire," 66.
50. On the evolution of the Ottoman polemics against the *kızılbaş*, see Eberhard, *Osmanische Polemik gegen di Safawiden.* On the sixteenth-century articulation of "heresy" and heresy trials, see Ocak, *Osmanlı Toplumunda Zındıklar.*
51. See Imber, "The Persecution of the Ottoman Shī'ites according to the *Mühimme Defterleri*," 245–73. See also Clayer, *Mystiques, état et société*, 63–141.
52. For an overview of the confessionalization thesis, see Schilling, "Confessionalization," 21–36. Also see Harrington and Smith, "Confessionalization, Community, and State Building in Germany," 77–101.
53. On the genealogy of concepts of social disciplining and confessionalization, see Hsia, "Social Discipline and Catholicism," 167–80.
54. See Farr, "Confessionalization and Social Discipline in France," 276–93;

de Boer, "Social Discipline in Italy," 294–307; Deventer, "'Confessionalization,'" 403–25; and Craciun, Ghitta, and Murdock, *Confessional Identity in East Central Europe*.

55. On confessionalization "from below" versus "from above," see de Boer, "Social Discipline in Italy," 294–307. I am greatly indebted to Derin Terzioğlu for discussing with me the merits of the confessionalization thesis in the Ottoman context and sharing her unpublished work "Sunni Traditionalism Ottoman-Style: The Kadızadelis Revisited."

56. For a more detailed discussion of this process and desiderata for future study, see the Conclusion.

57. See Goldstone, "The Problem of the 'Early Modern' World," 249–84; and Starn, "The Early Modern Muddle," 296–307.

58. The list of academic titles in "early modern" history and literature continues to grow. At the same time, major research institutions continue to organize symposia, conferences, and seminars revolving around the concept of "early modernity," which suggests that the current field of research is not ready to dispense with this notion anytime soon. A conference that took place at the University of Michigan in April 2009 was entitled "Comparative Early Modernities," and the Newberry Library organized a symposium, "Comparative Early Modern Legal History," in April 2010. In both cases contributors included scholars working on non-European contexts.

59. Subrahmanyam, "Connected Histories," 735–62.

60. Burke, "Can We Speak of an 'Early Modern' World?" 10.

61. On the etymology and history of this term, see Droogers, "Syncretism," 7–24.

62. See the collection of essays on syncretism in Stewart and Shaw, *Syncretism/Anti-syncretism*; Viswanathan, "Beyond Orientalism"; and Rutherford, "After Syncretism," 196–205.

63. This theory drew most significantly on Frederic W. Hasluck, *Christianity and Islam*, as well as on early studies by Ömer L. Barkan, most notably his article "Osmanlı imparatoluğunda bir iskan ve kolonizasyon metodu olarak vakıflar ve temlikler I," 279–386.

64. Examples of studies employing this paradigm abound, but see in particular Vryonis, *Decline of Medieval Hellenism*, and "Religious Changes and Patterns in the Balkans," 151–76. See also Melikoff, "Les voies de pénétration," 159–70; Norris, *Islam in the Balkans*; and Balivet, *Romanie byzantine et pays de Rûm turc*.

65. For a critique of this theory, see Krstić, "The Ambiguous Politics of 'Ambiguous Sanctuaries.'"

66. See particularly the works by Norris and Balivet cited earlier.

67. Lindner, *Nomads and Ottomans in Medieval Anatolia*; Kafadar, *Between Two Worlds*; and Lowry, *Nature of the Early Ottoman State*.

68. Commenting on the notable presence of Christians in the Ottoman army and administrative ranks throughout the fourteenth and fifteenth centuries, Cemal Kafadar suggested that Ottomans lived in a state of "metadoxy" (i.e., beyond any particular belief) and that they were not interested in defining and

enforcing an "orthodoxy." See *Between Two Worlds*, 76. Heath Lowry, on the other hand, labeled the fifteenth century as the "last phase of Ottoman syncretism" and argued that until the conquest of Syria and Egypt in 1516–17, the Ottomans did not care about religious differences. See *Nature of the Early Ottoman State*, 96.

69. See Balivet, "Aux origines de l'islamisation des Balkans ottomans," 11–20.

70. See Colpe, "Phenomenon of Syncretism and the Impact of Islam," 35–48.

71. See Hayden, "Antagonistic Tolerance," 205.

72. Richard Bulliet recently raised the question of whether sameness is not an equally productive source of conflict as difference in his *Case for Islamo-Christian Civilization*, 1–45.

73. See Stewart and Shaw, "Introduction: Problematizing Syncretism," in *Syncretism/Anti-syncretism*, 7.

74. Barkey, *Empire of Difference*, 114.

75. See İnalcık, "Islam in the Ottoman Empire," 19–29; and Itzkowitz, *Ottoman Empire and the Islamic Tradition*; as well as passing references in works of secondary literature.

76. See, for instance, Asad, *Idea of an Anthropology of Islam*; Bowen, *Muslims through Discourse*; Manger, *Muslim Diversity*; and Headley, *Durga's Mosque*.

77. Ocak, "Islam in the Ottoman Empire," 183–98.

78. Asad, *Idea of an Anthropology of Islam*, 7–8.

79. In this respect I draw significantly on the work of Talal Asad in his *Genealogies of Religion*.

80. Asad, *Idea of an Anthropology of Islam*, 14–16.

81. Lybyer, *Government of the Ottoman Empire in the Time of Suleiman*; and Gibbons, *Foundation of the Ottoman Empire*.

82. Köprülü, *Origins of the Ottoman Empire*. The work was originally published in Paris in 1935 as *Les origines de l'empire ottoman*.

83. In the Balkans, Bosnian, Macedonian, and Serbian scholars led the way in publishing and analyzing Ottoman census records from the fifteenth and sixteenth centuries. See, for instance, Šabanović, *Krajište Isa-Bega Isakovića*; Stojanovski and Sokoloski, *Opširen popisen defter* 4; and Lukač, *Vidin i vidinskija sandjak prez 15–16. vek*.

84. For a detailed discussion of the studies based on Ottoman census records and the dynamic of conversion in the Balkans, see Minkov, *Conversion to Islam in the Balkans*, 28–63. On conversion dynamics in various regions of Rumeli, see also, for instance, Lopašić, "Islamization of the Balkans with Special Reference to Bosnia," 163–86; Lowry, *Fifteenth Century Ottoman Realities*; Gjeorgiev, "Islamisierung im makedonisch-albanisch Grenzgebiet," 7–14; and Norman, "An Islamic City?"

85. See İnalcık, *Hicri 835 Tarihli Suret-i Defter-i Sanacak-i Arvanid*. This issue will be discussed in more detail in Chapter 2.

86. For instance, see the influential study by Gandev, *Bulgarskata narodnost prez 15. vek*.

87. Reviews and critiques of the nationalist Balkan literature on conversion

can be found in Zhelyazkova, "Islamization in the Balkans as a Historiographical Problem," 223–66; Todorova, "Conversion to Islam as a Trope," 130–36; Minkov, *Conversion to Islam in the Balkans*, 28–63; and Aleksov, "Adamant and Treacherous," 158–90. See also Kiel, *Art and Society of Bulgaria in the Turkish Period*; and Zhelyazkova, *Spread of Islam in the Western Balkan Lands.*

88. See Minkov, *Conversion to Islam in the Balkans*; and Baer, "Islamic Conversion Narratives of Women," 425–48, and *Honored by the Glory of Islam.*

89. See Bennassar and Bennassar, *Les Chrétiens d'Allah*; Matar, "England and Mediterranean Captivity," 1–54; García-Arenal and Wiegers, *A Man of Three Worlds*; Dursteler, *Venetians in Constantinople*, 103–29; Davis, *Trickster Travels*; and Rothman, "Becoming Venetian," 39–75.

90. See Rothman, "Between Venice and Istanbul," 123–39, 155–209; Dursteler, *Venetians in Constantinople*, 61–102; Greene, "Trading Identities," 121–48; and Agoston, "Information, Ideology, and Limits of Imperial Policy," 75–103.

91. Jewish conversion to Islam in the Ottoman Empire is the subject of two recent studies: Şişman, "A Jewish Messiah"; and Baer, *Honored by the Glory of Islam*, 121–38.

## *Chapter One*

1. For this argument see Kerime Üstünova's introduction to Kutbeddin İzniki, *Mukaddime*, 5. However, there is a possibility that other anonymous works of the same genre written in Turkish existed prior to the *Mukaddime*. For example, Şinasi Tekin speaks of an *'ilm-i hāl* entitled *Risāletü'l-İslām* written in Anatolian Turkish, which he dates to the first half of the fourteenth century, and suggests the Karasi province as its place of origin. See his "XIV. Yüzyılda Yazılmış *Gazi*lik Tarikasi," 139–63.

2. On the Topkapı copy, see Üstünova's introduction to İzniki's *Mukaddime*, 13. For a reference in a convert's writing, see Murad b. Abdullah, *Kitāb*, 36b. This convert and his opus will be discussed in more detail in Chapter 4.

3. *Mukaddime*, 139.

4. The concept of the textual community was first articulated by the medievalist Brian Stock in *The Implication of Literacy*. However, the concept is closely related to the idea of the "interpretative community" that literary theorist Stanley Fish proposed in his landmark study, *Is There a Text in This Class?*

5. On this issue see Swanson, "Literacy, Heresy, History and Orthodoxy," 283.

6. For a discussion of the concept of interpretative community and diversity within Islam, see Abou El Fadl, "The Ugly Modern and the Modern Ugly," 39, and *Speaking in God's Name*, 106–9; for its application in the study of other scriptural traditions, see Vanhoozer, "Scripture and Tradition," 149–69.

7. See Goody, "Question of Interface in Turkey," 12.

8. This phenomenon had a basis in the peculiar nature of the Qur'an as either the spoken word or a recitation that was written down, thus making it a text of a different order from that of the Jewish and Christian scriptures. See Graham, "Qur'an as Spoken Word," 23–40.

9. Roger Chartier warns that "the 'popular' cannot be found ready-made in a set of texts or habits that need to be identified, listed and described. Above all, the 'popular' can indicate a kind of relation, a way of using cultural products or norms that are shared, more or less by the society in large, but understood, defined, and used in styles that vary." See his "Popular Appropriations: The Readers and Their Books," in *Forms and Meanings*, 89.

10. On the universalizing and indigenizing aspects of Islamization, see Geertz, *Islam Observed*, 14–15; and Renard, *Islam and the Heroic Image*, 14. See also Bowen, "What Is 'Universal' and 'Local' in Islam?" 258–61.

11. On the development of Turkish as a literary language in medieval Anatolia, see Kut, "Turkish Literature in Anatolia," 27–45. On early Ottoman translations, mostly from Persian, see Pistor-Hatam, "The Art of Translation," 305–16.

12. For the case of Indonesia, see Cummings, "Scripting Islamization," 559–86. For the same development in Africa, see Goody, *The Logic of Writing*.

13. The meaning of the Arabic word *sa'āt* here is dual: it denotes the final hour on the Day of Judgment and refers to the hours when daily prayers are supposed to be performed.

In Rumeli collections, which are significantly smaller than the Anatolian and Istanbul ones, the frequency of these works stands out. In the case of Bulgaria, the survey of existing manuscripts is a particular challenge since no systematic catalogue exists and Ottoman books from Muslim villages throughout Bulgaria are still in the process of being collected and stored in the National Library in Sofia. I thank for her assistance Zorka Ivanova, former head librarian of the Oriental Collection, who compiled a working catalogue of the collection and is in charge of processing the books collected in various parts of Bulgaria. In the case of Bosnia I consulted the following catalogues: Nametak and Trako, *Katalog arapskih, persijskih, turskih i bosanskih rukopisa*; Hasandedić, *Katalog arapskih, turskih i persijskih rukopisa*; Boškov, *Katalog turskih rukopisa franjevačkih samostana*; and Dobrača et al., *Katalog arapskih, turskih i persijskih rukopisa*, vols. 1–8.

14. See Üstünova's introduction to İzniki, *Mukaddime*, 21–26.

15. *Mukaddime*, 145–46.

16. For an excellent discussion of this concept, see Smith and Haddad, *The Islamic Understanding of Death and Resurrection*.

17. Österreichische National Bibliothek, Vienna, MS A.F. 437, 22a–28b. See also Flügel, *Die arabischen, persischen und türkischen Handschriften*, vol. 3, 535, entry 2006. The manuscript itself is extremely interesting as it contains numerous orthographic mistakes that would typically be made by a new Muslim or someone unused to Arabic script.

18. *Mukaddime*, 150.

19. Ibid., 162.

20. See Birgili [Ott. Tr. Birgivi] Muhammed Efendi, *Vasiyyet-name*. There are indications that the work was so popular that women throughout the Ottoman Empire often commissioned its copying and donated it to libraries in pious institutions in North Africa for the Turkish-speaking Muslims appointed to serve in those regions. Copies of the *Vasiyetnāme* donated by women can

be found in the Tunisian Zeytuniye Library. See Yüksel, "Müslüman Türk Alimi," 33.

21. See Tekin, "XIV. Yüzyılda Yazılmış *Gazi*lik Tarikasi," 148.

22. *Mukaddime*, 165. It is interesting to compare this exposition on understanding *shahada* to the *fetva*s from the seventeenth century regarding the same issue. See Chapter 6 for this discussion.

23. He also discusses how to read the Qur'an if one does not know Arabic or whether a prayer is valid if the imam or the believer himself mispronounces the words. Ibid., 161. A special section is devoted to the issue of mispronouncing the Qur'an and the mistakes that invalidate the prayer. Ibid., 194–95.

24. In the section on ritual ablution he routinely mentions that ablution is compulsory after having sex with a woman or a boy: "Adamun āleti 'avrata ya oğlana şol sünnet yirine dek girse ikisine dahi bile gusl vācib olur." Ibid., 167.

25. For an excellent study of religious and political trends in the seventeenth century and the competing claims to protection of religious purity during the controversial Kadızadeli period, see Terzioğlu, "Sufi and Dissident," 92–275.

26. The range of topics covered by Birgivi in *Tarīkat-ı Muhammadiye* can be discerned from the recent publication of this work, although it is not a translation of the original but a modern commentary. See Birgivi, *The Path of Muhammad.*

27. Unlike al-Ghazali, Birgivi does not endorse the ritual Sufi dance (*semā'*) and the mystical experiences such as "uncovering" (*keşf*) and inspiration (*ilhām*). See Radtke, "Birgiwis *Tariqa Muhammadiyya*," 172.

28. On Birgivi's other works, see Yüksel, "Birgivi," 191–94.

29. Interestingly, a copy of Birgivi's *Vasiyetnāme* from AH 1095 (1683) includes stipulations that one should not rebel against the sultan even if he is an oppressor, and that one should direct only positive, not negative prayers toward the sultan. See Birgili Muhammad Efendi, *Vasiyyet-name*, 106 and 119, respectively.

30. *Kitāb-ı Üstüvānī* was collected by an anonymous student of the famous Kadızadeli preacher whose sermons and teachings were inspired by Birgivi's puritan views on Sufi practices, such as *semā'* and *devrān*. See Yurdaydın, "Üstüvanī Risalesi," 71–78. In the wake of violence against Sufis in the provinces and Istanbul, Üstüvani Mehmed Efendi was exiled to Cyprus in 1656. On his role in the Kadızadeli movement, see Zilfi, *The Politics of Piety*, 140–43.

31. See Yazıcızade Ahmed Bican, *Envārü'l-āşıkīn*, 927.

32. Ibid., 928.

33. See *Manākıb al-'Ārifīn* by Eflaki, cited in Imber, "What Does *ghazi* Actually Mean?" 173.

34. Yazıcızade Ahmed Bican, *Envārü'l-āşıkīn*, 929.

35. The number of surviving manuscript copies of the *Muhammediye* in the libraries in Turkey and in the lands of the former Ottoman Empire is rivaled only by that of the Qur'an and of Birgivi's *Tarīqat al-Muhammadiya.*

36. Analyses of probate records (*tereke*) in Bursa court registers suggest that if there were one book that a Muslim was likely to have, it was the Qur'an. The second most likely is the *Muhammediye.* The study shows that converted slaves often possessed a copy of the *Muhammediye*, presumably as a type of catechism. See Karataş, "XVI. Yüzyılda Bursa'da Yaygın Olan Kitaplar," 92–93.

37. See *Evliya Çelebi Seyahatnamesi*, vol. 5, 162–63.

38. Arpaguş, *Osmanlı Halkının Geleneksel İslam Anlayışı*, 26.

39. See Öztürk, "Muhammediyye'nin İki Yazma Nüshası ve İki Kadın Müstensih," 333–38.

40. The rapprochement between Sufism and the legalistic Islam that is usually considered a domain of the *'ulemā* took place during the "Middle" Islamic period. The synthesis of the two by al-Ghazali (d. 1111) is usually mentioned as a turning point in the process. Nevertheless, the trend continued to develop in the centuries after his death. Most of the early Ottoman scholars are representative of this convergence of the mystical and jurisprudential modes of religious discourse. See Berkey, *Popular Preaching and Religious Authority*, 91.

41. Yazıcızade Mehmed, *Muhammediye*, vol. 2, 390 (couplet 5924), 563 (couplets 8351–52).

42. For an excellent discussion of the eschatological dimension in the works of the Yazıcızade brothers, as well as of Gallipoli's special place in apocalyptic discourses circulating in Rumeli, see Yerasimos, *La fondation*, 60–61, 193–99.

43. See Yazıcızade Mehmed, *Muhammediye*, 398 (couplets 6034–36).

44. Yazıcızade Ahmed Bican, *Envārü'l-āşıkīn*, 407.

45. Imber, "What Does *ghazi* Actually Mean?" 173.

46. In Istanbul libraries there are about fifty copies of the text, with the earliest manuscript dating to AH 881 (ca. 1477) (Atatürk Library, Yeni bağışlar, K. 311). The text was also extraordinarily popular in Ottoman Rumeli—the Gazi Husrev Library in Sarajevo has about twenty copies collected from throughout Bosnia, and the small manuscript collection in the Oriental Section of the National Library in Sofia, Bulgaria, has six copies. There are also two lithograph-printed editions from the nineteenth century (AH 1273 and AH 1294). The text seems to have aroused only a limited interest from linguists who subjected it to analysis for its old Anatolian Turkish language. For example, see Yelten, "Hibetullah b. İbrahim'in *Sa'atnames*i ve Eserde Dudak Uyumunun Durumu," 585–93. Based on its linguistic features Vasfı Mahir Kocatürk tentatively dated it to the fourteenth century. See his *Türk Edebiyatı Tarihi*, 198–99.

47. Hibetullah b. İbrahim, *Sa'ātnāme*, Atatürk Library, K. 311, 10b, "Andan yaranları Hibetullah çevre yanında otururlardı. Yusuf b. Abdullah ve Ali b. Muhammad itdiler, 'Ya şeyh, oku işidelim, ol mübārek du'ān buyurun.'" [His companions sat around Hibetullah. Yusuf b. Abdullah and Ali b. Muhammad said: "Hey, *şeyh*, let us hear you recite that holy prayer of yours."]

48. The intermediary is called Ramazan and likely represents a personification of the traditional Muslim fast. See Lozanova, "'Mŭkite v groba' (*azab al-qabr*)," 255.

49. See Berkey, *Popular Preaching and Religious Authority*, 73–75.

50. On the nature of textual authority and its relationship to oral authority, see Messick, *The Calligraphic State*, 15–36. On transmission of religious knowledge, see Berkey, *Transmission of Knowledge in Medieval Cairo*.

51. Hibetullah b. İbrahim, *Sa'ātnāme*, 3b.

52. Ibid., 6b–7a.

53. See, for example, Süleymaniye Library, Fatih 2644.

54. See, for example, Süleymaniye Library, Yazma bağışlar 3693.

55. See Süleymaniye Library, Mesih Paşa 109.

56. See Süleymaniye Library, Serez 1634. This copy was endowed by two women, Ayşe b. Kadir and Hatice b. Ömer Kara batak. Also see Yazma bağışlar 3398, a manuscript from the *vakıf* of a certain Fatma. Under call number 499 in the Oriental Collection in the National Library in Sofia is a copy that belonged to Hatice Hatun, the daughter of El-Hac Hasan Gaferalla, the imam of Samokov (Bulgaria). See also entries 2567, 2569, and 2572 on copies endowed by women in Dobrača et al., *Katalog arapskih, turskih i persijskih rukopisa*, vol. 3. Most of these copies date from the seventeenth century.

57. The work was composed in Persian in the twelfth century but was translated into Turkish, probably early in the fourteenth century, and attained great popularity among the Turkish-speaking population. For a copy from 1341, see Hazai, "Vorstudien zur Anatolisch-Türkischen Version des *Tezkaratu l-awliya* von Fariduddin 'Attar," 269–333.

58. Ibid., 277–79.

59. See And, *Culture, Performance and Communication in Turkey*. According to And, storytellers were divided into many categories according to their style and repertoire. They performed popular romances, legends, pseudohistoric romances, epic tales of individual exploits, or religious narratives. See ibid., 111. Also see Dedes, *Battalnāme—Part I*, 43–84.

60. On the patronymic "ibn Abdullah" (son of the slave of God) as the marker of conversion, see Chapter 3.

61. For the complete list, see Bilici, "Les bibliothèques vakıf-s à Istanbul au XVIe siècle," 57.

62. See Folaron, "Oral Narrating and Performing Traditions."

63. Aşıkpaşazade, *Osmanoğulları'nın Tarihi*, 298.

64. On this issue, see Kafadar, *Between Two Worlds*, 97–98; and Yürekli, "Legend and Architecture in the Ottoman Empire."

65. On Aşıkpaşazade's political and spiritual allegiances, see Kafadar, *Between Two Worlds*, 99–103, 128–29; and Karamustafa, "Origins of Anatolian Sufism," 82n. See also Terzioğlu, "Sufis in the Age of State Building and Confessionalization." I thank the author for making this essay available to me ahead of publication.

66. Metin And writes of an incident in 1616 when a fierce fight broke out between two storytellers, Hayli Ahmed Çelebi and Saçakçi-zade. The former took the side of Kasim, one of the sons of Hamza from the cycle of the *Hamzanāme*; the latter favored Kasim's brother Badi. In the end Saçakçi-zade stabbed Haylı Ahmed Çelebi to death. See And, *Culture, Performance and Communication in Turkey*, 110.

67. For a recent reconsideration of the literature on early Ottoman "popular" Islam and its development in the milieu of thirteenth- and fourteenth-century Anatolia, see Karamustafa, "Origins of Anatolian Sufism," 67–95, especially 87–88.

68. Ibid, 92–93. See also Balivet, *Islam mystique*, 5–34. Balivet focuses more on the interaction between Islam and Christianity in medieval Anatolia and on what he calls Sufi universalism. He particularly emphasizes the confluence

of the Arabo-Andalusian mysticism represented by Ibn Arabi (1165–1240) and Persian–Central Asian mysticism of Mevlana Celaluddin Rumi (1207–73).

69. See Chodkiewicz, "Diffusion of the Ibn 'Arabī's Doctrine."

70. See Chodkiewicz, *Seal of the Saints*, 47–59.

71. See Chittick, "Disclosure of the Intervening Image," 52.

72. Although he drew on previous Sufi thinkers, Ibn Arabi was first to give coherence to the doctrine of sanctity (*walaya*). See Chodkiewicz, *Seal of the Saints*, 53, 58, 91–92, 94–95; see also Kunitzsch and de Jong, "al-Kutb."

73. Morris, "The Mahdi's Helpers," in Ibn al-'Arabi, *The Meccan Revelations*, vol. 2, 68.

74. See Aubin, "L'avènement des Safavides reconsideré," 1–130; and Newman, *Safavid Iran*, 13–25.

75. Chittick, *Ibn Arabi*, 3.

76. See Chodkiewicz, "La reception de la doctrine d'Ibn 'Arabi dans le monde ottoman," 97–120; and Jane Clark, "Early Best-Sellers in the Akbarian Tradition."

77. See İhsanoğlu, "Ottoman Educational and Scholarly-Scientific Institutions," 371–74.

78. See Tahrali, "Influence of Ibn 'Arabi on the Ottoman Era," 43–54.

79. Recep Cici emphasizes that all the authors of the earliest Ottoman *'ilm-i hāls* were at the same time Sufis and experts in Islamic law (*fākihs*), like Kutbeddin Izniki, his son Kutbeddinzade, Molla Fenari, Abdürrahman Aksarayi, and Şükrullah Amasyavi. See his *Osmanlı Dönemi İslam Hukuku Çalışmaları*, 316.

80. Geertz, *Islam Observed*, 15.

81. Renard, *Islam and the Heroic Image*, 14.

82. For a critique of this approach and of the concept of syncretism, see Chapter 2.

83. On frontier lords, see Lowry, *Nature of the Early Ottoman State*, 55–94.

84. *Muhammediye*, 594 (couplets 8817–18).

85. Ibid. (couplets 8823–24).

86. On this issue, see Yerasimos, *La fondation*, 143–59. According to Muslim legends and *hadiths*, Constantinople, known as a sinful, ungodly town full of pagan temples, was to be destroyed upon Muslim conquest, not turned into the capital of a Muslim polity. By incorporating it into his imperial project, Mehmed II became one in a line of impious emperors. See ibid., 85.

87. See Terzioğlu, "Sufis in the Age of State Building and Confessionalization." See also Holbrook, "Ibn 'Arabī and Ottoman Dervish Traditions."

88. *Tarih-i Edirne*.

89. For a detailed biography of Şeyh Bedreddin, see Balivet, *Islam mystique*; see also Ocak, *Osmanlı Toplumunda Zındıklar ve Mülhidler*, 143–202.

90. See Balivet, *Islam mystique*, 69–88.

91. Halil b. İsmail b. Şeyh Bedrüddin, *Simavna Kadısıoğlu* Şeyh *Bedreddin Manakıbı*, 6.

92. The rebellion drew on the parts of Rumeli that were conquered earliest (Edirne, Seres, Dimetoka), the areas inhabited by the Christianized Turks, and the so-called Gagauz (Dobruca and Deliorman), as well as on the parts of

western Anatolia inhabited by Christians (Chios, Karaburun). See Balivet, *Islam mystique*, 70–85.

93. On modern followers of Şeyh Bedreddin (*Bedreddinīs*), see Melikoff, "La communauté *kızılbaş* du Deli Orman," 407. In modern Turkey Bedreddin's legacy is also embraced by the left, mostly due to Nazim Hikmet's vision of Bedreddin as a proponent of sharing communal resources and ensuring equality and justice for all, expressed in his poem *Şeyh Bedrettin Destanı*.

94. The *fetva* that Mevlana Haydar al-Acemi proclaimed regarding Şeyh Bedreddin stated that it was lawful to kill him but not to confiscate his possessions. This implied that he did not transgress against the *sharia* but that he was a political rebel. See Ocak, *Osmanlı Toplumunda Zındıklar*, 176.

95. For an illuminating discussion on this issue, see Terzioğlu, "Sufi and Dissident," 357–69.

96. See Halil b. İsmail, *Simavna Kadısıoğlu* Şeyh *Bedreddin Manakıbı*, 92.

97. See Zhukov, "The Cathars, *Fraticelli*, and Turks," 188–95.

98. On *yürük*s in Rumeli, see the classic study by Gökbilgin, *Rumeli'de Yürükler, Tatarlar ve Evlād-ı Fātihān*, 14–16. On the alliances between the *yürük*s and the frontier lords in charge of the raiding troops (*akıncı*s), see Kiprovska, "The Mihaloğlu Family," 204–6.

99. The *vilāyetnāme* of Seyyid Ali is presently known to exist only in several eighteenth- and nineteenth-century manuscripts. I have used three different versions of the text: one from AH 1202 (ca. 1788) (*Seyyid 'Ali Sultan Vilāyetnāmesi*, Yapı Kredi Library), which is almost identical to the version published in facsimile by Bedri Noyan in his *Seyit Ali Sultan Velayetnamesi*. The third copy is a version copied by hand by John Birge in the Bektaşi tekke in Cairo, preserved but not catalogued in the Hartford Seminary Library. I thank the librarian, Steven Blackburn, for finding this manuscript among Birge's papers upon my request.

100. See Melikoff, "Le problème bektaşi-alevi," 83.

101. See *Saltuk-nāme*, vol. 1, 10. On his father's side Saltuk is said to descend from Hüseyn, and from his mother's side, from Hasan. He is also a descendant of Battal *Gāzī*, the eponymous hero of the epic *Battalnāme*.

102. See the transcription notes on the *Vilāyetnāme* of Otman Baba taken in A. Gölpınarlı's hand, *Journal of Turkish Studies* 9 (1995), 72. A manuscript of the *Vilāyetnāme* has recently been published but without a critical apparatus and with many mistakes. See Gö'çek Abdal, *Vilayetname-i Şahi*. For the parts not transcribed by Gölpınarlı, the most reliable is the relatively late manuscript preserved in Milli Kütüphane in Ankara, as *Otman Baba Vilayetnamesi*. See also İnalcık, "Dervish and a Sultan," 19–36.

103. *Demir Baba Vilayetnamesi*, 75. There are two known manuscripts of this text, both very recent and unreliable. One was published by Noyan; the other comes from Bulgaria and was recently used by Nevena Gramatikova for her study "Zhitieto na Demir Baba," 400–433.

104. See Beldiceanu-Steinherr, "La conquête d'Adrianople par les Turcs," 439–61. The protagonist of the Edirne conquest, rather than Ottoman sultan Murad I, in fact may have been Hacı İlbeği, one of the warriors who crossed into Rumeli with Süleyman Paşa, who is described as a cousin of Şeyh Bedreddin in

the latter's *menākıbnāme*. Beldiceanu-Steinherr also suggested that Hacı İlbeği may have been Seyyid Ali Sultan. See her "La vita de Seyyid 'Ali Sultan," 275–76. For more on this issue, see Krstić, "Narrating Conversions to Islam," 67.

105. See Beldiceanu-Steinherr, "En marge d'un acte concernant le pencik et les akinci," 33–34. This enabled them to create real dynasties; however, it also made them unsuitable candidates for the highest positions in the state or for the hand in marriage of Ottoman princesses (unlike the *devşirme* conscripts or the voluntary converts to Islam from among Balkan nobility). See Lowry, *Nature of the Early Ottoman State*, 55–66.

106. According to İdris Bitlisi, Hacı İlbeği, who conquered Dimetoka and possibly Edirne, which made him one of the heroes of the Rumeli conquests, was poisoned by Murad I's vizier, Lala Şahin. See Trako, "Pretkosovski dogadjaji u Hešt Bihištu Idrisa Bitlisija," 159–203.

107. Thus, for example, we have traces of a partnership between Mihaloğlu Ali Bey and Otman Baba in the latter's hagiography written in 1483; and the Mihaloğlu family of raider commanders sponsored the rebuilding of the Seyyid Gazi temple in Anatolia between 1493 and 1512. The descendants of Evrenos Gazi sponsored the remodeling of the shrine of Hacı Bektaş in Anatolia in approximately the same period. See Yürekli, "Legend and Architecture in the Ottoman Empire," 64, 128–29; 174–75. Yürekli also discusses the conjuncture of discontents from all walks of Ottoman society around the shrines in Anatolia that at this time were being incorporated into the Bektaşi network of shrines. For a discussion further substantiating the relationship between the family of the Mihaloğulları and dervish *tekke*s of Otman Baba, Demir Baba, and others, see Kiprovska, "The Mihaloğlu Family."

108. See Faroqhi, "Conflict, Accommodation and Long-Term Survival," 171–84; and Karamustafa, "*Kalenders, Abdāls, Hayderīs*," 125–27.

109. See Zarinebaf-Shahr, "Qızılbaş 'Heresy' and Rebellion in Ottoman Anatolia," 1–13.

110. On this process, see Gramatikova, "Islamic Unorthodox Trends in Bulgarian Lands," 192–284. It is important to point out that groups that identified themselves as Bektaşi were not necessarily homogenous; in fact, Bektaşi communities from Rumeli and Anatolia developed some interesting differences over time. For instance, in modern times the former venerate regional saints to the exclusion of those from Anatolia, even Hacı Bektaş himself, and they have adopted features of Sevener as opposed to Twelver Shi'ism. See Melikoff, "Les voies de pénétration de l'hétérodoxie islamique en Thrace et dans les Balkans," 159–61.

111. See Kiprovska, "The Mihaloğlu Family," 193.

112. See Karamustafa, *God's Unruly Friends*.

113. Georgius de Hungaria, *Tractatus*, 373–89.

## *Chapter Two*

1. See Mihailović, *Memoirs of a Janissary*, 191. Konstantin Mihailović took part in the Ottoman siege of Constantinople in 1453 as a member of the Serbian contingent sent by despot Djuradj Branković. He was later captured by the Otto-

mans at the siege of Novo Brdo in 1455 and enlisted in the janissary corps, but the nature of his duties while in Ottoman service remains unknown. In 1463, he was left in Bosnia with a garrison of janissaries, but after King Matthias Corvinus of Hungary conquered the fortress of Zvečaj, Mihailović joined the Christian army.

2. See Stewart and Shaw, "Introduction: Problematizing Syncretism," in *Syncretism/Anti-syncretism*, 7.

3. See Hayden, "Antagonistic Tolerance," 205.

4. For the latest survey of research based on Ottoman census records dating to the fifteenth century and the rates of conversion in the Ottoman Balkans, see Minkov, *Conversion to Islam in the Balkans*, 28–63.

5. See, for instance, İnalcık, *Hicri 835 Tarihli Suret-i Defter-i Sanacak-i Arvanid*; Delilbaşı, "Christian *Sipahis*," 87–114; and Lowry, *Fifteenth Century Ottoman Realities*.

6. Examples abound, but see particularly Hasluck, *Christianity and Islam under the Sultans*; Vryonis, *Decline of Medieval Hellenism*, 363–96; and Ocak, "Bazı Menakibnamelere Göre," 31–42.

7. The classic study on this subject is Ömer L. Barkan's "Osmanlı İmparatoluğunda bir İskan ve Kolonizasyon Metodu olarak Vakıflar ve Temlikler I." For a more recent study of Anatolia, see Wolper, *Cities and Saints*, 42–59.

8. For a detailed discussion of this issue, see Krstić, "Narrating Conversions to Islam," 92–103.

9. Radushev, "Smisŭlŭt na istoriografskite mitove za islamizatsiyata," 152–97.

10. See DeWeese, *Islamization and Native Religion*, 159.

11. *Saltuk-nāme*, vol. 1, 18–19.

12. Ibid., 145.

13. See Aşıkpaşazade, *Osmanoğullari'nın Tarihi*, 345–46; and Babinger, *Die Frühosmanischen Jahrbücher des Urudsch*, 9–10. For discussion of Köse Mihal's conversion in later chronicles, see Levend, *Ġazavāt-nāmeler ve Mihaloğlu Ali Bey'in ġazavāt-nāmesi*, 181–83.

14. See particularly İnalcık, "Ottoman Methods of Conquest," 104–29, and "Stefan Duşan'dan," 137–84; Kunt, "Transformation of *Zimmi* into Askeri," 55–68; and Lowry, *Nature of the Early Ottoman State*, 45–94.

15. Lowry, *Nature of the Early Ottoman State*, 140–41; and Gökbilgin, *Rumeli'de Yürükler*, 16.

16. See İnalcık, "Stefan Duşan'dan," 168.

17. See ibid. Also see Delilbaşı, "Christian *Sipahis*," 87–95; and Necipoğlu, *Byzantium between the Ottomans and the Latins*, 142–45.

18. See İnalcık, "Stefan Duşan'dan," 168–69.

19. See the imperial orders of Mehmed II and Bayezid II reproduced in Lowry, *Nature of the Early Ottoman State*, 50–55. See also Kiprovska, "The Mihaloğlu Family," 203, who suggests that many *akıncı*s were also drawn from the communities of the *yürük*s (nomadic Turkmen) who were settled in the areas close to the seat of the *akıncı* commander's power, from Vize northward to the mouth of the Danube.

20. For a detailed study on sons of Balkan nobility who ascended to the post of grand vizier, see Lowry, *Nature of the Early Ottoman State*, 115–30.

21. The story is recounted in Vaporis, *Witnesses for Christ*, 32–36. See also Karlin-Hayter, "La politique religieuse des conquerants ottomans," 353–58.

22. İnalcık and Oğuz, eds., *Gazavāt-ı Sultān Murād b. Mehemmed Hān*, 17.

23. As one anthropologist argues, "The greater the blurring of and ambiguities between socially constructed categories of difference," the more "over-determined hatred and repudiation unleashed in denial of 'confusions' or lack of fine partitions between the antagonists." See Tambiah, *Leveling Crowds*, 276.

24. Scholars studying conversion in different historical settings have argued that the production of conversion narratives is essentially a response to contradiction, typically resulting from a need to justify the present self in contrast to the former self. See, for instance, Stromberg, *Language and Self-Transformation*, 18; and García-Arenal, "Dreams and Reason," 89–118.

25. See Nicholas de Nicolay, *The Nauigations into Turkie*, 126.

26. Ibid., 127.

27. For a critical edition of the text from 1481 along with a German translation, see Georgius de Hungaria, *Tractatus*.

28. See, for instance, chapters 15 and 16 in ibid., 287–307.

29. Joachimism pervades the entire account, but see, for instance, ibid., 173.

30. See Rambo and Farhadian, "Converting," 30.

31. See Dedes, *Battalnāme—Part I*, 23.

32. For the legend, see Mihailović, *Memoirs of a Janissary*, 31–33. For the commentary, see Beldiceanu-Steinherr, "Péchés, calamités et salut par le triomphe de l'islam," 31.

33. For other examples of stories circulating among the janissaries, see Bojanić-Lukač, "Sırp-Hırvat destanlarından üç yeniçeri destanı," 63–68, and "Sırp-Hırvat halk destanlarında Fatih'in oğlu Şehzade Mustafa," 344–49.

34. Mihailović, *Memoirs of a Janissary*, 7.

35. See Schiltberger, *Bondage and Travels of Johann Schiltberger*, 65–67.

36. See Çetin, *Türk edebiyatında Hazreti 'Ali cenknameleri.*

37. See Terzioğlu, "Sufis in the Age of State Building and Confessionalization"; and Rudolf Tschudi, "Bektāshiyya," in *Encyclopaedia of Islam*.

38. See Georgius de Hungaria, *Tractatus*, 194–95.

39. Unfortunately, slavery in the early Ottoman period has not been investigated in detail by historians of conversion, presumably because it is hard to trace in the administrative records. For instance, York Norman suggests that only by looking at the endowment charters (*vakfiyye*) of the Bosnian frontier lords following the conquest of the region in 1463 can we begin to understand the role that slavery played in the conversion of the local population to Islam. Enslaved as a consequence of the Bosnian king's refusal to surrender, a significant number of Bosnians do not appear in the census records because they were considered private or pious endowment property. See Norman's "An Islamic City?" 40–74.

40. See Yürekli, "Legend and Architecture in the Ottoman Empire," 134.

41. Ibid.

42. Zeynep Yürekli convincingly argues that the convergence of the images

of a dervish and a warrior in the *vilāyetnāmes* can be explained by the patronage of the raider commanders for the holy men's cults during the course of the fifteenth century, when many of these narratives were first written down. Thus, we have traces of a partnership between Mihaloğlu Ali Bey and Otman Baba in the latter's hagiography written in 1483. The Mihaloğlu family of raider commanders sponsored the rebuilding of the Seyyid Gazi temple between 1493 and 1512. The descendants of Evrenos Gazi sponsored the remodeling of the shrine of Hacı Bektaş in approximately the same period. See ibid., 64, 128–29, 174–75.

43. See especially Imber, "What Does *ghazi* Actually Mean?" 165–78. Imber points out that the word *ghazi* could refer to an Islamic soldier in general, specifically to a freebooter. The jurists used it as a synonym for *mujāhid* (the one who undertakes *jihad*), whereas the Sufis understood it in a spiritual sense, as someone who struggled against the sinful self (*nefs*). See also Kafadar, *Between Two Worlds*, 91; and Darling, "Contested Territory," 134.

44. For more on this antagonism, see Yerasimos, *La fondation*; and Kafadar, *Between Two Worlds*, 138–50.

45. Upon the conquest of Constantinople, Çandarlı Halil was executed because of his close relations with Byzantium and opposition to the idea of attack on the Byzantine capital. On the Çandarlı family, see Imber, *The Ottoman Empire*, 161.

46. See Abel, "Un *hadit* sur la prise de Rome dans la tradition eschatologique de l'islam," 1–14; and Yerasimos, *La fondation*, 183–99.

47. Yerasimos, *La fondation*, 201–10.

48. See Kafescioğlu, *Constantinopolis/Istanbul*, 109–30, 188–96.

49. Aşıkpaşazade, *Osmanoğullarɪ'nın Tarihi*, 488–89.

50. For instance, in a fascinating text from Murad III's reign (1574–95), written probably in 1585, the author takes aim at the supposed "superficial" conversion of Bosnian Muslims, which he blames (unfoundedly) on Mesih Paşa, a prominent convert to Islam from the Byzantine Palaiologos family who began his rise to the rank of vizier in Mehmed II's time and later served as a grand vezir under Bayezid II. See Moačanin, "Mass Islamization of the Peasants in Bosnia," 353–58. I am grateful to Andras Riedlmayer of Harvard University, head of the Bosnian Manuscript Ingathering Project, for providing me with a copy of this manuscript (MS 4811/II) whose original from the Oriental Institute in Sarajevo burned in 1992. On Mesih Pasha, see Hedda Reindl Kiel, "Mesih Paşa," in *İslam Ansiklopedisi*, vol. 29, 309–10.

51. See Argyriou, "La littérature grecque," 259. See also Balivet, "Deux partisans," 381.

52. Argyriou, "La littérature grecque," 260.

53. See Balivet, "Deux partisans," 383.

54. See İnalcık, "Status of the Greek Orthodox Patriarch," 195–213. On the struggle for unification of the Latin and Orthodox churches in the last two centuries of Byzantium, see Nicol, *Last Centuries of Byzantium*.

55. The sultan was reportedly not satisfied with the first version of Gennadios's treatise, presumably because of its length but also because of its anti-

Muslim polemical character. Gennadios then produced a shorter version that survives. See Halasi-Kun, "Gennadios' Turkish Confession of Faith," 5–7.

56. See Argyriou and Lagarrique, "Georges Amiroutzes," 29–229.

57. For more on Mehmed's interest in Roman imperial heritage as explicit in his cultural politics, see Raby, "El Gran Turco," and "Mehmed the Conqueror's Greek Scriptorium," 15–34; and Osterhout, "The East, the West and the Appropriation of the Past," 165–76.

58. İnalcık, "Policy of Mehmed II," 229–49.

59. See Turan, "The Sultan's Favorite," 142–59.

60. *Saltuk-nāme*, vol. 1, 72; and Noyan, *Seyit Ali Sultan Velayetnamesi*, 88.

61. See Düzdağ, *Barbaros Hayreddin Paşanın Hatiraları*, vol. 1, 557–66.

62. For the episode, see Aşıkpaşazade, *Osmanoğulları'nın Tarihi*, 355–59. Also see Wittek, "The Taking of Aydos Castle," 662–72; and Hickman, "The Taking of Aydos Castle," 399–407.

63. For example, in the *Saltuknāme*, an episode describes Hacı İlbeği's abduction of Dimetoka (Didymoteicho) beğ's daughter. After a spectacular escape, the Muslim hero kept the girl intact for forty days and then "used her." The narrator comments that he did so because God ordered that one should wait forty days before engaging a slave girl (*cāriye*) sexually. *Saltuk-nāme*, vol. 2, 143. For other examples, see Flemming, "Aşikpaşazades Blick auf Frauen," 69–96.

64. For a detailed discussion of the laws governing interfaith marriages in Islam, see Friedmann, *Tolerance and Coercion in Islam*, 160–93.

65. For a more detailed discussion of women's conversion, see Chapter 6 in this volume. On *kebin* (from Persian *kābīn*) marriages, see Imber, "Guillaume Postel on Temporary Marriage," 179–83.

66. See Friedmann, *Tolerance and Coercion in Islam*, 188.

67. This is the contention of Stefan Gerlach, the Lutheran chaplain to the Habsburg embassy in Constantinople in the 1570s. See Gerlach, *Türkiye Günlüğü*, vol. 1, 274.

68. For a detailed discussion of such practices, see Vryonis, *Decline of Medieval Hellenism*, 485–97. It is important to emphasize that such phenomena as baptism were often meaningfully Christian in the first one or two generations, only to be given a distinctly Muslim meaning over the long term.

69. See Halil b. İsmail b. Şeyh Bedrüddin, *Simavna Kadısıoğlu Şeyh Bedreddin Manakıbı*, 12–13.

70. See, for instance, Melikoff, "Les voies de penetration," 167. Further examples abound in Norris, *Islam in the Balkans*; and Vryonis, *Decline of Medieval Hellenism*, 351–402, and "Religious Changes and Patterns in the Balkans," 151–76.

71. Atatürk Library, *Sa'ātnāme*, Yeni bağışlar, K. 311, 72a–b.

72. Süleymaniye Library, *Menākıb-ı Mahmūd Paşa*, Aya Sofya 1940/2, 68b–71a.

73. Ibid., 72a.

74. See Stavrides, *The Sultan of Vezirs*, 73–112.

75. See, for example, Kafadar, *Between Two Worlds*, 71–72.

76. *Saltuk-nāme*, vol. 1, 35–38. There are several scenes in which Sarı Saltuk's

sermons make the Christians cry, but this is the first and most elaborate episode that features this phenomenon.

A frequent epithet of Jesus/İsa in the Qur'an is *al-masīh*, which means "messiah," and he is the only one in the Qur'an referred to by this title. See Wensinck, "al-Masīh."

77. *Saltuk-nāme*, vol. 1, 71–72.

78. For a similar paradigm in other conversion narratives in the Islamic tradition, see DeWeese, *Islamization and Native Religion*, 167–68.

79. See Khalidi, *The Muslim Jesus*, 6. This Muslim Gospel as an entire corpus was not the exclusive preserve of any single mood, party, or sect in Islam.

80. For an analogous Byzantine Christian-Muslim fictional debate, see Argyriou, "Une 'controverse entre un Chrétien et un Musulman' inédite," 237–45.

81. See *Bir rahip ile bir pir-i Müslim arasında İsa A. S. hakkında*, İzzet Koyunoğlu City Museum Library of Konya, MS 10812.

82. Georgius de Hungaria, *Tractatus*, 243.

83. See Başbakanlık Osmanlı Arşivi (BOA), Mühimme Defterlerı, 25, p. 69, entry 750.

84. See BOA KK Ru'us, 239 (AH 989), p. 55.

85. See ibid., p. 230.

86. See BOA A. RSK, 1473 (AH 999–1000), p. 121.

87. See, for instance, the memoirs of the priest Synadynos from Serres in Macedonia, who discusses conversions among Orthodox clerics in the beginning of the seventeenth century. Odorico, *Conseils et mémoires de Synadynos*, 89–91.

88. Numerous copies of this text exist under different titles. I used the manuscript at Topkapı Sarayı Library, R. 1319, entitled *Kavānīn-i zümre-yi Bektāşiyān* (The Laws of the Bektaşis). A facsimile with a Russian translation has been published by I. E. Petrosyan, as *Mebde-i kanun-i ienicheri odzhzaqı tarihi*.

89. *Kavānīn-i zümre-yi Bektāşiyān*, 9b. "Kānūn eylediler ve kāfir evlādını cem' eylemek lazım geldiğinde ana bir oğlunu alalar ve papāz oğlunu ve kāfir arasında her aslı iyü olan kāfirin oğlunu alalar."

90. See Veinstein, "Sokollu Mehmed Paşa."

91. Georgius de Hungaria, *Tractatus*, 290–93.

92. On this development, see Turan, "Marriage of Ibrahim Pasha."

## *Chapter Three*

1. See also Niccoli, *Prophecy*, 169; Dionisotti, "La guerra d'Oriente nella letteratura Veneziana del Cinquecento," 479; Fleischer, "Shadows of Shadows," 51–52; and Turan, "The Sultan's Favorite," 260–69.

2. See Yates, *Astraea*; and Pagden, *Lords of All the World*.

3. On Ottoman-Habsburg imperial rivalry in the first half of the sixteenth century see Necipoğlu, "Süleyman the Magnificent and the Representation of Power." On the "millenarian conjunction" and interimperial rivalry, see Fleischer, "The Lawgiver as Messiah," 159–77, "Shadows of Shadows," 51–62,

and "Imperialism and the Apocalypse." See also Subrahmanyam, "Turning the Stones Over," 129–61.

4. The classic study of Ottoman impact on the success of the Protestant Reformation is Fischer-Galati's *Ottoman Imperialism and German Protestantism.*

5. According to census records from different regions in the Balkans, rates of conversion in both rural and urban communities were on a marked rise compared to those of the fifteenth century. See Minkov, *Conversion to Islam in the Balkans*, 41–52. At the same time, European travelers and diplomats to the Ottoman court testify to a significant number of European Jews and Christians converting in the Ottoman Imperial Council and obtaining special privileges and stipends, often to the dismay of the born Muslims. See Gerlach, *Türkiye Günlüğü*, vol. 1, 308, also 188, 291.

6. The transcription of the text into modern Turkish was published by İsmail H. Danişmend in *Fatih ve İstanbul*, 212–70. For the Cem Sultan affair, see İnalcık, "A Case Study in Renaissance Diplomacy," 209–33.

7. The *Gurbet-nāme-i Sultān Cem* is in fact an expanded version of a narrative known as *The Events That Befell Sultan Cem* (*Vākıʿāt-ı Sultān Cem*), which was written in AH 920 (1514), and it appears to be inspired by several scenes in the *Vākıʿāt* where Cem Sultan remains consistent in his Muslim faith despite the alleged attempts by his captors, most notably Pope Innocent VIII, to convert him to Christianity. See the transcription of the Ottoman text and the French translation of the *Vākıʿāt* in Vatin, *Sultan Djem*, 208–10.

8. Danişmend, "Gurbet-nāme-i Sultan Cem," 227–28. See also Fleischer, "Shadows of Shadows," 53.

9. See Goffman, "Negotiating with the Renaissance State," 61–74; and Burke, "Early Modern Venice," 389–419.

10. For a recent reconsideration of Ottoman-Venetian relations in the early sixteenth century, as well as the relationship between the Ottoman military expeditions into central Europe and their ambitions to conquer Rome, see Turan, "The Sultan's Favorite," 240–335.

11. See Danişmend, "Gurbet-name-i Sultan Cem," 247.

12. Throughout the early modern era Muslims found learning foreign languages deeply problematic because it was considered impious to learn the languages of the infidels and open oneself to the possibility of being proselytized in the process. See Veinstein, "The Ottoman Administration," 610.

13. "Banu al-Asfar" was a term early Arab authors gave to the Christians, especially the Byzantines and later Europeans. See Fierro, "Al-Asfar," 175. Literally, the term means "the blond people."

14. The prophecies about Süleyman's being the last of the Ottoman sultans were circulating in Europe in the first half of the sixteenth century. This theory was laid out in Paolo Giovio's *Commentario de la Cose de'Turchi*. See Miyamoto, "Influence of Medieval Prophecies," 138.

15. Murad b. Abdullah, *Kitāb*, 48a–49b.

16. See, for example, Teply, *Sagen und Legenden um die Kaiserstadt Wien*; Setton, *Western Hostility to Islam*; Miyamoto, "Influence of Medieval Prophecies";

Yerasimos, "De l'arbre à la pomme," 153–92; and Fodor, "View of the Turk in Hungary," 99–131.

17. Fleischer, "The Lawgiver as Messiah," 160–67; and Subrahmanyam, "Turning the Stones Over," 136–43.

18. Fleischer, "Shadows of the Shadows," 56–57.

19. Fleischer, "The Lawgiver as Messiah," 162.

20. For example, in a conversation with a Venetian envoy İbrahim Paşa reportedly said that in their youth he and Süleyman read together a book of prophecy that foretold that a man named "İbrahim" would rise to high office and that Süleyman would fulfill the will of God by conquering the Roman Empire. See Finlay, "Prophecy and Politics in Istanbul," 22. For a detailed discussion of Süleyman's and İbrahim Paşa's imperial image-making strategies and experimentation with apocalyptic expectations, see Turan, "The Sultan's Favorite," 254–355.

21. See Fleischer, "Seer to the Sultan," 296.

22. See Flemming, "Sahib-kiran und Mahdi," 164–67.

23. See Finlay, "Prophecy and Politics in Istanbul," 1–31. See also Muljačić, "Jedno nepoznato izvješće iz Dubrovnika," 33–46.

24. See Jacobs, *Islamische Geschichte in jüdischen Chroniken*, 168–84.

25. For post-Byzantine apocalyptic literature in Greek, see Argyriou, *Les exégèses grecques*. For a discussion of a late sixteenth-century illustrated Byzantine apocalyptic history that contains the history of the Ottoman sultans by Georgios Klontzas, a Greek artist from Crete, see Volan, "Last Judgments and Last Emperors," 141–273.

26. The belief in the imam who will return in glory as a *mahdi* before the Day of Judgment was central to both Sevener and Twelver Shi'ism. See Madelung, "al-Mahdī."

27. See Ocak, *Osmanlı Toplumunda Zındıklar*, 268–304.

28. For the millenarian revolts, see Sohrweide, "Der Sieg der Safawiden," 164–86.

29. For heresy trials, see Ocak, *Osmanlı Toplumunda Zındıklar*, 268–304; for measures against Shi'ites and their Turkmen followers, see Savaş, *XVI. Asırda Anadolu'da Alevîlik*, 102–18.

30. See Reeves, *Influence of Prophecy*, 359–76; Niccoli, *Prophecy and People*, 172–77; and Headley, "Rhetoric and Reality," 241–70. On Pseudo-Methodius, see Alexander, *The Byzantine Apocalyptic Tradition*.

31. See Reeves, *Influence of Prophecy*, 367.

32. Fleischer, "Shadows of Shadows," 52; and Finlay, "Prophecy and Politics in Istanbul," 17–25.

33. For the background, see Harvey, *Muslims in Spain*, 264–90; also see Coleman, *Creating Christian Granada*, 177–201. For the latest research on this fascinating subject, see Aguilera and García-Arenal, *Los plomos del Sacromonte*.

34. See Wiegers, "The 'Old' or 'Turpiana' Tower," 191–205; and Van Koningsveld and Wiegers, "The Parchment of the 'Torre Turpiana,'" 327–58.

35. Two early modern translations (or rather, reconstructions) of this text survive. The English translation of a text reconstructed by Franciscan Arabist Bartolome de Pettorano in 1642 is published in Harvey, *Muslims in Spain*, 391–92.

The translation into English, as well as the original text in Arabic of Ahmed b. Qasim al-Hajari's reading of the *Book of the Truth of the Gospel* from around 1637, is published in Van Koningsveld, al-Samarrai, and Wiegers, *Kitāb nāsir al-dīn*, 253–54.

36. Harvey, *Muslims in Spain*, 391–92. See also Van Koningsveld, al-Samarrai, and Wiegers, *Kitāb nāsir al-dīn*, 253–54.

37. On theories about the authorship of the *Lead Books*, see Wiegers, "The Persistence of Mudejar Islam?" 498–518; and García-Arenal and Rodríguez Mediano, "Médico, traductor, inventor," 187–231.

38. For the background, see Hess, "The Moriscos," 1–25. For a detailed discussion of the Ottoman involvement in the western Mediterranean throughout the sixteenth century, see Hess, *The Forgotten Frontier.*

39. Murad b. Abdullah, *Kitāb*, 131a–132b.

40. Danişmend, "Gurbet-nāme-i Sultan Cem," 228.

41. Thirty faithful followers of İsa appear in a marginal note appended to Ibn Hisham's (d. 833) story of Salman the Persian. According to the story Salman was attracted to Christianity and became a disciple of a holy man in Mosul—the annotator adds that his master belonged to thirty men who handed down the true religion amid the corruption of Christianity. See Stern, "Abd al-Jabbar's Account," 181.

42. These three individuals are supposed to be the spiritual heads of the Melkite, Nestorian, and Jacobite communities.

43. See Martin, *Venice's Hidden Enemies*, 99–122.

44. See Dán and Pirnát, *Antitrinitarianism*; Burchill, *The Heidelberg Antitrinitarians*; and Balázs, *Early Transylvanian Antitrinitarianism.*

45. See Isom-Verhaaren, "An Ottoman Report," 299–318.

46. The diary of Stefan Gerlach is a mine of information on these individuals led by the famous Heidelberg anti-trinitarian Adam Neuser.

47. See Finlay, "Al servizio del sultano," 93. I thank Ebru Turan for this reference.

48. Interestingly, some true self-narrative writers, such as Niyazi-i Mısri, gave their autobiographical writings the generic title *mecmū'a*, which could also be rendered as "journal." See Terzioğlu, "Man in the Image," 150.

49. See Flügel, *Die arabischen, persischen und türkischen Handschriften*, vol. 3, 535, entry 2006.

50. A study on this particular *mecmū'a* was published by Mittwoch and Mordtman as "Die Wiener Sammelhandschrift," in *Literaturdenkmäler aus Ungarns Türkenzeit*, 70–87. Transcription of the German, Latin, Hungarian, and Croatian poems can be found in the same work, 100–130.

51. For instance, in MS 2050 in the Oriental Collection of the "SS Cyril and Methodius" National Library, Sofia, the Psalms of David are followed by the self-narrative of conversion with a polemical treatise by a former Jew, Yusuf b. Abi Abdüdeyyan. On this text, see Chapter 4.

52. I was able to locate seven copies of this text, the oldest at the Süleymaniye Library in Istanbul (Serez 2015) and dating to AH 950 (1543/44). There are three more copies in the same library; one in the Oriental Collection of the

National Library in Sofia, Bulgaria, dating from AH 994 (1586/87) (Serrac b. Abdullah, *Mecmūʿatü'l-letā'if*, Op. 2461); one in the Bibliothèque Nationale in Paris, dating from AH 1033 (1624/25) (see Blochet, *Catalogue des manuscripts turcs*, vol. 1, Supplement turc no. 8); and another in the Nationalbibliothek in Vienna, without a date (see Flügel, *Die arabischen, persischen und türkischen Handschriften*, vol. 3, 126, entry 1685; MS Mixt. 708).

53. See Blochet, *Catalogue des manuscripts turcs*, vol. 2, no. 899.

54. Serrac b. Abdullah, *Mecmūʿatü' l-letā'if*, 2a. This is how the author himself described the contents of the miscellany: "First Chapter—The counsels for the kings in the words of the Qur'an and *hadith*, saints, and the first four caliphs; Second Chapter—Expounds the blessings of holy war on land and sea through citations from the Qur'an and the *hadith*; Third Chapter—Relates the histories of the prophets mentioned in the Qur'an, the counsels from the Psalms of David, and the stories composed about saints and prophets; Fourth Chapter—Proves unity of God [*vahdāniyyet*] with citations from the Qur'an, *hadith*, New Testament, and Pentateuch. Declares the religion of the Christians and Jews false and explains the scriptural distortions of the four Gospels. Enumerates the kings of Rum from the birth of Jesus until Muhammad's time; Fifth Chapter—Relates the questions Christians and Jews pose to us and our answers to them."

55. See the *mecmūʿa* catalogued as Mihrişah Sultan 443, Süleymaniye Library. This beautifully copied collection seems to have belonged to an Ottoman administrator, as it contains numerous official letters in the margins of the main text. It contains a number of texts suggesting that its compiler was a convert. For instance, one of the first entries is the "Stipulations for the Ritual Prayer Translated into Turkish" (*Şurūt as-salāt Türkçe tercümesiyle*). In this text the ritual prayer in Arabic was written with wide spaces in between, while the translation into Turkish and instructions on how to pray were located in little bubbles between the lines. This translation and instructions on how to do the ritual prayer suggest that the owner of the compilation was a convert. The texts that follow include the fourth and fifth chapters from the *Collection of Pleasantries*.

56. Murad b. Abdullah, *Kitāb*, 81a–85a.

57. See ibid., 126b. In addition, the *şeyh* points out the priests' inadequacy to purify anybody of sins, since they themselves are sinful. This stance is remarkably similar to "Donatism," a belief that the effectiveness of the sacraments depends on the moral character of the minister that was declared a heresy during the early Christian era but resurfaced in the context of the Protestant-Catholic debate.

58. The text of the Italian manuscript was transcribed and translated into English by Ragg and Ragg in *The Gospel of Barnabas*.

59. See Wiegers, "Muhammad as Messiah," 273–74. The Spanish manuscript was published by Luis F. Bernabé Pons.

60. See Van Koningsveld, "The Islamic Image of Paul," 217–18. Also see Wiegers, "The Persistence of Mudejar Islam?" 511–12, on Moriscos in Istanbul.

61. This argument is advanced, for example, by Luis Bernabé Pons, *El evangelio de San Bernabe;* Mikel de Epalza, "Le milieu hispano-moresque," 159–83; Wiegers, "Muhammad as Messiah"; and Slomp, "The Gospel of Barnabas," 81–109.

62. See Wiegers, "Muhammad as Messiah," 246.
63. Ragg and Ragg, *The Gospel of Barnabas*, chaps. 42–45.
64. See Wensinck, "al-Masīh."
65. See Khalidi, "Role of Jesus in Intra-Muslim Polemics," 146–56.
66. For a detailed discussion, see Ocak, *Osmanlı Toplumunda Zındıklar*, 230–38.
67. Ibid., 238.
68. See Balivet, "Chrétiens secrets et martyrs christiques en Islam Turc," 231–54.
69. This is my translation of the excerpt in Italian cited in ibid., 236.
70. Gerlach, *Türkiye Günlüğü*, vol. 1, 78–80.
71. On Hamza Bali, see Ocak, *Osmanlı Toplumunda Zındıklar*, 290–304.
72. One of the chapters of the *Futuhāt* is dedicated to the *īsāvī* type of saints, the heirs of Jesus, such as Mansur al-Hallaj, for whom Jesus' suffering and sacrifice were an inspiration. Ibn Arabi warns his readers about misjudging the behavior of a saint who through his privileged contact with a pre-Islamic prophet, whose spiritual heir he is, may be led to invoke the name of Moses or Jesus when he is in agony. That does not mean, Ibn Arabi says, that the saint has become a Jew or a Christian. See Chodkiewicz, *Seal of the Saints*, 75–88.
73. Ibid., 99. See also Khalidi, *The Muslim Jesus*, 3–45.
74. See Terzioğlu, "Sufis in the Age of State Building and Confessionalization."
75. Martin, *Venice's Hidden Enemies*, 121.
76. See Rycaut, *The Present State of the Ottoman Empire*, book 2, chap. 12, 131.
77. See Pagden, *Lords of All the World*, 26; and Reeves, *Influence of Prophecy*, 359–76.
78. See Necipoğlu, *The Age of Sinan*, 30.
79. See al-Tikriti, "*Kalam* in the Service of the State," 131–50; and Dressler, "Inventing Orthodoxy," 151–76.
80. On this issue, see Necipoğlu, *The Age of Sinan*, 54; and Winter, *The Shiites of Lebanon*, chap. 1.

## Chapter Four

A substantial portion of this chapter has been published as "Illuminated by the Light of Islam and the Glory of the Ottoman Sultanate: Self-Narratives of Conversion to Islam in the Age of Confessionalization," *Comparative Studies in Society and History* 51, no. 1 (Jan. 2009): 35–63. Copyright © 2009 Society for the Comparative Study of Society and History. Reprinted with the permission of Cambridge University Press.

1. Murad B. Abdullah, *Kitāb*, 148a–b.
2. See, for example, Questier, *Conversion, Politics and Religion*, 12–39; Carlebach, *Divided Souls*; and Pollmann, "A Different Road to God," 47–64.
3. On Ottoman self-narratives and the concept of autobiography in the Ottoman context, see Kafadar, "Self and Others," 121–50; and Terzioğlu, "Man

in the Image," 139–65. For further examples of self-narratives, see Fleischer, *Bureaucrat and Intellectual*; Kafadar, "Mütereddit bir mutasavvıf," 168–222; and Faroqhi, *Subjects of the Sultan*, 192–203.

4. See Kafadar, "Self and Others," 125–38.

5. Ibid., 125–26.

6. Murad b. Abdullah, *Kitāb*, 149a.

7. See Ács, "Tarjumans Mahmud and Murad," 307–16.

8. See Stefan Gerlach, *Türkiye Günlüğü*, vol. 1, 98; and Matuz, "Die Pfortendolmetscher zur Herrschaftszeit Süleyman des Prächtigen," 54.

9. Murad b. Abdullah, *Kitāb*, 149a.

10. On the proselytization to captives of war brought to Istanbul, see Gerlach, *Türkiye Günlüğü*, vol. 1, 186. On manumission and the role of conversion in this process in the Ottoman Empire, see Fisher, "Studies in Ottoman Slavery," 49–56.

11. Bulliet, "Conversion Stories," 123–33; and Calasso, "Récits de conversions," 19–48.

12. Calasso, "Récits de conversions," 20; and Bulliet, "Conversion Stories," 131.

13. See Nock, *Conversion*, 7. For the argument concerning difference between Nock's definition and the implications of *aslama*, see Calasso, "Récits de conversions," 33. See also Fredricksen, "Paul and Augustine," 3–34.

14. See, for example, Comaroff and Comaroff, *Of Revelation and Revolution*, vol. 1, 249; Asad, "Comments on Conversion," 263–73; and Keane, "From Fetishism to Sincerity," 674–93. On the relationship between the post-Tridentine conversion narratives and the accounts of Paul and Augustine, see Pollman, "A Different Road to God," 48–52; and Carlebach, *Divided Souls*, 88–123.

15. Bulliet, "Conversion Stories," 131.

16. See Reynolds et al., *Interpreting the Self*, 194.

17. On Samuel, see García-Arenal, "Dreams and Reason," 94–100; Stroumsa, "On Jewish Intellectuals," 191–97; and Husain, "Conversion to History," 3–34. On Turmeda, see Epalza, *Fray Anselm Turmeda*.

18. See García-Arenal, "Dreams and Reason," 93–94.

19. See Epalza, *Fray Anselm Turmeda*, 92–118; and García-Arenal, "Dreams and Reason," 96–97, 101.

20. Rummel, *Confessionalization of Humanism*, 10.

21. Murad participated in peace negotiations between the Habsburg ambassadors and the Ottoman Porte in the 1550s and 1570s as a second imperial dragoman. In the meantime, he wrote the *Guide* during 1556–57, produced a text in Ottoman Turkish that is inspired by (rather than a translation of, as it has been maintained) Cicero's *De senectute* at the commission of the Venetian *bailo* Marino di Cavalli around 1559, and translated the *Guide* into Latin in 1567–69. Sometime between 1580 and 1582 he wrote a number of religious hymns in Ottoman Turkish on the unity of God, which he presented in a parallel translation into Hungarian and Latin. Finally, as an elderly man dismissed from imperial service because of his "immoderate enjoyment of wine," he translated an anonymous Ottoman chronicle into Latin for Philip Haniwald of Eckersdorf

in return for a small per diem. This translation became one of the central texts of the *Codex Hanivaldanus*. On his works, including the short reference to his treatise, see Babinger, "Der Pfortendolmetsch Murad und seine Schriften," 33–54. On his work as an imperial interpreter, see Matuz, "Die Pfortendolmetscher," 54–55; and Ács, "Tarjumans Mahmud and Murad," 310.

22. Murad b. Abdullah, *Kitāb*, 153a.

23. Ibid., 150b.

24. On the history of *tahrīf* as a polemical trope, see Aydın, *Müslümanların Hristiyanlara Karşı Yazdığı Reddiyeler*, 145–84.

25. Murad b. Abdullah, *Kitāb*, 12a–b.

26. On this issue, see Abdul-Raof, *Qur'an Translation*.

27. See Gerlach, *Türkiye Günlüğü*, vol. 1, 101–3, 156, 239.

28. On Murad's hymns, see Babinger et al., *Literaturdenkmäler*, 45–51.

29. On the subject of anti-trinitarianism in Europe and relevant literature see Chapter 3, notes 43 and 44. See also Mout, "Calvinoturcismus und Chiliasmus," 72–84.

30. For the hymns, see Babinger et al., *Literaturdenkmäler*, 55–69.

31. Chittick, *Sufism*, 22.

32. Most notably, Yazıcızade Mehmed, Kutbeddin Mehmed Izniki, *Mevlana* Rumi, al-Ghazali, Lami Çelebi, and Ibn Arabi. See Krstić, "Narrating Conversions to Islam," 204–5.

33. Murad b. Abdullah, *Kitāb*, 150b–151a. See also Krstić, "Narrating Conversions to Islam," 198.

34. Murad b. Abdullah, *Kitāb*, 48a–49b. The translation of this passage on prophecies is given in Chapter 3. See also Miyamoto, "Influence of Medieval Prophecies," 125–45.

35. Murad b. Abdullah, *Kitāb*, 131a–132b.

36. See Fleischer, "The Lawgiver as Messiah."

37. See Imber, *Ebu's-su'ud*, 98–110; and Necipoğlu, *The Age of Sinan*, 29.

38. Traditionally, Muslim caliphs could not interpret or add to the holy law, which was the prerogative of religious scholars. However, as Haim Gerber points out, "*kanun* and *sharia* were enmeshed and the Ottoman ruler intervened into an area of legislation where Ottoman sultans never dared to intervene before or after." See Gerber, *State, Society and Law*, 88–89.

39. See Parker, *The Grand Strategy of Philip II*, 95.

40. See Newman, *Safavid Iran*, 37.

41. See Ocak, *Osmanlı Toplumunda Zındıklar*, 230–304. See also Dressler, "Inventing Orthodoxy," 153–76.

42. See Necipoğlu, *The Age of Sinan*, 29, 47–59; and Heyd, *Studies in Old Ottoman Criminal Law*, 24–32, 93–131.

43. For instance, in Ayıntab, the *mahalle* that was known in 1536 under the name *Mahalle-i Kayacik* became, in the 1543 *tahrīr defteri*, *Mahalle-i Kızılca Mescid*; similarly, *Mahalle-i Sıkkak* became by 1543 *Mahalle-i Mescid-i Hoşkadem*. Out of twenty-eight neighborhoods, twenty-four were renamed according to the local *mescids*, while six were broken into smaller neighborhoods

and divided according to the local *mescid*. For other examples, see Özdeğer, *Onaltıncı Asırda Ayıntāb Livāsı*, 121–24. I thank Leslie Peirce for this reference.

44. See de Boer, *Conquest of the Soul*; and Hsia, *Social Discipline*, 122–42.

45. See Clayer, *Mystiques, état et société*, 76–77.

46. See Newman, *Safavid Iran*, 13–38; Abisaab, *Converting Persia*, 15–30; and Babayan, *Mystics, Monarchs, and Messiahs*, 349–66. See also Quinn, *Historical Writing*, 76–86.

47. See Gerlach, *Türkiye Günlüğü*, vol. 1, 292–93.

48. See Abisaab, *Converting Persia*, 47. On the issue of falsification of the Qur'an, see Nöldeke, *Geschichte des Qorāns*, vol. 2, 93–110.

49. See Terzioğlu, "Imperial Circumcision Festival of 1582," 85–86.

50. Ibid., 86. In 1578 Stefan Gerlach reports on the conversion of a Safavid governor's chief steward (*kahya*), who crossed into the Ottoman territory with the governor's entire household. Gerlach explains that the *kahya* had openly admitted that the Safavid Shi'a religion was wrong and was brought to convert in front of the Imperial Council. See Gerlach, *Türkiye Günlüğü*, vol. 2, 795.

51. See Terzioğlu, "Imperial Circumcision Festival of 1582," 85. On the court politics surrounding the production of this manuscript, see Fetvacı, "Vezirs to Eunuchs," 211–14.

52. Murad states that he translated his work into Latin so that infidels in all parts of *Firengistān*, such as Hungary, Germany, Poland, Bohemia, France, Portugal, and Spain, can be "softened" toward Islam. *Kitāb*, 148b.

53. See Ocak, "Les réactions socio-religieuses," 73–75; Fleischer, "From Şeyhzade Korkud to Mustafa Ali," 67–77; and Fodor, "State and Society," 217–40.

54. At the very end of his account Murad writes: "It is my foremost desire to spend my transitory life in ensuring the eternity and auspicious hereafter of the exalted sovereign of the world in the felicitous time of his sultanate. . . . It is hoped that having distinguished the truth from the illusory, I will put my trust in God by consenting to God's decree, and having attained right guidance with God's grace and favor, I will befriend all the believers and all other groups with Islam before the last hour." *Kitāb*, 153b.

55. See Matar, *Turks, Moors, and Englishmen*, 109–27.

56. See Fleischer, "The Lawgiver as Messiah," 172–73; and Necipoğlu, *The Age of Sinan*, 36–38.

57. See Minkov, *Conversion to Islam in the Balkans*, 67–77, 195–96.

58. For instance, his personal letters suggest that he sought patronage from the Transylvanian *voyvoda* Stephan Bathory in 1572 and 1573. See Szalay, *Erdély és a Porta*, 57–59, 112–14. Gerlach states that in December 1576 David Ungnad, the Habsburg ambassador to Constantinople, intervened with Sokollu Mehmed Paşa to secure financial support for Murad, who had not been receiving income for years. See Gerlach, *Türkiye Günlüğü*, vol. 2, 480.

59. See Murad b. Abdullah, *Kitāb*, 149b–150a; and Babinger et al., *Literaturdenkmäler*, 143. On the changes in patron-client relations in the reign of Murad III and patronage practices of these viziers and other members of the court, see Fleischer, *Bureaucrat and Intellectual*, 70–190; and Fetvacı, "Vezirs to Eunuchs."

60. See Gerlach, *Türkiye Günlüğü*, vol. 1, 239.

61. Besides the complete manuscript in the British Library, about a third of the account, also in Murad's hand, is in the Österreichischer Nationalbibliothek in Vienna (A.F. 180).

62. I am using manuscript N.F. 380, from the Österreichischer Nationalbibliothek in Vienna. Another manuscript of the same work from the Süleymaniye Library (Ali Nihat Tarlan 144) carries the copying date of AH 1035 (1625), which is the *terminus ante quem*.

63. Österreichischer Nationalbibliothek, Vienna, N.F. 380, 227b.

64. See Runciman, *The Great Church in Captivity*, 215–17.

65. See Podskalsky, *Griechische Theologie*, 194–95.

66. Österreichischer Nationalbibliothek, Vienna, N.F. 380, 227b–228a.

67. See de Boer, *Conquest of the Soul*, 60.

68. Österreichischer Nationalbibliothek, Vienna, N.F. 380, 227b–228a.

69. Ibid., 230b.

70. For this episode in the *Tuhfa*, see Epalza, *Fray Anselm Turmeda*, 212–18.

71. Ibid., 48.

72. For dissemination of the *Tuhfa* in Ottoman Turkish and Turkish, see ibid., 48–54, 177–79.

73. Several copies survive in the Süleymaniye Library in Istanbul: Ali Nihat Tarlan 144; and Giresün Yazmaları 3610.

74. See Yerasimos, "De l'arbre à la pomme," 153–92.

75. This is borne out by an entry entitled *kānūn-i nev müslim* (Law of the New Muslim) in the collection of Ottoman laws compiled in 1677–78 by Tevkii Abdurrahman Paşa. See "Kanunname," *Milli Tetebbular Mecmuası* I (İstanbul, 1331), 542. Converts' petitions to the sultan and the Imperial Council, asking for stipends and appointments, also boomed beginning in the early seventeenth century. See Minkov, *Conversion to Islam in the Balkans*, 145–63.

76. Başbakanlık Archives, Istanbul, Ali Emiri collection, 757.

77. Marc Baer explores this development throughout his *Honored by the Glory of Islam*, especially 63–80, 105–19.

78. See Le Strange, *Don Juan of Persia*, 299, 29.

79. Ibid., 299–303.

80. See Rothman, "Becoming Venetian," 39–75.

81. I am using MS 2050, 91a–107b, from AH 1088 (1677/78), preserved in the Bulgarian National Library in Sofia. I thank Stoyanka Kenderova and Zorka Ivanova for making this manuscript available to me. Several other copies of this account also survive in the Süleymaniye Library in Istanbul (see, for example, Giresün Yazmaları 3610, where this account appears together with Mehmed's and Turmeda's; and Giresün Yazmaları 102 and 3574), as well as in other European collections (MS Leiden Cod. Or. 25.756 [Ar. 5836)].

82. Bulgarian National Library, Sofia, MS 2050, 92b.

83. I thank Judith Pfeiffer of Oxford University, who will soon publish a critical edition of this text, for this reference based on a manuscript in Süleymaniye Library (Bağdatlı Vehbi Efendi 2022), which I did not have a chance to consult.

84. See Zilfi, "The Kadizadelis," 258; Baer, "The Great Fire of 1660," 161–63,

and *Honored by the Glory of Islam*, 63–120. For a recent reconsideration, see also Terzioğlu, "Sufi and Dissident," 190–277.

85. In her research project proposal "The Age of the Kadızadelis," Derin Terzioğlu delineates the relationship between the seventeenth-century reform discourse and its sixteenth-century antecedents within the framework of Ottoman confessionalization and state building.

86. Professional rivalry was an important dimension of the movement, as the mosque preachers (*vāizān*) occupied a less distinguished place in the Ottoman religious hierarchy than the jurists trained in the Istanbul *medreses*, who held lucrative professorships and judgeships and often were intimately connected to Sufi circles. As Derin Terzioğlu points out, however, no one social group can be identified with the Kadızadeli movement because its ideology resonated with and was appropriated by different segments of Ottoman society.

87. See Zilfi, "The Kadizadelis," 264.

88. Ibid., 262.

89. Baer, "Great Fire of 1660," 162–63.

90. See Şişman, "A Jewish Messiah," 3.

91. On the phenomenon in the Ottoman context, see ibid.; and Baer, *Honored by the Glory of Islam*, 121–38. For the European context, see Carlebach, *Divided Souls*, 67–87.

92. See Carlebach, *Divided Souls*, 95–100.

93. Ibid., 115–23.

94. In the nineteenth century, parts of the Black Sea region were still undergoing a process of conversion and Islamization, with numerous Christians becoming both Muslims and Muslim teachers and prayer leaders. See Meeker, *A Nation of Empire*, 265–78.

95. The earliest of the four copies of this text I was able to locate is MS Mixt 689, Österreichische Nationalbibliothek in Vienna, which dates to AH 1062 (1653). Other copies come from the Süleymaniye Library in Istanbul, Vahid Paşa Public Library in Kütahya, and the National Library of Tunisia. I thank my colleague Günhan Börekci of Ohio State University for first bringing this text to my attention.

96. The narrative in question belongs to the Sufi genre of *sohbetnāme*, a record of conversation and companionship, usually between a master and a disciple. On this genre, see Kafadar, "Self and Others," 126–28; and Terzioğlu, "Man in the Image," 145.

97. Österreichische Nationalbibliothek, Vienna, MS Mixt 689, 4a–b; and Süleymaniye Library, Istanbul, Saliha Hatun 112/2, 79b.

98. For a detailed discussion of the challenges the Ottoman dynasty was facing, especially in terms of the politics of reproduction, in the early to mid-seventeenth century, see Börekci, "İnkirāzın Eşiğinde Bir Hanedan," 45–96.

99. For a discussion of the Ottoman observers of "decline" and of the modern historiographical "decline paradigm" (which views Ottoman history from 1560 to 1922 as a prolonged decline), see Fleischer, "Royal Authority," 198–220; Howard, "Ottoman Historiography," 52–77; and Kafadar, "The Question of Ottoman Decline," 30–71.

100. For the manuscripts of *Papasnāme*, see note 95.

101. Reported in Abou-El-Haj, "The Narcissism of Mustafa II," 115–31.

102. For the latest study on Müteferrika, see Sabev, *İbrahim Müteferrika ya da ilk Osmanlı matbaa serüveni*. On his Unitarian background, see Berkes, "İlk Türk Matbaası Kurucusunun Dinī ve Fikrī Kimliği," 715–37.

103. The manuscript, which is most likely an autograph, is located in the Süleymaniye Library (Esad Efendi 1187) and was recently published by Halil Necatioğlu as *Matbaacı İbrahim-i Müteferrika ve Risāle-i İslāmiye (tenkidli metin)*.

104. Müteferrika relates that from early childhood he was persistent in studying the Old Testament, the Gospels, and the Psalms. Having perfected his knowledge of the scriptures and being appointed to perform sermons, he felt a great desire to secretly study the "old sections" of the Old Testament that had been forbidden to him by the master teachers. He says that he first studied a verse in Greek that announced Muhammad's arrival as the last in the line of prophets, a concept removed from numerous places in the books he had studied previously. Having embraced divine guidance, he confronted his teachers, asserting that they had altered the holy books and refused to believe in Muhammad. He then decided to translate into Turkish some verses from the holy books in Greek that predict the coming of Muhammad as the Prophet of the Last Age. See Necatioğlu, *Risāle-yi İslāmiye*, 55–56.

105. Ibid., 56.

106. On converts' petitions, see Minkov, *Conversion to Islam in the Balkans*, 145–98. On conversion in court records, see Baer, "Islamic Conversion Narratives of Women," 438–52.

107. We know, for instance, that a partially completed manuscript of Murad's treatise was obtained and bequeathed to the Oriental collection of the Imperial Library in Vienna by Sebastian Tengnagel, the librarian from 1608 to 1636. See Flügel, *Die arabischen, persischen und türkischen Handschriften*, vol. 3, 13. Other manuscripts discussed in this chapter are also available in London, Vienna, Tunis, Sofia, and other cities both within and far beyond the boundaries of the former Ottoman Empire. For location of specific manuscripts, please consult the Bibliography.

108. These were the conclusions of the workshop "Language and Cultural Mediation in the Mediterranean, 1200–1800," organized by E. Natalie Rothman and Eric Dursteler as part of the Tenth Mediterranean Research Meeting in Florence and Montecatini Terme, March 25–28, 2009.

109. For a series of fascinating essays on this topic, see Hamilton, van den Boogert, and Westerweel, *The Republic of Letters and the Levant*, especially Neudecker, "From Istanbul to London?" 173–96.

## *Chapter Five*

1. *Christopher Angell*.

2. Gerlach laments the Orthodox Greek patriarch's poor knowledge of Greek during his stay in Constantinople in the mid-1570s and points to the superb linguistic skills of Lutheran scholars in Tübingen. See *Türkiye Günlüğü*, vol. 1, 225, 233.

3. See Matar, "England and the Mediterranean Captivity," 1–52; Vitkus, *Turning Turk*; and Burton, *Traffic and Turning.*

4. The most notable exception is the so-called Martyrs of Cordoba (850–59), although the deliberate nature of their martyrdom makes them more similar to the later Ottoman neomartyrs than to the early Christian witnesses for Christ. See Wolf, *Christian Martyrs*; and Coope, *The Martyrs of Córdoba.* For other examples of martyrdom in the pre-Ottoman period, see Zachariadou, "The Neomartyr's Message," 51–63; and El-Leithy, "Coptic Culture."

5. See Gregory, *Salvation at Stake.*

6. See Eberhard, *Osmanische Polemik gegen die Safawiden*, 191, 196.

7. See Chelkowski, "Ta'ziyeh," 3; and Calmard, "Le patronage de ta'ziyeh," 122–23.

8. See Stewart, "Husayn b. 'Abd al-Samad al-Āmilī's Treatise," 164.

9. On Jews seeking martyrdom in the sixteenth and seventeenth centuries, see Gross, *Spirituality and Law*, 59–100; and Bodian, *Dying in the Law of Moses.*

10. See Zachariadou, "The Neomartyr's Message," 56.

11. Vryonis, *Decline of Medieval Hellenism*, 341–43. See also Karlin-Hayter, "La politique religieuse des conquérants ottomans," 357.

12. See Pashou, *Neon martyrologion para tou osiou Nikodimou tou Hagioretiou.* I thank Manolis Galenianos for his help with translation from Greek.

13. An earlier, seventeenth-century collection of neomartyrologies by Ioannes Karyophilles is also known, but it contains only twelve vitae of martyrs who died between 1650 and 1683. See Balatsoukas, *To neomartyrologio tou Ioannou Karyophilli.* I thank Phokion Kotzageorgis for making this work available to me. Summary translations of texts from Karyophilles' and Hagiorites' collections, as well as additional ones not included in them, have recently been published as summary translations into English by Vaporis in *Witnesses for Christ.* Vaporis's collection includes about 170 narratives.

14. Vaporis, "The Price of Faith," 195.

15. Ibid., 198.

16. The oldest preserved manuscript of George of Sofia's vita is written in Old Church Slavonic and dates to the third quarter of the sixteenth century, some fifty years after the event supposedly took place. It is stored at the Hilandar monastery at Mount Athos. This text has been published with a critical apparatus by Dimitrije Bogdanović as "Žitije Georgija Kratovca," 203–67. I thank Aleksandar Fotić for this reference. For an abridged English translation, see Vaporis, *Witnesses for Christ*, 45–58.

17. In almost every neomartyrology the accused is given three opportunities to repent and return to Islam, between which he has time to contemplate his choices in a prison cell. The third refusal to embrace Islam, according to neomartyrologies, precipitated a death penalty. This description of the Ottoman legal procedure in the case of apostasy seems to correspond with the actual Ottoman jurisprudential practice. According to the Hanefi legal tradition, apostasy was punishable by death, but opinions varied as to what efforts, if any, should be invested in converting the apostate back to Islam. See Heffening, "Murtadd."

18. Bogdanović, "Žitije Georgija Kratovca," 244, 252.

19. Ibid., 257.
20. See Vaporis, *Witnesses for Christ*, 64–65, 68–69, 76, 79.
21. See the fifteenth-century narratives in Vaporis, *Witnesses for Christ*, 31–44.
22. See entry 1070 in *6 Numaralı Mühimme Defteri*, vol. 2, 70.
23. See Faroqhi, "An Orthodox Woman Saint," 383–94. For the neomartyrology, see Vaporis, *Witnesses for Christ*, 83–86.
24. See Carayon, *Relations inédites*, 278.
25. On this issue, see Zachariadou, "'A Safe and Holy Mountain,'" 127–34.
26. On taxation and Ottoman-Athonite relations in the fifteenth century, see Kolovos, "Negotiating for State Protection," 199–210. See also Kotzageorgis, "Fiscal Status of the Greek Orthodox Church," 73.
27. See Fotić, *Sveta Gora i Hilandar u Osmanskom Carstvu*, 79.
28. Ibid.
29. On the intricacies of the legal argument and the negotiations between the Ottoman government and the monks in this affair, see Kermeli, "Central Administration versus Provincial Arbitrary Governance," 189–202. For Ebussuud's argument, see ibid., 194.
30. Ibid., 194.
31. See Kotzageorgis, "Fiscal Status of the Greek Orthodox Church," 73–77, especially note 35.
32. Vaporis, "The Price of Faith," 212–15. For a discussion on other supporters of neomartyrdom and compilers of neomartyrologies in the early nineteenth century, when martyrs for faith began to be considered "ethnomartyrs," see Tzedopoulos, "Ethnike homologia kai symvolike sten Hellada tou 19ou aiona," 107–43. I would like to thank Manolis Galenianos for assistance with the translation.
33. See Nihoritis, *Sveta Gora i bŭlgarskoto novomŭchenichestvo*, 64–65.
34. Ibid., 173–74. On this issue, also see Eliou, "Pothos martyriou," 267–84.
35. See Frend, *Martyrdom and Persecution*, 353. Frend observes that this change in attitude martyrdom represented Christianity's "graduation" from a sect to a universal church prepared to live in harmony with the state, rather than in opposition to it, as in the first two centuries.
36. See Laurent, "L'idée de la guerre sainte," 71–98. Anna Komnena's astonishment at the sight of Frankish armed monks and prelates participating in the First Crusade also shows how foreign the idea of a holy man as a warrior was to a Byzantine mind.
37. See Nihoritis, *Sveta Gora i bŭlgarskoto novomŭchenichestvo*, 25.
38. When John ended up being martyred after all, Patriarch Jeremias I (1522–46) decided to send money to the *kadı* and ask him to postpone the sentence until after the Orthodox Christians had celebrated Easter. The *kadı* concurred, and John was executed after Easter celebrations. See Vaporis, *Witnesses for Christ*, 64–66.
39. The vita of Makarios the Tailor was published for the first time in a twelve-volume nineteenth-century collection of neomartyrologies compiled by Constantine Doukakis, *Megas synaxaristes* (Athens, 1889–96). For the English translation, see Vaporis, *Witnesses for Christ*, 86–90.

40. See the introduction to Nikodemos Hagiorites' *New Martyrologion*, in Vaporis, "The Price of Faith," 200.

41. Ibid., 207.

42. Fredrick Hasluck writes in his essay "Neo-martyrs of the Orthodox Church" that "it was generally held that the guilt of apostasy could be purged only by martyrdom, so that a permanent refuge in a monastery was impossible." See Hasluck, *Christianity and Islam under the Sultans*, 456. A modern apologist of the phenomenon of new martyrdom asserts, "The desire for atonement of former apostates who suffered from a guilty conscience was ever present. Undoubtedly some sought martyrdom because of the Church's teaching that martyrdom was a second baptism, which meant catharsis of all sins. . . . The lapsed Christians under the Turks were often rebuked by saintly monks and devout clergymen." See Constantelos, "The 'Neomartyrs,'" 230.

43. On his appointment and the rights given to the Orthodox Christian community, see Braude, "Foundation Myths," 69–88.

44. Braude suggests that Mehmed II tried to create a patriarchal seat based in Istanbul for the Armenians in order to win the community's loyalty away from his Akkoyunlu and Karakoyunlu rivals in eastern Anatolia. However, this patriarchal seat only gained more importance and institutional shape in the eighteenth century. See Braude, "Foundation Myths," 82.

45. Although established historiography conventionally uses the word *millet* to denote the structure through which the Ottomans administered and taxed its non-Muslim subjects, recent revisionist studies show that this term was a nineteenth-century creation and in the early modern era the religious communities were referred to as *tā'ife*. On this debate, see Braude, "Foundation Myths"; and Goffman, "Ottoman Millets," 135–58.

46. See Masters, *Christians and Jews*, 61–67.

47. The relationship between the patriarchs and Mount Athos was an ambivalent one since Mount Athos was a convenient place of exile for the high-ranking Orthodox clergy, especially former patriarchs. For example, Patriarch Jeremias II managed to obtain a *fermān* exiling his predecessor Mitrophanes III to Mount Athos under the accusation that the latter was inciting a rebellion among the metropolitans and preventing the collection of taxes. Those patriarchs and metropolitans who fell out of grace with the church would be sent against their wills to confinement at Mount Athos. See Fotić, *Sveta Gora i Hilandar u Osmanskom Carstvu*, 81.

48. On the influence of the old Byzantine imperial family of Kantakouzeni, especially of Michael Kantakouzenos, known as Şeytanoğlu (the Son of the Devil), on the politics surrounding the appointments to the Orthodox patriarchate, see Runciman, *The Great Church in Captivity*, 197.

49. See Papademetriou, "Ottoman Tax Farming," 13.

50. Ibid., 162–64.

51. The average length of the patriarchal term in the sixteenth century was 3.1 years, and there were thirty-two changes; in the seventeenth century the term lasted 1.9 years on average, and there were fifty-three changes. See ibid., 143.

52. See, for example, the neomartyrology of Damaskenos the Monk, who

died in 1681, where Patriarch Dionysios asks Damaskenos to postpone his intended martyrdom while he is on the patriarchal throne. Vaporis, *Witnesses for Christ*, 133.

53. For the early modern world in this period, see the essays in Parker and Smith, *General Crisis of the Seventeenth Century*. For the Ottoman experience, see İnalcık, "Military and Fiscal Transformation," 283–337; Barkey, *Bandits and Bureaucrats*; Tezcan, "Ottoman Monetary Crisis"; and Börekci, "İnkirāzın Eşiğinde Bir Hanedan."

54. For background, see Peirce, *The Imperial Harem*; and Börekci, "İnkirāzın Eşiğinde Bir Hanedan."

55. See Piterberg, *An Ottoman Tragedy*, 10–29, 71–132.

56. For a discussion on Spanish *arbitristas*, who like the Ottoman *nasīhatnāme* writers lamented the decline of their polity's vitality, see Kamen, "The Decline of Spain"; and Israel, "The Decline of Spain." For the Venetian case, see Grubb, "When Myths Lose Power."

57. Literature on Ottoman "decline," both early modern and modern, is abundant. For discussion on this issue, see, for example, Howard, "Genre and Myth," and "Ottoman Historiography"; Fleischer, *Bureaucrat and Intellectual*, 95–105, 226–27; and Kafadar, "Myth of the Golden Age."

58. See Baer, *Honored by the Glory of Islam*, 63–119.

59. See Sariyannis, "Aspects of 'Neomartyrdom.'"

60. See Jennings, *Christians and Muslims in the Ottoman Cyprus*; Gradeva, "Orthodox Christians in the Kadi Courts"; and Baer, "Islamic Conversion Narratives of Women."

61. See Minkov, *Conversion to Islam in the Balkans*, 75–78.

62. See, for example, Skilliter, *William Harborne*; de Groot, *Ottoman Empire and the Dutch Republic*; Goffman, *Ottoman Empire and Early Modern Europe*, 131–88, and *Izmir and the Levantine World*; Dursteler, *Venetians in Constantinople*; and Burton, *Traffic and Turning*.

63. See Masters, *Christians and Jews*, 68–97; and Van Den Boogert, *The Capitulations and the Ottoman Legal System*.

64. See Runciman, *The Great Church in Captivity*, 230.

65. See Nicolaidis, "Scientific Exchanges," 185. See also Fedalto, *Ricerche storiche sulla posizione giuridica ed ecclesiastica dei Greci a Venezia*; and Tiepolo and Tonetti, *I Greci a Venezia*.

66. For the career of one such individual, see Hartnup, *"On the Beliefs of the Greeks."*

67. See reports on the progress of the mission in Carayon, *Relations inédites*.

68. See Tsirpanlis, *Significance of Jeremias II's Correspondence*; and Podskalsky, *Griechische Theologie*, 101–17.

69. See Runciman, *The Great Church in Captivity*, 285. See also Hadjiantoniou, *Protestant Patriarch*; and Podskalsky, *Griechische Theologie*, 154–230.

70. See the vita of Iakovos the Monk and his disciples, who died in 1520 as a result of a slanderous denunciation against them by the metropolitan of Arta, in Vaporis, *Witnesses for Christ*, 58–59.

71. See Runciman, *The Great Church in Captivity*, 224.

72. See Pantazopoulos, *Church and Law*, 91–107.

73. See Vacalopoulos, *History of Macedonia*, 216–17.

74. See Frazee, *Catholics and Sultans*, 73–74.

75. Carayon, *Relations inédites*, 101–3.

76. This theme has pervaded Jesuit reports since the Society's establishment in the Ottoman Empire. For a particularly vociferous critique, see a report from Constantinople dated to 1695 in Carayon, *Relations inédites*, 245. The missionary says that "the ignorance of the Greeks is so great that for the most part they cannot tell any difference between their own church and the Catholic one save for the outer differences, which is to say in the ceremonies that they observe and we do not. They do not know what they should believe, nor what we believe, so they are constantly vulnerable to falling into error of the heretics that approach them. Their own priests, far from instructing them, are for the most part in need of being instructed themselves. Their patriarch dreams of maintaining his dignity, which is constantly open to auction/bargaining."

77. Indeed, since the late sixteenth century, Orthodox Christian clergy had learned important educational and proselytizing strategies from the Jesuits, which they then applied to strengthen the boundaries of their own confessional community. For instance, Nikodemos Hagiorites, the great opponent of Rome and promoter of the new martyrs, was profoundly influenced by Ignatius Loyola's *Spiritual Exercises* in his famous work *Unseen Warfare* (Venice, 1796). In a way, his exposure to Western spiritual trends during his schooling in Naxos and Smyrna, both of which witnessed Jesuit activities, ensured the enduring appeal of his works in the Orthodox Christian world. See Bobrinskoy, "Encounter of Traditions in Greece," 450.

78. On Padua-educated intellectuals spearheading learning in Athens and other cities under Ottoman rule, see Nicolaidis, "Scientific Exchanges," 187–88. See also Runciman, *The Great Church in Captivity*, 261.

79. See Petkanova Toteva, *Damaskinite v bŭlgarskata literatura*, 111–12.

80. Ibid., 118.

81. For the Byzantine period, see Runciman, *The Great Church in Captivity*, 49. For later developments, see ibid., 232–33.

82. Carayon, *Relations inédites*, 209.

83. Zachariadou, *The Neomartyr's Message*, 62–63.

84. See Argyriou, "Pachomios Roussanos et l'Islam," 143–64.

85. Gregory, *Salvation at Stake*, 165.

86. Ibid., 288–97.

87. For literature on this issue, see notes 3 and 62.

88. *Christopher Angell*, B2b.

89. See Patterson, "Beginning of Orthodox-Anglican Relations," 39–56.

90. See Davey, "Metrophanes Kritopoulos," 57–77; and Runciman, *The Great Church in Captivity*, 269.

91. Degenhardt, "Catholic Martyrdom," 83.

92. See especially Dimock, *New Turkes*. Both Catholic and Protestant polemicists likened their opponents to Turks. For the precedent in the Protestant tradition, see Henrich and Boyce, "Martin Luther," 250–66.

93. See Puchner, "Jesuit Theater," 209.
94. Ibid., 210.
95. Ibid., 214.
96. See Kotzageorgis, "'Messiahs' and Neomartyrs in Ottoman Thessaly," 226.
97. See Gerlach, *Türkiye Günlüğü*, vol. 1, 170, for his short and detached description of the death of an Orthodox Christian who is identified in Vaporis's collection as the neomartyr John the Cabinetmaker (d. February 26, 1575). He mentions two further incidents, one in February 1578 (vol. 2, 727) of a soldier who had become a Muslim but then returned to Christianity and was executed, and one in May 1578 (vol. 2, 789) of a young man from Cafa on the Black Sea who was tricked into saying the Muslim profession of faith but refused to become a Muslim and escaped to Italy.
98. Carayon, *Relations inédites*, 183–93.
99. Ibid., 191.
100. See Vaporis, *Witnesses for Christ*, 113, 151.
101. On Karyophilles, see Podskalsky, *Griechische Theologie*, 237–41. Karyophilles belonged to the intellectual circle of the "Calvinist" patriarch Cyril Lukaris. He held various high positions in the patriarchal church in Constantinople although he was not a cleric. In his written works he dealt with the issue of the Eucharist and transubstantiation and tried to distance himself from Protestantism. He compiled stories of twelve neomartyrs who died in Constantinople during the era of Mehmed IV (1648–93).
102. See Carayon, *Relations inédites*, 238.
103. See Balatsoukas, *To neomartyrologio tou Ioannu Karyophilli*, 38–46. For the English translation, see Vaporis, *Witnesses for Christ*, 123–26.
104. See Saphinaz-Amal Naguib, "The Martyr as Witness," 225.

## *Chapter 6*

1. For the bibliography, see Vaporis, *Witnesses for Christ*, 96–97. In his *Neon martyrologion* Nikodemos Hagiorites does not include Philothei but features the life of another, earlier female martyr known as Matrona of Volisos in Chios, who died in 1462. Since Matrona of Volisos actually lived and died while Chios was still under Genoese control, her story will not be included in the present discussion. Hagiorites includes the vita of this saint because most of the miracles attributed to her transpired in the Ottoman period. For a detailed discussion, see Walsh, "Women Martyrs," 71–91.
2. Vaporis, *Witnesses for Christ*, 83–86.
3. See the list in ibid.
4. See Faroqhi, "An Orthodox Woman Saint," 383–94.
5. The event took place in the time of Patriarch Jeremias II, the protégé of Michael Kantakouzenos, also known as Şeytanoğlu. Kantakouzenos, who had close connections to Sokollu Mehmed Paşa, was famous for manipulating the patriarchal throne and other lucrative tax farms. This was the era when the concept of *pīşkeş* became institutionalized. See Papademetriou, *Ottoman Tax Farming*,

125–72. The power of the Greek archons, the remnants of the old Byzantine aristocracy, should therefore not be underestimated.

6. See the discussion on Christophoros Angelles's neomartyrology in Chapter 5.

7. A Jesuit report from 1642 mentions that there were ten to twelve female monasteries in Athens, one even housing about sixty women. See Carayon, *Relations inédites*, 145–50.

8. See Greene, "Trading Identities," 121–48.

9. For recent studies based on neomartyrologies, see Gradeva, "Apostasy in Rumeli," 29–74; and essays in *Archivum Ottomanicum* by Gara, "Neomartyr without a Message," 155–76; Kotzageorgis, "'Messiahs' and Neomartyrs in Ottoman Thessaly," 219–32; and Sariyannis, "Aspects of 'Neomartyrdom,'" 249–62.

10. For insightful discussion on the issue of tolerance as imperial policy in the Ottoman Empire, see Rodrigue, "Difference and Tolerance in the Ottoman Empire"; Barkey, *Empire of Difference*, 110, 114; and Makdisi, *Artillery of Heaven*, 33–35.

11. For the translation of the text from Old Church Slavonic into Bulgarian, see Ivanova, *Stara bŭlgarska literatura*, vol. 4, 308–76. The neomartyrology was originally written by Matei Gramatik, a learned monk from Sofia who was Nikola's contemporary. The text, however, survives in only one copy from 1564, written by a priest, Lazar from Kratovo. See ibid., 615.

12. See Baer, Makdisi, and Shryock, "CSSH Discussion," 929.

13. See Nirenberg, *Communities of Violence*; and MacEvitt, *Crusades and the Christian World of the East.*

14. On *dhimma* in the Ottoman Empire, see Braude and Lewis, "Introduction," in *Christians and Jews*, vol. 1, 1–33. See also Masters, *Christians and Jews*, 16–40.

15. See also, for example, the cases of John the Merchant from Trebizond (d. 1492), Michael Mavroeides from Adrianople (d. late fifteenth century), and Nicholas the Peddler from Ichtys (d. 1554) in Vaporis, *Witnesses for Christ.*

16. Spandounes, *Origins of the Ottoman Emperors*, 133.

17. The incidence of such denunciations increases in later centuries. For the sixteenth century, see the vita of Iakovos the Shepherd and his disciples Iakovos the Deacon and Dionysios the Monk, all martyred in 1520, and Damianos the Monk from Myrichovo (d. 1568) in Vaporis, *Witnesses for Christ*, 58 and 81, respectively.

18. For this narrative, see ibid., 40. This neomartyrology is based on the story of John the New of Trebizond, who died in the 1330s in Akkerman. Although the earliest text of John's martyrdom, written by Grigorii Tsamblak around 1402, asserts that he was executed by the Tatar authorities for refusing to convert to Islam after he promised to do so, there is no mention of Jews. Later hagiographic tradition changed the narrative to make it more contemporary by situating it in the Ottoman period. For the original version of the vita, see Ivanova, *Stara bŭlgarska literatura*, 606.

19. For the original story, see Balatsoukas, *To neomartyrologio tou Ioannou Kariophilli*, 30–32. For the English version, see Vaporis, *Witnesses for Christ*, 111.

20. On the theory that Christian converts introduced anti-Semitic tendencies into Ottoman society, see Gradeva, "Apostasy in Rumeli," 41; and Shaw, *Jews of the Ottoman Empire*, 84.

21. Stefan Gerlach recounts an interesting episode from Constantinople in 1577 when a Jew publicly offended Jesus, and Christians appealed to the sultan, demanding that the Jew be executed. See Gerlach, *Türkiye Günlüğü*, vol. 2, 622–23. Another very telling example is the narrative of Albert Bobovius, alias Santuri Ali Ufki Bey (ca. 1610–75), a Polish convert to Islam who gives a disparaging image of the Jews when explaining their privileged position in Ottoman society during the seventeenth century. See Ali Ufki Bey, *Topkapı Sarayı'nda Yaşam*, 40.

22. See Braude and Lewis, "Introduction," in *Christians and Jews*, 25; and Benbassa and Rodrigue, *Sephardy Jewry*, 44–45.

23. See Vaporis, *Witnesses for Christ*, 109.

24. Ibid., 130.

25. See, for instance, BOA MHM 25 (AH 981 / 1573), cases 169, 218, 326, and 560.

26. See Düzdağ, *Şeyhülislām Ebussuūd Efendi Fetvaları*, 93. Such attempts seem to be more present in the later *fetva* collections. See Dimitrov, "Fetvi," 35.

27. For Ebussuud's *fetva*, see Düzdağ, *Şeyhülislām Ebussuūd Efendi Fetvaları*, 89, no. 360. For the *fetva* of Abdurrahim Efendi (*şeyhü'l-islām* 1715–16), see Velkov, Kalitsin, and Radushev, *Osmanski izvori za islyamizatsionnite protsesi na Balkanite*, 295, no. 72.

28. See Vaporis, *Witnesses for Christ*, 123, for the vita of Nicholas the Grocer, who died in 1672 after being tricked into pronouncing *shahada* by his Turkish teacher. For the *fetva* of Abdurrahim Efendi, see Velkov, Kalitsin, and Radushev, *Osmanski izvori za islyamizatsionnite protsesi na Balkanite*, 294–95.

29. Examples of conversion under threat abound in Vaporis's collection, *Witnesses for Christ*. For the *fetva* of Abdurrahim Efendi, see Velkov, Kalitsin, and Radushev, *Osmanski izvori za islyamizatsionnite protsesi na Balkanite*, 295.

30. For example, to the question whether a Christian or a Jew (*Zeyd-i zimmi*) who pronounces the *shahada* but does not explicitly reject the old religion (*teberrā eylemese*) should be ordered to become a Muslim, Ebussuud's answer was no. See Düzdağ, *Şeyhülislām Ebussuūd Efendi Fetvaları*, 89.

31. See Velkov, Kalitsin, and Radushev, *Osmanski izvori za islyamizatsionnite protsesi na Balkanite*, 294–95.

32. See ibid., 300.

33. On a detailed discussion of this issue, see Gradeva, "Apostasy in Rumeli," 45. Also see Akgündüz, *Osmanlı Devletinde şeyhülislāmlık*, 220–21.

34. According to Abu Hanifa (AH 80–148 / 699–767), the founder of the Hanefi school of law observed that in the Ottoman Empire, if a person was forcibly converted to Islam and later reverted to his former religion, he was not considered an apostate and could not be killed. See Friedmann, *Tolerance and Coercion in Islam*, 104.

35. See Vaporis, *Witnesses for Christ*, 88.

36. Their parallel in ancient martyrologies are the Roman judge/ruler and

the mob. For a typology of actors in the early martyrologies, see Delahaye, *Les passions des martyres*, 173–83.

37. See ibid., 178.

38. For discussion on how the local judges in Patmos and Kos, who had to deal with the issue of confiscation of the monastic properties at Mount Athos in 1568, simultaneously negotiated the need to keep the monks content and satisfy the requirements of Islamic law, see Eugenia Kermeli, "Central Administration versus Provincial Arbitrary Governance," 196–202.

39. For example, see the account of Michael Mavroeides' martyrdom in Vaporis, *Witnesses for Christ*, 42.

40. According to Ronald Jennings, the number of witnesses to a case (*şuhūdü'l-hāl*) was often enormous and included men who attended the hearing due to personal interest in the case, men who possessed information about the particular case, and men who happened to be in attendance at the court at the given time. See Jennings, "Limitations of the Judicial Powers," 162.

41. See Dimitrov, "Fetvi," 35. As Jennings demonstrates, imperial authority could easily have overshadowed the authority and initiative of the *kadı*. The *kadı*s were dismissed or appointed at the Porte's will. The Porte could order a reopening of the case, if complaints were received, but did not interfere in the actual legal procedure. The other rival of the *kadı* was the provincial authority, such as the governor of the given district (*sancak beğ*) or the governor of the entire province (*beğlerbeğ*). Whenever they stood unchecked by imperial authority, they could encroach on the legitimate sphere of the *kadı*. As the *kadı* had no police force or soldiers, he was much less powerful. See ibid., 151–55.

42. According to Gradeva, the Ottoman courts in Anatolia and the Balkans were open to all of its subjects excluding, in theory, only those of "suspicious morals." See Gradeva, "Apostasy in Rumeli," 51. As Jennings also shows, the numerous witnesses present at a trial could in fact account for the presence of the "crowd."

43. On this point, see also Rodrigue, "Difference and Tolerance in the Ottoman Empire."

44. See Ginio, "Childhood, Mental Capacity and Conversion," 110–11; and Minkov, *Conversion to Islam in the Balkans*, 166–92.

45. See Vaporis, *Witnesses for Christ*, 79–80.

46. See Ginio, "Childhood, Mental Capacity and Conversion," 99; and Friedmann, *Tolerance and Coercion in Islam*, 109–15.

47. Ginio, "Childhood, Mental Capacity and Conversion," 104.

48. For Onofrii's case, see Nihoritis, *Sveta Gora i bŭlgarskoto novomŭchenichestvo*, 84; and Vaporis, *Witnesses for Christ*, 307. For the Jewish boy's case, see Mina Rozen, "The Incident of the Converted Boy: A Chapter in the History of the Jews in Seventeenth-Century Jerusalem," *Cathedra* 14 (1980): 65–80 [in Hebrew], quoted in Ginio, "Childhood, Mental Capacity and Conversion," 98.

49. Ginio, "Childhood, Mental Capacity and Conversion," 105–6.

50. See also the vitae of Nicholas the Baker's Assistant (d. 1617) and John the Apprentice Tailor from Thasos (d. 1652) in Vaporis, *Witnesses for Christ*.

51. See, for example, the vitae of Theophanes the Monk (d. 1559), Nicholas the Baker's Assistant from Metsovo, Epeiros (d. 1617), Demetrios the Son of a Priest from Philadelphia (d. 1657), and Damaskenos the Monk from Constantinople (d. 1681), who was an orphan who converted to save himself from punishment, in ibid.

52. Vaporis, *Witnesses for Christ*, 185.

53. See Ginio, "Childhood, Mental Capacity and Conversion," 101; and Friedmann, *Tolerance and Coercion in Islam*, 109–15.

54. "*Question*: After *Zeyd-i zimmi* accepts Islam, are his minor children considered Muslim as well? *Answer*: Yes, they are." See Velkov, Kalitsin, and Radushev, *Osmanski izvori za islyamizatsionnite protsesi na Balkanite*, 294.

55. "*Question*: *Zeyd-i zimmi* accepted Islam. Hind, his minor daughter, also accepted Islam by way of her father. However, when she came of age, she did not confirm her loyalty to the Muslim religion and became an apostate. If in the meantime she dies, where should Hind be buried—in a Muslim or in an infidel graveyard? *Answer*: One like that cannot be buried. She should be thrown into some hole like a dog and be left there!" Also, "*Question*: If Hind who is a Christian accepts Islam and then, God forbid, becomes an apostate, what should be done with her? *Answer*: She should be imprisoned and forced into Islam." See ibid.

56. On the views of Abu Hanifa, see Friedmann, *Tolerance and Coercion in Islam*, 134–39. For a *fetva* by Abdürrahim Efendi stating that a minor son of a convert should not be killed but beaten for refusing to confirm his adherence to Islam when coming of age, see Velkov, Kalitsin, and Radushev, *Osmanski izvori za islyamizatsionnite protsesi na Balkanite*, 294.

57. For parallels with earlier Byzantine hagiographies, see Talbot, *Holy Women of Byzantium*.

58. See Walsh, "Women Martyrs," 72.

59. The most important studies are Baer, "Islamic Conversion Narratives of Women," 425–58; and Minkov, *Conversion to Islam in the Balkans*, 166–92.

60. See Vaporis, *Witnesses for Christ*, 161.

61. See ibid., 179, 230, 348.

62. See Velkov, Kalitsin, and Radushev, *Osmanski izvori za islyamizatsionnite protsesi na Balkanite*, 294.

63. See Baer, "Islamic Conversion Narratives of Women," 445–48.

64. See Minkov, *Conversion to Islam in the Balkans*, 170–71.

65. Rycaut, *Present State of the Greek and Armenian Churches*, 314–17.

66. David Nirenberg observes a similar situation in medieval Spain. See his *Communities of Violence*, 127–65.

67. For a detailed discussion of the laws governing interfaith marriages in Islam, see Friedmann, *Tolerance and Coercion in Islam*, 160–93.

68. Interestingly, other sources from the period suggest that there was a custom of marrying converts, both men and women, to other converts. It seems that this practice was tacitly condoned by the Ottoman authorities. See, for instance, anecdotes in Gerlach, *Türkiye Günlüğü*, vol. 1, 134; and Bennassar and Bennassar, *Les Chrétiens d'Allah*, 290–91.

69. It was very significant that according to Orthodox Christian custom, the bride had to bring a dowry, whereas Muslim grooms, in the case of regular marriage, usually paid a bride price for their wives. In the case of concubinage, the offspring of the relationship stayed with the father, whereas the woman usually returned to her father after the expiration of the contract. See Vryonis, "Experience of Christians," 203.

70. See Gradeva, "Orthodox Christians in the Kadi Courts," 37–69.

71. See ibid., 186–87. Also see Jennings, "Women in the Early Seventeenth-Century Ottoman Judicial Records," 53–114.

72. According to Orthodox Christian law, when a divorce took place, the husband did not have to return the premarital donation given to him by the prospective bride's family. In Islamic law, however, the wife had the right to full recovery of the premarital donation. See Pantazopoulos, *Church and Law*, 57; also Baer, "Islamic Conversion Narratives of Women," 434.

73. See Angelov, "Eschatological Views of Medieval Bulgaria," 46.

74. See Petkanova Toteva, *Damaskinite v bŭlgarskata literatura*, 118.

75. See Rothman, "Between Venice and Istanbul," 123–39, and *Trans-imperial Subjects*; and Vanzan, "In Search of Another Identity," 327–33.

76. For a detailed text of Maddalena's deposition, see Rothman, "Between Venice and Istanbul," 130–31.

77. See Vanzan, "In Search of Another Identity," 329.

78. See Bennassar and Bennassar, *Les Chrétiens d'Allah*, 294–96. For a detailed discussion of the implications a slave woman's conversion had for her relationship to her master, see Baer, "Islamic Conversion Narratives of Women," 444–48. Also see Toledano, "Slave Dealers," 53–68.

79. See Rothman, "Between Venice and Istanbul," 125–39, and "Narrating Conversion and Subjecthood."

80. See Dutton, "Conversion to Islam," 151–65.

81. See Bennassar and Bennassar, *Les Chrétiens d'Allah*, 48.

82. *Relazioni* and *dispacci* sent by the Venetian *bailo*s from the Ottoman Empire demonstrate that not all women from the Veneto-Ottoman contact zone were passive victims of circumstance in the process of conversion, as the high-profile case of Beatrice Michiel shows. This Venetian woman opted to escape to Istanbul and convert to Islam as a means to escape marriage with a Venetian *cittadino originario* (original citizen). See Dursteler, "Fatima Hatun née Beatrice Michiel," 355–82.

83. See Peirce, *Morality Tales*. Through a series of case studies Peirce shows how women could use the court strategically to seek the community's sympathy and exculpate themselves through an assertion of their own morality juxtaposed to the immorality of their antagonist.

84. Baer, "Islamic Conversion Narratives of Women," 431.

85. See Mahmood, "Anthropology."

86. Interestingly, this phenomenon has significant echoes in modern debates on conversion to Islam. New research on recent female converts to Islam in Europe suggests that many women embrace Islam precisely because it permits them "to stay at home and take care of children" instead of expecting them to

fulfill both female and male gender roles through raising children while having successful careers. From the perspective of some feminist critics, these female converts are therefore asking to be bound precisely by the ties that women should be attempting to overcome. See van Nieuwkerk, "Gender, Conversion, and Islam," 104.

87. See Minkov, *Conversion to Islam in the Balkans*, 171–72.

88. Ibid., 170–71.

89. On this issue, see also Veinstein, "Femmes d'Avlonya (Vlorë)," 207.

90. See *5 Numaralı Mühimme Defteri*, 14 Muharram AH 973.

91. On this issue, see Rothman, "Between Venice and Istanbul," 369–85, and "Mediating Converts, Commensurating Differences." See also Hardwick, "Looking for the Universal in the Local," book forum on Leslie Peirce's *Morality Tales* in *Journal of Women's History*, 181–85.

92. This competitive cultural interaction recently led one scholar to suggest that in the sixteenth century, Venetian religious and trading policies were "Ottomanized." See Husain, "Introduction: Approaching Islam," 17.

## Conclusion

1. Selim Deringil, "'There Is No Compulsion in Religion,'" and "'The Armenian Question.'"

2. Terzioğlu's current research project, "Age of the Kadızadelis," promises to significantly contribute to this objective.

3. For the background, see Şimşek, "Osmanlı cemiyetinde para vakıfları üzerinde münakaşalar."

4. See Imber, *Ebu's-su'ud*, 144.

5. Ibid. See also Buzov, "The Lawgiver and His Lawmakers," 252–58.

6. Gökbilgin, "Rüstem Paşa ve Hakkındaki İthamlar," 48.

7. For a discussion of the concept of *merdümzāde* and its significance in both Celalzade's work and in Selim I's bid for power, see Çıpa, "Centrality of the Periphery," 156–63.

8. See Celalzade Mustafa, *Selīmnāme*, 54b–55a, 48b, as cited in ibid., 160, 157.

9. See Necipoğlu, *The Age of Sinan*, 34–35, 48–49.

10. Terzioğlu, "Age of the Kadızadelis."

11. Tezcan, "The Ottoman *Mevali* as 'Lords of the Law.'" See also Zilfi, *The Politics of Piety*. As Tezcan argues, high-ranking Ottoman judges and professors of law came to constitute a privileged social group and attain a rank of nobility of sorts, passing the status to their sons.

12. See in particular Hagen, "Ottoman Understandings of the World"; and Terzioğlu, "Sufi and Dissident."

13. See Kerima Filan, "Sufije i kadizadelije u osmanskom Sarajevu."

14. Hagen, "Ottoman Understandings of the World," 246.

15. See Winter, *The Shiites of Lebanon*, 20.

16. Von Schlegell, "Sufism in the Ottoman Arab World," 100.

17. See Hathaway, "The Grand Vezir and the False Messiah."

18. See Flemming, "Die Vorwahhabitische Fitna im osmanischen Kairo, 1711"; and Peters, "Battered Dervishes of Bab Zuwayla."

19. See Greene, *A Shared World*, 25–28. For the fiscal reform in Syria, see Winter, *The Shiites of Lebanon*, 74–76.

20. Tezcan, "The Second Empire." Tezcan actually views the period between the 1580s and 1703 as the first half of the "Second Empire" era, during which the Ottoman dynasty still resisted acknowledging the power of all other political players (e.g., the *sipahīs*, the *a'yān* [notables], the janissaries, the *'ulemā*) who encroached on its absolute power and fought for a say in ruling the state. In the eighteenth century, Tezcan argues, the dynasty acknowledged these other players and balance in the government was achieved.

# Bibliography


## *Catalogues and Reference Works*

Blochet, Edgar, ed. *Catalogue des manuscrits turcs*. Bibliothèque National, Department des manuscrits. Paris: Bibliothèque National, 1932–33.

Boškov, Vančo, ed. *Katalog turskih rukopisa franjevačkih samostana u Bosni i Hercegovini*. Sarajevo: Orijentalni Institut, 1980.

Dobrača, Kasim, et al., eds. *Katalog arapskih, turskih i persijskih rukopisa: Gazi Husrev-Begova Biblioteka u Sarajevu*. 8 vols. Sarajevo: Starješinstvo Islamske vjerske zajednice za SR BiH, 1963–.

*Encyclopaedia of Islam*. 2nd ed. Edited by P. Bearman, Th. Bianquis, C. E. Bosworth, E. van Donzel, and W. P. Heinrichs. Brill, 2010. Brill Online. http://www.brillonline.nl/subscriber/entry?entry=islam_title_islam.

Flügel, Gustav, ed. *Die arabischen, persischen und türkischen Handschriften der Kaiserlich-Königlichen Hofbibliothik zu Wien*. 3 vols. Vienna: K. K. Hof- und staatsdruckerei, 1865–67.

Hasandedić, H., ed. *Katalog arapskih, turskih i persijskih rukopisa*. Mostar: Arhiv Hercergovine, 1977.

İslam Araştırma Merkezi (İSAM). Computerized Database of Manuscript Collections in Turkey. Üsküdar, Istanbul. http://ktp.isam.org.tr/.

Nametak, Fehim, and Salih Trako, eds. *Katalog arapskih, persijskih, turskih i bosanskih rukopisa iz zbirke Bosnjačkog Instituta*. Vol. 1. Zürich: Bosnjački institut, 1997.

Rieu, Charles, ed. *Catalogue of the Turkish Manuscripts in the British Museum*. London, 1888.

Schmidt, Jan, ed. *Catalogue of Turkish Manuscripts in the Library of Leiden University and Other Collections in the Netherlands*. Vol. 1. Leiden: Legatum Warnerianum, 2000.

## Unpublished Primary Sources

Atatürk Library (Istanbul Belediye Kütüphanesi), Istanbul

Hibetullah b. İbrahim. *Sa'ātnāme*. Yeni bağışlar, K. 311.

Başbakanlık Osmanlı Arşivi (BOA), Istanbul

Ali Emiri, Birinci Ahmed (BOA Ali Emiri), dosya 757.
Bab-ı Asafī Ru'us Kalemi (BOA A. RSK): 1453, 1459, 1473.
Kamil Kepeci, Ru'us Kalemi (BOA KK Ru'us): 230, 239, 246.
Mühimme Defterlerı (BOA MHM): 1, 2, 4, 7, 8, 10, 12, 13, 25.

British Library, London

Murad b. Abdullah. *Kitāb tesviyetü't-teveccüh ilā'l-hak*. MS Add. 19894.

Cebeci Provincial Public Library, Ankara

Küçük Abdal. *Otman Baba Vilāyetnāmesi*, MS 495.

Hartford Seminary Library, Connecticut

*Seyyid Ali Sultan Velāyetnāmesi* (John Birge's copy). Not catalogued.

İzzet Koyunoğlu City Museum Library, Konya

"Bir rahip ile bir pir-i Müslim arasında İsa A. S. hakkında." MS 10812.

National Library, Republic of Tunisia

*Papasnāme*, MS 1459, folios 39b–69a.

Oriental Collection, "SS Cyril and Methodius"
National Library, Sofia, Bulgaria

Hibetullah b. İbrahim. *Sa'ātnāme*. MSS 265, 499, 614, 1790, 2230, 2457.
Serrac b. Abdullah. *Mecmū'atü'l-letā'if*. MS 2461.
Yusuf b. Abi Abdüdeyyan (self-narrative of conversion with anti-Jewish polemic, entitled *Kepenekcizāde risālesi*). MS 2050/2.

Österreichische Nationalbibliothek, Vienna

*Eğer sorsalar . . .* (a catechism in a question-and-answer format). A.F. 437, 22a–28b.
*Mecmū'a*. MS Mixt 2006.
Mehmed b. Abdullah (self-narrative of conversion with anti-Christian polemic). N.F. 380.
Murad b. Abdullah. *Kitāb tesviyetü't-teveccüh ilā'l-hak*. A.F. 180.
*Papasnāme*. MS Mixt 689.

Süleymaniye Library, Istanbul

Hibetullah b. İbrahim. *Sa'ātnāme*. Fatih 2644.
———. *Sa'ātnāme*. Mesih Paşa 109.
———. *Sa'ātnāme*. Serez 1634.

———. *Sa'ātnāme.* Yazma bağışlar 3398.
———. *Sa'ātnāme.* Yazma bağışlar 3693.
İbrahim Müteferrika. *Risāle-i İslamīye.* Esad Efendi 1187.
*Mecmū'a.* Mihrişah Sultan 443.
Mehmed b. Abdullah (catalogued as Kadi Mahmud b. Hasan Atinalı). *Hazret-i Muhammed'e Dair Tevrat Zebur ve İncildeki Nasların Tahrifi Hakkında.* Ali Nihat Tarlan 144. 57b–60a.
*Menākıb-ı Mahmūd Paşa.* Aya Sofya 1940/2.
*Papasnāme.* Saliha Hatun 112/2.
Yusuf b. Abi Abdüddeyyan ("Yusuf b. Ebu Abdüdeyyan" in the Süleymaniye online catalogue, http://www.suleymaniye.gov.tr/Yordam.htm). *Reddu İtikadati Yahud* [*sic*]. Giresün Yazmaları 3610, 30b–45b.
———. *Reddu İtikadati Yahud* [*sic*]. Giresün Yazmaları 3574, 133b–164a.
———. *Risale fi'l-Hilafiyyat* (same text as previous entry but here titled differently; also the name of the author is given in the catalogue as Yusuf b. Ebi Abdüdeyyan). Giresün Yazmaları 102.

### Topkapı Sarayı Museum Library, Istanbul

*Kavānīn-i zümre-yi Bektāşiyān.* Revan MS 1319.

### Vahid Paşa Provincial Public Library, Kütahya

*Papasnāme.* MS 1545.

### Yapı Kredi Library, Istanbul

*Seyyid 'Ali Sultan Vilāyetnāmesi.*

## *Published Primary Sources*

*5 Numaralı Mühimme Defteri: Özet ve İndeks (973 / 1565–1566).* Ankara: T. C. Başbakanlık Devlet Arşivleri Genel Müdürlüğü, 1994.
*6 Numaralı Mühimme Defteri: Özet-Transkripsiyon ve İndeks (972 / 1564–1565).* Vol. 2. Ankara: T. C. Başbakanlık Devlet Arşivleri Genel Müdürlüğü, 1995.
*12 Numaralı Mühimme Defteri: Özet-Transkripsiyon ve İndeks (978–979 / 1570–1572).* Vol. 2. Ankara: T. C. Başbakanlık Devlet Arşivleri Genel Müdürlüğü, 1996.
Albèri, Eugenio. *Relazioni degli ambasciatori Veneti al senato.* Series 3. Vol. 2. Florence: Tipografia all'insegna di Clio, 1844.
Ali Ufki Bey. *Topkapı Sarayı'nda Yaşam.* Edited by S. Yerasimos and A. Berthier. Translated by A. Berktay. Istanbul: Kitap Yayınevi, 2002.
Aşıkpaşazade. *Osmanoğulları'nın Tarihi.* Edited by K. Yavuz and M. A. Yekta Saraç. Istanbul: K Kitapliği, 2003.
Babinger, Franz, ed. *Die Frühosmanischen Jahrbücher des Urudsch Nach den Handschriften zu Oxford und Cambridge erstmals herausgegeben und eingeleitet.* Hanover, 1925.

Balatsoukas, Sotirios, ed. *To neomartyrologio tou Ioannou Karyophilli.* Thessaloniki, 2003.
Birgili Muhammed Efendi. *Vasiyyet-name.* Edited by M. Duman. Istanbul: R Yayınları, 2000.
Birgivi Muhammed Efendi. *The Path of Muhammad* [*al-Tariqah al-Muhammadiyyah*] and *The Last Will and Testament* [*Vasiyyetname*] by Imam Birgivi. Foreword by Shaykh Abdul Mabud. Introduction by Vincent J. Cornell. Interpreted by Shaykh Tosun Bayrak al-Jerrahi an-Halveti. Bloomington, Ind.: World Wisdom, 2005.
Carayon, Auguste, ed. *Relations inédites des missions de la Compagnie de Jésus à Constantinople et dans le Levant au XVIIe siècle.* Paris, 1864.
*Christopher Angell, a Grecian Who Tasted of Many Stripes and Torments Inflicted by the Turkes for the Faith Which He Had in Christ Jesus.* 2nd ed. Oxford, 1618. *Early English Books* online. http://gateway.proquest.com.ezaccess.libraries.psu.edu/openurl?ctx_ver=Z39.88-2003&res_id=xri:eebo&rft_id=xri:eebo:image:176819.
Danişmend, İsmail Hami. "Gurbet-nāme-i Sultan Cem ibni Sultan Muhammed Hān." *Fatih ve Istanbul* 2, no. 12 (1954): 212–70.
Düzdağ, M. E., ed. *Barbaros Hayreddin Paşanın Hatiraları.* Vol. 1. Istanbul: Tercüman, n.d.
———. *Şeyhülislām Ebussuūd Efendi Fetvaları Işığında 16. Asır Türk Hayatı.* Istanbul: Enderun Kitabevi, 1983.
*Evliya Çelebi Seyahatnamesi.* Vol. 5. Edited by Y. Dağlı, S. A. Kahraman, and I. Sezgin. Istanbul: Yapı Kredi Yayınları, 2001.
Georgius de Hungaria. *Tractatus de moribus, condicionibus et nequicia turcorum. Traktat über die Sitten, die Lebensverhältnisse und die Arglist der Türken.* Edited and translated by Reinhard Klockow. Vienna: Böhlau, 1994.
Gerlach, Stefan. *Tagebuch der von zween Glorwüdrigsten Römischen Kaysern Maximiliano un Rudolpho . . . an die Ottomannische Pforte zu Constantinopel Abgefertigten.* Frankfurt am Main: Verlegung Johann David Zunners, 1674.
———. *Türkiye Günlüğü.* 2 vols. Edited by Kemal Beydili. Translated by Türkis Noyan. Istanbul: Kitap Yayınevi, 2006.
Gö'çek Abdal. *Vilayetname-i Şahi* [*Vilayetname-i Otman Baba*]. Edited by Şevki Koca. Istanbul: Can Yayınları, 2002.
Halil b. İsmail b. Şeyh Bedrüddin. *Simavna Kadısıoğlu Şeyh Bedreddin Manakıbı.* Edited by A. Gölpınarlı and I. Sungurbey. Istanbul: Eti Yayınevi, 1967.
Ibn al-ʿArabi. *The Meccan Revelations.* 2 vols. Edited and translated by Michel Chodkiewicz in collaboration with William C. Chittick and James W. Morris. New York: Pir Press, 2005.
Ivanova, K., ed. *Stara bŭlgarska literatura.* Vol. 4. Sofia: Bŭlgarski pisatel, 1986.
Kutbe'd-dīn İznikī. *Mukaddime (Giriş-İnceleme-Metin-Sözlük).* Edited and with an introduction by Kerime Üstunova. Bursa: Uludağ Üniversitesi, 2003.
Mihailović, Konstantin. *Memoirs of a Janissary.* Translation and commentary by B. Stolz and S. Soucek. Ann Arbor: University of Michigan Press, 1975.

Necatioğlu, H., ed. *Matbaacı İbrahim-i Müteferrika ve Risāle-yi İslāmiye (tenkidli metin).* Ankara: Elif Matbaacılık Tesisleri, 1982.
Nicolay, Nicolas de. *The Nauigations into Turkie.* Amsterdam: Da Capo Press, 1968. First published in London, 1585.
Noyan, Bedri, ed. *Demir Baba Vilayetnamesi.* Istanbul: Can Yayınları, 1976.
———. *Seyit Ali Sultan Velayetnamesi.* Ankara: Ayyıldız Yayınları, n.d.
Odorico, Paolo, ed. *Conseils et mémoires de Synadynos, prêtre de Serrès en Macédoine (XVIIe siècle).* Paris: Éditions Association "Pierre Belon," 1996.
Rycaut, Paul. *The Present State of the Greek and Armenian Churches.* London: Printed for John Starkely, 1687.
———. *The Present State of the Ottoman Empire.* London, 1670.
*Saltuk-nāme (of Ebu'l Hayr-i Rumi).* Edited by A. H. Akalın. 3 vols. Ankara: Milli Kültür Bakanlığı, 1987.
Schiltberger, Johannes. *The Bondage and Travels of Johann Schiltberger.* Translated by J. B. Telfer. London: Hakluyt Society, 1879.
Spandounes, Theodore. *On the Origins of the Ottoman Emperors.* Edited and translated by D. Nicol. Cambridge: Cambridge University Press, 1997.
*Tarih-i Edirne (Hikayet-i Beşir Çelebi).* Edited by İ. H. Ertaylan. Istanbul: Edebiyat Fakültesi Yayınları, 1960.
Yazıcızade, Ahmed Bican. *Envārü'l-āşıkīn.* 3 vols. Edited by A. Kahraman. Istanbul: Tercüman, n.d.
Yazıcızade, Mehmed. *Muhammediye.* Vol. 2. Edited by A. Çelebioğlu. Istanbul: Milli Eğitim Bakanlığı Yayınları, 1996.

## *Secondary Sources*

Abdul-Raof, Hussein. *Qur'an Translation: Discourse, Texture and Exegesis.* New York: Routledge, 2001.
Abel, A. "Un *hadit* sur la prise de Rome dans la tradition eschatologique de l'islam." *Arabica* 5, no. 1 (1958): 1–14.
Abisaab, Rula J. *Converting Persia: Religion and Power in the Safavid Empire.* London: I. B. Tauris, 2004.
Abou El Fadl, Khaled. *Speaking in God's Name: Islamic Law, Authority and Women.* Oxford: Oneworld, 2001.
———. "The Ugly Modern and the Modern Ugly: Reclaiming the Beautiful in Islam." In *Progressive Muslims: On Justice, Gender and Pluralism*, edited by Omid Safi, 33–77. Oxford: Oneworld, 2003.
Abou-El-Haj, Rifa'at. "The Narcissism of Mustafa II (1695–1703): Psychohistorical Study." *Studia Islamica* 40 (1974): 115–31.
———. "The Ottoman Nasihatname as a Discourse over "Morality." *Revue d'histoire maghrebine* 47–48 (1987): 15–30.
Ács, Pál. "Tarjumans Mahmud and Murad. Austrian and Hungarian Renegades as Sultan's Interpreters." In *Europa und die Türken in der Renaissance*, edited by W. Kühlmann and B. Guthmüller, 307–16. Tübingen: Frühe Neuzeit, 2000.
Addas, Claude. *Quest for the Red Sulphur: The Life of Ibn 'Arabī.* Cambridge: Islamic Texts Society, 1993.

Agoston, Gabor. "Information, Ideology, and Limits of Imperial Policy: Ottoman Grand Strategy in the Context of Ottoman-Habsburg Rivalry." In *Early Modern Ottomans: Remapping the Empire*, edited by Virginia Aksan and Daniel Goffman, 75–103. New York: Cambridge University Press, 2007.

Aguilera, Manuel Barrios, and Mercedes García-Arenal, eds. *Los plomos del Sacromonte: Invención y tesoro*. Valencia: Impremta Palacios, 2006.

Akgündüz, M. *Osmanlı Devletinde şeyhülislāmlık*. Istanbul: Beyan, 2002.

Aleksov, Bojan. "Adamant and Treacherous: Serbian Historians on Religious Conversion." In *Myths and Boundaries in South-Eastern Europe*, edited by P. Kolstø, 158–90. London: Hurst, 2005.

Alexander, Paul. *The Byzantine Apocalyptic Tradition*. Edited by Dorothy de F. Abrahamse. Berkeley: University of California Press, 1985.

Alouche, Adel. *The Origins and Development of the Ottoman-Safavid Conflict (906–962 / 1500–1555)*. Berlin: Klaus Schwarz Verlag, 1983.

Al-Tikriti, Nabil. "*Kalam* in the Service of the State: Apostasy and the Defining of Ottoman Islamic Identity." In *Legitimizing the Order: The Ottoman Rhetoric of State Power*, edited by H. Karateke and M. Reinkowski, 131–50. Leiden: Brill, 2005.

And, Metin. *Culture, Performance and Communication in Turkey*. Tokyo: ILCAA, 1987.

Angelov, Dimitar. "The Eschatological Views of Medieval Bulgaria as Reflected in the Canonical and Apocryphal Literature." *Bulgarian Historical Review* 4 (1990): 21–47.

Argyriou, Asterios. "Une 'Controverse entre un Chrétien et un Musulman' inédite." *Revue des sciences religieuses* 41 (1967): 237–45.

———. *Les exégèses grecques de l'apocalypse à l'epoque turque (1453–1821)*. Thessaloniki: Hetaireia Makedonikon Spoudon, 1982.

———. "La littérature grecque de polémique et d'apologétique à l'adresse de l'Islam au XVe siècle." *Byzantinische Forschungen* 12 (1987): 253–77.

———. "Pachomios Roussanos et l'Islam." *Revue d'histoire et de philosophie religieuses* 51 (1971): 143–64.

Argyriou, A., and G. Lagarrique. "Georges Amiroutzes et son dialogue sur la foi au Christ tenu avec le sultan des Turcs." *Byzantinische Forschungen* 11 (1987): 29–229.

Arpaguş, Hatice K. *Osmanlı Halkının Geleneksel Islam Anlayışı ve Kaynakları*. Istanbul: Çamlıca Yayınları, 2001.

Asad, Talal. "Comments on Conversion." In *Conversion to Modernities*, edited by Peter van der Veer, 263–73. New York: Routledge, 1995.

———. *Genealogies of Religion*. Baltimore: Johns Hopkins University Press, 1993.

———. *The Idea of an Anthropology of Islam*. Washington, D.C.: Georgetown University Center for Contemporary Arabic Studies, 1986.

Aubin, Jean. "L'avènement des Safavides reconsideré." *Moyen Orient et Océan Indien* 5 (1988): 1–130.

Aydın, Mehmet. *Müslümanların Hristiyanlara Karşı Yazdığı Reddiyeler ve Tartışma Konuları*. Ankara: Diyanet Vakfı, 1998.

Babayan, Kathryn. *Mystics, Monarchs, and Messiahs*. Cambridge, Mass.: Harvard University Press, 2002.

———. "Sufis, Dervishes and Mullas: The Controversy over Spiritual and Temporal Dominion in Seventeenth Century Iran." In *Safavid Persia: The History and Politics of an Islamic Society*, edited by C. Melville, 117–38. London: I. B. Tauris, 1996.

Babinger, Franz. "Der Pfortendolmetsch Murad und seine Schriften." In *Literaturdenkmäler aus Ungarns Türkenzeit*, edited by F. Babinger, R. Gragger, E. Mittwoch, and J. H. Mordtmann, 33–54. Berlin: W. de Gruyter, 1927.

Babinger, F., R. Gragger, E. Mittwoch, and J. H. Mordtmann, eds. *Literaturdenkmäler aus Ungarns Türkenzeit*. Ungarischen Institute an der Universität Berlin. Berlin: Walter de Gruyter, 1927.

Baer, Marc D. "The Great Fire of 1660 and the Islamization of Christian and Jewish Space in Istanbul." *International Journal of Middle Eastern Studies* 36 (2004): 158–81.

———. *Honored by the Glory of Islam: Conversion and Conquest in Ottoman Europe*. Oxford: Oxford University Press, 2008.

———. "Honored by the Glory of Islam: The Ottoman State, Non-Muslims, and Conversion to Islam in Late Seventeenth-Century Istanbul and Rumelia." Ph.D. diss., University of Chicago, 2001.

———. "Islamic Conversion Narratives of Women: Social Change and Gendered Religious Hierarchy in Early Modern Ottoman Istanbul." *Gender & History* 16, no. 2 (2004): 425–48.

Baer, Marc D., Ussama Makdisi, and Andrew Shryock. "CSSH Discussion: Tolerance and Conversion in the Ottoman Empire: A Conversation." *Comparative Studies in Society and History* 51, no. 4 (2009): 927–40.

Balázs, Mihály. *Early Transylvanian Antitrinitarianism (1566–1571)*. Baden-Baden: Éditions V. Koerner, 1996.

Balivet, Michel. "Aux origines de l'islamisation des Balkans ottomans." *Revue du monde musulman et de la Méditeranée* 66, no. 4 (1992): 11–20.

———. "Avant les *jeunes de langue*: Coup d'oeil sur l'apprentissage des langues turques en monde chrétien, de Byzance à Guillaume Postel (VIe–XVIe siècles)." In *Istanbul et les langues orientales. Actes du colloque organizé par l'IFEA et l'INALCO à l'occasion du bicentenaire de l'École des Langues Orientales, Istanbul, 29–31 mai 1995*, edited by F. Hitzel, 67–77. Paris: L'Harmattan, 1997.

———. *Byzantins et Ottomans*. Istanbul: ISIS, 1999.

———. "Byzantins judaïsants et juifs islamisés, des *kühan* (*kahin*) aux *chionai* (*chionis*)." In *Byzantins et Ottomans*, 151–80.

———. "Chrétiens secrets et martyrs christiques en Islam Turc: Quelques cas à travers les textes (XIIIe–XVIIe siècles)." In *Byzantins et Ottomans*, 231–54.

———. "Deux partisans de la fusion religieuse des chretiens et des musulmans au XVe siècle: Le turc Bedreddin de Samavna et le grec George de Trebizonde." *Byzantina* 10 (1980): 363–96.

———. *Islam mystique et revolution armée dans les Balkans ottomans: Vie du Cheikh Bedreddin le "Hallaj des Turcs" (1358/59–1416)*. Istanbul: ISIS, 1995.

———. "Miracles christiques et islamisation en chrétienté seldjoukide et ottomane entre le XIe et le XVe siècle." In *Byzantins et Ottomans*, 217–30.

———. "Mystiques musulmans dans les Balkans ottomans." In *Byzantins et Ottomans*, 255–70.

———. *Romanie byzantine et pays de Rûm turc: Histoire d'un espace d'imbrication gréco-turc*. Istanbul: ISIS, 1994.

———. "Le saint turc chez les infidèles: Thème hagiographique ou péripétie historique de l'islamisation du Sud-East Européen?" In *Byzantins et Ottomans*, 205–16.

Barkan, Ö. L. "Essai sur les donnés statistiques des registres de recensement dans l'Empire Ottoman au XVe et XVI siècles." *Journal of the Economic and Social History of the Orient* 1 (1957): 9–37.

———. "Osmanlı İmparatorluğunda bir İskan ve Kolonizasyon Metodu Olarak Sürgünler." *İstanbul Üniversitesi İktisat Fakültesi Mecmuası* 9, nos. 1–4 (1949–50): 524–69; 13, nos. 1–4 (1951–52): 56–78; 15, nos. 1–4 (1953–54): 209–37.

———. "Osmanlı İmparatoluğunda bir İskan ve Kolonizasyon Metodu Olarak Vakıflar ve Temlikler I: İstila devirlerinin kolonizatör dervişleri ve zaviyeleri." *Vakıflar Dergisi* 2 (1942): 279–386.

Barkey, Karen. *Bandits and Bureaucrats: The Ottoman Route to State Centralization*. Ithaca, N.Y.: Cornell University Press, 1994.

———. *Empire of Difference: The Ottomans in Comparative Perspective*. New York: Cambridge University Press, 2008.

Beldiceanu-Steinherr, Irène. "La conquête d'Adrianople par les Turcs: La pénétration turque en Thrace et la valeur des chroniques ottomans." *Travaux et memoires* 1 (1965): 439–61.

———. "En marge d'un acte concernant le pencik et les akinci." *Revue des études islamiques* 37 (1969): 21–47.

———. "Péchés, calamités et salut par le triomphe de l'Islam. Le discours apocalyptique relatif à l'Anatolie (fin XIIIe–fin XVe s.)." In *Les traditions apocalyptiques au tournant de la chute de Constantinople*, Actes da la Table Ronde d'Istanbul (April 13–14, 1996), edited by B. Lellouch and S. Yerasimos, 19–34. Istanbul: L'Institut Français d'Études Anatolienne, 1999.

———. "La Vita de Seyyid 'Ali Sultan et la conquête de la Thrace par les Turcs." In *Proceedings of the Twenty-seventh International Congress of Orientalists, Ann Arbor, Michigan, August 13, 1967*, 275–76. Wiesbaden, 1971.

Benbassa, Esther, and Aron Rodrigue. *Sephardi Jewry*. Berkeley: University of California Press, 2000.

Bennassar, B., and L. Bennassar. *Les Chrétiens d'Allah: L'histoire extraordinaire des renégats, XVIe–XVIIe siècles*. Paris: Perrin, 1989.

Berkes, Niyazi. "İlk Türk Matbaası Kurucusunun Dinī ve Fikrī Kimliği." *Belleten* 26, no. 104 (1962): 715–37.

Berkey, Jonathan P. *Popular Preaching and Religious Authority in the Medieval Islamic Near East*. Seattle: University of Washington Press, 2001.

———. *The Transmission of Knowledge in Medieval Cairo: A Social History of Islamic Education*. Princeton, N.J.: Princeton University Press, 1992.

Bernabé Pons, Luis F. *El evangelio de San Bernabe: Un evangelio islamico español*. Alicante: Universidad de Alicante, 1995.

Bilici, Faruk. "Les bibliothèques vakıfs à Istanbul au XVIe siècle, prémices de grandes bibliothèques publiques." *Revue des mondes musulmans et de la Méditerranée* (special issue entitled *Livres et lecture dans le monde ottoman*) 87–88 (1997): 39–60.

Biller, P., and A. Hudson, eds. *Heresy and Literacy, 1000–1300*. Cambridge: Cambridge University Press, 1994.

Birge, John. *The Bektashi Order of Dervishes*. London: Luzac, 1965.

Bobrinskoy, Boris. "Encounter of Traditions in Greece: St. Nicodemus of the Holy Mountain (1749–1809)." In *Christian Spirituality III: Post-Reformation and Modern*, edited by Louis Dupre and Don E. Saliers, 447–57. New York: Crossroads, 1989.

Bodian, Miriam. *Dying in the Law of Moses: Crypto-Jewish Martyrdom in the Iberian World*. Bloomington: Indiana University Press, 2007.

Bogdanović, Dimitrije. "Žitije Georgija Kratovca." *Zbornik istorije književnosti* 10 (1976): 203–67.

Bojanić-Lukač, Dušanka. "Un chant à la gloire de Mahomet en Serbe." *Wiener Zeitschrift für die Kunde des Morgenlandes* 76 (1986): 57–63.

———. "Sırp-Hırvat destanlarından üç yeniçeri destanı." In *Türkische Miszellen: Festschrift R. Anhegger*, edited by B. Flemming, J. Bacque-Grammont, M. Gökberg, and I. Ortaylı, 63–68. Istanbul: L'Institut Français d'Études Anatoliennes d'Istanbul, 1987.

———. "Sırp-Hırvat halk destanlarında Fatih'in oğlu Şehzade Mustafa." *I. Milletler arasi Türkoloji Kongresi (Istanbul, 15–20. X. 1973)* (1979): 344–49.

Börekci, Günhan. "İnkirāzın Eşiğinde Bir Hanedan: III. Mehmed, I. Ahmed, I. Mustafa ve 17. Yüzyıl Osmanlı Siyasī Krizi." *Dīvān* 14, no. 26 (2009): 45–96.

Bowen, John. *Muslims through Discourse: Religion and Ritual in Gayo Society*. Princeton, N.J.: Princeton University Press, 1993.

———. "What Is 'Universal' and 'Local' in Islam?" In "Communicating Multiple Identities in Muslim Communities." Special issue, *Ethos* 26, no. 2 (1998): 258–61.

Braude, Benjamin. "Foundation Myths of the *Millet* System." In *Christians and Jews in the Ottoman Empire: The Functioning of a Plural Society*, edited by Benjamin Braude and Bernard Lewis, vol. 1, 69–88. New York: Holmes and Meier, 1982.

Braude, Benjamin, and Bernard Lewis, eds. *Christians and Jews in the Ottoman Empire: The Functioning of a Plural Society*. Vol. 1. New York: Holmes and Meier, 1982.

Braudel, Fernand. *The Mediterranean and the Mediterranean World in the Age of Philip II*. Translated by Sian Reynolds. New York: Harper and Row, 1972.

Brummett, Palmira. "Visions of the Mediterranean: A Classification." *Journal of Medieval and Early Modern Studies* 37, no. 1 (2007): 9–55.

Bulliet, Richard. *The Case for Islamo-Christian Civilization*. New York: Columbia University Press, 2004.

———. "Conversion Stories in Early Islam." In *Conversion and Continuity: Indigenous Christian Communities in Islamic Lands, Eighth to Eighteenth Centuries*, edited by M. Gervers and R. J. Bikhazi, Papers in Medieval Studies 9, 123–33. Toronto: Pontifical Institute of Medieval Studies, 1990.

———. *Conversion to Islam in the Medieval Period: An Essay in Quantitative History*. Cambridge, Mass.: Harvard University Press, 1979.

———. "Process and Status in Conversion and Continuity." In *Conversion and Continuity*, 1–12.

Burchill, Christopher J. *The Heidelberg Antitrinitarians*. Baden-Baden: Éditions V. Koerner, 1989.

Burke, Peter. "Can We Speak of an 'Early Modern' World?" *International Institute for Asian Studies Newsletter* 43 (2007): 10.

———. "Early Modern Venice as a Center of Information and Communication." In *Venice Reconsidered*, edited by J. J. Jeffreys and D. Romano, 389–419. Baltimore: Johns Hopkins University Press, 2000.

Burton, Jonathan. *Traffic and Turning: Islam and English Drama, 1579–1624*. Newark: University of Delaware Press, 2005.

Buzov, Snježana. "The Lawgiver and His Lawmakers: The Role of Legal Discourse in the Change of Ottoman Imperial Culture." Ph.D. diss., University of Chicago, 2005.

Calasso, Giovanna. "Récits de conversions, zèle dévotionnel et instruction religieuse dans les biographes des 'gens de Basra' du *Kitab al-Tabaqat* d'Ibn Sa'd." In *Conversions islamiques: Identités religieuses en Islam méditeranéen*, edited by M. García-Arenal, 19–48. Paris: Maisonneuve et Larose, 2002.

Carlebach, Elisheva. *Divided Souls: Converts from Judaism in Germany, 1500–1750*. New Haven, Conn.: Yale University Press, 2001.

Casale, Giancarlo. "The Ethnic Composition of Ottoman Ship Crews and the 'Rumi' Challenge to Portuguese Identity." *Medieval Encounters* 13 (2007): 122–44.

———. *The Ottoman Age of Exploration*. New York: Oxford University Press, 2010.

Çetin, İsmet. *Türk edebiyatında Hazreti Ali cenknameleri*. Ankara: Kültür Bakanlığı, 1997.

Çetin, Osman. *Sicillere Göre Bursa'da İhtida Hareketleri ve Sosyal Sonuçları (1472–1909)*. Ankara: Türk Tarih Kurumu, 1994.

Chartier, Roger. *Forms and Meanings*. Philadelphia: University of Pennsylvania Press, 1995.

Chelkowski, Peter. "Ta'ziyeh: Indigenous Avant-Garde Theater of Iran." In *Ta'ziyeh: Ritual and Drama in Iran*, edited by Peter J. Chelkowski, 1–12. New York: New York University Press, 1979.

Chittick, W. C. "Disclosure of the Intervening Image: Ibn 'Arabi on Death." *Discourse* 24, no. 1 (2002): 51–62.

———. *Ibn 'Arabi: Heir to the Prophets*. Oxford: Oneworld, 2005.

———. "On the Cosmology of *Dhikr*." In *Paths to the Heart: Sufism and the Christian East*, edited by J. Cutsinger, 48–63. Bloomington, Ind.: World Wisdom, 2002.

———. *Sufism: A Short Introduction.* Oxford: Oneworld, 2000.

Chodkiewicz, Michel. "The Diffusion of Ibn 'Arabi's Doctrine." *Journal of the Muhyiddin Ibn 'Arabi Society* 9 (1991). http://www.ibnarabisociety.org/articles/diffusion.html.

———. "La reception de la doctrine d'Ibn 'Arabi dans le monde ottoman." In *Sufism and Sufis in Ottoman Society*, edited by Ahmet Y. Ocak, 97–120. Ankara: Türk Tarih Kurumu, 2005.

———. *Seal of the Saints: Prophethood and Sainthood in the Doctrine of Ibn 'Arabi.* Cambridge: Islamic Texts Society, 1993.

Cici, Recep. *Osmanlı Dönemi İslam Hukuku Çalışmaları (kuruluştan Fatih devrinin sonuna kadar).* Bursa: Arasta Yayınları, 2001.

Çıpa, Erdem H. "The Centrality of the Periphery: The Rise of Selīm I, 1487–1512." Ph.D. diss., Harvard University, 2007.

Clark, Jane. "Early Best-Sellers in the Akbarian Tradition." *Journal of the Muhyiddin Ibn 'Arabi Society* 33 (2003). http://www.ibnarabisociety.org/articlespdf/bestsellers.pdf.

Clayer, Natalie. *Mystiques, état et société: Les Halvetis dans l'aire balkanique de la fin du XVe siècle à nos jours.* Leiden: Brill, 1994.

Clucas, Lowell M. "Eschatological Theory in Byzantine Hesychasm: A Parallel to Joachim da Fiore." *Byzantinische Zeitschrift* 70, no. 2 (1977): 324–46.

Coleman, David. *Creating Christian Granada.* Ithaca, N.Y.: Cornell University Press, 2003.

Colpe, Carsten. "The Phenomenon of Syncretism and the Impact of Islam." In *Syncretistic Religious Communities in the Near East*, edited by K. Kehl-Bodrogi, B. Kellner-Heinkele, and A. Otter-Beaujean, 35–48. Leiden: Brill, 1997.

Comaroff, Jean, and John Comaroff. *Of Revelation and Revolution.* Vol. 1. Chicago: University of Chicago Press, 1991.

Constantelos, D. J. "The 'Neomartyrs' as Evidence for Methods and Motives Leading to Conversion and Martyrdom in the Ottoman Empire." *Greek Orthodox Theological Review* 23 (1978): 216–34.

Coope, Jessica A. *The Martyrs of Córdoba: Community and Family Conflict in an Age of Mass Conversion.* Lincoln: University of Nebraska Press, 1995.

Craciun, Maria, Ovidiu Ghitta, and Graeme Murdock, eds. *Confessional Identity in East Central Europe.* Aldershot, U.K.: Ashgate, 2002.

Cummings, W. "Scripting Islamization: Arabic Texts in Early Modern Makassar." *Ethnohistory* 48, no. 4 (2001): 559–86.

Dán, Róbert, and Antal Pirnát, eds. *Antitrinitarianism in the Second Half of the 16th Century.* Budapest: Akadémiai Kiadó, 1982.

Darling, Linda. "Contested Territory: Ottoman Holy War in Comparative Context." *Studia Islamica* 91 (2000): 133–63.

Davey, Colin. "Metrophanes Kritopoulos and His Studies at Balliol College from 1617 to 1622." In *Anglicanism and Orthodoxy 300 Years after the "Greek College" in Oxford*, edited by Peter M. Doll, 57–77. Oxford: Peter Lang, 2006.

Davis, James C. *Pursuit of Power: Venetian Ambassadors' Reports on Turkey,*

*France, and Spain in the Age of Philip II, 1560–1600*. New York: Harper Torchbooks, 1970.

Davis, Natalie Z. *Trickster Travels: A Sixteenth-Century Muslim between Worlds*. New York: Hill and Wang, 2006.

De Boer, Wietse. *The Conquest of the Soul: Confession, Discipline, and Public Order in Counter-Reformation Milan*. Leiden: Brill, 2001.

———. "Social Discipline in Italy: Peregrinations of a Historical Paradigm." *Archiv für Reformationsgeschichte* 94 (2003): 294–307.

Dedes, Yorgos. *Battalnāme: Part I: Introduction and English Translation*. The Sources of Oriental Languages and Literatures 33. Cambridge, Mass.: Harvard University Press, 1996.

Degenhardt, Jane H. "Catholic Martyrdom in Dekker and Messinger's *The Virgin Martir* and the Early Modern Threat of 'Turning Turk.'" *English Literary History* 73 (2006): 83–117.

De Groot, Alexander H. *The Ottoman Empire and the Dutch Republic: A History of the Earliest Diplomatic Relations, 1610–1630*. Leiden: Nederlands Historisch-Archaeologisch Institut, 1978.

Delahaye, Hypolite. *Les passions des martyres et les genres littéraires*. Brussels: Société des Bollandistes, 1966.

Delilbaşı, Melek. "Christian *Sipahis* in the Tırhala Taxation Registers (15th and 16th Centuries)." In *Provincial Elites in the Ottoman Empire*, edited by A. Anatastasopoulos, 87–114. Herakleion: Crete University Press, 2005.

Demetriades, V. "The Tomb of *Gazi* Evrenos Bey at Yenitsa and Its Inscription." *Bulletin of the School of Oriental and African Studies* 39 (1976): 328–32.

Deringil, Selim. "'The Armenian Question Is Finally Closed': Mass Conversions of Armenians in Anatolia during the Hamidian Massacres of 1895–1897." *Comparative Studies in Society and History* 51, no. 3 (2009): 344–71.

———. "'There Is No Compulsion in Religion': On Conversion and Apostasy in the Late Ottoman Empire: 1839–1856." *Comparative Studies in Society and History* 42, no. 3 (2000): 547–75.

Deventer, Jörg. "'Confessionalization': A Useful Theoretical Concept for the Study of Religion, Politics, and Society in Early Modern East-Central Europe?" *European Review of History* 11, no. 3 (2004): 403–25.

DeWeese, Devin. *Islamization and Native Religion in the Golden Horde: Baba Tükles and Conversion to Islam in Historical and Epic Tradition*. University Park: Pennsylvania State University Press, 1994.

Dimitrov, Strashimir. "Fetvi za izkorenyavane na bulgarskata mirogledna sistema sred pomohamedanchenite bulgari." *Vekove* 2 (1987): 27–39.

———. "Some Aspects of Ethnic Development, Islamisation and Assimilation in Bulgarian Lands in the 15th–17th Centuries." In *Aspects of the Development of the Bulgarian Nation*, edited by G. Yanakov. Sofia: Bulgarian Academy of Sciences, 1991.

Dimock, Matthew. *New Turkes: Dramatizing Islam and the Ottomans in Early Modern England*. Hampshire, U.K.: Ashgate, 2005.

Dionisotti, Carlo. "La guerra d'oriente nella letteratura veneziana del cinquecento." In *Venezia e l'Oriente fra tardo medioevo e rinascimento*, edited by Agostino Pertusi, 471–93. Florence: Sansoni, 1966.

Dressler, Markus. "Inventing Orthodoxy: Competing Claims for Authority and Legitimacy in the Ottoman Safavid Conflict." In *Legitimizing the Order: The Ottoman Rhetoric of State Power*, edited by H. Karateke and M. Reinkowski, 151–76. Leiden: Brill, 2005.

Droogers, A. "Syncretism: The Problem of Definition, the Definition of the Problem." In *Dialogue and Syncretism: An Interdisciplinary Approach*, edited by J. Gort, H. Vroom, R. Fernhout, and A. Wessels, 7–24. Grand Rapids, Mich.: Eerdsmans Publishing, 1989.

Dursteler, Eric. "Fatima Hatun née Beatrice Michiel: Renegade Women in the Early Modern Mediterranean." *The Medieval History Journal* 12, no. 2 (2009): 355–82.

———. *Venetians in Constantinople: Nation, Identity and Coexistence in the Early Modern Mediterranean*. Baltimore: Johns Hopkins University Press, 2006.

Dutton, Yasin. "Conversion to Islam: The Qur'anic Paradigm." In *Religious Conversion: Contemporary Practices and Controversies*, edited by C. Lamb and M. D. Bryant, 151–65. London: Cassell, 1999.

Eaton, Richard. "Approaches to the Study of Conversion to Islam in India." In *Approaches to Islam in Religious Studies*, edited by R. C. Martin, 106–23. Tucson: University of Arizona Press, 1985.

Eberhard, Elke. *Osmanische Polemik gegen die Safawiden im 16. Jahrhundert nach arabischen Handschriften*. Freiburg im Breisgau: Klaus Schwarz Verlag, 1970.

El-Cheikh, Nadia, and C. E. Bosworth. "Rūm." In *Encyclopaedia of Islam*, 2nd ed., edited by P. Bearman, Th. Bianquis, C. E. Bosworth, E. van Donzel, and W. P. Heinrichs. Brill, 2010. Brill Online. http://www.brillonline.nl/subscriber/entry?entry=islam_COM-0939.

Eliou, F. "Pothos martyriou: Apo tis vevaiotetes sten amfisvetese tou M. Gedeon. Symvole sten istoria ton neomartyron." *Istorika* 12, no. 23 (1995): 267–84.

El-Leithy, Tamer. "Coptic Culture and Conversion in Medieval Cairo, 1293–1524." Ph.D. diss., Princeton University, 2005.

Elmer, P., ed. *Challenges to Authority*. New Haven, Conn.: Yale University Press, 2000.

Emecen, Feridun. "Gaza'ya Dair: XIV. Yüzyıl Kaynakları Arasında Bir Gezinti." In *Prof. Hakkı Dursun Yıldız Armağanı*, 191–97. Istanbul: Türk Tarih Kurumu, 1995.

Emiralioğlu, M. Pınar. "Cognizance of the Ottoman World: Visual and Textual Representations in the Sixteenth-Century Ottoman Empire (1514–1596)." Vol. 1. Ph.D. diss., University of Chicago, 2006.

Epalza, Mikel de. *Fray Anselm Turmeda ('Abdallāh al-Taryumān) y su polémica islamo-cristiana*. 3rd ed. Madrid: Hyperion, 1994.

———. "Le milieu hispano-moresque de l'évangile islamisant de Barnabé (XVIe–XVIIe siècle)." *Islamochristiana* 8 (1982): 159–83.

Faroqhi, Suraiya. "Bektashis: Report on Current Research." In *Bektachiyya*, edited by Alexandre Popovic and Gilles Veinstein, 9–28. Istanbul: ISIS, 1995.

———. "Conflict, Accommodation and Long-Term Survival: The Bektashi Order and the Ottoman State (Sixteenth–Seventeenth Centuries)." In *Bektachiyya*, 171–84.

———. "An Orthodox Woman Saint in an Ottoman Document." In *Syncrétismes et hérésies dans l'Orient seldjoukide et ottoman des XIIIe–XVIIIe siècles*, edited by Gilles Veinstein, 383–94. Leuven: Peeters, 2005.

———. *Subjects of the Sultan: Culture and Daily Life in the Ottoman Empire.* London: I. B. Tauris, 2000.

Farr, James R. "Confessionalization and Social Discipline in France, 1530–1685." *Archiv für Reformationsgeschichte* 94 (2003): 276–93.

Fedalto, Giorgio. *Ricerche storiche sulla posizione giuridica ed ecclesiastica dei Greci a Venezia nei secoli XV e XVI.* Florence: Olschki, 1967.

Fetvacı, Emine. "Vezirs to Eunuchs: Transitions in Ottoman Manuscript Patronage, 1566–1617." Ph.D. diss., Harvard University, 2005.

Fierro, Maribel. "Al-Asfar." *Studia Islamica* 77 (1993): 169–81.

Filan, Kerima. "Sufije i kadizadelije u osmanskom Sarajevu." *Anali Gazi Husrev-begove Biblioteke* 29–30 (2009): 163–86.

Filipović, Nedim. "A Contribution to the Problem of Islamization in the Balkan under the Ottoman Rule." In *Ottoman Rule in Middle Europe and the Balkan in the 16th and 17th Centuries.* Paper presented at the 9th Joint Conference of the Czechoslovak-Yugoslav Historical Committee, 305–58, Prague, 1978.

Finkel, Caroline. *Osman's Dream.* London: John Murray, 2005.

Finlay, Robert. "Al servizio del Sultano: Venezia, i Turchi e il mondo cristiano, 1523–1538." In *Renovatio Urbis: Venezia nell'età di Andrea Gritti*, edited by Manfredo Tafuri, 78–118. Rome: Officina Edizioni, 1984.

———. "Prophecy and Politics in Istanbul: Charles V, Sultan Süleyman, and the Habsburg Embassy of 1533–1534." *Journal of Early Modern History* 2, no. 1 (1998): 1–31.

Fischer-Galati, Stephen A. *Ottoman Imperialism and German Protestantism 1521–1555.* New York: Octagon Books, 1972.

Fish, Stanley. *Is There a Text in This Class?: The Authority of Interpretative Communities.* Boston: Harvard University Press, 1980.

Fisher, Alan. "Studies in Ottoman Slavery and the Slave Trade II: Manumission." *Journal of Turkish Studies* 4 (1980): 49–56.

Fisher, C. G., and A. Fischer. "Topkapı Sarayı in the Mid-seventeenth Century: Bobovi's Description." *Archivum Ottomanicum* 10 (1985–87): 5–81.

Fleischer, Cornell H. *Bureaucrat and Intellectual in the Ottoman Empire: The Historian Mustafa Ali (1541–1600).* Princeton, N.J.: Princeton University Press, 1986.

———. "From Şeyhzade Korkud to Mustafa Ali: Cultural Origins of the Ottoman *nasihatname*." In *Proceedings of the IIIrd Congress of the Social and Economic History of Turkey (Princeton, 24–26 August 1983)*, edited by H. Lowry and R. Hattox, 67–77. Istanbul: ISIS Press, 1990.

———. "Imperialism and the Apocalypse, 1450–1550." *Annales*, forthcoming.

———. "The Lawgiver as Messiah: The Making of the Imperial Image in the Reign of Süleyman." In *Soliman le Magnifique et son temps: Actes du Colloque de Paris, Galeries Nationales du Grand Palais, 7–10 mars 1990*, edited by G. Veinstein, 159–77. Paris: La Documentation Française, 1992.

———. "Royal Authority, Dynastic Cyclism, and 'Ibn Khaldūnism' in Seventeenth Century Ottoman Letters." *Journal of Asian and African Studies* 18 (1983): 198–220.

———. "Seer to the Sultan: Haydar-i Remmal and Sultan Süleyman." In *Cultural Horizons: Festschrift in Honor of Talat Halman*, edited by J. L. Warner, 290–99. Syracuse, N.Y.: Syracuse University Press, 2001.

———. "Shadows of Shadows: Prophecy and Politics in 1530s Istanbul." *International Journal of Turkish Studies* 13, nos. 1–2 (2007): 51–62.

Fleming, Kate E. "Two Rabbinic Views of Ottoman Mediterranean Ascendancy: The *Chronica de los reyes otomanos* and *Seder elijahu zuta*." In *A Faithful Sea: The Religious Cultures of the Mediterranean, 1200–1700*, edited by Adnan Husain and K. E. Fleming, 99–120. Oxford: Oneworld, 2007.

Flemming, Barbara. "Aşikpaşazades Blick auf Frauen." In *Arts, Women and Scholars: Festschrift Hans Georg Majer*, edited by Sabine Prätor and Christoph Neumann, vol. 1, 69–96. Istanbul: Simurg, 2002.

———. "Sahib-kiran und Mahdi: Türkische Endzeiterwartungen im Ersten Jahrzehnt der Regierung Süleymans." In *Between the Danube and the Caucasus*, edited by Gy. Kara, 43–62. Budapest: Akademiai Kiado, 1987.

———. "Die Vorwahhabitische Fitna im osmanischen Kairo, 1711." In *İsmail Hakkı Uzunçarşılı'ya Armağan*, 55–65. Ankara: Türk Tarih Kurumu, 1976.

Fodor, Pál. "State and Society, Crisis and Reform, in 15th–17th Century Ottoman Mirror for Princes." *Acta Orientalia Academiae Scientiarum Hungaricae* 40, nos. 2–3 (1986): 217–40.

———. "The View of the Turk in Hungary: The Apocalyptic Tradition and the Red Apple in Ottoman-Hungarian Context." In *Les traditions apocalyptiques au tournant de la chute de Constantinople, Actes de la Table Ronde d'Istanbul (13–14, avril 1996)*, edited by B. Lellouch and S. Yerasimos, 99–131. Istanbul: L'Institut Français d'Études Anatolienne, 1999.

Folaron, Deborah. "Oral Narrating and Performing Traditions in the History of Modern Middle Eastern and Maghrebian Theatre and Drama." http://www.teatroestoria.it/Docs/Links/Anto/FOL-2002-01.htm.

Fotić, Aleksandar. *Sveta Gora i Hilandar u Osmanskom Carstvu, XV–XVII vek*. Belgrade: Balkanološki institut SANU, 2000.

Frazee, Charles A. *Catholics and Sultans: The Church and the Ottoman Empire, 1453–1923*. Cambridge: Cambridge University Press, 1983.

Fredricksen, Paula. "Paul and Augustine: Conversion Narratives, Orthodox Traditions, and the Retrospective Self." *Journal of Theological Studies* 37 (1986): 3–34.

Frend, W. H. C. *Martyrdom and Persecution in the Early Church*. Oxford: Blackwell, 1965.

Friedmann, Yohanan. *Tolerance and Coercion in Islam*. Cambridge: Cambridge University Press, 2003.

Gandev, Hristo. *Bulgarskata narodnost prez 15. vek*. Sofia: Nauka i izkustvo, 1972.

Gara, Eleni. "Neomartyr without a Message." *Archivum Ottomanicum* 23 (2005/2006): 155–76.

García-Arenal, Mercedes. "Dreams and Reason: Autobiographies of Converts in Religious Polemics." In *Conversions islamiques: Identités religieuses en Islam méditeranéen*, edited by Mercedes García-Arenal, 89–118. Paris: Maisonneuve et Larose, 2002.

García-Arenal, Mercedes, and Fernando Rodríguez Mediano. "Médico, traductor, inventor: Miguel de Luna, Cristiano Arábigo de Granada." *Crónica Nova* 32 (2006): 187–231.

García-Arenal, Mercedes, and Gerard Wiegers. *A Man of Three Worlds: Samuel Pallache, a Moroccan Jew in Catholic and Protestant Europe*. Baltimore: Johns Hopkins University Press, 2003.

Geertz, Clifford. *Islam Observed: Religious Development in Morocco and Indonesia*. Chicago: University of Chicago Press, 1971.

Gerber, Haim. *State, Society and Law in Islam*. New York: SUNY Press, 1994.

Gibbons, Herbert Adams. *The Foundation of the Ottoman Empire, 1300–1403*. Oxford: Clarendon, 1916.

Gilsenan, Michael. *Recognizing Islam: Religion and Society in the Modern Arab World*. New York: Pantheon Books, 1983.

Ginio, Eyal. "Childhood, Mental Capacity and Conversion to Islam in the Ottoman State." *Byzantine and Modern Greek Studies* 25 (2001): 90–119.

Ginzburg, Carlo. *The Cheese and the Worms: The Cosmos of a Sixteenth-Century Miller*. Translated by J. Tedeschi and A. Tedeschi. Baltimore: Johns Hopkins University Press, 1980.

Gjeorgiev, Dragi. "Islamisierung im makedonisch-albanisch Grenzgebiet in den ersten Jahrhunderten der osmanischen Herrschaft (15. und 16. Jahrhundert)." *Wiener Zeitschrift zur Geschichte der Neuzeit* 5, no. 2 (2005): 7–14.

Goffman, Daniel. *Izmir and the Levantine World, 1550–1650*. Seattle: University of Washington Press, 1990.

———. "Negotiating with the Renaissance State: The Ottoman Empire and the New Diplomacy." In *The Early Modern Ottomans*, edited by Virginia Aksan and Daniel Goffman, 61–74. Cambridge: Cambridge University Press, 2007.

———. *The Ottoman Empire and Early Modern Europe*. Cambridge: Cambridge University Press, 2002.

———. "Ottoman Millets in the Early Seventeenth Century." *New Perspectives on Turkey* 1 (1994): 135–58.

Gökbilgin, T. M. *XV–XVI. Asırlarda Edirne ve Paşa Livası (Vakıflar-Mülkler-Mukataalar)*. Istanbul: Üçler Basımevi, 1952.

———. *Rumeli'de Yürükler, Tatarlar ve Evlād-ı Fātihān*. Istanbul: Osman Yalçın Matbaası, 1957.

———. "Rüstem Paşa ve Hakkındaki İthamlar." *Tarih Dergisi* 8 (1955): 11–50.

Goldstone, Jack. "The Problem of the 'Early Modern' World." *Journal of the Economic and Social History of the Orient* 41, no. 3 (1998): 249–84.

Gölpınarlı, Abdülbaki. "Otman Baba Vilâyet-nāmesi." *Journal of Turkish Studies* 19 (1995): LV–CV.

Goody, Jack. *The Logic of Writing and the Organization of Society*. Cambridge: Cambridge University Press, 1986.

———. "Question of Interface in Turkey." *Revue du monde musulman et de la Méditerannée* (issue entitled "Oral et écrit dans le monde turco-ottoman") 75–76, nos. 1–2 (1995): 11–18.

Gradeva, Rossitsa. "Apostasy in Rumeli in the Middle of the Sixteenth Century." *Arab Historical Review for Ottoman Studies* 22 (2000): 29–74.

———. "Orthodox Christians in the Kadi Courts: The Practice of the Sofia Sheriat Court, Seventeenth Century." *Islamic Law and Society* 4 (1997): 37–69.

Graham, W. A. "Qur'an as Spoken Word: An Islamic Contribution to the Understanding of Scripture." In *Approaches to Islam in Religious Studies*, edited by R. C. Martin, 23–40. Tucson: University of Arizona Press, 1992.

Gramatikova, Nevena. "Isl'amski neortodoksalni techeniya v Bŭlgarskite zemi." In *Istoriya na M'usl'umanskata Kultura po Bŭlgarskite Zemi*, edited by Rossitsa Gradeva, 192–284. Sofia: IMIR, 2001.

———. "Zhitieto na Demir Baba i sazdavaneto na rukopisi ot M'usl'umanite ot heterodoksnite techenia na isl'ama v severoiztochna Bulgaria (izvor za kulturnata i religioznata im istoriya)." In *M'usl'umanskata Kultura po Bŭlgarskite Zemi*, edited by Rossitsa Gradeva and Svetlana Ivanova, 400–433. Sofia: IMIR, 1998.

Greene, Molly. *A Shared World: Christians and Muslims in the Early Modern Mediterranean*. Princeton, N.J.: Princeton University Press, 2000.

———. "Trading Identities: The Sixteenth-Century Greek Moment." In *A Faithful Sea: The Religious Cultures of the Mediterranean, 1200–1700*, edited by Adnan Husain and K. E. Fleming, 121–48. Oxford: Oneworld, 2007.

Gregory, Brad. *Salvation at Stake: Christian Martyrdom in Early Modern Europe*. Cambridge, Mass.: Harvard University Press, 1999.

Gross, Abraham. *Spirituality and Law: Courting Martyrdom in Christianity and Judaism*. Lanham, Md.: University Press of America, 2005.

Grubb, James. "When Myths Lose Power: Four Decades of Venetian Historiography." *Journal of Modern History* 58 (1986): 43–94.

Guenther, A. M. "The Christian Experience and Interpretation of the Early Muslim Conquest and Rule." *Islam and Christian-Muslim Relations* 10, no. 3 (1999): 363–78.

Hadjiantoniou, George. *Protestant Patriarch: The Life of Cyril Lucaris (1572–1638), the Patriarch of Constantinople*. Richmond, Va.: John Knox Press, 1961.

Hagen, Gottfried. "Ottoman Understandings of the World in the Seventeenth Century." Afterword in Robert Dankoff, *Evliya Çelebi: An Ottoman Mentality*, 207–48. Leiden: Brill, 2004.

Halasi-Kun, Tibor. "Gennadios' Turkish Confession of Faith." *Archivum Ottomanicum* 12 (1987–92): 5–7.

Hamilton, Alastair, Maurits H. van den Boogert, and Bart Westerweel, eds. *The Republic of Letters and the Levant*. Leiden: Brill, 2005.

Hardwick, Julie. "Looking for the Universal in the Local: Morality Tales from the Western End of the Mediterranean." *Journal of Women's History* 18, no. 1 (2006): 181–85.

Harrington, Joel F., and Helmut W. Smith. "Review: Confessionalization, Community, and State Building in Germany, 1555–1870." *The Journal of Modern History* 69, no. 1 (1997): 77–101.

Harris, W. V., ed. *Rethinking the Mediterranean.* Oxford: Oxford University Press, 2005.

Hartnup, Karen. *"On the Beliefs of the Greeks": Leo Allatios and Popular Orthodoxy.* Leiden: Brill, 2004.

Harvey, L. P. *Muslims in Spain, 1500–1614.* Chicago: University of Chicago Press, 2005.

Hasluck, Fredrick W. *Christianity and Islam under the Sultans.* Edited by M. Hasluck. 2 vols. Oxford: Oxford University Press, 1929.

Hathaway, Jane. "The *Evlād-i 'Arab* ('Sons of the Arabs') in Ottoman Egypt: A Rereading." In *Frontiers of Ottoman Studies*, edited by C. Imber and K. Kiyotaki, vol. 1, 203–16. London: I. B. Tauris, 2005.

———. "The Grand Vezir and the False Messiah: The Sabbatai Sevi Controversy and the Ottoman Reform in Egypt." *Journal of the American Oriental Society* 117, no. 4 (1997): 665–71.

Hayden, Robert. "Antagonistic Tolerance: Competitive Sharing of Religious Sites in South Asia and the Balkans." *Current Anthropology* 43, no. 2 (2002): 205–19.

Hazai, György. "Vorstudien zur Anatolisch-Türkischen Version des *Tezkaratu l-awliya* von Fariduddin 'Attar." *Archivum Ottomanicum* 20 (2002): 269–333.

Headley, John M. "Rhetoric and Reality: Messianic, Humanist, and Civilian Themes in the Imperial Ethos of Gattinara." In *Prophetic Rome in the High Renaissance Period*, edited by Marjorie Reeves, 241–70. Oxford: Clarendon Press, 1992.

Headley, Stephen C. *Durga's Mosque: Cosmology, Conversion and Community in Central Javanese Islam.* Singapore: Institute of Southeast Asian Studies, 2004.

Heffening, W. "Murtadd." In *Encyclopaedia of Islam*, 2nd ed., edited by P. Bearman, Th. Bianquis, C. E. Bosworth, E. van Donzel, and W. P. Heinrichs. Brill, 2010. Brill Online. http://www.brillonline.nl/subscriber/entry?entry=islam_SIM-5554.

Henrich, Sarah, and James L. Boyce. "Martin Luther: Translations of Two Prefaces on Islam." *Word & World* 16, no. 2 (1996): 250–66.

Hess, Andrew C. *The Forgotten Frontier: A History of the Sixteenth-Century Ibero-African Frontier.* Chicago: University of Chicago Press, 1978.

———. "The Moriscos: An Ottoman Fifth Column in Sixteenth-Century Spain." *American Historical Review* 74, no. 1 (1968): 1–25.

Heyd, Uriel. *Studies in Old Ottoman Criminal Law.* Oxford: Clarendon Press, 1973.

Hickman, William. "The Taking of Aydos Castle: Further Considerations on a Chapter from Aşikpaşazade." *Journal of the American Oriental Society* 99, no. 3 (1979): 399–407.

Holbrook, Victoria. "Ibn 'Arabī and Ottoman Dervish Traditions: The Melami Supra-Order (Part One)." *Journal of the Muhyiddin Ibn 'Arabi Society* 9 (1991). http://www.ibnarabisociety.org/articles/melami1.html.

Horden, Peregrine, and Nicholas Purcell. *The Corrupting Sea: A Study of the Mediterranean History*. Oxford: Blackwell, 2000.

Howard, Douglas. "Genre and Myth in the Ottoman Advice for Kings Literature." In *Early Modern Ottomans*, edited by V. Aksan and D. Goffman, 137–66. Cambridge: Cambridge University Press, 2007.

———. "Ottoman Historiography and the Literature of 'Decline' of the Sixteenth and Seventeenth Centuries." *Journal of Asian History* 22 (1988): 52–77.

Hsia, Ronnie Po-Chia. "Social Discipline and Catholicism in Europe of the Sixteenth and Seventeenth Centuries." In *Chiesa cattolica e mondo moderno. Scritti in onore di Paolo Prodi*, edited by A. Prosperi, P. Schiera, and G. Zarri, 167–80. Bologna: Il Mulino, 2007.

———. *Social Discipline in the Reformation: Central Europe 1550–1750*. New York: Routledge, 1989.

Husain, Adnan A. "Conversion to History: Negating Exile and Messianism in al-Sama'wal al-Maghribī's Polemic against Judaism." *Medieval Encounters* 8, no. 1 (2002): 3–34.

———. "Introduction: Approaching Islam and the Religious Cultures of Medieval and Early Modern Mediterranean." In *A Faithful Sea: The Religious Cultures of the Mediterranean, 1200–1700*, edited by Adnan Husain and K. E. Fleming, 1–26. Oxford: Oneworld, 2007.

İhsanoğlu, Ekmeleddin. "Ottoman Educational and Scholarly-Scientific Institutions." In *History of the Ottoman State*, edited by E. İhsanoğlu, vol. 2, 371–74. Istanbul: IRCICA, 2002.

Imber, Colin. *Ebu's-su'ud: The Islamic Legal Tradition*. Stanford: Stanford University Press, 1997.

———. "Guillaume Postel on Temporary Marriage." In *Frauen, Bilder und Gelehrte: Festschrift Hans Georg Majer*, edited by S. Prätor, vol. 1, 179–83. Istanbul: Simurg, 2002.

———. "A Note on 'Christian' Preachers in the Ottoman Empire." *Osmanlı Araştırmaları* 10 (1990): 59–67.

———. *The Ottoman Empire, 1300–1650: The Structure of Power*. New York: Palgrave Macmillan, 2002.

———. "The Persecution of the Ottoman Shī'ites according to the *Mühimme Defterleri*, 1565–1585." *Der Islam* 56, no. 2 (1979): 245–73.

———. "What Does *ghazi* Actually Mean?" In *The Balance of Truth: Essays in Honour of Professor Geoffrey Lewis*, edited by C. Balım-Harding and C. Imber, 165–78. Istanbul: ISIS, 2000.

İnalcık, Halil. "A Case Study in Renaissance Diplomacy: The Agreement between Innocent VIII and Bayezid II on Djem Sultan." In *Ottoman Diplomacy: Conventional or Unconventional?* edited by A. Nuri Yurdusev, 209–33. New York: Palgrave Macmillan, 2003.

———. "Dervish and a Sultan: An Analysis of the Otman Baba *Vilāyetnāmesi*."

In *The Middle East and the Balkans under the Ottoman Rule*, 19–36. Bloomington: Indiana University Press, 1993.

———. *Hicri 835 Tarihli Suret-i Defter-i Sanacak-i Arvanid*. Ankara: Türk Tarih Kurumu, 1954.

———. "Islam in the Ottoman Empire." *Cultura Turcica* 5–7 (1968–70): 19–29.

———. "Military and Fiscal Transformation in the Ottoman Empire, 1600–1700." *Archivum Ottomanicum* 6 (1980): 283–337.

———. "Osmanlı İdare, Sosyal ve Ekonomik Tarihiyle İlgili Belgeler: Bursa Kadı Sicillerinden Seçmeler." *Belgeler* 10, no. 14 (1980–81): 1–91; 13, no. 17 (1988): 1–41.

———. "Ottoman Methods of Conquest." *Studia Islamica* 2 (1954): 103–29.

———. "The Policy of Mehmed II toward the Greek Population of Istanbul and the Byzantine Buildings of the City." *Dumbarton Oaks Papers* 23 (1969–70): 229–49.

———. "Rūmī." In *Encyclopaedia of Islam*, 2nd ed., edited by P. Bearman, Th. Bianquis, C. E. Bosworth, E. van Donzel, and W. P. Heinrichs. Brill, 2010. Brill Online. http://www.brillonline.nl/subscriber/entry?entry=islam_SIM-6336.

———. "The Status of the Greek Orthodox Patriarch under the Ottomans." *Turcica* 21–23 (1991): 407–36.

———. "Stefan Duşan'dan Osmanlı İmparatorluğuna: XV. Asırda Rumeli'de hiristiyan sipahiler ve menşeleri." In *Fatih Devri Uzerinde tetkikler ve Vesikalar*, 137–84. Ankara: Türk Tarih Kurmu, 1954.

———. "The Yürüks: Their Origins, Expansion and Economic Role." In *The Middle East and the Balkans under the Ottoman Empire: Essays on Economy and Society*. Bloomington: Indiana University Press, 1993.

İnalcık, H., and M. Oğuz. *Gazavāt-ı Sultān Murād b. Mehemmed Hān*. Ankara: Türk Tarih Kurumu, 1989.

Isom-Verhaaren, Christine. "An Ottoman Report about Martin Luther and the Emperor: New Evidence of the Ottoman Interest in the Protestant Challenge to the Power of Charles V." *Turcica* 28 (1996): 299–318.

Israel, Jonathan. "The Decline of Spain: A Historical Myth?" *Past and Present* 91, no. 1 (1981): 170–80.

Itzkowitz, Norman. *Ottoman Empire and the Islamic Tradition*. Chicago: University of Chicago Press, 1972.

Jacobs, Martin. "Exposed to All the Currents of the Mediterranean: A Sixteenth-Century Venetian Rabbi on Muslim History." *Association for Jewish Studies Review* 29, no. 1 (2005): 33–60.

———. *Islamische Geschichte in jüdischen Chroniken*. Tübingen: Mohr Siebeck, 2004.

Jennings, Ronald C. *Christians and Muslims in the Ottoman Cyprus, 1570–1640*. New York: New York University Press, 1993.

———. "Limitations of the Judicial Powers of the Kadi in 17th C. Ottoman Kayseri." *Studia Islamica* 50 (1979): 151–84.

———. "Some Thoughts on the Gazi-Thesis." *Wiener Zeitschrift für die Kunde des Morgenlandes* 76 (1986): 151–61.

———. "Women in the Early Seventeenth-Century Ottoman Judicial Records:

The Sharia Court of Anatolian Kayseri." *Journal of the Economic and Social History of the Orient* 18 (1975): 53–114.

Kafadar, Cemal. *Between Two Worlds*. Berkeley: University of California Press, 1995.

———. "Mütereddit bir mutasavvıf: Üsküp'lü Asiye Hatun'un Rüya Defteri, 1641–43." *Topkapı Sarayı Müzesi Yıllık* 5 (1992): 168–222.

———. "The Myth of the Golden Age: Ottoman Historical Consciousness in the Post-Süleymanic Era." In *Süleyman the Second and His Time*, edited by H. İnalcık and Cemal Kafadar, 37–48. Istanbul: ISIS Press, 1993.

———. "The Question of Ottoman Decline." *Harvard Middle Eastern and Islamic Review* 4 (1997–98): 30–75.

———. "A Rome of One's Own: Reflections on Cultural Geography and Identity in the Lands of Rum." In "History and Ideology: Architectural Heritage of the 'Lands of Rum,'" edited by S. Bozdoğan and G. Necipoğlu. Special issue, *Muqarnas* 24 (2007): 7–25.

———. "Self and Others: The Diary of a Dervish in Seventeenth Century Istanbul and First-Person Narratives in Ottoman Literature." *Studia Islamica* 69 (1989): 121–50.

Kafescioğlu, Çiğdem. *Constantinopolis/Istanbul: Cultural Encounter, Imperial Vision, and the Construction of the Ottoman Capital*. University Park: University of Pennsylvania Press, 2009.

Kaldy-Nagy, Gyula. "The Holy War (*jihad*) in the First Centuries of the Ottoman Empire." *Harvard Ukrainian Studies* 3–4 (1979–80): 467–73.

Kamen, Henry. "The Decline of Spain: A Historical Myth?" *Past and Present* 81 (1978): 24–50.

Kara, Mustafa. "Molla Ilāhī: Un précurseur de la Nakşibendiye en Anatolie." In *Naqshbandis*, edited by M. Gaborieau, A. Popovic, and T. Zarcone, 303–30. Istanbul: ISIS, 1990.

Karamustafa, A. *God's Unruly Friends*. Salt Lake City: University of Utah Press, 1994.

———. "*Kalenders, Abdāls, Hayderīs*: The Formation of the *Bektaşīye* in the Sixteenth Century." In *Süleyman the Second and His Time*, edited by H. İnalcık and C. Kafadar, 121–29. Istanbul: ISIS, 1993.

———. "Origins of Anatolian Sufism." In *Sufism and Sufis in Ottoman Society*, edited by Ahmet Y. Ocak, 67–95. Ankara: Türk Tarih Kurumu, 2005.

Karataş, A. İhsan. "XVI. Yüzyılda Bursa'da Yaygın Olan Kitaplar." Master's thesis, Uludağ University, Bursa, 1995.

Karlin-Hayter, P. "La politique religieuse des conquerants ottomans dans un texte hagiographique (a. 1437)." *Byzantion* 35 (1965): 353–58.

Keane, Webb. "From Fetishism to Sincerity: Agency, the Speaking Subject, and Their Historicity in the Context of Religious Conversion." *Comparative Studies in Society and History* 39, no. 4 (1997): 674–93.

Kermeli, Eugenia. "Central Administration versus Provincial Arbitrary Governance: Patmos and Mount Athos Monasteries in the 16th Century." *Byzantine and Modern Greek Studies* 32, no. 2 (2008): 189–202.

Khalidi, Tarif. *The Muslim Jesus*. Cambridge, Mass.: Harvard University Press, 2001.

———. "The Role of Jesus in Intra-Muslim Polemics of the First Two Islamic Centuries." In *Christian-Arabic Apologetics during the Abbasid Period (750–1258)*, edited by S. K. Samir and J. S. Nielsen, 146–56. Leiden: Brill, 1994.

Khoury, Adel-Théodore. *Les théologiens byzantins et l'Islam. Texts et auteurs (VIIIe–XIIIe siècles)*. Paris: Éditions Béatrice Nauwelaerts, 1969.

Kiel, Machiel. *Art and Society of Bulgaria in the Turkish Period*. Maastricht: Van Gorcum, 1985.

———. "Razprostranenie na Islyama v Bulgarskoto selo prez osmanskata epoha (XV–XVIII v.): Kolonizatsiya i Islamizatsiya." In *M'usl'umanskata Kultura po Bŭlgarskite zemi*, edited by R. Gradeva and S. Ivanova, 56–124. Sofia: IMIR, 1998.

Kiprovska, Mariya. "The Mihaloğlu Family: Gazi Warriors and Patrons of Dervish Hospices." *Osmanlı Araştırmaları* 32 (2008): 193–222.

Knysh, Alexander D. *Ibn 'Arabi in the Later Islamic Tradition*. Albany: State University of New York Press, 1999.

Kocatürk, Vasfı Mahir. *Türk Edebiyatı Tarihi*. Ankara: Edebiyat Yayınevi, 1970.

Kolovos, Elias. "Negotiating for State Protection: *Çiftlik*-Holding by the Athonite Monasteries (Xeropotamou Monastery, Fifteenth–Sixteenth C.)." In *Frontiers of Ottoman Studies: State, Province and the West*, edited by Colin Imber, Keiko Kiyotaki, and Rhoads Murphey, vol. 2, 199–210. London: I. B. Tauris, 2005.

Köprülü, M. F. *The Origins of the Ottoman Empire*. Edited and translated by G. Leiser. Albany: State University of New York Press, 1992.

Köse, Ali. *Conversion to Islam: A Study of Native British Converts*. London: Kegan Paul International, 1996.

Kotzageorgis, Phokion P. "About the Fiscal Status of the Greek Orthodox Church in the 17th Century." *Turcica* 40 (2008): 67–80.

———. "'Messiahs' and Neomartyrs in Ottoman Thessaly: Some Thoughts on Two Entries in a Mühimme Defteri." *Archivum Ottomanicum* 23 (2005/2006): 219–31.

Krstić, Tijana. "The Ambiguous Politics of 'Ambiguous Sanctuaries': F. Hasluck and Historiography on Syncretism and Conversion to Islam in 15th- and 16th-Century Rumeli." In *Archaeology, Anthropology and Heritage in the Balkans and Anatolia: The Life and Times of F. W. Hasluck*, edited by David Shankland and Keith Hopewood. Istanbul: Isis Press, forthcoming.

———. "Illuminated by the Light of Islam and the Glory of the Ottoman Sultanate: Self-Narratives of Conversion to Islam in the Age of Confessionalization." *Comparative Studies in Society and History* 51, no. 1 (2009): 35–63.

———. "Narrating Conversions to Islam: The Dialogue of Texts and Practices in the Early Modern Ottoman Balkans." Ph.D. diss., University of Michigan, 2004.

Kunitzsch, P., and F. de Jong. "al-Kutb." In *Encyclopaedia of Islam*, 2nd ed., edited by P. Bearman, Th. Bianquis, C. E. Bosworth, E. van Donzel, and W. P. Heinrichs. Brill, 2010. Brill Online. http://www.brillonline.nl/subscriber/entry?entry=islam_COM-0550.

Kunt, Metin İ. "Transformation of *Zimmi* into Askeri." In *Christians and Jews in the Ottoman Empire*, edited by B. Braude and B. Lewis, vol. 1, 55–68. New York: Holmes and Meier, 1982.

Kut, Günay. "Turkish Literature in Anatolia." In *History of the Ottoman State, Society and Civilization*, edited by E. Ihsanoğlu, vol. 2, 27–45. Istanbul: IRCICA, 2002.

Laurent, V. "L'idée de la guerre sainte et la tradition byzantine." *Revue historique du Sud-Est Européen* 23 (1946): 71–98.

Le Strange, Guy, ed. and trans. *Don Juan of Persia: A Shi'ah Catholic, 1560–1604*. New York: Harper and Brothers, 1926.

Levend, Agah Sırrı. *Ġazavāt-nāmeler ve Mihaloğlu Ali Bey'in ġazavāt-nāmesi*. 2nd ed. Ankara: Türk Tarih Kurumu, 2000.

Lindner, Rudi Paul. *Nomads and Ottomans in Medieval Anatolia*. Bloomington: Indiana University Press, 1983.

———. "Stimulus and Justification in Early Ottoman History." *Greek Orthodox Theological Review* 27 (1982): 207–24.

Lofland, John, and Norman Skonovd. "Conversion Motifs." *Journal for the Scientific Study of Religion* 20, no. 4 (1981): 373–85.

Lopašić, Aleksandar. "Islamization of the Balkans with Special Reference to Bosnia." *Journal of Islamic Studies* 5, no. 2 (1994): 163–86.

Lowry, Heath W. *Fifteenth Century Ottoman Realities: Christian Peasant Life on the Aegean Island of Limnos*. Istanbul: Eren, 2002.

———. *The Nature of the Early Ottoman State*. New York: State University of New York Press, 2003.

———. *Trabzon Şehrinin İslamlaşması ve Türkleşmesi, 1461–1583*. Translated by D. Lowry and H. Lowry. Istanbul: Boğazici Üniversitesi Yayınevi, 1998.

Lozanova, Galina. "'Mŭkite v groba' (*azab al-kabr*) ili ideyata za chasten (predvaritelen) sŭd u bŭlgarskite Musulmani." In *Proceedings of the International Symposium on Islamic Civilisation in the Balkans, Sofia, April 21–23, 2000*, edited by E. İhsanoğlu, 247–59. Istanbul: IRCICA, 2002.

———. "Sakralnata sreshtu realnata istoriya na Bulgarite m'usl'umani v Rodopite." In *M'usl'umanskata kultura po bulgarskite zemi*, edited by R. Gradeva and S. Ivanova, 451–63. Sofia: IMIR, 1998.

Lukač, Dušanka. *Vidin i vidinskija sandjak prez 15–16. vek*. Sofia: Nauka i izkustvo, 1975.

Lybyer, Albert H. *The Government of the Ottoman Empire in the Time of Suleiman the Magnificent*. London, 1913.

MacCulloch, D., M. Laven, and E. Duffy. "Recent Trends in the Study of Christianity in Sixteenth-Century Europe." *Renaissance Quarterly* 59 (2006): 697–731.

MacEvitt, Christopher Hatch. *The Crusades and the Christian World of the East: Rough Tolerance*. Philadelphia: University of Pennsylvania Press, 2008.

Madelung, W. "al-Mahdī." In *Encyclopaedia of Islam*, 2nd ed., edited by P. Bearman, Th. Bianquis, C. E. Bosworth, E. van Donzel, and W. P. Heinrichs. Brill, 2010. Brill Online. http://www.brillonline.nl/subscriber/entry?entry=islam_COM-0618.

Mahmood, Saba. "Anthropology." In *Encyclopedia of Women and Islamic Cultures*. Edited by Suad Joseph et al. Brill Online, 2008. http://www.brillonline.nl .proxy.uchicago.edu/subscriber/entry?entry=ewic_COM-0043.

Makdisi, Ussama. *Artillery of Heaven: American Missionaries and the Failed Conversion of the Middle East*. Ithaca, N.Y.: Cornell University Press, 2008.

Manger, Leif, ed. *Muslim Diversity: Local Islam in Global Contexts*. New York: Routledge, 1999.

Martin, John J. *Venice's Hidden Enemies*. Baltimore: Johns Hopkins University Press, 2004.

Masters, Bruce. *Christians and Jews in the Ottoman Arab World*. New York: Cambridge University Press, 2001.

Matar, Nabil. "Introduction: England and the Mediterranean Captivity, 1577–1704." In *Piracy, Slavery, and Redemption: Barbary Captivity Narratives from Early Modern England*, edited by Daniel Vitkus, 1–52. New York: Columbia University Press, 2001.

———. *Turks, Moors, and Englishmen in the Age of Discovery*. New York: Columbia University Press, 1999.

Matuz, Josef. "Die Pfortendolmetscher zur Herrschaftszeit Süleymans des Prächtigen." *Südost-Forschungen* 24 (1975): 26–60.

McGinn, Bernard. "Cabalists and Christians: Reflections on Cabala in Medieval and Renaissance Thought." In *Jewish Christians and Christian Jews*, edited by R. H. Popkin and G. M. Weiner, 11–34. Dordrecht: Kluwer Academic Publishers, 1994.

Meeker, Michael E. *A Nation of Empire: The Ottoman Legacy of Turkish Modernity*. Berkeley: University of California Press, 2002.

Melikoff, Irène. "La communauté *kızılbaş* du Deli Orman en Bulgarie." In *Bektachiyya*, edited by Alexandre Popovic and Gilles Veinstein, 401–12. Istanbul: ISIS, 1995.

———. "Le problème bektaşi-alevi: Quelques dernière considerations." In *Au banquet des Quarante*, 65–86. Istanbul: ISIS, 2001.

———. "Le problème kızılbaş." *Turcica* 6 (1975): 49–67.

———. "Les voies de pénétration de l'hétérodoxie islamique en Thrace et dans les Balkans aux XIVe–XVe siècles." In *The Via Egnatia under Ottoman Rule (1380–1699)*, edited by E. Zachariadou, 159–70. Rethymnon: Crete University Press, 1996.

Messick, Brinkley. *The Calligraphic State*. Berkeley: University of California Press, 1993.

Meyendorff, John. *A Study of Gregory Palamas*. London: Faith Street, 1964.

Minkov, Anton. *Conversion to Islam in the Balkans:* Kisve Bahası *Petitions and Ottoman Social Life, 1670–1730*. Leiden: Brill, 2004.

Mittwoch, E., and J. H. Mordtman. "Die Wiener Sammelhandschrift." In *Literaturdenkmäler aus Ungarns Türkenzeit*, edited by F. Babinger, R. Gragger, E. Mittwoch, and J. H. Mordtmann, 70–87. Berlin: W. de Gruyter, 1927.

Miyamoto, Yoko. "The Influence of Medieval Prophecies on Views of the Turks: Islam and Apocalypticism in the Sixteenth Century." *Journal of Turkish Studies* 17 (1993): 125–45.

Moačanin, Nenad. "Mass Islamization of the Peasants in Bosnia: Demystifications." In *Melanges Professor Machiel Kiel*, 353–58. Zaghouan: Fondation Temimi, 1999.

Morris, James W. "Ibn 'Arabi's 'Esotericism': The Problem of Spiritual Authority." *Studia Islamica* 71 (1990): 37–64.

Morrison, Karl F. *Conversion and Text: The Cases of Augustine of Hippo, Herman-Judah, and Constantine Tsatsos*. Charlottesville: University Press of Virginia, 1992.

Mout, M. E. H. N. "Calvinoturcismus und Chiliasmus im 17. Jahrhundert." *Pietismus und Neuzeit* 14 (1988): 72–84.

Muljačić, Žarko. "Jedno nepoznato izvješće iz Dubrovnika o stanju u Otomanskom Carstvu (1531)." *Anali Dubrovnik* 37 (1999): 33–46.

Mulsow, Martin. "Ambiguities of the *Prisca Sapientia* in Late Renaissance Humanism." *Journal of the History of Ideas* 65, no. 1 (2004): 1–13.

Murphey, Rhoads. "The Ottoman Resurgence in the Seventeenth-Century Mediterranean: The Gamble and Its Results." *Mediterranean Historical Review* 8, no. 2 (1986): 186–200.

Naguib, Saphinaz-Amal. "The Martyr as Witness: Coptic and Copto-Arabic Hagiographies as Mediators of Religious Memory." *Numen* 41 (1994): 223–54.

Nasr, Sayyed Hossein. "The Prayer of the Heart in Hesychasm and Sufism." In *Orthodox Christians and Muslims*, edited by N. M. Vaporis, 195–203. Brookline, Mass.: Holy Cross Orthodox Press, 1986.

Necipoğlu, Gülrü. *The Age of Sinan*. Princeton, N.J.: Princeton University Press, 2005.

———. "Creation of a National Genius: Sinan and the Historiography of 'Classical' Ottoman Architecture." *Muqarnas* 24 (2007): 141–84.

———. "Süleyman the Magnificent and the Representation of Power in the Context of Ottoman-Habsburg-Papal Rivalry." *The Art Bulletin* 71, no. 3 (September 1989): 401–27.

Necipoğlu, Nevra. *Byzantium between the Ottomans and the Latins: Politics and Society in the Late Empire*. New York: Cambridge University Press, 2009.

Neudecker, Hannah. "From Istanbul to London? Albertus Bobovius' Appeal to Isaac Basire." In *The Republic of Letters and the Levant*, edited by Alastair Hamilton, Maurits H. van den Boogert, and Bart Westerweel, 173–96. Leiden: Brill, 2005.

Neumann, Christoph. "Concepts of the Self among the Ottomans." Paper presented at the Symposium on Autobiographical Themes in Turkish Literature: Theoretical and Comparative Perspectives, Bosphorus University, Istanbul, May 15–17, 2003.

Newman, Andrew J. *Safavid Iran: Rebirth of a Persian Empire*. London: I. B. Tauris, 2006.

Niccoli, Olivia. *Prophecy and People in Renaissance Italy*. Princeton, N.J.: Princeton University Press, 1990.

Nicol, Donald. *The Last Centuries of Byzantium, 1261–1453*. Cambridge: Cambridge University Press, 1993.

Nicolaidis, Efthymios. "Scientific Exchanges between Hellenism and Europe:

Translations into Greek, 1400–1700." In *Cultural Translation in Early Modern Europe*, edited by Peter Burke and R. Po-Chia Hsia, 180–91. Cambridge: Cambridge University Press, 2007.

Nihoritis, Konstantinos. *Sveta Gora i bŭlgarskoto novomŭchenichestvo*. Sofia: "Prof. Marin Drinov," 2001.

Nirenberg, David. *Communities of Violence: Persecution of Minorities in the Middle Ages*. Princeton, N.J.: Princeton University Press, 1996.

Nock, A. D. *Conversion: The Old and the New in Religion from Alexander the Great to Augustine of Hippo*. Oxford: Clarendon Press, 1933.

Nöldeke, Theodore. *Geschichte des Qorāns*. Vol. 2. Leipzig: Dietrich, 1919.

Norman, York. "An Islamic City? Sarajevo's Islamization and Economic Development, 1461–1604." Ph.D. diss., Georgetown University, 2005.

Norris, H. T. *Islam in the Balkans*. London: Hurst, 1993.

Ocak, Ahmet Yaşar. "Bazı Menakibnamelere Göre XIII–XV. Yüzyılardaki İhtidalarda Heterodoks Şeyh ve Dervişlerin Rolü." *Osmanlı Araştırmaları* 2 (1981): 31–42.

———. "Din." In *Osmanlı Devleti ve Medeniyeti Tarihi*, edited by E. İhsanoğlu, vol. 2, 107–58. Istanbul: IRCICA, 1998.

———. "Islam in the Ottoman Empire: A Sociological Framework for a New Interpretation." *International Journal of Turkish Studies* 9, nos. 1–2 (2003): 183–98.

———. *Kültür Tarihi Kaynağı Olarak Menakıbnameler: Metodolojik Bir Yaklaşım*. Ankara: Türk Tarih Kurumu Basımevi, 1997.

———. *Osmanlı Toplumunda Zındıklar ve Mülhidler (15.–17. Yüzyıllar)*. Istanbul: Tarih Vakfı Yurt Yayınları, 1998.

———. "Les reactions socio-religieuses contre l'idéologie officielle otomane et la question de *zendeqa* ve *ilhad* (hérésie et athéisme) au XVIe siècle." *Turcica* 21–23 (1991): 71–82.

O'Malley, John W. *Trent and All That: Renaming Catholicism in the Early Modern Era*. Boston: Harvard University Press, 2000.

Öngören, Reşat. *Osmanlılar'da Tasavvuf: Anadolu'da Sufiler, Devlet ve 'ulema (XVI. Yüzyıl)*. Istanbul: Iz Yayıncılık, 2000.

Osterhout, Robert. "The East, the West and the Appropriation of the Past in Early Ottoman Architecture." *Gesta* 43, no. 2 (2004): 165–76.

Özbaran, Salih. *Bir Osmanlı Kimliği: 14.–17.Yüzyıllarda Rûm / Rûmi Aidiyet ve İmgeleri*. Istanbul: Kitap yayınevi, 2004.

———. "Ottomans as 'Rumes' in Portuguese Sources in the Sixteenth Century." *Portuguese Studies* 17 (2001): 64–74.

Özdeğer, Hüseyin. *Onaltıncı Asırda Ayıntāb Livāsı*. Istanbul: İstanbul Üniversitesi, 1988.

Öztürk, Zehra. "Muhammediyye'nin İki Yazma Nüshası ve İki Kadın Müstensih." *Türk Kültürü Incelemeleri Dergisi* 1 (1999): 333–38.

Pagden, Antony. *Lords of All the World: Ideologies of Empire in Spain, Britain and France c. 1500–1800*. New Haven, Conn.: Yale University Press, 1998.

Pantazopoulos, N. J. *Church and Law in the Balkan Peninsula during the Ottoman Rule*. Thessaloniki: Institute for Balkan Studies, 1967.

Papademetriou, Anastasios G. "Ottoman Tax Farming and the Greek Orthodox Patriarchate: An Examination of State and Church in Ottoman Society (15th–16th Century)." Ph.D. diss., Princeton University, 2001.

Parker, Geoffrey. *The Grand Strategy of Philip II*. New Haven, Conn.: Yale University Press, 1998.

Parker, Geoffrey, and Lesley M. Smith, eds. *The General Crisis of the Seventeenth Century*. New York: Routledge, 1997.

Pashou, P. V., ed. *Neon martyrologion para tou osiou Nikodimou tou Hagioretiou*. Athens: "Aster," Al. and E. Papademetriou, 1961.

Patterson, W. B. "Cyril Lukaris, George Abbot, James VI and I, and the Beginning of Orthodox-Anglican Relations." In *Anglicanism and Orthodoxy 300 Years after the "Greek College" in Oxford*, edited by Peter M. Doll, 39–56. Oxford: Peter Lang, 2006.

Peirce, Lesley. *The Imperial Harem: Women and Sovereignty in the Ottoman Empire*. New York: Oxford University Press, 1993.

———. *Morality Tales: Law and Gender in the Ottoman Court of Aintab*. Berkeley: University of California Press, 2003.

Peters, Rudolph. "The Battered Dervishes of Bab Zuwayla: A Religious Riot in Eighteenth-Century Cairo." In *Eighteenth-Century Renewal and Reform in Islam*, edited by Nehemia Levtzion and John O. Voll, 93–115. Syracuse, N.Y.: Syracuse University Press, 1987.

Petkanova Toteva, Donka. *Damaskinite v bŭlgarskata literatura*. Sofia: Bulgarian Academy of Sciences, 1965.

Petrosyan, I. E., ed. *Mebde-i kanun-i ienicheri odzhzaqı tarihi*. Moscow: Nauka, 1987.

Philippidis-Braat, Anna. "La captivité de Palamas chez les Turcs: Dossier et commentaire." *Travaux et memoires* 7 (1979): 109–218.

Pistor-Hatam, Anja. "The Art of Translation: Rewriting Persian Texts from the Seljuks to the Ottomans." In *Essays on Ottoman Civilization: Proceedings of the XIIth Congress of CIEPO (Praha, 1996)*, 305–16. Praha, 1998.

Piterberg, Gabriel. *An Ottoman Tragedy: History and Historiography at Play*. Berkeley: University of California Press, 2003.

Podskalsky, Gerhard. *Griechische Theologie in der Zeit der Türkenherrschaft (1481–1821)*. Munich: C. H. Beck, 1988.

Pollmann, Judith. "A Different Road to God: The Protestant Experience of Conversion in the Sixteenth Century." In *Conversion to Modernities: The Globalization of Christianity*, edited by Peter van der Veer, 47–64. New York: Routledge, 1995.

Popović, Alexandre. *Cultures musulmanes balkaniques*. Istanbul: ISIS, 1994.

———. *L'Islam balkanique: Les musulmans du sud-est européen dans la période post-ottomane*. Berlin: Otto Harrassowitz, 1986.

Pratt, Mary Louise. "The Arts of the Contact Zone." *Profession* 91 (1991): 33–40.

Puchner, Walter. "The Jesuit Theater on the Islands of the Aegean Sea." *Journal of Modern Greek Studies* 21 (2003): 207–22.

Questier, Michael. *Conversion, Politics and Religion in England, 1580–1625*. Cambridge: Cambridge University Press, 1996.

Quinn, Sholeh A. *Historical Writing during the Reign of Shah 'Abbas*. Salt Lake City: University of Utah Press, 2000.

Raby, Julian. "El Gran Turco, Mehmet the Conqueror as a Patron of the Arts of Christendom." Ph.D. diss., Oxford University, 1980.

———. "Mehmed the Conqueror's Greek Scriptorium." *Dumbarton Oaks* 37 (1983): 15–34.

Radtke, Bernd. "Birgiwis *Tariqa Muhammadiyya*: Einige Bemerkungen und Überlegungen." *Journal of Turkish Studies* 26 (2002): 159–74.

Radushev, Evgenii. "Smisŭlŭt na istoriografskite mitove za islamizatsiyata." In *Balkanski Identichnosti*, edited by E. Radushev and S. Fetvadzhieva, vol. 3, 152–97. Sofia: Open Society Fund, 2003.

Ragg, Lonsdale, and Laura Ragg, eds. and trans. *The Gospel of Barnabas*. Oxford: Clarendon Press, 1907.

Rambo, Lewis R. *Understanding Religious Conversion*. New Haven, Conn.: Yale University Press, 1993.

Rambo, L. R., and C. E. Farhadian. "Converting: Stages of Religious Change." In *Religious Conversion: Contemporary Practices and Controversies*, edited by C. Lamb and M. Darrol Bryant, 23–34. New York: Cassell, 1999.

Reeves, Marjorie. "The Abbot Joachim's Sense of History." In *The Prophetic Sense of History in Medieval and Renaissance Europe*, 782–96. Aldershot, U.K.: Ashgate, 1999.

———. *The Influence of Prophecy in the Later Middle Ages: A Study in Joachimism*. Oxford: Clarendon Press, 1969.

Reindl Kiel, Hedda. "Mesih Paşa." *İslam Ansiklopedisi*. Vol. 29, 309–10. Ankara: Türkiye Diyanet Vakfı, 2004.

Renard, John. *Islam and the Heroic Image: Themes in Literature and the Visual Arts*. Columbia: University of South Carolina Press, 1993.

Reynolds, D. F., ed. *Interpreting the Self: Autobiography in the Arabic Literary Tradition*. Berkeley: University of California Press, 2001.

Rodrigue, Aron. "Difference and Tolerance in the Ottoman Empire: An Interview with Aron Rodrigue." Interview by Nancy Reynolds. *Stanford Electronic Humanities Review* 5, no. 1. http://www.stanford.edu/group/SHR/5-1/text/rodrigue .html.

Rothman, E. Natalie. "Becoming Venetian: Conversion and Transformation in the Seventeenth-Century Mediterranean." *Mediterranean Historical Review* 21, no. 1 (2006): 39–75.

———. "Between Venice and Istanbul: Trans-imperial Subjects and Cultural Mediation in the Early Modern Mediterranean." Ph.D. diss., University of Michigan, 2006.

———. "Mediating Converts, Commensurating Differences: Boundary-Marking and Boundary-Crossing in the Venetian-Ottoman Borderlands." *Journal of Medieval and Early Modern Studies*, forthcoming.

———. "Narrating Conversion and Subjecthood in the Venetian-Ottoman Borderlands." In *The Turn of the Soul: Representations of Religious Conversion in Early Modern Art and Literature*, edited by Harald Hendrix, Todd Richardson, and Lieke Stelling. Leiden: Brill, forthcoming.

———. *Trans-imperial Subjects: Boundary-Markers of the Early Modern Mediterranean.* Ithaca, N.Y.: Cornell University Press, forthcoming.

Rummel, Erika. *The Confessionalization of Humanism in Reformation Germany.* Oxford: Oxford University Press, 2000.

Runciman, Steven. *The Great Church in Captivity.* Cambridge: Cambridge University Press, 1968.

Rutherford, Danilyn. "After Syncretism: The Anthropology of Islam and Christianity in Southeast Asia. A Review Article." *Comparative Studies in Society and History* 44 (2002): 196–205.

Šabanović, Nazim. *Krajište Isa-Bega Isakovića: Zbirni katastarski popis is 1455. godine.* Sarajevo: Orijentalni Institut, 1964.

Sabev, Orlin. *İbrahim Müteferrika ya da ilk Osmanlı matbaa serüveni (1726–1746): Yeniden değerlendirme.* Istanbul: Yeditepe, 2006.

Šamić, Jasna. "Où sont les bektachis de Bosnie?" In *Bektachiyya*, edited by A. Popovic and G. Veinstein, 381–91. Istanbul: ISIS, 1995.

Samsel, Peter. "A Unity with Distinctions: Parallels in the Thought of St Gregory Palamas and Ibn Arabi." In *Paths to the Heart: Sufism and the Christian East*, edited by J. Cutsinger, 190–224. Bloomington, Ind.: World Wisdom, 2002.

Sariyannis, Marinos. "Aspects of 'Neomartyrdom': Religious Contacts, 'Blasphemy' and 'Calumny' in 17th Century Istanbul." *Archivum Ottomanicum* 23 (2005/2006): 249–62.

Savaş, Saim. *XVI. Asırda Anadolu'da Alevîlik.* Ankara: Vadi Yayınları, 2002.

Schilling, Heinz. "Confessionalization: Historical and Scholarly Perspectives of a Comparative and Interdisciplinary Paradigm." In *Confessionalization in Europe, 1555–1700*, edited by J. M. Headley, H. J. Hillerbrand, and A. J. Papalas, 21–36. Aldershot, U.K.: Ashgate, 2004.

Schilling, Heinz, and Istvan György Toth, eds. *Cultural Exchange in Early Modern Europe: Religion and Cultural Exchange in Europe, 1400–1700.* Vol. 1. Cambridge: Cambridge University Press, 2006.

Setton, Kenneth. *Western Hostility to Islam and Prophecies of Turkish Doom.* Darby, Penn.: Diane Publishing, 1992.

Shatzmiller, Maya. "Marriage, Family, and the Faith: Women's Conversion to Islam." *Journal of Family History* 21, no. 3 (1996): 235–66.

Shaw, Stanford. *The Jews of the Ottoman Empire and the Turkish Republic.* New York: New York University Press, 1991.

Şimşek, Mehmet. "Osmanlı cemiyetinde para vakıfları üzerinde münakaşalar." *Ankara İlahiyat Fakültesi Dergisi* 27 (1985): 207–20.

Şişman, Cengiz. "A Jewish Messiah in the Ottoman Court: Sabbatai Sevi and the Emergence of a Judeo-Islamic Community (1666–1720)." Ph.D. diss., Harvard University, 2004.

Skilliter, Susan. *William Harborne and the Trade with Turkey, 1578–1582: A Democracy Study of the First Anglo-Ottoman Relations.* London: British Academy, 1977.

Slomp, Jan. "The Gospel of Barnabas in Recent Research." *Islamochristiana* 23 (1997): 81–109.

Smith, Jane I., and Yvonne Y. Haddad. *The Islamic Understanding of Death and Resurrection*. Oxford: Oxford University Press, 2002.

Sohrweide, Hanna. "Der Sieg der Safawiden in Persien und seine Ruckwirkungen auf der Schiiten Anatoliens im 16. Jahrhundert." *Der Islam* 41 (1965): 164–86.

Starn, Randolph. "The Early Modern Muddle." *Journal of Early Modern History* 6, no. 3 (2002): 296–307.

Stavrides, Theoharis. *The Sultan of Vezirs: The Life and Times of the Ottoman Grand Vezir Mahmud Pasha Angelović (1453–1474)*. Leiden: Brill, 2001.

Stern, S. "Abd al-Jabbar's Account of How Christian Religion Was Falsified by the Adoption of Roman Custom." *Journal of Theological Studies* 19 (1968): 129–76.

Stewart, Charles, and Rosalind Shaw, eds. *Syncretism/Anti-syncretism*. London: Routledge, 1994.

Stewart, Devin J. "Husayn b. 'Abd al-Samad al-Āmilī's Treatise for Sultan Suleiman and the Shī'ī Shāfi'ī Legal Tradition." *Islamic Law and Society* 4, no. 2 (1997): 156–99.

Stock, Brian. *The Implication of Literacy: Written Language and Models of Interpretation in the Eleventh and Twelfth Centuries*. Princeton, N.J.: Princeton University Press, 1983.

Stoilova, Anka, and Zorka Ivanova. "On Two New Collections of Books in the Arabic Script Preserved in Bulgaria" [in Bulgarian]. In *M'usl'umanskata kultura po bŭlgarskite zemi*, edited by R. Gradeva and S. Ivanova, 380–96. Sofia: IMIR, 1998.

Stojanovski, Aleksandar, and Metodija Sokoloski, eds. *Opširen popisen defter 4 (1467–1468)*. Skopje: Arhiv na Makedonija, 1971.

Stromberg, Peter G. *Language and Self-Transformation: A Study of the Christian Conversion Narrative*. Cambridge: Cambridge University Press, 1993.

Stroumsa, S. "On Jewish Intellectuals Who Converted in the Early Middle Ages." In *The Jews of Medieval Islam: Community, Society and Identity*, edited by D. Frank, 180–97. Leiden: Brill, 1995.

Subrahmanyam, Sanjay. "Connected Histories: Notes towards a Reconfiguration of Early Modern Euroasia." *Modern Asia Studies* 31, no. 3 (1997): 735–62.

———. "Turning the Stones Over: Sixteenth-Century Millenarianism from the Tagus to the Ganges." *Indian Economic and Social History Review* 40, no. 2 (2003): 129–61.

Swanson, R. N. "Literacy, Heresy, History and Orthodoxy: Perspectives and Permutations for the Later Middle Ages." In *Heresy and Literacy, 1000–1530*, edited by P. Biller and A. Hudson, 279–93. New York: Cambridge University Press, 1994.

Szalay, Laszlo, ed. *Erdély és a Porta, 1567–78*. Pest: Lauffer és Stolp, 1862.

Tahrali, M. "A General Outline of the Influence of Ibn 'Arabi on the Ottoman Era." *Journal of the Muhyiddin Ibn 'Arabi Society* 26 (1999): 43–54.

Talbot, Alice-Mary, ed. *Holy Women of Byzantium*. Washington, D.C.: Dumbarton Oaks Research Library, 1996.

Tambiah, Stanley. *Leveling Crowds: Ethnonationalist Conflicts and Collective Violence in South Asia*. Berkeley: University of California Press, 1996.

Tekin, Şinasi. "XIV. Yüzyılda Yazılmış *Gazilik* Tarikasi '*Gaziliğin* Yolları' Adlı Bir Eski Anadolu Türkçesi Metni." *Journal of Turkish Studies* 17 (1989): 139–63.
Teply, Karl. *Sagen und Legenden um die Kaiserstadt Wien*. Vienna: Böhlau, 1980.
Terzioğlu, Derin. "The Age of the Kadızadelis: Social and Moral Regulation in the Seventeenth-Century Ottoman Empire." Unpublished grant proposal submitted to the Koç University Research Center for Anatolian Civilizations for 2009–10.
———. "The Imperial Circumcision Festival of 1582: An Interpretation." *Muqarnas* 12 (1995): 84–100.
———. "Man in the Image of God in the Image of the Times: Sufi Self-Narratives and the Diary of Niyāzī-i Mısrī (1618–94)." *Studia Islamica* 94 (2002): 139–65.
———. "Sufi and Dissident in the Ottoman Empire: Niyāzī-ı Mısrī (1618–1694)." Ph.D. diss., Harvard University, 1999.
———. "Sufis in the Age of State Building and Confessionalization." In *The Ottoman World*, edited by Christine Woodhead. London: Routledge, forthcoming.
Tezcan, Baki. "The Ottoman *Mevali* as 'Lords of the Law.'" *Journal of Islamic Studies* 20, no. 3 (2009): 383–407.
———. "The Ottoman Monetary Crisis of 1585 Revisited." *Journal of the Economic and Social History of the Orient* 52, no. 3 (2009): 460–504.
———. "The Second Empire: The Transformation of the Ottoman Polity in the Early Modern Era." *Comparative Studies of South Asia, Africa and the Middle East* 29, no. 3 (2009): 556–72.
Tiepolo, Maria F., and Eurigio Tonetti, eds. *I Greci a Venezia: Atti del Convegno internazionale di studio, Venezia, 5–7 novembre 1998*. Venice: Istituto Veneto di Scienze, 2002.
Todorova, Maria. "Conversion to Islam as a Trope in Bulgarian Historiography, Fiction and Film." In *Balkan Identities*, edited by Maria Todorova, 129–57. New York: New York University Press, 2004.
Toledano, Ehud. "Slave Dealers, Pregnancy, Abortion, and the World of Women: The Story of a Circassian Slave-Girl in Mid-Nineteenth-Century Cairo." *Slavery and Abolition* 2, no. 1 (1981): 53–68.
Trako, Salih. "Pretkosovski dogadjaji u Hešt Bihištu Idrisa Bitlisija." *Prilozi za orijentalnu filologiju* 20–21 (1970–71): 159–203.
Tsirpanlis, Constantine. *The Historical and Ecumenical Significance of Jeremias II's Correspondence with the Lutherans (1573–1581)*. New York: American Institute for Patristic and Byzantine Studies, 1982.
Tŭpkova-Zaimova, Vasilka, and Anisava Miltenova. *Istoriko-apokaliptichnata knizhnina vŭv Vizantija i v srednovekovna Bŭlgariya*. Sofia: Univerzitetsko Izdatelstvo "Sv. Kliment Ohridski," 1996.
Turan, Ebru. "The Marriage of Ibrahim Pasha (ca. 1495–1536): The Rise of Sultan Süleyman's Favorite, Ibrahim Pasha, to the Grand Vizirate and the Politics of Elites in the Early Sixteenth-Century Ottoman Empire." *Turcica* 41 (2010): 3–36.
———. "The Sultan's Favorite: İbrahim Pasha and the Making of the Ottoman Universal Sovereignty in the Reign of Sultan Süleyman (1516–1526)." Ph.D. diss., University of Chicago, 2007.

Tzedopoulos, G. "Ethnike homologia kai symvolike sten Hellada tou 19ou aiona: Oi ethnomartyres." *Mnemon* 24 (2002): 107–43.

Unghvary, A. S. *The Hungarian Protestant Reformation in the Sixteenth Century under the Ottoman Impact*. Lewiston, N.Y.: Edwin Mellen Press, 1989.

Vacalopoulos, Apostolos E. *History of Macedonia, 1354–1833*. Thessaloniki: Institute for Balkan Studies, 1973.

Van den Boogert, Maurits H. *The Capitulations and the Ottoman Legal System*. Leiden: Brill, 2005.

Vanhoozer, Kevin J. "Scripture and Tradition." In *The Cambridge Companion to Postmodern Theology*, edited by K. J. Vanhoozer, 149–69. New York: Cambridge University Press, 2003.

Van Koningsveld, P. S. "The Islamic Image of Paul and the Origin of the Gospel of Barnabas." *Jerusalem Studies in Arabic and Islam* 20 (1996): 217–28.

Van Koningsveld, P. S., Q. al-Samarrai, and G. Wiegers, eds. and trans. *Kitāb nāsir al-dīn 'alā'l-qawm al-kāfirīn*. Madrid: Agencia Española de Cooperación Internacional, 1997.

Van Koningsveld, P. S., and Gerard A. Wiegers. "The Parchment of the 'Torre Turpiana': The Original Document and Its Interpreters." *Al-Qantara* 24, no. 2 (2003): 327–58.

Van Nieuwkerk, Karin. "Gender, Conversion, and Islam." In *Women Embracing Islam: Gender and Conversion in the West*, edited by Karin van Nieuwkerk, 95–119. Austin: University of Texas Press, 2006.

Vanzan, Anna. "In Search of Another Identity: Female Muslim-Christian Conversions in the Mediterranean World." *Islam and Christian-Muslim Relations* 7, no. 3 (1996): 327–33.

Vaporis, Nomikos. "The Price of Faith: Some Reflections on Nikodemos Hagiorites and His Struggle against Islam, Together with a Translation of the 'Introduction' to His *New Martyrologion*." *Greek Orthodox Theological Review* 23 (1978): 194–215.

———, ed. *Witnesses for Christ: Orthodox Christian Neomartyrs of the Ottoman Period, 1437–1860*. New York: Saint Vladimir Seminary Press, 2000.

Vatin, Nicolas. *Sultan Djem: Un prince ottoman dans l'Europe du XVe siècle d'après deux sources contemporains: Vāki'āt-ı Sultan Cem, oeuvres de Guillaume Caoursin*. Ankara: Imprimerie de la Société turque d'histoire, 1997.

Veinstein, Gilles. "Femmes d'Avlonya (Vlorë) vers le milieu du XVI siècle (d'après les actes des cadis)." In *Festschrift Hans Georg Majer: Arts, Women and Scholars*, edited by Sabine Prätor and Christoph Neuman, vol. 1, 195–208. Istanbul: Simurg, 2002.

———. "The Ottoman Administration and the Problem of Interpreters." In *The Great Ottoman-Turkish Civilisation*, vol. 3, *Philosophy, Science and Institutions*, edited by K. Çiçek, 607–15. Ankara: Yeni Türkiye, 2000.

———. "Sokollu Mehmed Pasha." In *Encyclopaedia of Islam*, 2nd ed., edited by P. Bearman, Th. Bianquis, C. E. Bosworth, E. van Donzel, and W. P. Heinrichs. Brill, 2010. Brill Online. http://www.brillonline.nl/subscriber/entry?entry=islam_SIM-7090.

Velkov, A., M. Kalitsin, and E. Radushev, eds. *Osmanski izvori za islyamizatsion-*

*nite protsesi na Balkanite (XVI–XIX v.)* Sofia: Izdatelstvo na Bŭlgarskata Akademiya na Naukite, 1990.

Viswanathan, Gauri. "Beyond Orientalism: Syncretism and the Politics of Knowledge." *Stanford Electronic Humanities Review* 5, no. 1 (1996). http://www.stanford.edu/group/SHR/5-1/text/viswanathan.html.

Vitkus, Daniel. *Turning Turk: English Theater and the Multicultural Mediterranean, 1570–1630*. New York: Palgrave Macmillan, 2003.

Volan, Angela. "Last Judgments and Last Emperors: Illustrating Byzantine Apocalyptic History in Late- and Post-Byzantine Art." Ph.D. diss., University of Chicago, 2005.

Von Schlegell, Barbara Rosenow. "Sufism in the Ottoman Arab World: Shaykh ʿAbd al-Ganī al-Nāblusī (d. 1143/1731)." Ph.D. diss., University of California, Berkeley, 1997.

Vryonis, Speros. *The Decline of Medieval Hellenism in Asia Minor and the Process of Islamization from the Eleventh to the Fifteenth Century*. Los Angeles: University of California Press, 1971.

———. "The Experience of Christians under Seljuk and Ottoman Domination, Eleventh to Sixteenth Century." In *Conversion and Continuity: Indigenous Christian Communities in Islamic Lands, Eighth to Eighteenth Centuries*, edited by M. Gervers and R. J. Bikhazi, Papers in Medieval Studies 9, 185–216. Toronto: Pontifical Institute of Medieval Studies, 1990.

———. "Religious Changes and Patterns in the Balkans, 14th–16th Centuries." In *Aspects of the Balkans*, edited by H. Birnbaum and S. Vryonis Jr., 151–76. The Hague: Mouton, 1972.

Walsh, E. M. "The Women Martyrs of Nikodemos Hagiorites' *Neon Martyrologion*." *Greek Orthodox Theological Review* 36, no. 1 (1991): 71–91.

Wensinck, A. J. "al-Masīh." In *Encyclopaedia of Islam*, 2nd ed., edited by P. Bearman, Th. Bianquis, C. E. Bosworth, E. van Donzel, and W. P. Heinrichs. Brill, 2010. Brill Online. http://www.brillonline.nl/subscriber/entry?entry=islam_SIM-5012.

Wiegers, Gerard A. "Muhammad as Messiah: A Comparison of the Polemical Works of Juan Alonso with the Gospel of Barnabas." *Bibliotheca Orientalis* 52, nos. 3–4 (1995): 245–91.

———. "The 'Old' or 'Turpiana' Tower in Granada and Its Relics according to Ahmad b. Qasim al-Hajari." *Res Orientales* 8 (1996): 191–205.

———. "The Persistence of Mudejar Islam? Alonso de Luna (Muhammad Abū'l-ʿĀsī), the *Lead Books*, and the *Gospel of Barnabas*." *Medieval Encounters* 12, no. 3 (2006): 498–518.

Winter, Stefan. *The Shiites of Lebanon under Ottoman Rule, 1516–1788*. New York: Cambridge University Press, 2010.

Wittek, Paul. *The Rise of the Ottoman Empire*. London: Royal Asiatic Society, 1938.

———. "The Taking of Aydos Castle: A Ghazi Legend and Its Transformations." In *Arabic and Islamic Studies in Honor of Hamilton A. R. Gibb*, edited by George Makdisi, 662–72. Leiden: Brill, 1965.

Wolf, Kenneth B. *Christian Martyrs in Muslim Spain*. Cambridge: Cambridge University Press, 1988.

Wolper, Sarah. *Cities and Saints*. University Park: Pennsylvania State University Press, 2003.

Yates, Frances A. *Astraea: The Imperial Theme in the Sixteenth Century*. New York: Routledge, 1975.

Yelten, M. "Hibetullah b. Ibrahim'in *Sa'atname*si ve Eserde Dudak Uyumunun Durumu." *Türk Dili ve Edebiyatı Dergisi* 28 (1998): 585–93.

Yerasimos, Stephane. "De l'arbre à la pomme: La généalogie d'un thème apocalyptique." In *Les traditions apocalyptiques au tournant de la chute de Constantinople*, Actes da la Table Ronde d'Istanbul (April 13–14, 1996), edited by B. Lellouch and S. Yerasimos, 153–92. Istanbul: L'Institut Français d'Études Anatolienne, 1999.

———. *La fondation de Constantinople et de Sainte-Sophie*. Paris: L'Institut Français d'Études Anatoliennes, 1990.

Yüksel, Emrullah. "Birgivi." In *İslam Ansiklopedisi*, vol. 6, 191–94. Istanbul: Türkiye Diyanet Vakfı, 1992.

———. "Müslüman Türk Alimi olarak İmam Birgivi'nin Osmanlı Döneminde ve Günümüz Türkiyesinde Yeri." In *İmam Birgivi*, edited by Mehmet Şeker, 32–37. Ankara: Türkiye Diyanet Vakfı, 1994.

Yurdaydın, H. "Üstüvanī Risalesi." *Ankara Üniversitesi Ilahiyat Fakültesi* 10 (1962): 71–78.

Yürekli, Zeynep. "Legend and Architecture in the Ottoman Empire: The Shrine of Seyyid Gazi and Hacı Bektaş." Ph.D. diss., Harvard University, 2005.

Zachariadou, Elisabeth. "The Neomartyr's Message." *Kentro Mikrasiatikon Spoudon* 8 (1990–91): 51–63.

———. "Religious Dialogue between Byzantines and Turks during the Ottoman Expansion." In *Religionsgespräche im Mittelalter*, edited by B. Lewis and F. Niewohner, 289–304. Wiesbaden: Harrassowitz, 1992.

———. "'A Safe and Holy Mountain': Early Ottoman Athos." In *Mount Athos and Byzantine Monasticism*, edited by Anthony Bryer and Mary Cunningham, 127–34. Aldershot, U.K.: Variorum, 1996.

———. "The Worrisome Wealth of Čelnik Radić." In *Studies in Ottoman History in Honour of Professor V. L. Ménage*, edited by C. Heywood and C. Imber, 383–97. Istanbul: Isis Press, 1994.

Zarcone, Thierry. "Nouvelles perspectives dans les recherches sur les Kizilbas-Alevis et les Bektachis de la Dobroudja, de Deli Orman et de la Thrace orientale." *Anatolia Moderna* 4 (1995): 1–11.

Zarinebaf-Shahr, Fariba. "Qızılbaş 'Heresy' and Rebellion in Ottoman Anatolia during the Sixteenth Century." *Anatolia Moderna* 7 (1997): 1–13.

Zhelyazkova, Antonina. "The Bulgarian Ethnic Model." *East European Constitutional Review* 10, no. 4 (2001): 62–66.

———. "Islamization in the Balkans as a Historiographical Problem: The Southeast-European Perspective." In *The Ottomans and the Balkans*, edited by S. Faroqhi and F. Adanır, 223–66. Leiden: Brill, 2002.

———. "The Penetration and Adaptation of Islam in Bosnia from the Fifteenth to the Nineteenth Century." *Journal of Islamic Studies* 5, no. 2 (1994): 187–208.

———. "The Problem of Authenticity of Some Sources on the Islamization of the Rhodopes, Deeply Rooted in Bulgarian Historiography." *Études balkaniques* 4 (1990): 105–11.

———. *The Spread of Islam in the Western Balkan Lands under Ottoman Rule (15th–18th Centuries)* [in Bulgarian]. Sofia: Bulgarian Academy of Sciences, 1990.

Zhukov, Konstantine A. "The Cathars, *Fraticelli*, and Turks: A New Interpretation of Berkludje Mustafa's Uprising in Anatolia, c. 1415." In *The Proceedings of the XVIIIth International Byzantine Congress*, edited by I. Shevchenko, G. Litavrin, and W. Hanak, vol. 2, 188–95. Shepherdstown, West Virginia: 1996.

Zilfi, Madeline C. "The Kadizadelis: Discordant Revivalism in Seventeenth-Century Istanbul." *Journal of Near Eastern Studies* 45, no. 4 (1986): 251–69.

———. *The Politics of Piety: The Ottoman Ulema in the Postclassical Age (1600–1800)*. Minneapolis: Biblioteca Islamica, 1988.

# Index


Abbot, George, 140. *See also* Anglicans
Abdürrahim Efendi, 155, 157, 211n27, n28, 213n56
*'Acem*, 5, 175n10
*'acemioğlan* (janissary cadet), 5, 127
*'akāid* (catechetical literature), 27, 29
*akıncı* (raider), 56, 186n98, 188n19
Akylina from Zagliveri, 155–56. *See also* neomartyrs; conversion
Aleppo, 119, 134
Alexander the Great, 38, 62
al-Ghazali. *See* Ghazali, al-
Ali b. Abu Talib, 6, 59–60, 74, 107–8, 123
Ali Efendi, 151
Ali Ufki Bey (Albertus Bobovius), 211n21
al-Kaşşaş. *See* Kaşşaş, al-
al-Maghribi. *See* Maghribi, al-
al-Nablusi. *See* Nablusi, al-
al-Tarjuman. *See* Tarjuman, al-
Ahmed I, 72, 110, 112–13
ambiguous sanctuaries, 16
Amiroutzes, George, 63
Anatolia, 16, 21, 24, 27, 29, 33, 35, 39, 41–42, 44–45, 47–48, 53, 55–56, 59, 61, 73–74, 76, 81–82, 92, 95, 107, 123–24, 170, 173, 177n38, 184n68, 187nn107–110, 206n44, 212n42
Angeles, the Goldsmith, 149–50. *See also* neomartyrs
Angelles, Christophoros, 121, 139, 145, 210n6
Anglicans, 122, 135, 139–40
anti-trinitarianism, 87, 94, 105, 195n46. *See also* Unitarianism
*Apocalypse of Pseudo-Methodius*, 12, 80
apocalypticism: 177n45; apocalyptic discourse, 77, 80–82, 85, 183n42; apocalyptic expectations, 81, 82, 94, 194n20; apocalyptic imagery, 12, 117, 159, 177n45; apocalyptic texts, 12, 82,194n25. *See also* millenarianism
apostasy/apostate, 2, 122, 124, 127–129, 131, 133, 147, 149–51, 153–58, 160, 164, 171, 204n17, 206n42, 211n34; female, 155–58, 160, 213n55. *See also* neomartyrs
*'Arab*, 5–6, 83, 131, 172–73, 175nn10–11
Arabic: in instruction of new Muslims, 28–29, 33, 182n23; language, 5, 74, 103, 195n35; literature/texts, 3, 83, 88, 91, 101–2; translation from, 26, 35, 89–90; Ottoman texts in, 31, 32,111, 181n13, 196n55; script, 27, 82, 99, 118, 181n17
Argyre of Bursa, 156–57. *See also* neomartyrs; conversion
Arius, 86–87
Armenians, 131, 206n44
Asad, Talal, 19, 179n79
Aşıkpaşazade, 38–39, 55, 62, 65
*aslama* (to surrender), 101–2; 198n13. *See also* conversion
Athens, 99, 110–11, 116, 118, 121, 127, 137, 143–45, 210n7
Athos, Mount, 127–28, 131, 136, 204n16, 205n26, 206n47, 212n38; Athonite monasteries, 128–9; monks of, 127, 129, 131–32, 135–39, 142; Xeropotamou, 141; Iviron, 138. *See also* Holy Mountain

Attar, Feridüddin, 37
Aya Sofya (Hagia Sophia), 62, 71
*'azāb al-qabr* (the torments of the grave), 30, 183n48

Baer, Marc, 162, 201n77
Balkans, 1, 3, 17, 21, 30, 123, 134, 169–70, 179n83, 188n4, 189n20, 193n5, 212n42
*Banu al-Asfar* (*Beni Asfer*, the blond people), 79, 193n13
Barbarossa, Hayreddin, 64–65, 67
Barkey, Karen, 18
Bathory, Stephen, 200n58
Battal Gazi, 38, 59, 186n101
*Battalnāme*, 38, 59, 186n101
Bayezid I, 44
Bayezid II, 48, 62, 74, 78, 170, 188n19, 190n50
Bedreddin, Şeyh, 41–46, 67, 185n89, 186nn93–94
Bektaşi: order, 48,60, 187n110, 192n88; propaganda, 48; network of saints, 47, 187n107. *See also* Hacı Bektaş
Berkey, Jonathan, 36
Bernardo, Lorenzo, 6, 173
Bible, 66, 85, 93, 104
Birgivi, Mehmed Efendi, 29–32, 115, 169, 172–73, 181n20, 182nn26–30, n35
Bitola, 69
*Bolus La'īn* ("Accursed Paul"), 86, 90. *See also* Paul, the Apostle
*Book of Daniel*, 12, 80
Borromeo, Carlo, 107
Bosnia, 21, 46, 95, 160, 171, 181n13, 183n46, 188n1, 189n39
Braude, Benjamin, 206n44
Braudel, Fernand, 7, 176n16
bribery, 116, 121, 133, 141, 144, 145, 175n3
Bulgaria, 2, 35, 60, 125, 156, 159–60, 181n13, 183n46, 184n56, 186n103, 196n52
Burke, Peter, 15
Bursa, 41, 55, 89, 124, 156, 182n36

caliph, 44; 80, 84, 106, 107–8, 196n54; Süleyman as, 80, 84, 106, 199n38;
caliphate, 27, 40; Istanbul as the seat of the, 111–12
Calvinist, 100, 135, 209n101. *See also* Lukaris, Cyril
Çandarlı Halil, 61, 190n45
canon law, 136
Capsali, Eliyahu, 81
*Casa dei Catecumeni*, 160
Caseti, Nicolas, 141. *See also* neomartyrs
catechism, 3, 24, 30, 41, 88–89, 137, 182n36
Catholic: church, 13, 141; community, 107; discourse on martyrdom, 24, 122–23, 129, 139; missionaries, 6, 110, 122, 131, 135–36, 208n76; polemic against Protestants, 14, 77, 84, 99, 103, 107, 120, 122, 196n57, 208n92; reformation, 135–36, 160, 166; states, 100; vs. Orthodox, 2, 62, 138, 177n42
Cavalli, Marino di, 198n21
Celalzade, Mustafa, 170, 215n7
Cem Sultan, 54, 78–79, 85, 88, 193n7
census records, 20–21, 52–53, 65, 133, 179n83, n84, 188n4, 189n39, 193n5, 199n43
Charlemagne, 82
Charles V of Habsburg, 76–77, 79, 82, 106, 168
Charles VIII of France, 78
Chiones, 8–9
Chios, 11, 140, 151, 186n92, 209n1
Chittick, William, 41
Christianity, 6, 9, 16, 19, 36, 44, 59, 62–63, 66, 75, 77–78, 99, 101–2, 113, 116, 123, 127–29, 136–38, 144, 152, 193n7, 205n35, 209n97; Catholic, 112, 166; crypto-, 94, 124; Eastern/Orthodox, 11, 112, 128–29, 138, 147; Islam as a perfected version of, 24, 86, 95, 195n14; vs. Islam, 2, 24, 62–63, 68–70, 79, 83–88, 95, 98, 104, 184n68
Christians, 2, 6–8, 11, 20, 24–25, 44–45, 51–57, 59–60, 62–64, 67–71, 77, 80–82, 86–87, 92–93, 96, 98, 103, 108–11, 115, 119, 122–24, 126, 129–31, 133–38, 141–49, 152, 158–60, 168, 186n92, 192n76, 193n5,196n54, 202n94, 206n42, 211n21; Orthodox, 6, 81, 110,

122, 130, 133, 135, 138, 140–41, 144, 146, 149, 158, 205n38; in the Ottoman army, 51–64, 178n68
Chryse from Moglen, 156–57. *See also* neomartyrs; conversion
Çivizade, Muhyiddin Efendi, 94, 169
*Codex Hanivaldanus*, 199n21
community: -building, 13; confessional, 2; interpretative, 27, 43, 59–61, 73; Jewish, 23; moral, 66; Muslim, 2, 14, 26, 28, 31–32, 40, 42, 44, 46, 52, 64, 77, 88, 102; Orthodox, 14, 24, 63; textual, 27, 38
concubinage, 65, 136, 158, 214n69
confessionalization, 12–16, 23–24, 76, 165, 177n52, 178n55, 202n85; the age of, 15, 24, 96, 100, 103, 122–23, 139, 143, 145–46, 151, 163, 165–67; Ottoman, 115, 120, 171, 173–74
Constantine the Great, 75, 86–87, 123, 139
Constantinople, 6, 7, 93, 94, 100, 110, 115, 119, 131, 134–37, 140, 141, 149, 151, 156; Byzantine, 9, 62–64,79, 185n86; the conquest of, 11, 24, 43, 54, 61–63, 75–76, 80, 131; as Ottoman capital, 74. *See also* Istanbul
conversion, 1–3, 5–6, 10, 16–17, 23, 25, 30, 51–52, 76, 106–8, 122, 133; agents of, 52–53, 73, 150; of children, 153–56; to Christianity, 75, 83, 92, 101–2, 116, 122; forced, 92, 96, 122, 134, 150–51; in historiography, 19–23; of men, 55–67, 112, 153–54; of priests, 68–72, 116–18; self-narratives of, 2, 24, 88, 90, 98–120; to Shi'a Islam, 12; of soldiers, 55–64; while drunk, 146, 150; of women, 65–67, 144–46, 156–64
converts, 1–2, 5, 6, 18, 20–23, 26, 51, 67, 71–74, 95, 99, 108–9, 113, 116, 119–20, 126, 129–30, 133, 142, 146, 150, 155, 163, 166–70, 173, 187n105, 201n75, 211n20, 213n68, 214n86; as authors of polemical texts, 12, 31, 82, 84, 86, 88, 90–91, 95, 99, 103–20; Christian, 24, 86, 149; female, 22, 157, 159–61; German, 105; and imperial ideology, 24, 62, 76–84, 100–20; instruction of, 28, 30–31, 90, 167; Jewish, 8, 116, 161; in the Ottoman army, 52–53, 56–61, 64
Corvinus, Matthias, 188n1
Corydalleus, Theophilus, 111
court records, 21, 119, 133, 154–57, 162, 182n36
Crusius, Martin, 135

Davud-i Kayseri, 10, 29, 41
Day of Judgment, 8, 9, 11, 30, 31, 34, 35, 38, 76–77, 80, 86, 92, 94, 95–96, 112, 117, 119, 159, 169, 181n13, 194n26
*Debate Between a Monk and a Muslim Elder regarding İsa*, 71
*Deccāl* (Antichrist), 79–80
Dekker, Thomas, 140
Demetrius, Saint, 140
Demir Baba, 45–46, 187n107
dervish, 16, 38–39, 43, 47, 49, 53–54, 61–62, 71, 73, 187n107, 190n42
*Destān-ı Ahvāl-ı Kiyāmet* ("Epic about the Events Portending the Day of Judgment"), 38
*Destān-ı Kurubaş* ("Epic of the Dry Skull"), 38
*devşirme* (child levy), 1, 5, 56, 60, 61, 72, 108, 109, 169, 170, 187n105
DeWeese, Devin, 53, 192n78
*dhimma* (pact of protection), 18, 96, 147, 153, 164, 210n14
Dionysios, Patriarch, 207n52
Don Juan, of Persia, 113
dragoman (interpreter), 57, 90, 119, 198n21. See also *tercümān*
*Dürr-i Meknūn* ("Hidden Pearl") (Ahmed Yazıcızade), 43
Dursteler, Eric, 203n108

Ebu'l Hayr-ı Rumi, 54
Ebussuud Efendi, 93, 106, 128, 150, 168–69, 170, 172, 205n29, 211n27, n30
Edirne, 41, 43, 46, 56–58, 61, 89, 117, 185n92, 186n104, 187n106
Egypt, 14, 76, 81, 131, 172–74, 179n68
England, 121–22, 139–40
*Envārü'l-Āşıkīn* ("The Illuminations of the Enraptured") (Ahmed Yazıcızade), 32–35, 38

ethnomartyrs, 205n32
*Evlād-i fātihān* (descendants of the conquerors), 46
Evliya Çelebi, 7, 33, 176n19
Evrenos , 47, 55, 187n107, 190n42

*faraklıta* (Paraclete), 71
Faroqhi, Suraiya, 144–45
*fetva* (legal opinion of a Muslim jurisprudent), 21, 93, 108, 145, 150–52, 155, 157, 166, 169, 170, 172, 182n22, 186n94, 211n26, n27, n28, n29, 213n56
*Firengistān* (Western Europe), 98, 110, 144–45, 160, 200n52
Fleischer, Cornell H., 11, 80, 177n45, 200n59, 202n99
France, 78, 121, 127, 135, 139, 141, 200n52
Franciscans, 71, 93, 102, 139, 194n35; spiritual (Fraticelli), 11

Gallipoli, 32–33, 35, 42–43, 46, 183n42
*gazā* (holy war), 17, 35, 61, 65, 78, 89
*Gazavāt-ı Hayreddin Paşa* ("The Military Exploits of Hayreddin Paşa") (Seyyid Muradi), 64–65
*gazavātnāme* (narrative about military campaigns), 56, 67, 167
*gāzī* (warrior for faith), 33, 35, 42–43, 45–47, 53–57, 61–62
George of Hungary, 49, 58, 60, 71, 73
George of Trebizond, 62–63, 75
George the Goldsmith, 125–26, 148, 204n16. *See also* neomartyrs
George the Soldier, 56. *See also* neomartyrs
Gerlach, Stefan, 93, 100, 105, 107, 110, 135, 140–41, 191n67, 195n46, 200n50, n58, 203n2, 209n97, 211n21, 213n68
Ghazali, Abu Hamid al-, 31, 34, 182n27, 183n40, 199n32
Ginio, Eyal, 154–55
Gospel, 8, 69–70, 80, 83–86, 90–92, 104, 110, 111, 196n54, 203n104; "Muslim" 70, 192n79
*Gospel of Barnabas*, 91, 196n58
Granada, 83
Greek(s), 83, 110, 117, 121–22, 135, 137, 140–41, 143, 158; College, 110, 135, 137, 140; language, 57, 63, 67, 74, 103, 111, 118, 122, 137,140, 194n25, 203n104, 203n2, 204n12, 208n76, 210n5; philosophy/sciences, 103, 110
*Gurbet-nāme-i Sultān Cem* ("The Story of Cem Sultan's Exile"), 78–79, 84–88, 90, 95, 193n7

Habsburgs, 12–14, 23–24, 76, 79–80, 82–84, 87, 92, 95–96, 100, 103, 105–8, 113, 117, 119, 132, 135, 140, 167–68, 172, 191n67, 192n3, 198n21, 200n58
Hacı Bayram Veli, 32, 43
Hacı Bektaş, 38–39, 46, 48, 187n107, n110, 190n42. *See also* Bektaşi
Hacı İlbeği, 186n104, 187n106, 191n63
*hadith*, 29–30, 33–37, 89, 92, 104, 185n86, 196n54
Haga, Cornelius, 135
Hagen, Gottfried, 171
hagiography, 37, 44, 59, 187n107, 190n42. See also *menākıbnāme*; *vilāyetnāme*
Hagiorites, Nikodemos, 124, 129–31, 141, 156, 204n13, 208n77, 209n1. See also *Neon martyrologion*
Halil, Hafiz, 44
Hamza Bali, 93
*Hamzanāme* ("Book of Hamza"), 38, 184n66
Hanefi (legal tradition), 30, 115, 169, 204n17, 211n34
Haniwald, Philipp, 198n21
Hasluck, Fredrick, 178n63, 206n42
Hathaway, Jane, 173
Haydar, Remmal, 81
heresy, 20, 44, 48, 67, 82, 93, 94–95, 107, 133, 172, 177n50, 196n57
hesychasm, 9–11, 177n38
heterodoxy, 16–17, 48, 64, 67
Hibetullah b. İbrahim, 29, 35–36,183n47
*Hikāyet-i Beşir Çelebi* ("Story of Beşir Çelebi"), 43
Holy Mountain, 124–25, 127–28, 130, 154. *See also* Athos
*Holy Wars of Sultan Murad Son of Sultan Mehmed Han*, 56

*hubmesihleri* (lovers of the messiah), 95
humanist, 15, 62, 77, 100, 103–4, 106, 111, 122, 137, 139, 140, 168
Hungarians, 56
Husain, Adnan, 7
Hussein, Imam, 123

Ibn Arabi, Muhyiddin, 10–11, 27, 34, 39–46, 48, 80, 94, 184n68, 185n72, 197n72, 199n32
İbrahim Müteferrika, 99, 118, 203n104
İbrahim Paşa, 81, 87, 194n20
*Ifhām al-Yahūd* ("Silencing the Jews") (Samuel ibn Abbas ha-Ma'aravi), 102
*'ilm-i hāl* (manual of faith), 3, 24, 26–27, 29–32, 34–35, 167, 180n1, 185n79
imam, 31, 36, 37, 107, 152, 171, 182n23, 184n56; hidden, 12, 170, 194n26; Hussein, 123; of the Last Age, 11; Twelfth, 107
Imperial Council, 21, 71, 93, 110, 111, 113, 133, 157, 162, 193n5, 200n50, 201n75
*İncīl*, 33, 69, 80. *See also* Gospel
Innocent VIII, 78, 193n7
Inquisition, 1, 107, 161
Intermarriage. *See* marriage
İntizami of Foça, 108
Ioannina, 130, 146, 158
Iordanes the Coppersmith, 149. *See also* neomartyrs
Iran, 5, 12, 39, 76, 81, 92
İsa, 8, 38, 67, 68, 70–71, 79–80, 84–86, 90–95, 191n76, 195n41. *See also* Jesus
*īsāvī* (Christic), 94–95, 197n72
İshak, Hakim, 93
*İskendernāme*, 38
Islam: "Christianized," 16, 42; diversity within, 95, 180n6; essentialized, 19; Kadızadeli, 171; monolithic, 20; Ottoman, 19–20, 24, 26–28, 36, 39–42, 59, 67, 103, 167; "popular," 184n67; proselytization of, 116; regional, 19; Sunni, 97, 107–08, 168; syncretic, 17, 42; Twelver Shi'a, 12, 107, 113
Islamic law, 2, 18, 19, 34, 41, 49, 74, 93, 106, 109, 144, 145, 152, 154, 155, 157–62, 169, 185n79, 212n38, 214n72
Islamdom, 12, 13, 20, 76, 80, 95, 97, 100, 122, 168
Islamization, 27–29, 32, 39, 42, 46, 53, 54, 181n10, 202n94
Ismail, Shah, 12, 41, 76, 81, 106, 107
Istanbul, 14, 37, 38, 62, 72, 74, 79, 81, 87, 89, 90, 91, 92, 95, 99, 101, 104, 105, 109, 111–112, 115, 119, 134, 145, 149, 163, 181n13, 182n30, 183n46, 195n52, 196n60, 198n10, 201n73, n81, 202n86, n95, 206n44, 214n82. *See also* Constantinople
Italy, 58, 76, 78–79, 105, 121, 209n97
Iviron, 138. *See also* Athos, Mount
İzmir, 119, 134
İznik, 8, 10, 26, 41, 44, 185n79
İzniki, Kutbeddin Mehmed, 26, 28–33, 41, 180nn1–2, 185n79, 199n32

James I, 140
janissaries, 1, 39, 56, 59–60, 72–73, 132, 170, 187–188n1, 189n33, 216n19
Jeremias II, 135–136, 206n47, 209n5
Jerusalem, 86, 154
Jesuits, 3, 127, 135–42, 160, 208nn76–77, 210n7
Jesus, 8–9, 38, 56, 67, 69–71, 76, 79, 83–87, 90–95, 105–06, 118, 138, 147–48, 152, 173, 191n76, 196n54, 197n72, 211n21; Society of, 127, 135. *See also* İsa
Jews, 7–8, 11, 18, 23, 25, 45, 76–77, 80–81, 85–86, 89–90, 92–93, 96, 99, 102–104, 108, 114–116, 120, 123, 134, 147–150, 154, 157, 161, 173, 180n8, 193n5, 195n51, 196n54, 197n72, 210n18, 211n21, 211n29
Joachim of Fiore, 11, 58, 82
John VI Kantakouzenos, 138
John the Merchant, 149, 201n15. *See also* neomartyrs
John the Tailor, 130. *See also* neomartyrs; Malaxos, Nikolaos
Judaism, 16, 36, 66, 98–99
Justinian, 96

*kadı* (judge), 31, 44, 107, 125–26, 138, 141, 147–49, 152–55, 205n38, 212n41
*kadı sicilleri*, 21. *See also* court records

Kadızadeli, 13–15, 29, 32, 94, 100, 115, 117, 133, 169, 170–174, 182n25, 182n30, 202n86
Kafadar, Cemal, 5, 178n68
*kāfir* (non-believer), 33, 68, 150, 192n89
Kantakouzeni, 131, 206n48
Kantakouzenos, Michael ("Şeytanoğlu"), 206n48, 209n5
*kānūn* (sultanic law), 106, 168, 174, 192n89, 199n38, 201n75
Karaki, Ali, 106–107
Karyophilles, Ioannes, 141, 149, 204n13, 209n101. *See also* neomartyrology
Kaşşaş, Abu al-Gays Muhammad al-, 112
*kebin* (temporary marriage), 66, 136, 158, 191n65. *See also* concubinage
Kemalpaşazade, 93–94
*Kıssa-yı Temmim-i Dāri* ("Story of Temmim Dari"), 38
*Kitāb hakikāt al-injīl* ("Book of the Truth of the Gospel"), 83
*Kitāb-ı Üstüvānī* ("Üstüvani's Book"), 29, 31–32, 182n30
*Kitāb tesviyetü't-teveccüh ilā'l hak* ("The Guide for One's Turning toward Truth") (Murad b. Abdullah), 98, 103–04 109, 175n3, 180n2, 198n21, 200n52, n54
*kızılbaş* ("red-heads"), 12, 48, 81, 107, 108, 168, 177n48, n50. *See also* Ismail, Shah; Shi'a
Köprülü, Fazıl Ahmed Paşa, 173–174
Kratovo, 125–126, 210n11
*kul* (slave of the sultan), 170
*Künhü'l-Ahbār* ("The Essence of Histories") (Mustafa Ali), 3
Kyranna of Avysokka, 156–57. *See also* neomartyrs; conversion
Kyrillos the Tanner, 154–55. *See also* neomartyrs

*Lead Books*, 83–84, 195n37
literacy, 27, 37–38, 99
Low Countries, 139
Loyola, Ignatius, 208n77
Lukaris, Cyril, 135, 140, 209n101
Luther, Martin, 87
Lutherans, 96, 100, 105, 135, 138, 140, 168, 191n67, 203n2

Maghribi, Samaw'al al-, 102, 116. *See also* Samuel ibn Abbas ha-Ma'aravi
*mahdi* (the rightly-guided one), 11–12, 40, 81–82, 92, 95, 194n26
Mahmood, Saba, 162
Mahmud Paşa, 69
Makarios the Tailor, 130, 151, 205n39. *See also* neomartyrs
Makdisi, Ussama, 147
Malaxos, Nikolaos, 130
Malkoç, 45, 47
Manastır, 69
Manuel II, Palaiologos, 176n28
marriage, 66, 136, 143, 158, 161, 163, 187n105, 214n82; conversion in the context of, 65–67, 160; interfaith, 65–67, 159, 191n64; temporary, 66, 191n65, 214n69
Martyrdom, 2, 24, 56, 122–33, 137–42, 143–46, 148, 151, 154–55, 157, 160, 204n4, n9, 205n35, 206n42, 207n52, 210n18, 212n39; martyrs, 33, 35, 83, 152, 159, 204n4, n13, 205n32, 209n1. *See also* neomartyrs
Massinger, Philip, 140
Mecca, 34, 93
*mecmū'a* (miscellany, collection), 2, 77, 88–90, 195n48, n50, n52, 196n54
*Mecmū'atü'l-letā'if* ("Collection of Pleasantries") (Serrac b. Abdullah), 88, 90, 195n52, 196n54
Medina, 79, 92
Mediterranean, 3, 6–8, 11, 13, 15, 22–23, 45, 75–76, 82, 91–92, 94, 103, 110, 113, 120, 133–34, 145, 160, 163, 165, 167–168, 173, 176n16, n19, 195n38
Mehmed I, 44
Mehmed II, 24, 27, 43, 46, 47, 49, 54, 61–65, 69, 74–75, 131, 167, 169, 185n86, 188n19, 190n50, 206n44
Mehmed IV, 115, 117, 174, 209n101
Mehmed b. Abdullah (Mehmed of Athens), 99, 110–113, 116, 118, 137
Melami-Bayrami, 43, 81, 93
*Menākıb-ı Mahmūd Paşa* ("Life and Deeds of Mahmud Paşa"), 69
*menākibnāme* (life and deeds of a Muslim holy man), 3, 45–46, 167, 187n104. See

also hagiography; *vilāyetnāme*
*merdümzādes*, 170
messiah, 45, 75–77, 80–81, 83, 91–95, 115, 167, 192n76; Muhammad as, 91–92, 95. See also *mahdi*; Jesus; İsa
Mesih Paşa, 190n50
*Mevlid-i Nebī*, 38
Michiel, Beatrice, 214n82
Mihailović, Konstantin, 51–52, 57–59, 65, 187–188n1
Mihal, Köse, 47, 55, 60, 188n13
Mihalloğlular, 45, 47, 48, 55, 188n19
Mihaloğlu Ali Bey, 60–61, 187n107, 190n42
Milan, 107
millenarian(ism), 11–12, 15, 42, 45, 50, 58, 76, 81–82, 91, 167, 192n3, 194n28. *See also* apocalypticism
*millet* (religious community), 206n45
Minkov, Anton, 133–134
Mir Husayn, 108
Mitrophanes III, 206n47
Mohács, Battle of, 79, 100
Molla Fenari, 41, 185n79
Molla Gürani, 69
Molla Kabız, 93
Morea, 127
Moriscos, 76, 83–84, 91–92, 95, 112
Moses, 8, 44, 67, 197n72
mosque, 14, 28, 36–38, 60, 107, 115, 133, 147, 169–171, 202n86
*müceddid* (the renewer of religion), 81. *See also mahdi*
*müfti* (jurisprudent), 169
Muhammad, the Prophet, 6, 8–9, 22, 29–31, 34, 38, 43, 46, 56, 59, 62, 70–71, 79, 81, 84–86, 91–95, 104, 106–107, 111–112, 114, 117, 118, 123, 147–149, 172, 182n26, 196n54, 203n104
*Muhammediye* ("The Story of Muhammad") (Mehmed Yazıcızade), 29, 32–35, 38, 41, 43, 182n35, 36
*mühimme defterleri*, 71, 127. *See also* rescripts (of important imperial affairs)
*Mukaddime* ("The Introduction") (Kutbeddin İzniki), 26, 28–29, 31, 180n1
*mülk* (private property), 127
Murad II, 43, 49, 56, 58, 69, 127
Murad III, 88, 108–109, 190n50, 200n59
Murad b. Abdullah, 1, 79–80, 82, 84, 90, 98, 100–10, 111, 112, 113, 118, 175n3, 180n2, 198n21, 200n52, n54, n58. See also *Kitāb tesviyetü't-teveccüh ilā'l hak*
Muslims: 7, 8, 11, 16; Anatolian, 21, 56; "authentic/genuine," 17, 170, 173; born/old, 2, 28, 51, 73, 193n5; Bosnian, 190n50; "imperfect," 87; new, 2,6, 28–31, 55, 73, 134, 149–50; non-, 5, 6, 14, 52, 53,55–56, 60, 62–64, 68, 77, 109, 115, 133, 148, 162, 169, 174; Ottoman, 52, 145–46, 158; Rumeli, 32, 35, 47; Shi'a, 2,12, 48, 60, 76, 81–82, 96–97, 107, 113, 123, 172; Slavic-speaking, 95; Spanish, 83, 92, 96
Mustafa II, 117
Mustafa Ali, 3, 5
mystic/mysticism, 8,10–12, 16, 32, 33, 37, 39, 43–44, 48, 49, 53, 62, 73, 76, 92, 94–95, 99, 102, 105, 116–17, 167, 182n27, 183n40; of Ibn Arabi, 10–11, 40–45, 80, 94–95, 185n68

Nablusi, Abd al-Ghani al-, 172–73
narrative, 2–3, 21–24, 26, 38–50, 52–61, 64–66, 68–69, 72–73, 78, 82, 85–86, 90–91, 95; of captivity, 3, 57–58, 59, 98; of conversion, 2, 53, 68, 99, 102–3, 110, 113–16, 145, 164–66, 189n24, 198n14; polemical, 1, 2, 9, 24, 75, 77–79, 84–91, 93, 98–120, 138, 140, 166, 168, 171–73, 176n28, 196n51, 199n24; Rumeli, 42, 45, 50; self-, 2, 22, 24, 88, 90, 98–120
*nasīhatnāme* (advice literature),109, 207n56
neomartyrology, 2, 3, 24, 25, 125–64, 210n18; genre of, 122, 141; compilation of, 124, 141, 143–44, 204n13, 205n39, 210n11; self-, 139, 145; in dialogue with Ottoman sources, 145, 150–64
neomartyrs, 2, 123–43, 143–64; impresarios of, 125–142, 146, 149, 205n32; female, 144, 155–64; male, 123–154. *See also* Akylina from Zagliveri; Argyre of Bursa; Caseti, Nicolas; Chryse from Moglen; George the Goldsmith;

neomartyrs (*continued*)
George, the Soldier; Iordanes the Coppersmith; John the Merchant; John the Tailor; Kyranna of Avysokka ; Kyrillos the Tanner; Makarios the Tailor; Nicholas the Grocer; Philotei the Nun. *See also* Hagiorites, Nikodemos, neomartyrology; *Neon Martyrologion*
*Neon martyrologion* ("The New Compilation of Martyrs' Lives") (Nikodemos Hagiorites), 124, 129, 141, 156, 209n1. *See also* neomartyrology
Neophitos, 137
Neoplatonism/ Neoplatonic, 8–12
Neuser, Adam, 105, 195n46
New Testament, 11, 33, 89, 104, 111, 196n54
Nicaea, 8, 85. *See also* İznik
Nicholas the Grocer, 141, 211n28. *See also* neomartyrs
Nicolay, Nicolas de, 57
Nock, Arthur, 102, 198n13
North Africa, 82, 91–92, 139, 181n20
*Nusretnāme* (Silahdar), 117

Old Testament, 11, 66, 111, 114, 203n104
orality, 27, 30, 38, 53, 54, 59, 73, 183n50
Orhan, 8, 10, 45–46
Orthodox: Christians, 2, 6, 14, 23, 24, 51, 56, 63, 81, 99, 110, 112, 115, 121–42, 144, 146, 149, 158, 205n38; church, 2, 62, 69, 72, 135–36; monk/priest, 2, 71, 111, 116, 117, 135–37; theologians, 111; tradition, 2, 129. *See also* Patriarch; Patriarchate
orthodoxy, 14, 17, 20, 66, 107, 108, 130, 169, 171–74, 179n68; Eastern Orthodoxy, 9, 128–29, 135; Islamic, 16, 20, 97, 109, 115, 117, 133; Sunni, 12, 94, 95
Osman, 38, 42, 44, 55, 59, 78, 80
Osman II, 117
*Osmanlı* (Ottoman), 5
Otman Baba, 45–46, 186n102, 187n107, 190n42
Otranto, 58, 75
Ottoman: chroniclers, 46, 55, 93, 96; culture, 89; dynasty, 3, 12, 38–39, 42, 45, 74, 78, 80, 82, 84, 96, 99, 106, 116–18; Empire, 1–6, 12–16, 18–23, 25, 27, 33, 36, 40–41, 49–53, 72, 90, 92, 94–95, 97, 100, 105, 107–8, 115–16, 119, 122–23, 127, 131–32, 134–35, 139, 143–49, 151–52, 156–58, 161–67, 169, 171–73; government/ authorities, 2, 3, 6, 22, 46, 47, 61, 63, 72, 93, 95, 122, 127–28, 132, 135–36, 139, 145–46, 148; history, 7, 12,14,17, 18, 49, 52, 61, 72, 98, 115; identity, 54, 64, 66, 77, 95–97, 100, 167; imperial ideology, 7, 18, 24, 50, 80–82, 96, 106; imperial ritual, 64, 108, 168; institutions, 41; polity, 27–28, 37, 39–41, 47, 64, 94, 167; religious politics, 24, 52, 68, 72, 97; rule, 3, 17, 21–22, 24, 39, 110, 122, 138; society, 1, 17, 24, 27–28, 38, 41, 47, 49, 61, 73, 99, 109, 115, 133, 137, 144, 149–50, 175n3; soldiers/army/ military, 5–6, 17,23, 24, 44, 47–48, 52, 54–57, 64, 89, 93, 100, 108–9, 115, 117–18, 132–34, 156, 170, 175n11, 178n68, 193n10; state, 17, 21, 23, 52, 59–60, 72–73, 100, 117, 128, 174; sultan, 12, 24, 43, 45–47, 50, 60, 64, 74–84, 89, 95, 103, 106, 108, 113, 115, 117–19, 127, 131, 133, 156, 186n104, 193n14, 194n25, 199n38; vs. Rumi, 5; vs. Turk, 5, 67
Oxford, 121, 139

Padua, 111, 135, 137, 208n78
Palamas, Gregory, 8–11, 176n28
*Papasnāme* ("The Priest's Story"), 116–117
Paradise (*Cennet*), 8, 30, 34–37, 68, 70
Patriarch, 63, 124, 131, 135–36, 158, 159; 203n2, 206n47, n51; Cyril Lukaris, 135, 140, 209n101, 209n5; Dionysios, 207n52; Gennadios Scholarios, 63, 131; Jeremias I, 205n38; Jeremias II, 135–36, 206n47; John IV Aprenos, 124; Mitrophanes III, 135, 206n47; Neophitos, 137; Patrarchal Academy, 110, 137; Patriarchal church, 141
Patriarchate: of Constantinople, 63, 130–32, 135–36, 206n48; of Peć, 131

Paul, the Apostle, 86, 90, 101–102. See also *Bolus La'īn*
Peace of Augsburg, 13, 96, 168
Peć, 131
Peirce, Leslie, 162, 214n83
Pentateuch, 33, 89, 114, 196n54
Persian, 6, 43, 74, 83, 85, 107; language, 26, 28, 33, 49, 74, 88, 111, 181n11, 184n57, 185n68, 191n65, 195n41; literature, 3
Peter, the Apostle, 76, 78, 84, 106
Philip II, 106
Philip III, 113
Philothei, the Nun, 127, 143–45, 156, 160, 209n1. *See also* neomartyrs; conversion
Pius II, 63
Polemics, 8–11, 63, 70, 87, 103, 123; Muslim-Christian, 8–11, 70, 85, 100, 103, 107, 112, 120; intra-Muslim, 61; 177n50; Muslim-Jewish, 85, 102–04, 114–16; Orthodox-Catholic, 138; Orthodox-Muslim, 191n55, Protestant-Catholic, 84, 107, 208n92; Sunni-Shi'a, 123
Porte, 69, 98, 198n21, 212n41
preachers, 13, 14, 33, 45, 115, 133, 169, 171, 172, 202n86
priest, 53, 68–72, 90, 99, 111, 116–18, 125–27, 130, 132, 135–37, 141, 148, 192n87, 196n57, 208n76, 210n11, 213n51
Protestant, 2, 13, 23, 89, 96–97, 103, 122, 135, 140, 142, 161, 208n92, 209n101; martyrologies, 139; missionaries, 6, 122, 131, 135, 140; Reformation, 76–77, 104,123, 193n4; vs. Catholic, 14, 77, 84, 99, 107, 120, 196n57
Psalms of David, 89, 90, 111, 114, 195n51, 196n54, 203n104
Pseudo-Dionysius, 9
Pseudo-Methodius, 12, 80, 82

Qur'an, 29, 31, 33, 35–37, 62, 69, 70, 85, 87, 92–93, 99, 101, 104, 107–8, 112, 114, 151, 180n8, 182n23, n35, 192n76, 196n54
*qutb* (mystical axis of the saintly hierarchy), 40–41, 44–47, 50, 74, 81–82, 84

*re'āyā* (tax-paying commoner), 133
"Red Apple," 112, 119
*reddiye* (Muslim polemical genre), 100
Reinhard, Wolfgang, 13
renegade, 6, 20, 77, 104, 160–161
rescripts (of important imperial affairs), 71, 127–28, 144, 150, 163. See also *mühimme defterler*
*Risāle-yi Birgivī*. See *Vasiyetnāme*
*Risāle-yi islāmīye* ("Treatise on Islam") (İbrahim Müteferrika), 118, 203n104
Rome, 3, 7, 54, 61–63, 74–76, 78–79, 82, 85, 96, 110, 111, 112, 119, 123–124, 135–141, 168, 191n57,193n10, 194n20, 208n77, 211n36
Rothman, E. Natalie, 161, 203n108
Rum: lands of, 3–7, 13–14, 32, 35, 38, 44, 67, 74, 111, 165, 171–74, 175n6, n11, 196n54; sultan of, 43
Rumeli, 3, 6, 13, 14, 21, 41–48, 52–56, 60–63, 69, 74, 95, 124, 127, 138, 146, 158, 169, 172, 179n84, 183n42, 185n92, 186n104, 187n110; conquest of, 24, 27, 32, 41–43, 45–47, 187n106; Islamization of, 16, 20–21, 28–29, 32, 42–48, 52–54, 133; library collections in, 29, 181n13, 183n46; narratives, 45, 50
Rumi (inhabitant of the lands of Rum), 1, 3, 5, 51, 54, 64, 67–68, 74, 77, 172–73, 175n6
Rumi, Celaluddin, 185n68, 199n32
Russanos, Pachomios, 138
Rüstem Paşa, 1, 57, 100, 109, 170

*Sa'ātnāme* ("Book of The Hour") (Hibetullah b. İbrahim), 29, 68
Safavid, 5–6, 12–15, 24, 41, 48, 76, 80–82, 96–97, 100, 106–8, 113, 117, 119, 122, 123, 166–68, 170, 200n50
*sāhib-kırān* (the Master of Conjunction), 81. See *mahdi*; Süleyman ("The Magnificent")
saint, 16, 27, 31, 39–40, 45–47, 49, 54, 73, 86, 88, 94, 101–2, 114–115, 125, 129–130, 137, 140–141, 144, 156, 159, 187n110, 196n54, 197n72, 206n42, 209n1

Saltuk, Sarı, 45–46, 54, 64, 68–70, 73, 186n101, 191–192n76
*Saltuknāme*, 45, 54, 57, 59, 68–69, 186n101, 191n63
Samuel ibn Abbas ha-Ma'aravi (Samaw'al al-Maghribi), 102–3, 116
Sarajevo, 29, 171, 183n46, 190n50
Schilling, Heinz, 13
Schiltberger, Johann, 59
Scholarios, Gennadios, 63, 131
scholars, 7, 8, 10, 14, 16–19, 22, 39, 41, 43–44, 46, 48, 49, 52–53, 61, 66, 69, 80, 83, 91, 94, 99, 102, 119, 122, 145, 147, 166, 176n20, 178n58, 179n83, 189n24, 203n2; Ottoman, 29, 41, 43–44, 48–49, 62, 92, 94–95; religious, 19, 36, 38, 48–49, 62, 92, 94–95, 169, 171, 173, 183n40, 199n38, 216n19; Safavid, 108, 123
Selanik, 89, 137, 154–156. *See also* Thessaloniki
Selim I, 48, 76, 80, 170, 215n7
Selim II, 108, 128
Serbs, 23, 131, 172, 179n83, 187n1
Serrac b. Abdullah, 88–90
*şeyhü'l-islām* (chief jurisprudent of the Ottoman Empire), 41, 93–94, 106, 108, 128, 150–151, 155, 157, 169, 211n27
Seyyid Ali Sultan (Kızıl Deli), 45–46, 87n104
Seyyid Muradi, 64
*shahada* (Muslim profession of faith), 22, 31, 141, 150, 161, 182n22, 209n97, 211n28, 211n30
*sharia* (Holy Law), 106, 113, 128, 152–153, 157, 162, 164, 168, 174, 178n94, 199n38. *See also* Islamic law
Shi'a, 60, 76, 81–82, 97, 106–07, 113, 172, 200n50; propaganda, 48, 82; Safavids, 6, 48, 81, 96, 100, 107, 123; Shi'ism, 12, 107, 172, 187n110; -Sunni polarization, 13, 97, 120, 123
Sinan Paşa, 109
slavery/slaves, 22, 37, 58, 60, 66, 73, 89, 119, 127, 143, 144, 157, 160, 169, 175n2, 175n11, 182n36, 184n60, 189n39, 191n63, 214n78
Smyrna, 138, 141, 208n77
social disciplining, 12–16, 32, 97, 100, 107, 115, 133, 147, 151, 166, 168, 171, 173,177n53. *See also* confessionalization
Society of Jesus, 127, 135. *See also* Jesuits
sodomy, 109, 175n3
Sofia, 2, 29, 56, 90, 125, 146, 148, 210n11
Sokollu Mehmed Paşa, 72, 93, 109–110, 131, 200n58, 209n5
Somlyai, Balázs (Murad b. Abdullah), 100. *See also* Murad b. Abdullah
Spain, 76, 82–83, 88, 92, 96, 112–113, 200n52, 213n66
Spandounes, Theodore, 148
Studitis, Damaskinos, 137, 159
Subrahmanyam, Sanjay, 15, 80
Sufi, 10, 14, 16, 18, 27, 31–35, 37, 39–44, 48–50, 53, 62, 71, 81–82, 94–95, 99, 105, 107, 109, 114–118, 133, 166, 171–173, 177n38, 182n27, n30, 183n40, 184n68, 185n72, n79, 190n43, 202n86, n96; orders, 19, 31, 39, 43, 46, 49, 58, 73–74, 81, 107, 115, 166, 172; Sufism, 10–11, 19, 31, 37, 39, 41, 48, 73, 105. *See also* mysticism
Süleyman ("The Magnificent"), 7, 14, 64, 75–82, 84–85, 87–88, 90, 95–97, 99–100, 106–9, 128, 168, 170–71, 193n14, 194n20
Süleyman Paşa, 45–46, 186n104
*sunna* (normative legal practice based on words and deeds of the Prophet), 31, 115, 133
Sunni(s), 2, 6, 31, 107–08, 168, 174; Islam, 97, 107–08, 168; orthodoxy, 94–95; polarization between Shi'ites and, 2, 6, 13, 96–97, 100, 107, 120, 123; Sunnitization, 12–14, 94, 107, 128, 168–71; tradition, 91–92, 97
*Sūrnāme-yi hümāyūn* ("Imperial Festival Book") (Intizami of Foça), 108
Symeon the Goldsmith, 149. *See also* neomartyrs
syncretism/syncretic, 16–18, 20, 24, 28, 39, 42, 51–53, 64–73, 83, 95, 163, 179n68, 185n82; anti-syncretism, 18, 24, 52, 58, 64, 66, 70, 72, 95, 142, 147, 150, 159

Syria, 14, 76, 80, 131, 172, 174, 179n68

*Ta'bīr-i Rüyā* (Interpretation of Dreams), 38
Tahmasp, Shah, 76, 106–107, 168
*tahrīf* (distortion of scriptures), 70, 85, 104
*tahrīr defterleri. See* census records
*tā'ife* (group or party), 131, 206n45
Talikizade, 96
Tanzimat, 165–166
*taqiyya* (dissimulation), 123
*Tārih-i Edirne*, 43
*Tarīkat al-Muhammedīya* (The Muhammadan Path) (Birgivi Mehmed Efendi), 29, 31–32, 182n26
Tarjuman, al-Abdallah, 102. *See also* Turmeda, Anselm
*ta'ziyeh* (passion play), 123
Tengnagel, Sebastian, 203n107
*tercümān* (interpreter), 98, 107. *See also* dragoman
*tereke* (probate registers), 182n36
Terzioğlu, Derin, 171, 202n85–86, 215n2
*Tevārīh-i Āl-i Osmān* (The Chronicles of the House of Osman), anonymous, 38, 61; by Aşıkpaşazade, 38, 55; by various authors, 42
*Tevrāt*, 33. *See also* Pentateuch
Tezcan, Baki, 174, 215n11, 216n19
*Tezkiretü'l-evliyā* ("Biography of the Saints") (Feridüddin Attar), 37
Thessaloniki, 8–9, 137, 154. *See also* Selanik
Thrace, 21, 45–46, 67
*tımār* (land grant), 47, 55, 71, 127
Tirmidhi, Hakim, 46
Timur, 44
toleration, 16–18, 144–49, 163–64, 172, 210n10
*Tractatus de moribus, condicionibus et nequicia Turcorum* ("Treatise on the Beliefs, Customs and Perfidy of Turks") (George of Hungary), 58
translation, 36, 79, 89–90, 91, 138, 194n35; from Arabic into Ottoman Turkish, 32, 89, 112, 196n55; of the Bible, 85, 90, 103–05; from Croatian, Hungarian into Ottoman Turkish, 89; from Greek into Ottoman Turkish, 63, 203n104; from Italian into Ottoman Turkish, 198n21; from Ottoman Turkish into Latin, 98, 105, 109, 198n21, 200n52; from Persian into Ottoman Turkish, 181n11, 184n57; of the Qur'an, 104
Transylvania/Transylvanians, 58, 87, 100, 103, 105, 118, 200n58
*Treasure* (Damaskinos Studitis), 137–138, 159
Treaty of Amasya, 97, 168, 170
Trent, Council of, 99, 102, 107, 134
Tridentine, post-, 100, 111, 116, 136, 139, 166, 198n14
Trinity, 86
Tsamblak, Grigorii, 210n18
Tübingen, 135, 141, 203n2
*Tuhfat al-adīb fī al-radd 'alā ahl al-salīb* ("A Unique Find for the Intelligent Mind—A Treatise of Riposte to the People of the Cross") (Anselm Turmeda / Abdallah al-Tarjuman), 102
Turahan, 45, 47
Turk, 3, 5–6, 20, 51–52, 57, 58, 63, 66–67, 75, 93, 109, 139, 140, 158, 160; to turn, 8, 20, 139, 185n92, 206n42, 208n92
Turkish (language), 3, 23, 26–33, 35, 41, 63, 67, 73, 74, 88–90, 98–100, 105, 109, 112, 138, 180n1, 181n11, n20, 183n46, 196n55, 198n21, 201n72, 203n104
Turkmen, 12, 41, 44–45, 47, 55, 56, 81–82, 188n19, 194n29. See also *yürük*
Turmeda, Anselm, 102–103, 110, 112, 114, 116, 118, 201n81

*uc* (frontier), 42
*'ulemā* (Muslim religious scholars), 19, 171, 173, 183n40, 216n19. *See also* scholars
*umma* (community of believers), 172
Ungnad, David, 200n58
Unitarianism, 105. *See also* anti-trinitarianism
Universal Monarchy, 7–8, 12, 75, 96, 168
Uruc Bey, 113. *See* Don Juan of Persia
Üstüvani Mehmed Efendi, 29, 31–32, 182n30,

*vāizān* (mosque preachers), 202n86. *See also* preachers
*Vākı'āt-ı Sultān Cem* ("The Events that befell Sultan Cem"), 193n7
*vakıf* (pious endowment), 60, 62,63, 114, 127, 169, 189n39
Vani Mehmed Efendi, 115, 182n30
Vasıl, Şeyh, 90
*Vasiyetnāme* (or *Risāle-yi Birgivī*) ("The Testament" or "Birgivi's Treatise") (Birgivi Mehmed Efendi), 29–30, 32, 181n20, 182n29
Venice, 7, 79, 87, 92, 113, 127, 135, 136, 138, 145, 160–161
vezir, 1, 74, 93, 170, 172, 173, 190n50
Vienna, 15, 82, 88, 90, 100, 104, 108, 117, 168, 171, 174
*vilāyetnāme* (hagiography), 3, 45–47, 53–54, 167, 186n99, n102, 190n42. *See also* hagiography, *menākıbnāme*
Virgin Mary, 83
*Visions of Daniel*, 12
*vojnuks* (type of Christians soldiers in Ottoman army), 55–56
Vryonis, Speros, 158

Winter, Stefan, 171–172
Wittek, Paul, 17
women, 33–34, 37, 65–66, 68, 122, 124, 127, 133, 137, 138, 143–46, 153–164, 181n20, 184n56, 191n65, 201n7, 213n68, 214n82, n83, n86

Xeropotamou, 141. *See also* Athos, Mount

Yazıcızade Ahmed, 32–35, 42–43, 45, 62, 183n42
Yazıcızade Mehmed, 29, 32–35, 41–43, 45, 183n42
*yürük* (nomadic Turkmen), 45, 186n98, 188n19. *See also* Turkmen
Yusuf b. Abi Abdüdeyyan, 99, 114–116, 195n51
*Yūsuf ve Züleyha* (Yusuf and Züleyha), 38

Zaganos Paşa, 61
Zayn al-Din b. Ali al-Amili, 123
*Zebūr*, 89–90. *See also* Psalms of David
Zevi, Sabbatai, 115–116, 173
Zograph, Dicho, 159